FOREIGN FOLLIES

AMERICA'S NEW GLOBAL EMPIRE

DOUG BANDOW

Foreign Follies
by Doug Bandow

Printed in the United States of America

ISBN 1-59781-988-3

www.xulonpress.com

Dedication

Dedicated to Ted Galen Carpenter, my good friend and colleague who has done so much to promote a more peaceful world.

Table of Contents

Foreword

Congressman John J. Duncan, Jr. (R-TN)

I really cannot adequately express my very great admiration and respect for Doug Bandow.

I have read his columns, articles, and books for many years, and I have become one of his biggest fans.

In fact, in the last newsletter I sent to me 700,000 constituents in East Tennessee, I quoted something he wrote in an article for the American Conservative Magazine.

Mr. Bandow writes about very complicated issues in a very intelligent yet understandable and enjoyable way.

He has consistently and courageously expressed traditional conservative-libertarian views although this has hurt him in a time when our government and almost all major publications and think tanks are controlled by liberals or so-called neo-conservatives.

Yes he knows that "big government conservatives" are really not conservatives at all.

Doug Bandow's views and opinions are held by a big majority of the American people, even if not by the very powerful minority presently in control on our major institutions.

As syndicated columnist Georgia Anne Meyer wrote in late 2003: "Critics of the way against Iraq have said since the beginning on the conflict that Americans, still strangely complacent about overseas wars being waged by a minority in their name, will inevitably come to a point where they will see they have to have a government that provides services at home or one that seeks empire across the globe."

In this book, Doug Bandow forcefully advocates a traditional conservative, but more importantly, a traditional American foreign policy.

Most conservatives have always been against the U.S. attempting to be the policeman of the world. This is unnecessary, unaffordable, and unconstitutional.

Senator Robert Taft said many years ago: "No foreign policy can be justified except a policy devoted...to the protection of the liberty of the American people, with was only as the last resort and only to preserve that liberty."

A foreign policy such as this in scornfully and arrogantly described as isolationist. However, anyone who levels such a charge is resorting to name-calling and childish sarcasm rather than a serious discussion on the merits, or lack thereof, of an issue.

Doug Bandow and I know, as do a majority of the American people, that the best way to have friends around the world is to have trade and tourism, cultural and educational exchanges, and help put during humanitarian crises, but maintain a non-interventionist foreign policy.

We certainly do not need to spend several hundreds of billions each year to maintain our military-industrial war machine of turn the Department of Defense in the Department of Foreign Aid.

As the very popular columnist Charley Reese wrote recently: "What exists at this moment is a military-industrial complex with a vested interest in war and conflict. What exist at this moment are unnecessary wars in Afghanistan and Iraq. What exists at this moment is a government solicitous of corporate welfare, but one that doesn't give a hoot about the individual American."

This is the traditional conservative viewpoint; one that finds it horrible when the Defense Department's own Inspector General says, as he did after a year and half of our operation in Iraq, that $35 billion had been misspent, due to waste, fraud, and abuse, and another nine billion had simply been "lost."

Conservatives should not be defending this type of waste. They should be attacking it.

Almost 80% of House Republicans voted against President Clinton's bombings and military action in Bosnia and Kosovo. We had no vital national interest there, and that was the first time we changed NATO from a purely defensive body into an offensive one.

I believe most Republicans and talk radio hosts would have opposed war in Iraq had it been started by a Democratic President.

Now, finally, many conservation commentators and columnists have realized that there was nothing conservative about waging a preemptive was in Iraq, a country with a military budget only a little more than two-tenths of one percent of ours.

William F. Buckley, Jr., sometimes called the godfather of conservatism, wrote that if he had known in 2002 what he knew in 2004, he would have opposed the war in Iraq. He later wrote that we will soon reach a point where "steadfastness of purpose" becomes "stubbornness of pride."

I am not a pacifist and voted for the war in Afghanistan to respond to 9/11, but we have stayed far too long there. Recently, Kabul has been the scene of huge anti-American demonstrations.

Some have said we were wrong to go to war in Iraq, but now that we are there, we have to "stay the course" or "finish the job" and that we can't "cut and run."

However, if you find you are going the wrong way down the interstate, you don't just keep going. You get off at the next exit.

It seems that no matter which Party, too many in Washington want to be seen as world statesmen or men and women of action. They worry too much about their place in history. They certainly do not want to be called isolationists.

All those who have anything to do with foreign or defense policies know they will get more money, power and prestige if the U.S. gets involved in every major religious, ethnic, or political dispute around the world.

Governing or defending just the U.S. is simply not enough. How we need more Calvin Coolidges in our government today, or at least some who believe in the "more humble" foreign policy President George W. Bush advocated in his 2000 campaign.

Three years ago, I was part of a Congressional delegation that made a brief visit to Australia. Our Ambassador said that 80% of Australians were opposed to our actions in Iraq, but that the Australian government was supportive because it was "ahead of the people."

This was a very elitist attitude but was true of most countries and their leaders around the world.

Our interventionist foreign policies are isolating us from the rest of the world. We should not place our troops under U.N. command and we should not base our decisions on what any other country thinks.

But if we followed a much more neutral, less interventionist foreign policy and brought most of our military back to the U.S., we would have many more friends and our homeland would be much more secure.

Traditional conservatives have never believed in world government, even if run by the United States. It is far too expensive and elitist and far too removed from the control by the people.

Now, many are wondering if we are going to war in Iran, even as our national debt approaches nine trillion dollars with deficits of $300 to $400 billion adding to this every year for at least the next decade.

Doug Bandow wants us to get off this disastrous course we are on and head in a strong and more peaceful direction.

If *Foreign Follies* can somehow reach a large audience, this Nation will be a much better and safer place.

Preface

There are many to thank during a career that essentially began in May 1982, most obviously my colleagues at the Cato Institute, Copley News Service, and (long-ago folded) *Inquiry* Magazine. But I have worked with many principled and helpful editors, journalists, think-tankers, foundation staffers, political activists, business people, human rights workers, and even a few such political staffers and candidates over the years. To all I owe a great debt.

The idea for the companion collections of my articles, *Foreign Follies: America's New Global Empire* and *Leviathan Unchained: Washington's Bipartisan Big Government Consensus*, arose after what I term "the late unpleasantness," my fabled 15 minutes of fame arising after I acknowledged having been paid to write an occasional article by lobbyist Jack Abramoff. It was a serious mistake because it created a conflict in appearances, even though I wrote what I wanted about subjects that I found interesting. To fail to meet the expectations of those who did so much for me over the years is my greatest regret from what remains my mistake, and mine alone.

I began writing three decades ago in student newspapers and have promoted a consistent set of principles. There have been some shifts—many years ago I was noticeably more hawkish, but that stance disappeared along with my student days. The death penalty continues to confound me. But in the main, the essays that I wrote while attending Stanford Law School criticizing conscription, high taxes, unnecessary regulation, U.S. support for repressive Third World regimes, the minimum wage, foreign intervention, and socialized medicine sound little different, except for being a bit less polished, than my more recent offerings on the same subjects. I really couldn't have sold my opinion even had I been so inclined: the inconsistencies would have been too obvious to too many.

Although there are few people, other than family members, likely to be interested in what I wrote in the *Stanford Daily* in the late 1970s, many of my more recent offerings remain relevant. Although there is inevitably some overlap in multiple articles written on the same subjects over the years, their consistent message of individual liberty and limited government may be more important today than at almost any other time in our republic. Despite the rhetoric of liberty which infuses today's political debate, the Leviathan state has triumphed. And both major parties have joined in a bipartisan campaign to increase its power at every turn.

Essential to this project was my good friend Tom Freiling of Xulon Press, who so generously offered to publish *Foreign Follies: America's New Global Empire* and *Leviathan Unchained: Washington's Bipartisan Big Government Consensus*. To him and those around him, including Bryan Mullican, my most hearty thanks.

—Doug Bandow, September 2006

INTRODUCTION

Social Engineering Gone Global

The U.S. once was a republic, but that was long ago. Today there seems to be no problem any where on earth about which Washington is not concerned. No country, large or small, can long escape a hectoring lecture from the American Secretary of State, Secretary of Defense, or President.

More important, no nation can feel safe from U.S. pressure, including military force. Some countries have struck a reasonably good deal. For instance, the Europeans, Japanese, and South Koreans enjoy expensive protection from disappearing threats. Although they increasingly bridle at Washington's pretensions of leadership—there was, for instance, little enthusiasm for the Iraq war, irrespective of how many years America had supplied security guarantees—none of these prosperous and populous states seem ready to take on full responsibility for their own or their region's defense.

Far more countries make do only with foreign aid payments or trade preferences. In return they must put up with an endless stream of directives, demands, and exhortations. Many of America's preferences are perfectly reasonable, but few are worth imposing on the reluctant and recalcitrant. And rarely do even the friendliest states appreciate Washington's unending attentions.

Still, arrogance is one thing. Arrogance backed by the world's mightiest military is something quite different. The Cold War was a threatening, dangerous time, but it did constrain the U.S. from engaging in more frivolous interventions. With America's emergence as a hyperpower enjoying a unipolar moment, as the globe's only superpower—and on and on, as some would-be imperialists regularly remind the rest of us—more than a few policymakers in Washington want to take advantage of the country's opportunity to reorder the globe by force, if necessary.

Iraq has come to epitomize the vision that "what we say goes." Although some war advocates advanced legitimate national interest grounds for deposing Saddam Hussein, all have been utterly discredited by the war's aftermath. Rather than acknowledge error, the Bush administration turned Woodrow Wilson into its patron saint, suggesting that holding elections in Iraq justified the war as well as the occupation. Some Republican legislators and administration backers even cite garbage collection and port dredging as evidence of America's "success."

Every sensible American desires the emergence of a liberal society on the Euphrates, for the benefit of the U.S. as well as Iraq, but no realistic person should expect that result. Social engineering is difficult enough at home. It is extraordinarily difficult abroad. Iraq might eventually end up as the kind of society that we desire, but there are likely to be many more bloody detours along the way.

The essays in this volume unashamedly advocate a different foreign policy. America should be engaged in the world, confident in its ability to profit from free trade, committed to friendly political relations, ready to sample foreign cultures, and pleased to accept people fleeing political persecution and seeking a better life. Global problems, from the environment to poverty to refugees, warrant global cooperation that preserves liberty and prosperity as well. In this way the U.S. can advance the interests of its own people and of those who share our humanity across the globe.

But military action should be a last rather than a first resort. Washington should deploy coercive tools, such as sanctions, only when significant national interests are at stake. Military action lies at the very end of the continuum of force. War is costly, risky, and uncertain; its prosecution undermines liberties at home. Moreover, in an age of terrorism it encourages more, and more deadly, attacks on America's homeland. Military action is a blunt object ill-adapted to shape liberal societies.

That some people somewhere may benefit from U.S. military action matters less than the fact that Americans might suffer. The point is not that other people's lives are less valuable morally, but the U.S. government has a far greater responsibility to its own citizens. Absent a threat to their own political community, Americans—soldiers, Marines, sailors, and airmen as well as civilians—should not find their own lives placed at risk.

The result of a less-assertive America might be a messy world. But it will be messy irrespective of the pretensions of the would-be peacemakers and nation-builders. Our first priority should be to build a stable, safe, and prosperous republic at home. Such a society requires peace as well as free markets.

CHAPTER ONE

Foreign Policy

The Politics of Foreign Policy

The U.S. Congress continues to protect America's defense budget from serious reductions. Indeed, it has begun increasing outlays, with both parties competing to restore reductions previously agreed to.

However, military outlays should be an obvious target for American budget-cutters. Defense spending does not exist in a vacuum, but is the price of a nation's foreign policy. When the U.S. faced the threat of hegemonic communism—an aggressive Soviet Union aided by client states worldwide—it chose the policy of containment, which required a large military, numerous alliances, scores of bases, and an advanced-force presence around the globe. All told, Washington spent more than $13 trillion (in today's dollars) to win the Cold War.

But starting in 1989, all the assumptions underlying American foreign policy collapsed. The Central and Eastern European states overthrew communism, the Berlin Wall fell, the Warsaw Pact dissolved, and the Soviet Union disappeared. A military strategy and force structure designed to deter Soviet aggression was suddenly obsolete; the U.S. (and its allies) faced no adversary worthy of the name.

Military spending did not change accordingly, however. True, outlays have fallen, but only from the 1985 peak, up 55 percent from 1980, caused by the Reagan defense build-up. At roughly $270 billion, military outlays currently remain above the level of 1980, in inflation-adjusted terms. Indeed, President Bill Clinton is spending more than Richard Nixon spent in 1975 and almost as much as Lyndon Johnson spent in 1965, during the height of the Cold War. Outlays are running at 85 percent of the Cold War average, without a Cold War. Washington accounts for a larger share of the globe's military expenditures today than it did a decade ago, when it faced a hostile hegemonic threat.

But this is not enough for many policymakers. A number of leading conservatives have formed the Project for the New American Century. The organization is dedicated to promoting what analyst William Kristol characterizes as "benevolent hegemony." As he argues, "we need to increase defense spending significantly if we are to carry out our global responsibilities," which essentially means imposing order around the globe. Kristol advocates an annual increase of $60 to $80 billion. Groups like the Heritage Foundation are only somewhat less extreme; the latter proposes a hike of $20 to $25 billion a year.

Before leaving office, House Speaker Newt Gingrich proposed no specific number, but urged the Budget Committee to significantly up military outlays. He explained: "We have lived off the Reagan buildup about as long as we can. The fact is that our defense structure is getting weaker, our equipment is getting obsolete, and our troops are stretched too thin." Similarly, *National Review* magazine has called for "reversing the decline in our defense budget."

President Clinton, as is his wont, arrayed himself as a pale version of his critics. In 1997 he requested that Congress hike military spending. The administration boasted that for "the fifth time in four years ... the President increased defense spending above previously planned levels." Not surprisingly, one anonymous Pentagon official told the *New York Times* that "the Defense Department has fared well in the budget deliberations."

When the Pentagon finished its Quadrennial Defense Review, it advocated the warmed-over status quo. Defense Secretary William Cohen proposed preserving the current force structure, slightly paring manpower levels, and allowing inflation to slowly erode overall expenditures. He envisioned no change in strategy, with the Defense Department remaining committed to fighting two wars almost simultaneously. It is as if the Cold War never ended.

There is little serious partisan disagreement on this score. Secretary of State Madeleine Albright has been consciously building GOP support for administration policies. As she puts it, "both parties are led by people who understand the importance of American leadership." The administration even considered enlisting former Republican presidential nominee Robert Dole to promote its plans for NATO expansion and an extended stay in the Balkans.

What is the justification for a potentially huge military buildup? Some advocates contend that America is in danger of becoming a second-rate military power vulnerable to attack. Former Marine Commandant Charles Krulak spoke of a continuing "national demobilization." During the 1996 election campaign Robert Dole warned that "peace is threatened and dark forces are multiplying in almost every corner of the globe. All of us have seen how an enemy can rise suddenly and strike quickly when America seems unprepared." Columnist Harry Summers argued that if the U.S. doesn't have "military forces deployed around the world" Americans will find the enemy "at our throats." The Pentagon's two-war strategy, explained Secretary Cohen, "signals our resolve to friends and foes alike."

Where, however, are these foes? Today the U.S. dominates the globe, accounting for over a third of its military outlays. And Washington presides virtually without enemies. America and its friends account for about 80 percent of the world's military spending. States with civil, if at times uncomfortable, relations with the U.S., particularly China and Russia, account for the bulk of the rest. Even former Defense Department official Zalmay Khalilzad admits: "the U.S. is without peer. We face no global rival or a significant hostile alliance. Indeed, the world's most powerful and developed countries are our friends and allies. In modern times, no single nation has held such a predominant position as the United States does at present."

Yet, in a world so very different from that of the Cold War Washington spends even more compared to its allies and potential adversaries than before. U.S. outlays are more than thrice those of Moscow, nearly twice those of Britain, France, Germany, and Japan combined, and eight times those of China. As a share of GDP, American military expenditures are four times those of Japan, and two or more times those of most of its European allies. U.S. citizens spend more to defend South Korea than do the South Koreans. America's interests in the world are great, but the U.S. does not have more at stake in Europe than do the Europeans, or have a greater interest in the independence of South Korea than do the South Koreans. There is something very wrong with this picture.

Of course, as House National Security Committee Chairman Floyd Spence observes, "it's still a dangerous world." It is not particularly dangerous for America or Europe, however. As Colin Powell noted when he was chairman of the Joint Chiefs of Staff, "I'm running out of demons. ... I'm down to Castro and Kim Il Sung." The impoverished communist dictatorships of Cuba and North Korea may be ugly, but neither threatens American security. The mere fact that a conflict may break out somewhere in the world doesn't mean that it would be in Washington's interest to intervene, or that America's friends couldn't look after themselves.

The largest component of the Pentagon budget remains the traditional alliances, such as NATO. In Europe 100,000 U.S. soldiers stand guard lest phantom Soviet divisions roll West. While the future direction of Russia remains unclear, the Western Europeans, with a combined population of more than 400 million and GDP of $8 trillion compared to about 150 million and $1 trillion, respectively, for Moscow, are eminently capable of defending themselves. Britain and France possess independent nuclear deterrents. They, plus Germany, spend 25 percent more on the military than does Russia, which has been continually cutting defense outlays. It is time for the Europeans to take over NATO.

American-backed expansion into Central Europe makes even less sense than continued support for the Western Europeans. While the former communist satellites should be integrated into the West, the best means to do so is economically through the European Union. These struggling nations need access to Western markets, not the presence of Western soldiers. Yet the Western Europeans continue to dawdle, preferring to offer American military subsidies than risk increased European economic competition.

Moreover, America has no vital interest that warrants guaranteeing the borders of Poland, Hungary, Romania, the Baltic States, Ukraine, and whoever else ends up on a NATO wish list. These nations obviously matter more to Western Europe, but that means Western Europe should defend them. The Western European Union, EuroCorps, Organization for Security and Cooperation in Europe, and even an America-less NATO all provide potential frameworks for a European-organized, -funded, and -manned defense of the East.

But lack of national interest is obviously no bar to U.S. military intervention. Although Europe looks secure, NATO officials peer south as well as east, and see only trouble. Many alliance planners say that the greatest risks of conflict lie south of Europe. Explains Adm. T. Joseph Lopez, commander of NATO's Southern Command (AFSOUTH): "The next war could grow out of any number of explosive factors—economic difficulties, water shortages, religious fanaticism, immigration, you name it. There are many different forces of instability in the southern region." Naturally, he believes Washington must intervene, explaining that "I can think of no foreign theater more critical for the United States. We have to stay engaged, with a robust force and the political will to use it." Indeed, he advocates "engagement across the line," since that strategy is what won the Cold War. Of course, acknowledges Lopez, "instability is a difficult enemy to deal with."

Well, yes, as Washington is discovering in Bosnia. The U.S. is already deeply enmeshed in the Balkans, a region with no serious link to U.S. security. A European diplomat told the *Washington Post*: "Bosnia shows us the alliance only works when the United states takes the lead, and we need to keep the U.S. engaged where the action is likely to be." Bosnia shows that the alliance works? Despite the ongoing Western occupation, there is little support among any of the three hate-filled ethnic groups for preserving the artificial Bosnian state, a utopian goal of no practical value to America or even Europe.

Nevertheless, Washington is now using its military to support one nationalist politician over another in Serbian Bosnia. It turns out the kind of democracy Washington intends to bring to the Balkans—by seizing television and radio stations when it disapproves of their broadcasts and transferring control of police stations to factions it views as more pliant—is more representative of, say, Slobodan Milosevic than Gerhard Schroeder. But good policy doesn't seem to be the goal. As the *Weekly Standard* explained: "We need to make it clear, not just to Bosnians but to the world, that it's much safer to be our friend than our enemy." This seemed to be the basis of America's otherwise purposeless war on Serbia.

So great has been America's apparent success that an endless parade of officials and pundits warn against leaving Bosnia before people who have been battling each other for centuries learn to love each other. Naturally, Secretary of State Madeleine Albright favors expansive U.S. involvement: "To suggest, as some have, that America has no stake in the future of Bosnia is to propose that America abdicate its leadership role in Europe. To do so would shake the faith of allies, betray our responsibilities and ignore the lessons—learned at priceless cost in blood and treasure—of this century." Similarly, David Bosco of the Refugee Policy Group contended: "Backing down now would not only halt the peace process in Bosnia. It would signal to friends and foes alike the weakness of American commitments."

These sort of arguments about U.S. leadership, repeated endlessly during the war on Serbia by advocates of Pax Americana, are just plain silly. Leadership requires acting even when those on whose behalf one claims to be acting don't think the issue is important enough to act? That is the conduct of a sucker, not a leader. And what foes and what commitments are at stake? If Washington doesn't try to rebuild a Muslim-dominated Bosnia, then what? China will attack Taiwan, North Korea will attack South Korea, Russia will invade Germany? It would be an exercise in real leadership to ignore the Europeans' attempt at blackmail—threatening to remove their forces if President Clinton fulfilled his original commitment to bring U.S. soldiers home.

Unfortunately, the Balkans is only the start, at least if current Washington policy-makers have their way. Adm. Lopez says "if you take a macro-look at our theater, it's literally filled with instability and pockets of unrest." Examples include Albania, Algeria, Armenia, Azerbaijan, Bulgaria, Greece and Turkey, Libya, the Mideast, Syria, and Zaire. "With the end of the Cold War, the new enemy is instability, and it is manifested in this region more than in any other place in the world. Our business and our mission is to maintain stability."

Which, apparently, is why the U.S. has been aiding the militaries of Kazakstan, Kyrgyzstan, and Uzbekistan, areas never before thought to be of great strategic interest. Washington has been providing military aid to the latter; it has also established the United States-Uzbekistan Joint Commission to study military and political cooperation.

Moreover, last fall the U.S. conducted military exercises in the region. Explained Marine Gen. Jack Sheehan, commander of the U.S. Atlantic Command, if the UN ever authorized a "peace support operation," whatever that is, in the Central Asian nations, "then the United States is ready to stand beside them and participate." To this cheery thought he added: "there is no nation on the face of the earth that we cannot get to." He did not explain, however, why the U.S. or its NATO allies would want to get to such distant, impoverished nations, which border on Afghanistan, China, and Russia.

AFSOUTH is also advocating a "Mediterranean Initiative" that promotes military contacts with Egypt, Jordan, Mauritania, Morocco, and Tunisia. But Adm. Lopez wants more, much more—to expand the so-called Partnership for Peace, the precursor to NATO expansion into Central Europe, to such nations. And the Sixth Fleet has been conducting training exercises throughout West Africa. "I believe there's a need to make new friends," says Lopez, "so that NATO and the United States are viewed in a positive, rather than threatening, way." In other words, NATO will become kind of a big Peace Corps, only with nuclear weapons.

Is there no country over which America is unwilling to go to war? The answer, unfortunately, appears to be no. NATO officials suggest that "out-of-area" actions may become the alliance's primary focus in the future. For what conceivable purpose? Capt. Ken Golden, commander of an Amphibious Readiness Group attached to the Sixth Fleet, says "While a lot of Americans back home seem to think we don't have enemies anymore, I can tell you there's a lot of hatred out there. The world as we see it out here is a very unsettling and unstable place." Yes, but America's enemies—such as Cuba and North Korea—are simply pathetic. And most of the hatred would not be directed at the U.S. if Washington did not meddle in all sorts of faraway, irrelevant conflicts.

The case for maintaining 100,000 soldiers in East Asia is equally dubious. South Korea has 30 times the GDP and twice the population of North Korea. The former is a dominant trading nation, produces a wealth of hi-tech products, and has stolen away almost all of its adversaries' allies. The latter is impoverished, isolated, and incapable of feeding itself. It is as if the U.S. was dependent on outside support to deter Mexican aggression.

Similarly, a military presence imposed on Japan when it was a distrusted and war-torn former military dictatorship remains even though the latter is now the second-ranking economic power on earth, which has peacefully attained most that it could have hoped for from its World War II goal of a Greater East Asia Co-Prosperity Sphere. It was one thing to borrow money from Japan to defend Japan when Tokyo faced a potentially aggressive Soviet Union and was incapable of defending itself. It is quite another to do so when the threats against Japan have greatly diminished and Tokyo's defense capabilities have greatly increased.

And no replacement threats loom on the horizon. China is growing, but it seems assertive rather than aggressive, and its military expansion has so far been measured. Japan and the other East Asian states are capable of maintaining a sufficient military deterrent, and that won't change for many years. China remains poor and underdeveloped despite its recent explosive economic growth.

Germany and Japan are still feared by some neighbors, but neither has a double dose of original sin and is unlikely to attack powerful neighbors, many of whom possess nuclear weapons. Brazil, India, Indonesia, and other nations may eventually evolve into regional powers, but the U.S. has no reason to treat them as enemies and plenty of time to respond if they become hostile. Outlaw states like Iraq and North Korea pose local conventional threats that should be contained by their neighbors, not the U.S. The problem of nuclear proliferation is more complex, but not easily resolvable through conventional military means by Washington.

Of course, the globe remains an uncertain place, and new threats could arise over the long-term. But that doesn't require Washington to attempt to micromanage a world that will always be unsettled. Secretary of State Albright says of her interventionist views: "my mind-set is Munich." There was only one Hitler, however, and Europe's circumstances during the 1930s were unique. Thus, the U.S. need not confront militarily every nation with which it has a disagreement. Rather, Washington should remain wary and watchful, prepared to play the role of distant balancer should a potential hegemonic threat arise that cannot be contained by friendly states. America will be better able to meet genuine future threats if it does not exhaust itself attempting to maintain a dominance, benevolent or not, that is sure to be resisted by many friends as well as foes.

Another alternative mission is trying to rebuild failed societies, which could also absorb significant military forces. In fact, it already has. As John Hillen, of the Center for Strategic and International Studies, puts it, "the United States has had difficulty saying no to almost any call for military action in the past five years," undertaking some 50 different military missions all over the world. And there could be even more demands for U.S. intervention in the future. Today some 30 Third World brushfires are raging. National Security adviser Sandy Berger talks of using U.S. power as "the decisive force for peace in the world." Sen. Richard Lugar, one of the GOP's leading foreign policy spokesmen, argues that "we have an unparalleled opportunity to manage the world."

But Somalia vividly demonstrated how difficult it is for officials in Washington to reach inside and manipulate other societies, let alone to resolve ancient hatreds and political divisions. U.S. military pressure helped halt the fighting in the Balkans, but only after allowing the very partition that Washington had long resisted. In Kosovo Washington's war of aggression has strengthened Albanian extremists, the most destabilizing force in the region. American involvement has simply suppressed regional antagonisms, not resolved them.

Nor is there any reason to try to fix broken states. That tragedy abounds in a world so full of opportunity is perhaps the great anomaly of our age. But failing to recognize the inherent limitation on the ability of Washington to "manage" other countries ensures that officials will only compound tragedy elsewhere by sacrificing the lives of U.S. (and potentially European) citizens as well.

Of course, some politicians seem unconcerned about the prospect of risking the lives of U.S. servicemen for any number of dubious purposes. Then-U.N. Ambassador Albright asked Colin Powell, "What's the point in having this superb military that you're always talking about if we can't use it?" That's easy to say if one doesn't have any family members or friends in the military. But as Powell retorted, GIs are "not toy soldiers to be moved around on some kind of global game board." The American people obviously agree, given their reaction to the disaster in Somalia. This has led to criticism by some foreign policy elites. Writes Thomas Friedman of the New York Times, "We can't lead if we don't put our own people at risk." But real leadership does not mean sacrificing soldiers' lives for interests irrelevant to their own political community.

Even in distant wars with some plausible security implications, like the Balkans, other nations, in this case the Europeans, have far more at stake than does the U.S. Moreover, nonintervention offers the surest method to contain such conflicts. Alliances proved to be transmission belts of war in World War I, drawing ever more peripheral powers into a conflict that proved disastrous for every one of them. In contrast, the same nations erected firebreaks to war when fighting broke out in Yugoslavia in 1991. Thus, the conflict burned longer than the First World War without spreading.

The final refuge of those who support big military budgets is "leadership." Republican presidential nominee Bob Dole made that undefined term his 1996 campaign mantra. Vice President Al Gore matched Dole by telling the Veterans of Foreign Wars convention that "America must act and lead." Former House Speaker Newt Gingrich made much the same pitch: "You do not need today's defense budget to defend the United States. You need today's defense budget to lead the world." Secretary of State Madeleine Albright says that America must "accept responsibility and lead." William Kristol's Project for the New American Century proclaims: "we cannot safely avoid the responsibilities of global leadership."

There is virtually no limit to the responsibilities entailed by this popular goal. "At times," declares Joshua Muravchik of the American Enterprise Institute, the U.S. "must be the policeman or head of the posse—at others, the mediator, teacher, or benefactor. In short, America must accept the role of world leader." Zalmay Khalilzad cites as responsibilities of leadership preparing for such contingencies as tension in the Balkans, a China-Taiwan confrontation, and "an internal conflict in a key regional state," presumably meaning involvement in a civil war. This attitude even leads to support for intervention to simply demonstrate leadership. Former Secretary of State Warren Christopher called Bosnia "an acid test of American leadership." Having gotten involved, the

U.S. naturally now cannot leave without fulfilling its goals—in order to demonstrate leadership. UN Ambassador Richard Holbrooke, who negotiated the unrealistic agreement for an artificial, polyglot Bosnian state, declares that "failure is unthinkable. We cannot afford to fail."

However, the U.S. has the largest and most productive economy on earth. It is the leading trading nation. The American constitutional system has proved to be one of the world's more durable. U.S. culture permeates the globe. (Admittedly, this might not always be good for the rest of the world—MTV and Madonna are probably not America's best exports—but it exemplifies America's non-military dominance.) An outsize military is not required for "leadership."

Anyway, even significant budget cuts would leave Washington with the world's largest and most advanced military, far stronger than that of any other state or coalition of states. And those cuts would allow the economy, America's most important source of influence, to grow faster. Today, Washington's disproportionate military burden does more than divert precious economic resources down wasteful channels. It simultaneously relieves America's industrialized competitors from spending more on their militaries. This has allowed Japan and Europe, in particular, to gain an edge they otherwise would not have. Not surprisingly, such international dependents want to keep their generous U.S. subsidies: both Germany's Helmut Kohl and France's Jacques Chirac shamelessly demanded a continued U.S. military presence in Europe even while cutting back their own militaries.

There are alternatives to unilateral U.S. hegemony. In some areas regional security organizations, like the Western European Union or an America-less NATO in Europe, could keep the peace. Another option is informal spheres of influence, where interested local powers help maintain stability in their own regions—essentially America's strategy in Central America. Finally, a rough balance of power may generally constrain potentially aggressive powers; such a system could evolve in both East Asia and Mideast if the U.S. reduced its dominant presence.

No one wants America to be weak, or vulnerable to potential enemies, which is why defense spending on training and technology should remain priorities. This is also why policymakers should beware turning the military into something else, either through social experimentation, such as the feminization of training and standards, or involvement in humanitarian missions. Of the latter, warns a Foreign Policy Research Institute task force, "U.S. forces engage in the politics, ambiguities and complexities of 'peacefighting,' often at the expense of their 'war-fighting' skills and training."

Washington needs to match forces to missions, and to do so it must reconsider strategies made obsolete by a changing world. Zalmay Khalilzad worries that the collapse of the U.S.S.R., "the common enemy that helped bring" America's disparate alliances together, creates the danger "that these alliances will weaken and eventually collapse." But the disappearance of the threat that animated such military organizations *should* lead to their disappearance, at least as originally formed. The U.S. should adjust its force structure for a post-Cold War world by shifting defense responsibilities onto allies and eliminating units currently dedicated to those tasks. Doing so would allow a radical restructuring—from, for instance, 1.4 million to 900,000 servicemen. The military budget could be cut to some $170 billion, down from nearly $270 billion today.

Although Joshua Muravchik complains that the U.S. media "has given the American people a very distorted picture of our military effort" by suggesting that defense outlays are too high, it is really the politicians seeking higher military outlays who are misleading the American people. Polls find rising support for sizable cuts in military outlays when U.S. voters find out how much Washington actually spends compared to its allies and potential adversaries.

The U.S. spends far more than is necessary to protect America and its vital interests around the world. In the absence of a threatening global hegemon, Washington should again become a normal nation, with a normal military.

November 1999

Isolationist Myths

When Texas Gov. George W. Bush recently inveighed against "isolation," he joined a chorus in which President Clinton is the lead member. When the Republican Congress voted to cut the administration's foreign aid budget, the President predictably responded by denouncing "a new isolationism in this country." Yet what is now routinely termed "isolationism" is actually responsible internationalism.

Opposition to attacking Yugoslavia, occupying Bosnia, invading Haiti, expanding NATO, increasing foreign aid, opposing the test ban and Law of the Sea treaties, paying more dues to the UN, continuing draft registration, and any number of other international initiatives have been met with the epithet "isolationist." Rather than debate the issues, global interventionists prefer to smear their opponents.

Despite a persistent xenophobic strain in U.S. politics, Americans have always been active around the globe. Their "isolationism" primarily reflected George Washington's sensible advice to avoid unnecessary military entanglements.

Indeed, most alleged isolationists were anything but. Many of the strongest opponents of Woodrow Wilson's League of Nations were internationalists who wanted the U.S. to act unilaterally. Many critics of Franklin Delano Roosevelt simply saw no need to get involved in another European killfest.

Today the charge of isolationism is errant nonsense. The same Republican Senate that Clinton attacked for killing the Comprehensive Test Ban Treaty (CTBT) approved the expansion of NATO. The Republican Congress that cut the President's foreign aid budget nevertheless had approved nearly $13 billion in outlays.

Indeed, the real danger today is promiscuous intervention, not isolation. On issue after issue, foolish and unnecessary meddling is making America as well as other nations less prosperous and secure.

Consider the CTBT. People of good will can differ, but the treaty's verifiability and impact on America's nuclear arsenal are problematic.

The more obscure Law of the Sea Treaty, which remains in Senate limbo, would create essentially a second United Nations to govern international seabed mining. The costly, bureaucratic system would impede economic development and discriminate against American companies.

As for foreign aid, supporters simply assume that throwing good money after bad will achieve something positive. Yet there is no correlation between foreign assistance and economic growth; waste and fraud have been epidemic everywhere from Bosnia to Indonesia to the Philippines to Russia.

Then there's the administration's dubious strategy of foreign policy as social work, as Michael Mandelbaum of Johns Hopkins University has called it. U.S. military intervention has created an artificial, unstable Bosnian state, transformed Haiti from a military into a presidential dictatorship, and promoted the ethnic cleansing of Serbs rather than of Albanians in Kosovo. Opposition to putting Americans at risk in all these endeavors was eminently reasonable.

Similarly, expanding NATO has increased U.S. defense responsibilities in a region with little impact on American security. Continuing expansion may draw Washington into irrelevant regional squabbles, while needlessly exacerbating already potent nationalistic sentiments in Russia.

Paying off America's dues to the UN before reforms were made has ensured that reforms will never be made, since Washington's only leverage was its unpaid dues. The UN will remain simultaneously profligate and ineffective.

Even the House vote to defund the Selective Service System, and its continuing registration of young men for the draft, has been cited as evidence of isolationism. Yet the U.S. dominates the globe militarily and could defeat any conceivable enemy with its existing active and reserve forces. This vestige of the Cold War deserves to die.

The new isolationists, warns President Clinton, "are saying America does not need to lead either by effort or by example." They believe that "we should bury our heads in the sand behind a wall." This is false, and he knows it.

The U.S. will be a superpower in spite of itself: it possesses the world's largest and most productive economy, one of the most stable political systems and attractive political philosophies, and the most pervasive culture. America's influence is guaranteed if it participates naturally in the global economy, compassionately accepts immigrants and refugees, and cooperates with other states to solve global problems.

Washington need not, however, subsidize every foreign nation, global agency, and international initiative. At the very least it should determine that the programs it is being asked to support, such as foreign aid, actually work. It should also expect other parties, especially those which have more at stake, to pay more.

Moreover, it is good sense, not isolationism, to reserve military intervention for issues of vital national concern. Washington's responsibility to Americans in uniform demands no less.

The end of the Cold War has reduced the international dangers facing the U.S. Those who want America to do everything everywhere should drop the ad hominem. Instead of trashing their opponents as isolationists, they should make their case—if they can.

December 1999

Defending Whom?

Over the weekend Attorney General John Ashcroft warned that more terrorism is likely, while Defense Secretary Donald Rumsfeld predicted that terrorists would eventually deploy biological, chemical, and possibly even nuclear weapons. These frightening possibilities illustrate the superficial appeal of President George W. Bush's plan to create a cabinet-level Office of Homeland Security.

But the plan raises an equally obvious question. What is the Department of Defense protecting, if not America's homeland?

The devastating terrorist attacks of 11 September demonstrated that the U.S. is open to attack. But a "coordinator," even with the political skill of Pennsylvania Gov. Tom Ridge, is unlikely to do much without statutory authority. Just like the so-called Drug Czar.

Yet creating another formal bureaucracy carries dangers of its own. As the writer Randolph Bourne once observed, "war is the health of the state." Powers supposedly temporarily granted during emergencies frequently persist long afterwards.

Here, as elsewhere, the President and Congress should let the panic spawned by the terrorist attack fade, rather than act in haste. Otherwise Americans might find themselves stuck with a new agency that is ineffective but intrusive, pointless but expensive.

Even more fundamental, however, is the question: why is a new bureaucracy needed? After all, shouldn't the Department of Defense be defending America's homeland?

Theoretically the Pentagon is deterring traditional foreign military threats. Yet much of what the U.S. armed forces do has nothing to do with protecting Americans. Which is one reason why the U.S. was ill-prepared for the terrorist strikes and why terrorists want to attack America.

Despite charges of declining military strength, the U.S. is a colossus without peer. America accounts for one-third of the world's military outlays, spends as much as the next seven countries combined, and is allied with all of the globe's major industrialized states.

No state offers a conventional match. Only Russia has a significant nuclear force capable of devastating the U.S. The Chinese arsenal will grow and smaller nations might eventually develop limited nuclear capabilities, but Washington is well able to guard against such threats, especially if it deploys a meaningful missile defense.

With so few genuine threats against which to guard, the Pentagon has focused on other tasks: protecting populous and prosperous allies throughout Asia and Europe against phantom perils; endlessly but ineffectively striking at old enemies, such as Iraq; attempting to settle other nations' civil wars, as in Kosovo; and propping up artificial countries, like Bosnia. None of these have much to do with guarding America.

There are troops in Europe, but no Red Army to contain. There are soldiers policing the Balkans, a region of interest to Europe, but not America.

There are forces throughout East Asia, even though the Soviet Union is gone, North Korea is fading, and China remains far behind. The U.S. attacks Iraq to protect Kurds while abetting Turkey which attacks Kurds.

This globally interventionist foreign policy is obviously burdensome and expensive. Moreover, it has drawn attention away from real homeland defense. Instead of configuring the military to eliminate an illusive enemy that just hit two American cities, the Pentagon worries about defending its traditional ally, South Korea, which possesses 40 times the GDP and twice the population of its bankrupt adversary, North Korea—which itself has no capacity to threaten America.

Moreover, the attempt to play global social engineer has created many enemies who, sadly, are able and willing to attack America. Backing Israel against the Palestinians, seeking to enforce a broken peace against Iraq ten years on, allying with Saudi Arabia, supporting various ethnic groups, governments, and guerrilla forces in the Balkans, and supporting a weak Colombian regime against drug dealers and communist insurgents all thrust the U.S. into violent, hate-filled conflicts.

Gov. Ridge will find much work to do: preparing disaster response plans, coordinating federal intelligence and security efforts, and making sense of 40-plus agencies with related programs. But we would be far safer if only the Pentagon devoted more of its attention to homeland defense.

We need fewer army divisions designed for a NATO-Warsaw Pact confrontation—and more special forces trained to find and kill terrorists in distant lands. We need fewer air wings dedicated to stopping nonexistent communist aggression overseas—and more aircraft patrolling U.S. airspace to thwart assaults launched with private planes, hijacked or otherwise. We need less defense pork, ranging from obsolete bases to unnecessary weapons—and more money to counteract less obvious unconventional threats.

Most fundamentally, we need a foreign policy that emphasizes defending America, not allied states. And which accurately counts the cost of unnecessary meddling abroad, eschewing involvement where the benefits are negligible and the risks are significant.

There is no more important duty for the U.S. government than homeland defense. But the key to protecting Americans is not creating a new agency. The key is refocusing the attention of the Department of Defense on defense.

October 2001

Withdrawing U.S. Forces: A Good Start

President George W. Bush has proposed bringing home about one-third of U.S. troops stationed in Asia and Europe. It's a good start, but it doesn't go nearly far enough.

The administration shouldn't just plan on pulling back 60,000 or 70,000 troops (along with their families and support staff), and do so over the next decade. Washington should withdraw all 230,000 service personnel guarding against phantom enemies in Europe and protecting well-heeled friends in East Asia. And the U.S. should begin withdrawing them now, rather than in 2006, and finish in two or three years, rather than in ten.

From World War II through the Cold War, America was forced to adopt the role of global guardian. The enemies of freedom were obvious and dangerous: Nazism, fascism, and communism.

As President Ronald Reagan observed, the Soviet Union was an evil empire. The U.S. had little choice but to confront a succession of monstrous tyrannies backed by ample militaries.

However, the Cold War ended more than a decade ago. The Berlin Wall, the ultimate symbol of communist totalitarianism, now seems but a hazy memory. Now America's friends face few conventional threats and are capable of defending themselves.

Yet Washington retains its extensive network of commitments, bases, and garrisons created to contain the USSR and allied powers. American troop levels have fallen, but not nearly enough.

There is no serious military threat to Europe. Instability in the Balkans threatens to inconvenience neighboring states, not leave the continent under the control of a hegemonic antagonist.

Indeed, it is hard to spin a plausible, let alone likely, scenario involving Europe that threatens American security. An invasion of, say, Germany by Martians is about as likely as by Russians.

In East Asia the dangers are more real, with North Korea making threatening noises. But the South has 40 times the GDP and twice the population of Pyongyang. South Korea can outmatch any military fielded by the North.

Japan understandably looks at China with some unease, but Tokyo should construct a defensive force capable of deterring Chinese adventurism. Tokyo's neighbors prefer defense by America, but World War II is 60 years in the past. The U.S. has no obligation to pacify the region forever.

Beijing could become a serious rival of America; it is not likely to challenge the U.S. directly, however. Taiwan is the most obvious potential flashpoint, but no sane president would inaugurate a ground war with China. Thus, neither an army division in South Korea nor a Marine Expeditionary Force in Japan would perform any useful role in any conflict.

Still, critics contend, having troops nearby would better enable the U.S. to intervene in some future crisis. But most potential conflicts, whether in the Balkans or Southeast Asia or the Caucasus, would not warrant American involvement.

Moreover, allies often limit Washington's options. France would not even grant overflight rights to Washington to retaliate against Libya for the Berlin disco bombing.

Seoul and Tokyo would be unlikely to allow Washington to use their bases in a war with China, at least unless they were directly attacked. After all, neither wants to become a permanent enemy of the People's Republic.

Finally, changing technology has reduced the value of propinquity. As President Bush observed, our forces are "more agile and more lethal, they're better able to strike anywhere in the world over great distances on short notice."

The U.S. can use precision weapons to strike from American territory or international waters; quickly insert special forces for covert action or cooperation with allied forces; and bring naval air power to bear without land bases. A major conflict like that in Iraq would require an extended build-up, irrespective of where the forces were located.

In contrast, the benefits of withdrawing are obvious. As the President observed: "our service members will have more time on the home front, and more predictability and fewer moves over a career. Our military spouses will have fewer job changes, greater stability, more time for their kids and to spend with their families at home. The taxpayers will save money, as we configure our military to meet the threats of the 21st century. There will be savings as we consolidate and close bases and facilities overseas no longer needed to face the threats of our time and defend the peace."

One of the most important virtues of drawing down unnecessary foreign garrisons is to reduce the pressure on personnel resulting from the unexpectedly difficult and long occupation of Iraq. Roughly 40 percent of the 140,000 troops now stationed in Iraq are Reserve or National Guard.

No matter how patriotic soldiers are, they will not reenlist if they fear spending most of their lives abroad. The burden falls particularly heavily on members of the Guard and Reserve, who leave their jobs as well as families and often face career disruptions and severe economic hardships.

President Bush also contended that his proposal "will strengthen our alliances around the world, while we build new partnerships to better preserve the peace." Actually, pulling out troops would not improve existing relationships, which is perhaps the only sensible point made by his critics.

For instance, former UN Ambassador Richard Holbrooke complained of "the message that this administration continues to operate in a unilateral manner without adequately consulting its closest allies." That's certainly the attitude in foreign capitals.

Explains Holbrooke: "the Germans are very unhappy about these withdrawals. The Koreans are going to be equally unhappy." No one wants Washington to trim America's defense gravy train.

A few officials in Asia might actually fear for their security. Some Europeans complain that the Bush administration is retaliating for their opposition to the U.S. invasion of Iraq.

However, most critics most worry about the economic impact on local communities that now benefit from the presence of American forces. Wuerzburg city spokesman Ole Kruse explained that "Base closures would hit us very hard." Peter Lang, mayor of Baumholder, said: "The town would bleed to death."

Washington's response should be, so what? Proposals for drawing down U.S. forces were made long before the Iraq war and are justified by changing strategic realities, whatever the Bush administration's private intentions.

Moreover, Americans aren't responsible for making Germans and Koreans happy. In particular, the economic health of small German villages is a problem for Berlin, not Washington, which has the U.S. economy to consider.

Even some American devotees of the status quo complain that the nation's defenses will suffer. Charged Wesley Clark, who commanded President Bill Clinton's misbegotten war on Serbia and now supports Democratic presidential nominee John Kerry: the move would "significantly undermine U.S. national security." Holbrooke called the proposal "pretty alarming."

But even if trans-Atlantic ties loosened, the U.S. would be better off. America's alliances are largely security black holes, with Washington doing the defending and allies doing the carping. Withdrawal would force friendly states to take on full responsibility for their own defense, which would significantly enhance U.S. security.

Why should Americans patrol Bosnia, Kosovo, and Macedonia, which are of only peripheral interest to Europe, and of no concern to the U.S.? Japan should take on a front-line role in deterring potential Chinese adventurism. Why does Washington treat populous and prosperous South Korea as a perpetual defense dependent?

However, the Bush proposal only makes sense if the troops come home. They should not be based in different countries—Central and Eastern Europe or Australia, for instance, or worse yet, in Central Asia. The core threat against American security interests today is terrorism. Stationing troops in Poland or Australia would no more help destroy terrorist groups than has keeping forces in Germany or South Korea.

More troops should be brought home more quickly from Asia and Europe. U.S. forces, now at 140,000, must be withdrawn from Iraq as well. Continuing American participation in civil strife and guerrilla war creates more antagonism and encourages more terrorism at the cost of more body bags coming home.

Washington must accelerate the creation of a viable Iraqi government and security force, and get out. Baghdad's future must be decided by Iraqis.

America's overall security environment has changed dramatically over the last two decades. America's combat troop requirement has changed dramatically over the last two years.

President Bush recognizes that the status quo is untenable. His plan should be but the opening move towards full disengagement.

August 2004

Staying As Long As Who Wants Us To?

President George W. Bush may look forward to liberating foreign lands, but the majority of Americans believe that his chief priority is dealing with Iraq. How long we stay there ultimately must be decided based on American, not Iraqi, interests.

One reason the U.S. military is badly stretched is because Washington continues to maintain garrisons around the globe. Traditional commitments in Asia and Europe have been supplemented by sporadic intervention elsewhere, including the ongoing occupation of Iraq.

America should defend foreign nations and base troops overseas based on its interests, not those of other countries. U.S. deployments should advance Americans' security, not other people's desires.

Unfortunately, U.S. analysts and policymakers often ignore this fundamental principle. To resolve the problem of Iraq, for instance, Frederick Barton, Bathsheba Crocker, and Craig Cohen of the Center for Strategic and International Studies propose allowing "the Iraqis themselves" to vote on America's continued military presence.

That would be fine if the Iraqis said go. But their saying stay would offer no reason for the U.S. to stick around. Washington should bear the cost and risk soldiers' lives only if doing so serves American interests, irrespective of what the Iraqis think.

It's a common mistake. U.S. officials have routinely said that Washington plans on staying in South Korea as long as the South Koreans want us to stay. But why?

The Republic of Korea is well able to defend itself. That they prefer to save money by relying on the U.S. is no justification for America's security guarantee.

Thankfully, over the objection of the Korean government the Bush administration recently decided to bring home one-third of the existing garrison. But 25,000 U.S. troops will remain.

In fact, other nations and peoples routinely expect the U.S. to serve their interests. When the administration announced last year that it intended to withdraw two armored divisions from Germany, residents in towns hosting the forces complained.

They weren't worried about having to defend against, say, a Russian invasion. Rather, they feared losing the cash that U.S. soldiers bring.

Two years ago Icelanders made a similar complaint when Washington decided to close its air base at Keflavik. Washington reasonably pointed out that there no longer was a Soviet threat, but officials from Iceland—which doesn't bother to field its own military—were not convinced.

Warned Helgi Agustsson, Iceland's ambassador to the U.S.: "September 11th wasn't supposed to happen either. An enemy always looks for the weakest link." Petulantly, Prime Minister David Oddsson said that American naval vessels might not be welcome if the U.S. pulled out its F-15 fighters.

When violence erupted in East Timor, then occupied by Indonesia, in 1999. protestors gathered before America's embassy in Portugal—East Timor's one-time colonial master—demanding that Washington intervene. Never mind that Portugal had contributed to the problem and failed to field a military capable of acting. America should do something.

Equally presumptuous, though for far more understandable reasons, were Liberians in summer 2003. They had suffered decades of conflict and civil war. The murderous President Charles Taylor, who had emerged victorious a few years before in a three-sided civil war, was then beset by a growing insurgency.

Since Liberia was established by freed U.S. slaves, the west African nation was considered to be Washington's client. Two decades ago a U.S. Senate report concluded: "It is fair to say that in the eyes of other African and Western governments, Liberia's well-being is an American responsibility."

Liberians obviously felt the same way. One banner proclaimed at a demonstration in the capital of Monrovia: "Uncle Sam Must Come at Once." Doug Collier, a relief worker, said that Liberians asked him, "Why doesn't America come in and save us?"

Although Nigeria sent troops, that wasn't viewed as enough. A refugee exclaimed: "we like the Nigerians—but we want some few Americans or British, to help them out and ensure the stability of the country."

One can understand why Liberians wanted U.S. aid. But American troops are not pawns to be moved about the globe in someone else's international chess game.

This point befuddles even some of Washington's closest allies. After his election South Korean President Roh Moo-hyun complained that "So far, all changes in the size of U.S. troop strength here have been determined by the United States based on its strategic consideration, without South Korea's consent."

But upon what does he believe America's deployments should be based? South Korea's strategic consideration?

Bringing stability and democracy to Iraq is no mean task. And the U.S. cannot stay if it is not wanted. But an Iraqi desire that American forces remain is no cause to keep them there.

Even more so, the fact that South Koreans want to be defended, or that Germans enjoy the benefits of spending by American troops, is irrelevant to U.S. policy. America's force deployments must be based on America's strategic interests.

The U.S. is a great and good country. But its military should not be used to serve the interests of others. Only the protection of American interests warrants the sacrifice of American lives.

January 2005

CHAPTER TWO

The Impact On A Free Society

The Price of Intervention

"The era of big government is over," it has been said, but government continues to grow. Even when Congress rebuffs a presidential power grab, like Bill Clinton's proposed nationalization of health care, legislators soon surrender much of the same ground in smaller pieces.

The expanding welfare state is an obvious cause of our steadily eroding freedom. Since the New Deal, Uncle Sam has become a quixotic cross between Santa Claus and national nag. The average citizen doesn't finish paying the cost of government until July, according to Americans for Tax Reform.

But the growth of the state is not merely a domestic phenomenon. The transformation of Washington, D.C. from a sleepy, insular southern town into the center of a Leviathan state also reflects Uncle Sam's determination to dominate the world. The shift from republic to empire abroad sparked a related mutation at home.

In this way, conservatives who support global intervention promote big government. Unfortunately, some are clueless. For instance, Arch Puddington of Freedom House dismisses such concerns as "overheated rhetoric," given "the extraordinary prosperity and personal freedom that Americans have enjoyed in the postwar era." But while the U.S. is freer that most other nations, this reflects a vestigial philosophical heritage reaching back to the founding, not an immunity from the corrosive impact of military measures on liberty.

The Civil War first firmly impressed the national government on the national consciousness: new and confiscatory taxes, inflationary monetary policy, routine violations of civil liberties and democratic procedures, conscription, and more. As Robert Higgs pointed out in his seminal work, *Crisis and Leviathan*, while government usually shrinks at the conclusion of such conflicts, it never returns to its previous size.

This phenomenon was even more evident during World War I, perhaps America's bleakest time ever for free speech. Mere opposition to conscription and the conflict landed socialist Eugene Debs and a host of lesser-known figures in prison. Federal spending mushroomed, remaining at quadruple pre-war levels during the 1920s.

Washington also implemented war socialism, with pervasive government intervention in the economy. Many of those restrictions live on—as Ted Galen Carpenter points out in the *Freeman*, Richard Nixon used the 1917 Trading with the Enemy Act to control every wage and price in America. More subtly, government economic management introduced many businessmen to the benefits of state-supported cartels, preparing the ground for the costly excesses of the New Deal.

Similar was the experience of World War II. Not only was the economy and population conscripted in the ongoing military crusade, but many of the worst regulations, ranging from the military draft to rent control in New York City, survived the conflict. Equally long-lasting was the belief in executive infallibility, which led President Harry Truman to unilaterally take America into the Korean War and to attempt to seize the steel industry.

The Cold War spawned McCarthyism, FBI surveillance of domestic dissidents, peacetime conscription, the sprawling Military-Industrial Complex, the Vietnam imbroglio, and unending executive arrogance. Observes Burton Yale Pines, former Vice President of the Heritage Foundation: "today's mammoth federal government is the product not so much of the New Deal but of the massive power assembled in Washington to wage World War II and the Cold War."

At least the threat posed by the Soviet Union provided a plausible argument for sacrificing individual freedom to state power. But no longer: America's enemies are few and pathetic and its allies are capable of defending themselves. So advocates of a new imperium typically demand an international crusade for democracy.

However, occasional elections are not the same thing as liberty. As Fareed Zakaria points out in *Foreign Affairs*, many democracies around the globe, like Belarus, Slovakia, and Pakistan, are short on freedom. Even the U.S. is not immune from the authoritarian virus—consider the jackboot liberalism of the Clinton administration. We certainly should not sacrifice our freedom through global intervention in the often vain hope of bringing democracy, which so frequently means illiberal democracy, to other states.

Of course, some of those who back Cold War interventionism despite the end of the Cold War—including Puddington, who, ironically, works for an organization with "freedom" in its name—really don't believe in liberty. At least they don't believe it is important enough to interfere with their goals. They see war, conscription, big military budgets, high taxes, economic regulation, trade restrictions, and press controls as a small price to pay for the opportunity to play social engineer around the globe, especially if someone else is doing the paying.

Republican legislators and potential presidential candidates must realize that they can't have both limited government and global hegemony. The President is pursuing the latter. What says the GOP?

November 1997

Who's Number One?

Foreign policy has become a leading political issue: America is being portrayed as a beleaguered isle of freedom in a world threatened with a new Dark Ages. Yet the U.S. is safer today than at any time during the last half century. Washington should sharply cut military outlays.

While Al Gore and Bill Bradley spar over health care, the leading Republican candidates push to "strengthen" the military, a popular call in the upcoming South Carolina primary. For instance, Texas Gov. George W. Bush complains that "not since the years before Pearl Harbor has our investment in national defense been so low as a percentage of GNP." Sen. John McCain (R-Ariz.) sounds like an echo when he warns that "the last time we spent so little on defense was 1940—the year before Pearl Harbor."

Even more apocalyptic is conservative radio personality Rush Limbaugh, who warns that "we cannot survive more liberalism" at home or abroad. After all, he explains, "the world is far more dangerous than the day Ronald Reagan left office."

It is unclear, however, in what world they believe Americans to be living.

True, the percentage of GNP currently devoted to defense, about 3.2 percent, is lower than at any time since before World War II. Although that number fell to 3.5 percent in 1948, it climbed sharply with the onset of the Cold War and very hot Korean War. One must go back to 1940, when military outlays ran about 1.7 percent of GNP, to find a lower ratio.

But so what? America's GNP then was $96.5 billion, or about $1.2 trillion in today's dollars. That compares to a GNP of more than $8.7 trillion in 1999. In short, one percent of GNP today means eight times as much spending as in 1940.

Moreover, the U.S. was a military pygmy in 1940, with just 458,000 men under arms, up from around 250,000 during the mid-1920s through 1930s. America lagged well behind Britain, China, France, Germany, Japan, Russia—and even Italy.

Today Washington dominates the globe. It accounts for more than a third of the globe's defense outlays. It possesses the strongest military on earth: a well-trained force of 1.4 million employing the most advanced weapons. The U.S. spends as much on the military as the next seven nations combined, five of which are close allies.

In short, to suggest that America is weak, let alone as weak as before Pearl Harbor, is nonsense.

No less silly is the contention that the U.S. faces greater threats today than a decade ago. The world is messy, yes, and the end of the artificial stability of the Cold War unleashed a series of small conflicts in the Balkans. However, most of the globe's nasty little wars—such as Angola, Kashmir, Sri Lanka, and Sudan—began well before 1989. And none of these conflicts threatens the U.S. as did the struggle with the U.S.S.R. and its international satellite network.

Moreover, virtually every pairing today favors America's friends. The Europeans spend more on the military than does Russia; Japan's outlays exceed those of China; South Korea vastly outranges North Korea. America's implacable enemies are few and pitiful: Cuba, Iran, Iraq, Libya, North Korea, and Serbia collectively spend $12 to $13 billion on the military, less than U.S. allies like Israel and Taiwan, let alone the U.S.

A decade ago was not so rosy. Not only did the Soviet Union spend more than twice as much as does Russia, but it formally confronted America. The Warsaw Pact states spent as much as NATO's eight smallest members. Heavily militarized Third World communist nations, such as Angola, Ethiopia, North Korea, and Vietnam, threatened U.S. surrogates. Most important, the American homeland was at risk: today the possibility of a foreign attack on the U.S. is a paranoid fantasy.

Except in one form—terrorism. Although foreign governments, facing the threat of massive retaliation, are unlikely to strike America, ethnic, ideological, and religious groups might not be so hesitant. However, they are unlikely to do so out of abstract hatred of the U.S. To the contrary, most acts of violence, such as those perpetrated by Osama bin Laden, are in response to U.S. intervention abroad. Terrorism is the weapon of choice of the relatively powerless against meddling by the globe's sole superpower.

In this case, America's strength, represented by its global pervasive presence, is America's weakness. The solution is not more military spending, but greater military caution. The risk of terrorism must be added to the other costs of intervening in foreign quarrels with little relevance to U.S. security.

Should America's military be strengthened? Yes: problems with readiness, recruiting, and retention should be addressed and missile defenses should be constructed. But outlays could still be slashed by shrinking force levels to match today's more benign threat environment. The world is less, not more dangerous, than a decade ago. America is relatively stronger today than ever before, notwithstanding the misguided claims of Messrs. Bush and McCain.

February 2000

Treason Trials

Few people doubt that Bill Clinton has blundered disastrously in his war against Yugoslavia. But some pundits are busy seeking to taint those who criticize him as guilty of treason.

The administration itself has been working hard to silence its critics, particularly those on Capitol Hill. Secretary of State Madeleine Albright opposed proposals for a congressional vote on military action in early March, when the President was merely threatening air strikes. In late April the administration and its Democratic congressional allies sought to block any vote on the President's unauthorized warmaking.

Democratic legislators accused the GOP of "ambushing" the administration. Secretary Albright and Defense Secretary William Cohen fussed that any vote could be "misinterpreted" as a retreat from NATO solidarity. The President even promised to come back to Congress for approval of any plan to launch a ground war, though White House spokesman Joe Lockhart fueled GOP fears by explaining that Clinton would seek "support," not "approval" from Congress, meaning the President would feel free to ignore the results of any vote.

Nevertheless, the administration was circumspect in its criticism compared to some Kosovo hawks. Columnist Bill Press, for instance, termed GOP leaders Slobodan Milosevic's "best friends in Washington." Congress had "turned its back on a president and on our brave men and women in uniform in the middle of a war." Indeed, the GOP majority was guilty of "betrayal," of "giving aid and comfort to the enemy." Oh, he whined, "what ever became of patriotism?"

Republicans with the temerity to seek some solution other than flattening of Yugoslavia have come under attack from Michael Kelly, editor of *National Journal*. "It is customary, when the United States is at war, for members of Congress to support the nation, or at least to avoid giving support to the enemy," writes Kelly.

Thus, Kelly flays Majority Whip Tom Delay for considering the conflict to be "the president's war." Rep. Jim Saxton (R-NJ) is accused of "giving aid and comfort to the Yugoslavian war aims and working against the war aims of the United State" for observing that Belgrade's vicious crackdown was triggered by the imminence of U.S. military strikes. Rep. Curt Weldon (R-Pa.) faces a similar charge for meeting with Russian legislators to attempt to find a compromise to halt the conflict.

To not reflexively back the administration's strategy is thus to work "against the interests of the United States." The war is ours, not Bill Clinton's, argues Kelly, and those who fail to understand that "do not understand the idea of nationhood, and they call into question their own fitness to lead." Whew!

Actually, true patriotism does not require reflexive support of an administration, irrespective of how wrong its policy. The war against Yugoslavia—and it is a war, despite President Clinton's best effort to say otherwise—violates both the U.S. Constitution and international law.

Indeed, the threat to use force against Yugoslavia if it did not agree to the Rambouillet *diktat* was dubious enough. There was no international principle that authorized NATO to bomb Belgrade if it accept Washington's preferred solution. To the contrary, the 1980 International Convention of Treaties invalidates agreements achieved through coercion.

Far worse, however, was carrying through on the threat. In doing so, the President acted unilaterally, without the approval of Congress, as required by the U.S. Constitution. He transformed NATO, a defensive alliance, into a tool of offensive war, violating its basic purpose. And Washington initiated aggressive military action in violation of the U.N. Charter, which binds the members of NATO not less than other states.

The administration's calamitous bungling in Kosovo illustrates just why war should require congressional approval, NATO should remain a defensive alliance, and the U.N. Charter properly outlaws aggressive war, irrespective of the goodness of the expressed intentions. Sovereign states make no more important decisions; thus, those decisions should be widely debated and those who make them should be held widely accountable. Organizations created to protect a polyglot coalition from hegemonic aggression are not easily turned into regional policemen. And the U.N. prohibition against promiscuous international intervention provides one barrier, however week, to the spread of conflict.

If the administration is unwilling to follow the law, only Congress has the power to bring it to heel. Bill Press generously allowed that a legislative debate was permissible, but contended that "the time for that debate in Congress was before the war, not during."

But President Clinton and his aides did their best to prevent a debate, and openly promised to flout the results of any vote. Congress has an obligation to confront a lawless administration.

It is bad enough that the President believed he had the unilateral power to launch an undeclared, aggressive war against a state which had done nothing to the U.S. That he set not only unrealistic but unjust war goals also requires Congress to oppose him.

Rambouillet failed because the administration sought to impose a *diktat* that no serious country could accept—particularly phased independence for a rebellious province and a foreign military occupation. To maintain these objectives now will likely extend the conflict and intensify the hardship to Albanian refugees and Serb civilians alike.

Thus, no American should confuse the administration's goals with the nation's interest. Indeed, where the President and his aides are arrogant, ignorant, and incompetent, others must lead. That means attempting to fashion war aims that actually reflect American interests. That means putting peace before the President's poll ratings.

Patriotism is the last refuge for the scoundrel who has plunged the nation into a war in which it does not belong and simultaneously created a humanitarian and geopolitical crisis. The greatest service that Republican legislators and common citizens alike can render to their nation is to oppose the administration at every turn.

May 1999

The Volunteer Check on an American Empire

For the first time in six years the Army is likely to miss its annual recruiting goals. The Army National Guard is facing its worst personnel shortages in a decade. An unnecessary and badly managed war based on false claims is sapping the willingness of young Americans to enlist.

So far the Pentagon is rearranging deck chairs on the Titanic. The Army is hiking benefits for priority jobs and bumping up the age limit for enlistees. The Army Guard is adding recruiting centers and recruiters.

But "all of the services are competing for the same pool of people," admits Guard spokesman Lt. Col. Mike Milord. And none of these palliatives address the primary reason enlistments are falling: a growing reluctance of young people, reinforced by their parents' fears, to serve in Iraq.

Naturally, war supporters are taking cover behind scapegoats. Hindering prosecution of the war are critics who "work to undermine American support for our troops and the missions they serve," complains Melanie Morgan of the group Move America Forward.

Morgan recently directed her ire at anti-war artists whose work was promoted by California State Attorney General Bill Lockyer. These people "do the bidding of terrorists," she declared.

Columnist Thomas Lindaman railed against those who claim to support the troops but who criticize the war or even the President. The job of each citizen, he explains, is "to get your fellow citizens behind the efforts in Iraq, even if you disagree with the reasons for the war."

So much for principled dissent in a democracy. If the conflict in Iraq worsens, it is the fault of those who oppose it, not those who foolishly inaugurated it.

Some war advocates spotlight the ongoing recruiting crisis. For instance, Hollywood's Ben Stein blames the media.

"Why would anyone join the Army if he reads the newspapers and watches TV?" Stein asks. It would be different if "the media showed the military building schools, saving little children's lives, feeding families, getting sick people medical care" instead of "the military getting killed."

Alas, ignoring the consequences of the war won't make the deaths and maimings go away. And ignoring the consequences won't reverse the administration's blundering, such as failing to provide adequate body armor and armored vehicles to protect the troops.

War supporters reserve the lowest circle of hell, however, for those who are impeding military recruiting efforts. The latter range from parents who attempt to shield their children from recruiters' blandishments to activists organizing what they call a "counter-recruitment movement."

The capital's arm-chair warriors certainly don't intend to let reluctant would-be soldiers inhibit their plans. The Center for Security Policy declares: "Those who oppose our armed forces recruiters' visits to schools and universities or otherwise interfere with their activities will not prevent us from waging the war we have no choice but to fight. They may, however, require us to do so with forces that are obliged to serve rather than those who do so freely."

America's military commitments are seen as fixed, perhaps by a peculiar conjunction of the sun and moon. Thus, the Iraq conflict must continue, even if it entails sending press gangs across the land in search of warm bodies.

But a policy of promiscuous war-making is neither necessary nor natural for America. A refusal by those with the most at risk to implement the administration's counterproductive foreign policy should cause officials to reconsider America's course.

Why is Washington wasting tens of thousands of troops defending populous and prosperous allies like Japan and South Korea? Why does the U.S. man antiquated garrisons in Britain and Germany?

Why are there still American troops stationed in the Balkans patrolling Europe's backyard? Why should Uncle Sam deploy U.S. forces in conflicts when no American interests are at stake or other nations are capable of acting—in Haiti and Liberia recently and Somalia, Bosnia, and Kosovo before?

If Iraq is a "must war," then the Pentagon could concentrate its personnel on that conflict. Let wealthy allies and friends start carrying the burden of their own and their respective regions' defenses.

In any case, Iraq is not a must war. From the beginning it has been a war of choice, based on false premises and pursued by officials with hysterically optimistic expectations and criminally incompetent preparations. For this young men and women should be conscripted to fight if they choose not to join voluntarily?

Even if the invasion was necessary, the occupation is not. There are sound reasons to avoid a precipitous withdrawal. But those reasons are not important enough to justify a return to the draft if that's the only way to stay.

Indeed, the military's recruiting difficulties illustrate an important virtue of the volunteer military. It turns out that the All-Volunteer Force does not insulate the armed services from U.S. society, especially with the large-scale call-up of Guard and Reserve units. Most Americans have been personally touched by the Iraq conflict.

And they can, in turn, influence the war. The AVF's reliance on volunteers allows average people to resist—and eventually shut down—an unpopular conflict by simply refusing to join.

In contrast, a draft ensures a steady source of manpower, allowing the government to pursue an unpopular war. Although political opposition might eventually force a change in policy, this process took years in Vietnam's case.

Military service is honorable and necessary. Unfortunately, President Bush's misguided invasion of Iraq has caused increasing numbers of young people to tell Uncle Sam no thanks. That's yet another good reason for the administration to begin planning America's exit from Iraq.

September 2005

CHAPTER THREE

Terrorism

The Horror of Terror

Istanbul is a beautiful city sitting astride the Bosphorus. A sophisticated, tolerant city, it seamlessly mixes Occident and Orient. But now it has been stricken by the new cancer of our age: terrorism.

The attack on two Turkish synagogues is not just an instance of terrorism. It is the deliberate targeting of civilians no where near a war zone. And it reflects the virulent anti-Semitism that has despoiled our world for centuries.

It is hard for most people steeped in the humane, liberal values of Western civilization to understand the massacre of innocents. To slaughter to make a political point. But terrorism is not likely to disappear.

Indeed, it is a surprisingly common practice. Although Americans were taken unaware on September 11, many other peoples have long suffered from the murderous attention of domestic and foreign terrorists.

The attacks on Israelis have been frequent, in Israel and around the world. And killings continue, deterred neither by war measures or peace processes.

Kurdish rebels used terrorism against the Turkish government. Urban leftist terrorists once bedeviled Germany and Italy. Ethnic and religious separatists have killed in Northern Ireland and Spain.

Terrorism was a tool of leftists fighting military regimes in South America. Communist guerrillas routinely bomb urban targets, such as bars and nightclubs, in Colombia.

Chechens kill in Moscow. In Algeria terrorism was used against the French colonial overlords and continues today against the military-backed regime.

Tamils and Sikhs kill in India. Tamils also have routinely deployed terror against the majority Sinhalese in Sri Lanka, making the former the most prolific suicide bombers on earth.

Russian revolutionaries once killed Tsars and Tsarist officials. A Serbian terrorist shot down the Austro-Hungarian royal heir and his wife, triggering World War I. No other murder in human history—except perhaps that of Julius Caesar—had such profound consequences.

Terrorism is common, and will persist, because it is a tool of the weak versus the strong, a cheap military weapon to achieve expensive political goals. As long as there are people willing to kill to advance their ends, there will be terrorists.

Awful but unsurprising are attacks on military targets, such as the Marine Corps barracks in Lebanon, the USS Cole on its visit to Yemen, and the Italian military police headquarters in Iraq. Lacking the conventional weapons of war necessary to resist, opponents turn to the truck bomb. Horrific, careless of noncombatants, and brutally effective.

The Istanbul strikes—like those in Riyadh, Jakarta, Bali, and on the World Trade Center—take terrorism a step further. They are intended to kill noncombatants. The goal is not to resist foreign military power per se, but to murder and terrorize civilians. The willingness to kill, and kill indiscriminately, is expected to cow peoples and governments.

Yet the bombings of the two Turkish synagogues cap the murder of innocents with that age-old disease, anti-Semitism. It's been around for centuries, mixing discrimination with persecution.

The early variants were practiced in the name of Christianity, a bizarre justification of what was in fact a murderous assault on the roots of Christianity itself. Without the Jew Jesus, there is no Christianity. There is certainly nothing in his message to justify the Spanish Inquisition, Russian pogroms, or the polite social ostracism often practiced in Western Christian societies.

Today Christians, especially American evangelicals, have become among the strongest defenders of Judaism, even occasionally confusing support for Israelis against Palestinians with support for Jews against persecutors. Nevertheless, a Christian commitment to the life and dignity of all those created in God's image is the strongest barrier possible to anti-Semitism: The most monstrous anti-Jewish attack ever, the Nazi Holocaust, grew out of a movement that assaulted authentic Christianity with the same fervor that it destroyed tolerant humanism.

That terrorists claim to kill people in the name of God may be the greatest sacrilege. The Abu-Hafs al-Masri Brigades, a group linked to al-Qaeda, took credit for the Istanbul attacks: "The remaining operations are coming, God willing, and by God, Jews around the world will regret that their ancestors even thought about occupying the land of Muslims."

What kind of God urges his people to kill other people gathered to worship him? What kind of God urges people to kill other people today because of what their ancestors did years, decades, and centuries before? What kind of God urges people to kill other people, made in his image and of transcendent worth, to advance ephemeral political ends?

What kind of God is this?

If this is not the God of Islam, Muslims must speak out. Not just Islamic politicians themselves under attack—in Indonesia, Saudi Arabia, and Turkey, for instance. But clerics, imams, teachers, and ayatollahs. And common celebrants, those who regularly fill mosques for worship and daily drop to their prayer rugs.

Moreover, it is not enough to denounce attacks on Americans or Australians or Indonesians. It is necessary to denounce attacks on Jews. To say clearly that the God of Islam does not urge the children of Ishmael to murder the children of Isaac.

No one but the enemy gains from turning the War on Terrorism into a war between civilizations. But it certainly is a war between the civilized and uncivilized. And after atrocities like that in Istanbul, it is essential that Muslims as well as Christians declare against anti-Semitism, the blasphemy that refuses to die.

November 2003

The Price of Giving Offense

The tragic bombing of two U.S. embassies in Africa obviously illustrates the danger of serving a country, any country, abroad. But there is another, more important lesson directed at America. Even a superpower like the U.S. cannot intervene abroad without cost. Unfortunately, the price of attempting to run the world is ruined buildings and mangled bodies.

President Clinton acknowledged the connection in his radio address—though, of course, he didn't admit responsibility. He argued: "Americans are targets of terrorism, in part, because we have unique leadership responsibilities in the world, because we act to advance peace and democracy." To pull back would exhibit weakness, he claimed, so the U.S. has no choice but to "continue to take the fight to terrorists."

However, Washington doesn't "have" leadership responsibilities; it chooses leadership responsibilities. Few duties are absolute. Today's world is one in which almost every other country wants America to defend, subsidize, support, or otherwise aid them. If the definition of leadership responsibilities was what other nations desired, Washington would do, well, what it is doing now—defending, subsidizing, supporting, and aiding virtually every other state.

But Washington should consider costs, including the catastrophic human toll from terrorism, before deciding what responsibilities to fulfill. Terrorists kill for a cause. The bombers in Kenya and Tanzania were almost certainly retaliating for particular U.S. policies. Those who attacked the American military base in Dhahran, Saudi Arabia and the World Trade Center in New York were similarly motivated.

Of course, terrorism is a monstrous act. But it is a sadly rational response, since it is the only effective weapon for weak states or small groups confronting the world's dominant power. While the U.S. should deal forcefully with terrorist threats and retaliate when possible, Americans should not delude themselves that Washington is suffering only because it is busy promoting, as the President claimed, "peace and democracy" around the globe.

By stationing U.S. soldiers in Saudi Arabia, for instance, Washington is buttressing a totalitarian government. The Saudi royal family loots the economy, suppresses political opposition, and bans non-Muslim religions. Washington may view its support as a necessary bit of realpolitik. But America is suppressing, not aiding democracy.

For that reason, Mohammed Masari, a Saudi exile, terms U.S. forces "legitimate targets." Osama bin Laden, another critic of the Saudi regime—and leading suspect in the recent bombings—says that "Muslims burn with anger at America." They are war with Riyadh and Washington is openly siding with their enemies. The U.S. has made itself a target.

The bombings of the American embassy and Marine Corps barracks in Lebanon in 1983 were similar. In the name of "peace and democracy" the U.S. backed the ruling Christian faction against Muslim groups in what was a full-scale civil war. Washington even used its fleet to bombard Druze villages, filled with people who had never bothered America. That Muslims responded violently was tragic, but should not have surprised U.S. policymakers.

The Mideast is the fount of much terrorism against America. Washington has long aided Israel and ignored the plight of displaced Palestinians. The U.S. backed the Shah's brutal dictatorship in Iran and continues to support Saudi Arabia and the other Gulf autocracies. The war against Iraq and continuing military threats against Baghdad also fan passions.

The embers glow in other regions. Somalia demonstrated that not everyone wants to be "saved" by Washington. American policymakers publicly dismiss democracy when Islamic fundamentalists win elections in Algeria, Egypt, Jordan, and Turkey. Hypocrisy in the Balkans—condemning ethnic cleansing by Serbs while ignoring it by Croats—has left many people believing the U.S. stands for something other than "peace and democracy." Arrogant demands by Washington rankle in China, Russia, and elsewhere. For good reason, then, Charles Englehart of Kroll-Ogara, a business security firm says "There are a whole lot of people who hate America."

Of course, unpopularity is not necessarily a sign of being wrong. But U.S. policy is often glaringly misguided. Even when it isn't, Washington still needs to decide whether U.S. interests are important enough to warrant intervention. And that requires remembering that intervention begets terrorism.

The cost of terrorism is high enough today. As weapons of mass destruction spread, however, the price could become staggering. Imagine the use of biological, chemical, or nuclear weapons at the World Trade Center, in the heart of New York City's financial district. As potential terrorists' power grows, intervening for marginal international gains will become increasingly foolish.

Any nation is vulnerable to terrorism, but America is most at risk. By all means, Washington should combat terrorism. But the best defense is to give no offense. The twin bombings in East Africa offer two more reasons for not promiscuously meddling in overseas conflicts that don't concern the U.S. It is almost always innocent victims—embassy personnel and foreign civilians in the latest instance—rather than Washington policymakers who pay the terrorists' hideous bill.

August 1998

Interventionist Follies

Last year the U.S. attacked another sovereign state, conducting nightly bombing missions without losing a single serviceman. This month it sent a destroyer to refuel in the unimportant nation of Yemen and lost 17 sailors. Such is the threat of terrorism.

The problem is likely to grow only worse, especially if Al Gore is elected President and continues the administration's promiscuous intervention in small but bitter foreign conflicts. Attempts at nation-building risk turning all of America into a military front-line.

Moreover, Washington's high profile intervention in the burgeoning fight between Israel and the Palestinians makes additional incidents almost certain. Ayman el Zawahri, an associate of terrorist Osama bin Laden, has called for attacks on Americans and Israelis to avenge dead Palestinians; bin Laden has threatened assaults against the "enemies of Islam." Militants demonstrating as far away as Pakistan blame the U.S. for the killings.

Palestinians in Yemen cite their anger over the events in Israel. Yemeni President Ali Abdallah Salih says he would send troops to aid the Palestinians if his nation bordered Israel.

During the Cold War the Soviet Union used terrorism as another weapons to damage its chief global adversary. With the collapse of communism, however, terrorism is now the chief weapon of weak states and movements which have no other way to strike at the globe's sole superpower.

The awful consequences of terrorism are obvious: coffins arriving home, families devastated by grief. The causes seem less well understood, however, at least by Washington policymakers.

They usually react with shock, amazed that someone could wish us ill. President Bill Clinton announces: "We will find out who was responsible and hold them accountable."

That's appropriate, of course, but it doesn't go nearly far enough. American officials should also review U.S. policies which encourage terrorism.

The attack in Yemen didn't occur in a vacuum. This is a poor, strife-torn, tribalistic country, home to Islamic militants and haven for a variety of terrorist groups. In fact, Washington pulled out American military personnel in 1993 after a series of embassy and hotel bombings.

The USS Cole docked in Aden to refuel. But that is largely a pretense for a larger mission, to turn Yemen into a military ally. Reports Bill Gertz of the Washington Times: "Refueling U.S. warships in the Yemeni port of Aden is part of a broader U.S. government effort to develop closer ties with Yemen and to place an electronic eavesdropping post on a nearby island."

Thus, opponents of the regime—and war long raged between what were once two separate countries—are likely to see Washington as their enemy as well. Two groups, one with ties to Osama bin Laden's Al Qaida group, have denounced America's military presence. Other possible perpetrators include bin Laden and even Iraq's Saddam Hussein.

Last year, reports the State Department, there were 169 attacks on American targets. They were concentrated in Colombia (where the U.S. supports the government in its war against guerrillas and drug producers), Greece (in protest over the U.S. bombing of Serbia), and Nigeria and Yemen (where two embassy employees narrowly avoided being kidnapped).

But the highest profile, and most violent, incidents are usually tied to the Mideast. For instance, the 1998 bombings of the U.S. embassies in Dar es Salaam, Tanzania, and Nairobi, Kenya, were thought to be organized by bin Laden, who opposes America's support for Israel and unsavory alliance with the totalitarian monarchy that rules Saudi Arabia. Similar sentiments motivated the 1996 truck bombing that killed 19 U.S. soldiers at an American military installation near Dhahran, Saudi Arabia.

Back in the mid-1980s attacks were launched on American bases in Germany and Spain and a German disco frequented by U.S. soldiers. The first two offered convenient targets for terrorists angered with America's active international role, particularly in the Mideast. The latter was thought by some to be Iranian retaliation for the American shoot-down of an Iranian airliner while patrolling the Persian Gulf to aid Iraq during its war with Iran.

Far bloodier were the 1983 Lebanese bombings of the U.S. embassy and Marine barracks (as well as French military headquarters) in Beirut. Here the reason was even more obvious: American soldiers were sent in to back the minority Christian government, which controlled little more than Beirut, in its fight against Islamic forces. Washington even shelled hillside Muslim villages to demonstrate its power; no wonder Americans were targeted.

The potential for terrorism doesn't mean that it is never in America's interest to act. But it does mean that Washington must carefully calculate the risks before acting.

And in a world where weapons of mass destruction spread, the damage that could be inflicted not only overseas, but also at home—imagine the bombing of New York's World Trade Center with a nuclear weapon—could be huge. Which means the benefits of acting must be commensurately large.

Unfortunately, that is not the case today. The Clinton-Gore administration seems committed to the use of American forces in the most frivolous cases, such as turning a military dictatorship into a presidential dictatorship in Haiti, maintaining an artificial multiethnic state in Bosnia, and deciding which ethnic group can "cleanse" the other in Kosovo.

It apparently also thinks it can impose a settlement upon warring parties in the Mideast. Which means the attack on the USS Cole may be merely the beginning of another string of terrorist incidents.

October 2000

The Price of Terrorism

For the last decade it has seemed easy being the world's sole superpower. No longer. The U.S. has just paid a frightening price for its position in the world.

It is hard for most Americans, steeped in the humane, liberal values of Western civilization, to understand the massacre of innocents. To hijack planes and destroy office buildings. To murder to make a political point.

It has happened in the past, but even the Oklahoma City bombing was small-scale compared to this. A coordinated assault on the symbols of American economic, military, and political power. Killing hundreds, thousands of people, average people just going about their lives.

If this murderous attack was conducted by a nation, it was a traditional act of war, warranting war-like retaliation. If conducted by a group, then it was a lawless act of murder, warranting whatever form of justice can be best meted out where ever they may be.

The most obvious question is who? President George W. Bush promised to "hunt down the folks who committed this act," and hunt them down we should.

Although the U.S. must strike hard, it must strike accurately. No erroneous hits on innocent pharmaceutical plants. We must get the actual killers.

Moreover, any strike—one large and tough enough to appropriately retaliate for the murder of so many Americans—should be treated as an act of war in which the President and Congress share responsibility. President Bush should request congressional authorization for the necessary military measures. Let America's political leadership stand and act together.

But to retaliate is not enough. America must also rethink.

Until now Washington has acted as if there was little price to be paid for intervening around the globe. Two years ago the U.S. attacked another sovereign state, conducting nightly bombing missions without losing a single serviceman. War seemed, to Americans, like a video game.

No longer.

The U.S. can defeat any other nation. And any other country is likely to be deterred from striking America for years to come.

Over the long-term countries like China and India will grow more powerful, with larger and more deadly conventional weapons and nuclear arsenals. Current friends, including Europe, may grow more competitive and distant.

Even then, however, the U.S. is likely to possess sufficient power to deter any aggressor. Washington may no longer be able to impose its will on other nations, but they will certainly not be able to do so on America. In that sense, the U.S. will be relatively safe.

But not safe enough. It turns out that the seemingly powerless have power. Terrorism that once killed a dozen, a few score, or even a couple hundred has been turned loose on thousands.

Moreover, imagine the result had weapons of mass destruction been involved. If there were biological, chemical, or nuclear weapons on one of the planes.

Terrorism is evil. But it is the chief weapon of weak movements and states which have no other way to strike back.

They attack for a reason—in response to American involvement in their lands and struggles. Whoever brought down the twin towers of the World Trade Center did not do so because of irritation with American culture. They did so because of rage over Washington's intervention in what they saw as their affairs.

They are wrong to kill innocent Americans. But that's not the issue.

The issue is whether the stakes are high enough to pay the price. In the past it seemed to be a small risk. Now it turns out to be costly indeed.

Getting in the middle of the struggle between the Arabs and Israel guarantees that America will be a target. U.S. citizens and facilities have also been attacked because of Washington's aid to Colombia in its war against guerrillas and drug producers and America's bombing of Serbia.

The Saudi terrorist Osama bin Laden is partially motivated by U.S. support for the totalitarian Saudi Arabian government. Thwarting ethnic Albanian aspirations in the Balkans could create a new source of hostility.

The U.S. military has always been at risk when overseas. Now, however, the targets lie in America's homeland. We are all at risk.

The potential for terrorism doesn't mean that it is never in America's interest to act. But it does mean that Washington must carefully calculate the risks before acting. Especially in a world where weapons of mass destruction are likely to continue to spread.

In short, Washington needs to exercise more humility. The issue is not whether terrorists will drive us from the field. It is whether we have the good sense to stay off of fields on which we do not belong.

It is numbing to think that people care so little for life that they are willing to kill thousands for their own ends. We must hunt them down, as the President promised. And we must think twice before getting involved in conflicts that are likely to create more of them.

September 2001

The Price of Intervention

The horror of the World Trade Center bombing has generated national unity. It should also generate national reflection. If Americans fail to learn the right lessons from the attack, they risk more, and more deadly, terrorist assaults.

In the short-term, the goal should be to kill terrorists, destroy their resources, and cow their backers. In the long-term we must also reduce the sources of foreign hostility to the U.S.

Terrorism cannot be treated in isolation from American foreign policy. It's not that Americans deserved to die, that the blame falls on U.S. policymakers instead of the killers who hijacked and crashed four planes. Rather, terrorism must be understood as an inevitable consequence of global intervention.

Despite the claim that America's military is weak and underfunded, the U.S. stands as an international colossus. Accounting for one-third of the globe's defense outlays and allied with every significant industrialized state, America can defeat any other country.

Thus, terrorism has become a tool for weak nations or groups to strike back at a superpower. Without nuclear weapons, missiles, air wings, or carrier groups, they have no conventional mechanism for resisting the U.S. Terrorism is a form of asymmetrical warfare, a means to exploit the vulnerability of a free and liberal society.

The point is not that America deserves to be attacked. The point is that it will be attacked. And it will be attacked because of what it does as well as because of what it is.

President George W. Bush claimed in his speech that the terrorists hate "a democratically elected government," and "our freedoms, our freedom of religion, our freedom of speech, our freedom to vote and assemble and disagree with each other." This may be true. But alone it isn't why people try to kill us. And why they are willing to die trying to kill us.

Other countries have suffered from terrorism. In 1991 India's Prime Minister Rajiv Ghandi was killed by a suicide bomber. Sri Lanka's President Chandrilea Kumaratunga lost an eye in a similar attack last year.

These assaults did not spring from abstract hatred of Brahmin Indian culture or Sri Lankan democracy, but internal conflicts. In the latter case the bombing was part of an ongoing civil war between majority Sinhalese and minority Tamils.

So it is with the U.S. Terrorists might dislike Disneyland and loath MTV. They might fear abundant consumerism and hate sensual imagery. But they don't kill for that reason.

Terrorists strike the U.S. because they consider Washington to be at war with them. As the Defense Science Board reported four years ago: "Historical data show a strong correlation between U.S. involvement in international situations and an increase in terrorist attacks against the United States."

This was evident in the 1983 car bombing of the Marine Corps barracks in Beirut, a response to U.S. intervention on behalf of the minority Christian government in the midst of a protracted civil war. The 1996 truck bombing of the military barracks in Dhahran, Saudi Arabia, was retaliation for American support for that unpopular, thuggish government.

Nothing justifies terrorism. But it is not hard to imagine people who might wish America ill. For instance, some Colombians—communist guerrillas, right-wing paramilitaries, nonpartisan drug dealers—might seek a means to strike America for supporting the Bogota government.

There are almost certainly Serbs who lost family members during U.S. bombing two years ago who cheered the deaths of American citizens. Ethnic Albanians in Kosovo, who desire independence but are now blocked by Washington, might eventually see terrorism as a means to pressure their one-time benefactor.

Many Iraqis who have seen friends or family members starve during the decade-long U.S. embargo probably blame America. Osama bin Laden is apparently angered by America's alliance with the Saudi Arabian regime.

Most significant is the struggle between Israel and the Palestinians. There is no more virulent vortex of irrational hatred into which America has been sucked.

Yassir Arafat's government, like those of most of the surrounding Arab states, is steeped in blood. Yet Palestinians understandably bridle at more than three decades of outside military rule. Given America's strong support for Israel—guaranteeing not only its survival, but also its dominance—their anger and hostility has been transmitted to America.

To recognize the connection between U.S. actions and terrorist attacks leads to no automatic policy conclusion. Everyone of these policies has a justification, perhaps worth risking thousands of American lives.

But promiscuous intervention can no longer be undertaken in the belief that there will be no consequences. The American homeland itself is at risk. Put together Attorney General John Ashcroft's warning that more terrorism will occur and Defense Secretary Donald Rumsfeld's prediction that terrorists will eventually acquire biological, chemical, and even nuclear weapons, and you have catastrophe. The resulting danger must be considered in deciding when and where—and particularly if—to intervene.

Today we rightly focus on avenging the deaths of thousands of Americans. And on ensuring that those who killed them will not be able to kill again.

But we must begin to think beyond the present. The murder of American citizens is neither fair nor just. But it is a reality. That reality must shape the future direction of American foreign policy.

October 2001

The Danger of Being American

JAKARTA, INDONESIA—"It's dangerous here for Americans," said my cab driver. No question.

A few blocks away sat the J.W. Marriott, its facade broken and blackened. Scores of windows were blown out; mutilated blinds swayed in the wind. Wrecked autos sat as silent sentinels in the hotel driveway.

Westerners were almost entirely absent on Jakarta's streets. The Indonesians whom I visited worried about my safety. "People hate Americans," said one; "they are very much against Americans," allowed another. Osama Bin Laden posters still sell in some Islamic neighborhoods and rumors circulated that the CIA arranged the Marriott bombing.

During the war with Iraq the owner of Jakarta's McDonald's franchises let it be known that he was a Muslim. It was one city where I did not jog, even though I've run everywhere from Pyongyang, North Korea to Pristina, Kosovo.

Security precautions were ubiquitous. At the Sheraton, where I stayed, guards examined every car at driveway checkpoints. Another guard used an electronic wand to check guests and luggage entering the hotel. The clerk at the reception desk tried to reassure me: "you're safe here."

An upscale mall checked vehicles as they entered and an employee at the Hard Rock Cafe searched my backpack. Even as the Indonesian terrorist Hambali, thought to be involved in the bombings of both the Marriott and in Bali, was arrested, the American and Australian governments warned their citizens to avoid any Western-owned hotel in Jakarta. Hambali's group, Jemaah Islamiah, remains a potent threat.

To fear being murdered for one's nationality is humbling. The mere fact that Americans are resented doesn't prove that they or their government are wrong. But the fact that such sentiments pervade friendly and hostile nations alike should cause serious reflection.

Common is the "they hate us because we are beautiful" thesis, expressed in the aftermath of September 11 by President George W. Bush. And, no doubt, some people, particularly Islamists and other traditionalists, do resent a culture that they see as licentious and degrading.

But people typically don't kill because they dislike Disneyland, MTV, or liberal democracy. Instead, they attempt to isolate themselves.

Indeed, polls by John Zogby find that Muslims and Arabs like many of the attributes of Western culture. They like American products and freedoms.

What they don't like are policies of the U.S. government. It is such policies—long centered around Iraq, Israel, and Saudi Arabia—which have helped spark a hatred strong enough to kill. Alas, Zogby found that positive ratings towards America have collapsed with the war on Iraq. One Indonesian told me: "Even before, when America attacked Afghanistan, they were angry." But it's gotten "worse, much worse," with the attack on Iraq, he said.

This should surprise no one. Terrorism around the world, from the Tamils in Sri Lanka to the IRA in Northern Ireland, typically represents a particularly vicious battle front in an ongoing political struggle. Palestinians who murder Israeli civilians don't do so out of an abstract dislike of Jewish culture, but as part of a bloody struggle over a single piece of land. Killers of Americans at the World Trade Center, Australians in Bali, and Westerners in Jakarta perceive a crusade against Islam.

Were America's only critics Islamic tribalists, they could more easily be ignored. But antagonism towards the U.S. is increasingly evident even among friendly peoples and states.

A British conservative MP privately bemoans American support for Israel's Ariel Sharon. A Thai intellectual criticizes U.S. arrogance.

A Kuwaiti government official worries that restrictive immigration restrictions are losing America friends. A Portuguese tour guide rues U.S. unilateralism.

An Australian wonders how a superpower could act so frightened of a decrepit Mideast dictatorship. A German journalist denounces an administration so determined on war without allied support—but then so insistent on post-war allied aid.

Such criticism resonates given American ignorance about foreign affairs. Many fervent Christian supporters of Israel seem blissfully unaware that more than three million Palestinians live under Israeli control in the Gaza Strip and West Bank. There are obvious reasons to back Israel, but peace is unlikely to come as long as Palestinians live in conditions that neither Israelis nor Americans would accept.

Many Americans erroneously believed that Saddam Hussein was involved in the 9/11 atrocities. Whatever the argument for attacking Iraq in an attempt to remake the Mideast, it was not just another step in the war on terrorism.

Few Americans can imagine what it is like to have another power, however benign its behavior or worthy its intentions, constantly hector, criticize, and threaten. Yet Washington routinely acts as the world's governess.

Criticism doesn't mean Washington shouldn't act when it believes itself to be right and its action to be necessary. It doesn't mean the U.S. should flee unpopularity when great principles and interests are at stake.

But Americans must realize that they are hated for more than their beauty. Although Americans don't deserve to be in danger, U.S. policy often puts them at greater risk.

August 2003

CHAPTER FOUR

Humanitarian Intervention

Compounding the Somali Tragedy

The post-Cold War world is proving to be a disorderly place. Conflicts once restrained by the superpowers are now breaking out all over—in Africa, the Balkans, and the former Soviet Union. More wars could eventually explode in Eastern Europe and Southeast Asia.

Tragic though these conflicts are, they need not involve the U.S. The end of the superpower competition means the world is no longer a zero-sum game, with a foreign "loss" benefiting America's adversaries. In particular, the international chess game in which Somalia was Washington's pawn is long over.

Somalia's lack of geopolitical value does not lessen the humanitarian concern, of course. But the world today is full of tragedy—Angola, Armenia, Cambodia, Liberia, and Yugoslavia, to name just a few. The fundamental question is, should Washington compound the calamity by sending young Americans to their deaths in those conflicts? Is there any foreign cause for which 18-year-olds in this country are not expected to die?

Somalia has long been one of Africa's basket cases, an economically destitute nation ruled by a venal autocrat who opportunistically shifted his country from the Soviet to American orbit for his own gain. Like many other African states, Somalia was never a true nation, but rather arose as a colonial amalgam. Since the overthrow of Siad Barre in January 1991 the country has descended into chaos, with different warlords attacking each other and seizing relief workers' foodstocks.

The result has been mass starvation, prompting the out-going Bush administration's deployment of roughly 28,000 American troops. The Clinton administration has begun bringing some soldiers home, but the planned transfer to U.N. forces may take some time. Indeed, more than a few advocates of a "new colonialism" want the U.N., backed by the U.S. military, to turn Somalia into a protectorate and install an interim government.

Already the U.S. forces have stayed longer than President Bush originally promised. And while the U.N. Security Council has approved the operation and other nations have contributed forces, it, like the Korean and Persian Gulf wars, remains a largely American show. Washington is paying more than 80 percent of the cost and providing two-thirds of the soldiers.

Intervention for what appears to be almost completely humanitarian grounds is unprecedented. The only national interest-based arguments made in favor of the deployment are that it preserves America's international leadership role and promotes domestic morale by strengthening the population's "can-do" psychology. Neither of these is particularly persuasive, however. American prestige did not decline when Washington sat by as Ethiopia and Liberia disintegrated in civil wars. With the globe's largest economy and powerful military and most dominant culture and political ideology, Washington's influence is guaranteed. Countries are not likely to think less of the U.S. if it remains selective about where it puts its soldiers at risk.

As for promoting a sense of national purpose, Somalia is a diversion from pressing domestic issues. Americans' energies could be far more effectively devoted to helping their fellow citizens than hunting down snipers in Mogadishu.

Still, the humanitarian impulse cannot be cavalierly dismissed. The desire to save lives is obviously worthy. And a willingness to send humanitarian aid reflects the most generous impulses of the American people. But intervening militarily is a very different matter.

Yes, public officials have spared no effort patting themselves on the back for their international beneficence. The problem, however, is that they are being generous with other people's money, $583 million in the first three months alone, and lives. Although volunteers, most servicemen and women nevertheless joined with some patriotic notion of defending the U.S., not policing the world. An American Foreign Legion the Marines Corps is not. The only purpose that soldiers' lives should be put at risk is to protect their own political community.

While the dangers of Somalia pale compared to those of intervention in, say, the Balkans, they remain very real: by the end of January two Marines and one civilian employee had been killed and others had been wounded. This is neither a traditional U.N. peacekeeping operation that helps separate parties who really don't want to fight nor an attempt to shore up a respected central authority against a temporary threat. Rather, Somalia is no longer a nation, but rather a hodge-podge of violent gangs representing various clans and sub-clans, engaged in the sort of tribal warfare that has bedeviled the African continent for so long.

Although the arrival of American forces initially cowed the roving bands that had been terrorizing Somali refugees and foreign relief workers, the resulting "peace" is limited—gun-men engage in almost daily shoot-outs with U.S. soldiers, violent assaults against relief workers are increasing, and gangs steal food in outlaying areas as soon as the soldiers depart. Even today's relative calm is likely to last only so long as the American troops stay in place. The longevity of any artificial interim government would be no longer, which is why some Somalis have called for a long-term U.S. commitment. Plans for an early American departure are already fading: The bulk of the U.S. force is expected to remain in Somalia through April, at least.

Indeed, U.N. Secretary General Boutros Boutros-Ghali wants the U.S. to disarm the warlords before leaving: "The point of view of the United Nations, the point of view of the Security Council is that disarmament is a prerequisite." In essence, he is demanding that Washington pacify the entire country before the replacement U.N. troops are deployed. This is obviously no easy task, but otherwise the U.N. forces are unlikely to be able to prevent violence from steadily escalating, requiring either a new infusion of U.S. troops or a willingness to watch the land again sink into chaos. For this reason the American withdrawal is likely to be less than full. U.S. special envoy Robert Oakley, for one, says that Washington should remain a "major participant" in any U.N. force and current plans are for at least 5,000

Americans to remain in Somalia, along with some number of Marines offshore.

Yet the longer American soldiers are present, the greater the risk of retaliatory attacks on military and relief workers alike. Still, the likely loss of life is relatively small, and a few score deaths may seem a small price to pay for thousands or conceivably tens of thousands of Somalis saved. Of course, we will never know how many are alive only because of U.S. intervention.

The worst violence was always geographically limited, and some progress in restoring order had been made in those areas even before the arrival of the soldiers, with organizations like the Red Cross and Great Britain's Save the Children Fund reporting that 90 percent of their food shipments were being delivered. Rakiya Omaar and Alex de Waal, formerly of the human rights organization Africa Watch, point out that clan negotiations had virtually ended looting in the town of Baidoa for the preceding two months; alas, the agreement collapsed once the Marines arrived.

Many warlords have simply shifted their activities away from the arriving American troops. Reports Brigitte Doppler of the French Medecins Sans Frontieres, "The number of bandit attacks is increasing. The bandits have moved to places where we are working but where there are no coalition forces." Indeed, more foreigners were killed in Somalia in January than in the preceding two years.

In any case, the number of Somalis saved can't simply be compared with the number of Americans killed. While the Somalis' lives are no less valuable than those of American troops, the primary duty owed by this government is to its own citizens, including soldiers.

Intervention in Somalia also raises two disturbing issues of precedent. The first is, who will make American policy? American action appears to have been dictated by shocking television coverage. This is a poor means of deciding when American soldiers should be deployed around the globe. As military columnist Harry Summers observes, "Passions are a shaky foundation upon which to build a military commitment."

The second involves the criteria for intervention. We must be prepared either to say that Somali lives are more valuable than those of Armenians, Bosnians, and Liberians, or to garrison the globe for humanitarian reasons. While other nations, and especially the free-riding Europeans, might find that to be a pleasant prospect, it would not be in the interest of the American people, who would have to fund and man the operations. The end result would not only be great expense and loss of life, but also likely entanglement in a variety of esoteric, virulent struggles with no implications for American security. With the threat of terrorism and spread of both missiles and weapons of mass destruction, one or another foreign adventure might lead to unexpectedly expensive complications.

The response by some advocates of humanitarian intervention is: well, what about Hitler? If he was merely killing his own people, and not conquering other countries, shouldn't we still have intervened? That question cannot be answered without considering various country's relative interests at stake, capabilities of intervening, and costs of acting. The very same question could be asked of Stalin and Mao, both of whom slaughtered more people than did Hitler. Should the U.S. have intervened to halt the starvation of the Ukraine or great purges in the U.S.S.R.? Should Washington have deployed military forces to stop China's disastrous Great Leap Forward? Humanitarianism without regard for consequences and costs is good intentions run amok.

Thus, as difficult as it might be for people with America's "can-do" spirit to admit, not every international problem can be solved. Nor is it Washington's duty to try to resolve every one. What is going on in Somalia, and many other places around the globe, is pitiable. But these tragedies should not be expanded by involving the U.S. Officials have no right to risk the lives and treasure of Americans in conflicts that are not of vital concern their own political community.

February 1993

The Silence of the International Community

When white Europeans are dying, the Clinton administration acts. When black Africans are dying, Washington talks. Such is the hypocritical cynicism that passes for foreign policy today.

So shameless is Madeleine Albright's ritualistic incantation of the "international community" that United Nations Secretary General Kofi Annan has taken the U.S. to task. He complained to the New York Times: "Washington will not put an American officer on the ground" in Sierra Leone.

The administration's reluctance to act does seem extraordinary, given the President's promise, offered barely a year ago when he visited the Balkans, to stop ethnic cleansing anywhere in the world. But residents of East Timor soon learned what frightened civilians in Sierra Leone are realizing today: he was only kidding.

What he really meant was that if white Europeans were dying, their deaths were being covered on CNN, and their killers were adversaries of the U.S., then Washington might—MIGHT—act. Otherwise, millions could die and administration officials wouldn't bother to mention the problem, let alone attempt to solve it.

Administration hypocrisy is appalling. But the real problem is Washington's willingness to get involved in hopeless European conflicts, such as Bosnia and Kosovo, not its refusal to jump into even worse wars in Africa and Asia. Of course, Secretary General Annan wants Washington to put U.S. officers on the ground. It's easy to be generous with other people's lives.

However, America should not be the 911 number for the rest of the world.

First, UN peacekeeping can work only if there is peace to be kept. Despite persistent animosities in Cyprus, neither ethnic Greeks nor Turks have any desire to go to war again; the UN may be helping reduce potential incidents by separating the two sides. In Sierra Leone, in contrast, the UN was "enforcing" a temporary ceasefire, with no military disarmament or political solution.

Second, only a dozen or so countries, the usual industrialized states, have militaries capable of serious action. No one else counts.

Indeed, to rely on anyone else is dangerous. In Sierra Leone, for instance, Zambian "peacekeepers" managed to provide the rebels with hostages, armored personnel carriers, and uniforms. What American could possibly want U.S. officers on the ground serving with such a force?

Third, the world is full of tragedy. Unless 18-year-old Americans are going to be drafted to patrol a new empire, there is little that Washington can do.

After all, Sierra Leone is hardly the only African state in crisis. Ethiopia and Eritrea are fighting—again. The Angolan civil war has erupted—again. Conflict pervades the Democratic Republic of the Congo—again.

Killing and slavery continue in Sudan. Rwanda and Uganda are threatening each other. Zimbabwe's President Robert Mugabe has unleashed thugs on the white minority and black opposition in an attempt to maintain his hold on power.

Then there's Sri Lanka, where the Tamil insurgency is advancing. Kashmir, over which India and Pakistan have verged on war. Indonesia, wracked by sectarian violence and ethnic separatism. Russian suppression of Chechnyan independence. And more.

If Washington is not willing to intervene in all of these but still wants to act, then it needs a standard. Other than white Europeans dying on TV at the hands of an American foe.

One proposal, by Michael O'Hanlon of the Brookings Institution and former Rep. Stephen Solarz, is to use force when the death rate in another society exceeds the murder rate in our own. A creative idea, yes, but a bizarre guide for putting American soldiers at risk.

Another option would be to act where the greatest number of lives are at stake. But none of America's recent interventions—Kosovo, Bosnia, Haiti—would make the list. Indeed, Kosovo was a trivial conflict compared to a score of others around the globe. Whether the number of deaths and refugees, or the degree of social catastrophe, Washington has consistently refused to countenance any involvement in the worst, and usually most insoluble, cases.

In the end, nonintervention is the right option. Not because the lives of those in other nations are without value. But because the highest duty of the U.S. government is to this nation's citizens, including those in uniform.

Of course, the Secretary of State undoubtedly feels a sanctimonious glow as she wanders the globe prattling on about the demands of the "international community." American policymakers, no less than the UN Secretary General, are often generous with the lives of American soldiers.

But Americans' lives should be put at risk only when their own political community has something at stake. That's not the case in Sierra Leone. Nor was it the case in Kosovo.

There's no reason to expect anything other than unprincipled hypocrisy from the Clinton administration. Ironically, in the case of Sierra Leone, that's the best we can hope for. It is appalling that the President seems more interested in saving white Europeans than black Africans, but it would be even more appalling to risk American lives in attempting to put yet another failed state back together.

May 2000

Superpowers Don't Do Windows

Nigerian troops have arrived in Liberia and Liberian President Charles Taylor has fled into exile. Whether these peacekeepers, and the soldiers from Ghana, Mali, and Senegal who are to follow, will bring peace in the three-sided civil war is yet uncertain. What is certain, however, as U.S. Marines sit on ships offshore, is that bringing peace to Liberia is not America's responsibility.

The world is full of tragedy. A brutal communist insurgency burns in Nepal. Once stable Ivory Coast has dissolved into destructive civil war. In Colombia the military battles communist insurgents and right-wing militias, which fight each other while each produces and sells drugs.

As many as 4.7 million people have died in five years of war in Congo. A score of other nations endure instability, ethnic strife, and genocide. Such as Liberia, which has suffered successive bouts of devastating and deadly civil war.

America might be able to stop some of the fighting. It might be able to save some lives. But it can't do everything. And it should not try to do so.

The U.S. is better than any other state at war fighting. It possesses the finest military on earth. America could defeat any other power or combination of powers.

Which means Washington's most important international role is to prevent a hostile hegemonic power from dominating the Asian or European continents. No other state is capable of doing so. There is no more important foreign policy objective.

In contrast, the desire to impose cease-fires and remake societies, though worthy, pales in importance to the U.S. Washington should resist unnecessary entanglements in conflicts which threaten no important American interests.

Peacekeeping operations span a wide continuum, starting with genuine peacekeeping, where a cold peace has been achieved and an outside party can help separate the formerly warring parties—a Cyprus, Macedonia, or Sinai, perhaps. There are costs and risks, though they are measured: before committing itself, Washington should demand some interest of note as well as evidence of efficacy, that is, U.S. involvement is necessary and success is likely.

And America should limit its participation to reflect its limited interests. Provide temporary logistical aid. But leave the battlefield work to parties with a greater stake, such as surrounding states or former colonial powers.

Next are wars where the insertion of foreign forces is supposed to inaugurate peace, like Bosnia and Somalia, as well as Liberia. In these conflicts there is no political settlement. The risks of continued violence are real.

Worse, a long-term commitment—eight years and counting in Bosnia, four years to start in Kosovo—is almost inevitable. This sort of intervention should require a higher standard, with serious security issues at stake and a realistic end game for getting out.

Finally, there are real wars, whether they are called peacekeeping or not. The "police action" in Korea in 1950, the attack on Serbia over Kosovo in 1999, the two wars with Iraq. In these the costs and risks are potentially enormous.

To undertake real war should require a vital national interest, something important enough to sacrifice the lives of Americans. And something important enough to put effort into succeeding in both the war and the peace that follows.

War, no matter how small, is always serious business. Absent both a significant national interest and realistic assurance that intervention will not degrade America's fighting capabilities and turn Americans into targets, Washington should eschew involvement.

Other nations can deal with most conflicts. Not only are the Europeans and others capable of suppressing civil strife, if desired; they would provide a lower profile target in a world of terrorism.

Thus, if settling a guerrilla struggle in Kosovo was not important enough to make Europe act, it should not have been important enough to involve the U.S. If the west Africans weren't willing to intervene in Liberia, there was no need for Americans to do so.

Demonstrating reluctance before exercising its power makes sense in theory. Today, there are serious practical reasons to do so as well.

Today, the U.S. is very busy. Of the Army's 495,000 soldiers, 370,000 are deployed overseas.

Of 33 active-duty combat brigades, 21 have been deployed. Given other commitments and refitting, only three brigades currently are available as replacement forces for Iraq.

The Pentagon's latest deployment plan for Iraq, reports Esther Schrader of the Los Angeles Times, "relies on foreign troops that have not yet been committed by their governments, on two National Guard combat brigades that have not yet been trained for the mission, on an Army division that just returned home from Iraq, and on two new Army brigades that have not been certified by the Pentagon as combat-ready."

Yet should conflict break out on the Korean peninsula, should China and Taiwan end up at war, should some other serious, unexpected contingency occur, Washington would almost certainly be involved in a major conflagration. Should the security of America or its major allies be threatened, everyone would look to the U.S. for the answer.

Under such circumstances, it would be madness to undertake a new commitment of potentially limitless duration in Liberia. Instead of adding new policing duties, the U.S. should be shedding commitments.

The tragedies that abound throughout the world should tug at the hearts of compassionate people. However, the humanitarian gloss applied to peacekeeping missions, such as that of Liberia, does not eliminate the need to make hard decisions, demand the presence of serious national interests, and balance competing objectives.

Superpowers can do windows. But they should do so only if it is in their interest to do so.

August 2003

The Perils of Nation-Building

The U.S. easily conquered Iraq, but the war was only the beginning. Unfortunately, winning the peace is proving to be far more difficult. Destroying an unpopular, isolated dictatorship in a wreck of a country was one thing. Creating a liberal, multi-party, multi-ethnic democracy where one has never existed is quite another. Despite the positive tone that he has presented to the public, even President George W. Bush has been forced to acknowledge that America faces a "security issue in Iraq," a "massive and long-term undertaking."

Lest people grow discouraged, the administration has mounted a concerted PR campaign, mixing presidential speeches with congressional testimony and creation of an "Iraq Stabilization Group." But bombings, shootings, and killings of Americans and Iraqis alike continue, despite claimed improvement in the provision of services and security. The U.S. is almost alone in contributing troops to garrison Iraq and money to rebuild it. And polls find that a plurality of Iraqis have a negative view of America and a majority believes that Western-style democracy will not work.

Officially, the Pentagon proclaims that it will stay in Iraq "as long as necessary" and leave "as soon as possible." Superficially, that sounds like a sensible course. But real success for the administration seems ever more distant. Washington's only hope is to set modest goals and a private but firm departure date from Iraq.

Yet unexpected opposition to the U.S. occupation has forced the Pentagon to delay withdrawing American forces. More than 115 deaths and 1000 woundings of U.S. military personnel occurred in the first six months after President Bush declared the war over. Hostile Iraqis apparently took his challenge to "bring 'em on" seriously: they have launched multiple suicide bombings, routinely shot up military patrols, threatened aircraft flying into Baghdad airport, and even disabled the supposedly unstoppable M-1 Abrams tank.

Forget dropping to 30,000 soldiers by the end of 2003, as promised by Defense Secretary Donald Rumsfeld. Instead, analysts are talking about the necessity of pushing the total up from 160,000 to 200,000 or even 300,000. And few outside powers have proved willing to put their soldiers at risk to bail out an administration that was so adamant in going it alone when the war seemed easy. Indeed, what other government would want to subject its citizens to Washington's counterproductive leadership? Iraq is going to stay America's problem.

Yet just maintaining the current force will stretch the U.S. military. In peacetime the Army has traditionally aimed to deploy only a third of its units at any one time. With a force of ten divisions and several enhanced war-fighting brigades, author Frederick Kagan argues that the Army could support an Iraqi deployment of only three and two-thirds divisions, compared to the more than equivalent of five now on station.

The problem is made more acute by the fact that Iraq is not America's only foreign commitment. Of the Army's 495,000 soldiers, 370,000 are deployed overseas. Although tours in countries like Britain and Germany include families, few people want to join the Army if doing so means rarely seeing home.

Now much of a soldier's time overseas might be spent in war zones. Of 33 active-duty combat brigades, 21 have been deployed: 16 to Iraq, two each to Afghanistan and South Korea, and one in the Balkans. Given other commitments and refitting, only three brigades currently are available as replacement forces for Iraq.

"Every possible unit worldwide is being considered for possible rotations in different mixes and matches," explained one Defense Department official to the *Washington Post*. But that's just a stop-gap, and not a particularly realistic one at that. Moreover, it is particularly rough on the troops themselves.

A Council on Foreign Relations panel chaired by former Defense Secretary James Schlesinger warned that "even the lowest suggested requirements of 75,000 troops" in the occupation force would mean "that every infantryman in the U.S. Army spends six months in Iraq out of every 18 to 24." Army officials privately acknowledge that up to a quarter of soldiers might have to serve back-to-back overseas tours. Increase the Iraqi troop requirement and toss in a covey of new commitments—Philippines, Liberia, etc.—and U.S. servicemen and servicewomen won't see America again until they retire.

The unexpected occupation burden has forced the Pentagon to announce that tours in Iraq will be for one year, the same as in Vietnam and Korea and double the normal tour for "peacekeeping" missions.

"We've done it before, and we can do it again," said Abizaid. We can in the short-term. But "Either we find a fix to rotate those troops out and to keep the families content ... or we're going to suffer what I anticipate is a downturn in retention," warns military analyst Robert Maginnis.

Relying more on the reserves is another poor option. The Reserves and National Guard number 1.2 million, but about 210,000 were on active duty (down from 223,000 at the war's peak) in the fall of 2003. There are only 550,000 total in the Army Reserve or Army National Guard, however. Some already have served for more than a year. Frequent deployments are even more disruptive for reservists, who must leave their jobs as well as families and often face a ruinous loss in income.

That has led to political pressure to limit future call-ups: Sen. Robert Byrd (D-W.Va.) has proposed limiting deployments to one for six months in any year. Reservists, too, are less likely to sign up and stay in if they face frequent and lengthy stints abroad in a war zone. Michael Doubler, author of Civilian in Peace, Soldier in War: The Army National Guard, believes recruiting and retention are likely to suffer. Not uncommon are Army trucks in Iraq festooned with the sign "One Weekend A Month My Ass." As of September Army National Guard recruitments were well below Pentagon objectives.

The Marine Corps also could be drafted into occupation duty. But it is a small force, of 175,000, designed to respond to unexpected contingencies. Moreover, as of mid-2003 19 of 24 active duty and four of nine reserve battalions were deployed overseas. Many of them since have returned home, but immediate redeployment would be no less burdensome for the Marines as for the Army.

Despite the strain on the military, advocates of nation-building are advancing an expansive nation-building agenda. Argued *New York Times* columnist Nicholas D. Kristof, "To leave behind a stable Iraq, we must establish order, nurture a free press and independent police force, purge the civil service of Baath thugs, help Iraqis write a constitution and hold local and national elections. All that will take a year or more."

Actually, far more than a year, most everyone now acknowledges.

But that has not diminished the belief that the U.S. must stay, no matter how long it takes. Argues Harlan Ullman, associated with the Center for Strategic & International Studies: "We are now committed. The United States cannot cut and run. We have no choice but to make the best of the situation." Similarly, warns Fareed Zakaria of Newsweek, going home means "giving up." And of course George W. Bush, cosseted in the White House behind an ample Secret Service guard, says that anyone who believes "we will run from a challenge" is mistaken.

Giving up on expansive nation-building ambitions is the only sensible course of action, however. Unfortunately, there are few successful models upon which to draw for Iraq.

America's obvious successes are Germany and Japan, yet neither look like Iraq: both comprised ethnically homogenous populations, possessed democratic traditions, and sported an educated, professional class. The U.S. effort was widely viewed as legitimate by all major international players and the two countries' neighbors, which had suffered the most at their hands.

While many Germans and Japanese seemed to hold the same mixture of feelings evident in Iraq—relief at foreign liberation but resentment at foreign occupation—they had no illusion that American rule would be brief. Not so in Iraq. Abu Eslam Saqir, a spokesman for the Iran-friendly Supreme Council for the Islamic Revolution in Iraq, said: "We wanted the international community, including Americans, to help us get rid of Saddam's dictatorship, not impose their will on our nation."

Most important, Germany and Japan were real nations. Iraq is not and has never been one. It consisted of three provinces under the Ottoman empire and owes its current borders to British nation-builders. The cultural and political gulf among Kurds, Shias, and Sunnis is enormous. Moreover, the first two groups are drawn to allied peoples outside Iraq.

Unfortunately, Iraq looks more like several countries where American attempts at nation-building have been far less successful—disastrous even. In Somalia, for instance, the U.S. thrust itself into the bloody conflict among competing warlords in the name of delivering humanitarian relief. Local combatants successfully manipulated Washington to take sides.

The attempt to seize warlord Mohammed Aideed led to a vicious firefight in Mogadishu killing 18 U.S. Rangers and as many as a 1000 Somalis in 1993. The U.S. withdrew and the local combatants eventually wore themselves out. Today Somalia has achieved some degree of peace if not unity, without America's help.

In 1994 the Clinton administration used the threat of a U.S. invasion to force junta leader Raoul Cedros from power in Haiti. Washington installed Jean-Bertrand Aristide in his stead. Alas, Aristide, though more popular than Cedros, was no less authoritarian. Attempts to restore the economic infrastructure, train a police force, and promote democracy have largely come to naught. With great fanfare the U.S. managed to replace a military dictatorship with a presidential one.

The 1995 Dayton accord led to a nation-building exercise that continues in Bosnia, a purely artificial country. Never before independent, Bosnia is made up of three warring groups, two of which want to join co-religionists in neighboring states. Bosnia exists today only because of foreign military occupation now exceeding eight years. Bosnia is still ruled by a European "High Representative" who interferes with local elections, censors the media, and makes national policy. He has chosen the currency and national anthem. Corruption is rife, particularly in the Muslim conclave, which receives the most foreign aid.

A recent report from the Balkan think tank the European Stability Initiative concludes that the latest High Representative, Paddy Ashdown, displays a "bewildering conception of democracy politics." By essentially exercising dictatorial powers, he is acting like a "European Raj" whose policy "echoes the liberal imperialism of the past," warns the ESI. There is no reason to believe that such rule is ever going to turn Bosnia into a real country.

The experience in Kosovo is even worse. After going to war to stop ethnic cleansing, the U.S. presided over the territory while its erstwhile allies, the Kosovo Liberation Army, murdered hundreds of Serbs, ethnically cleansed nearly a quarter of a million Serbs, Jews, Gypsies, and non-Albanian Muslims, and despoiled Orthodox religious sites. Violence remains a serious problem as KLA members have taken over organized crime and formed the quasi-state's police force. Yet the West holds Kosovo in an autonomous limbo that satisfies no one: the Albanians want independence while the Serbs want to reassert Belgrade's control. After being empowered by Washington, the transformed KLA mounted attacks to the north in Serbia and to the east in Macedonia.

Examples in the Mideast and Muslim world look no better. Two decades ago many Shia Muslims in Lebanon greeted Israeli troops in Lebanon as liberators. The Shiites shared little affinity with Palestinian guerrillas who had dominated their territory and turned it into a target for Israeli military retaliation. But war raged among Muslim sects while Israel allied itself with contending Christian militias. Eventually residents hated occupation by Israel even more than by the PLO, and the Shia Hizbollah movement proved to be as deadly a foe as the PLO for Israel.

Lebanon offered no better an experience for America. In 1958 a temporary U.S. military intervention seemed to help stabilize the government. In 1983 The U.S. jumped into the ongoing Lebanese civil war on the side of the minority Christian government, which ruled little more than Beirut. Washington turned itself into a combatant, bombarding Muslim villages, and was rewarded with bomb blasts that killed 16 Americans at the U.S. embassy and 241 Marines at their airport barracks. President Ronald Reagan proclaimed that the attacks demonstrated that America was "accomplishing its mission." Indeed, "we are more resolved than ever" to persevere, he declared. But Washington quickly redeployed its forces on ship and sailed away.

Today Afghanistan is turning ugly. Although Washington expeditiously defenestrated the Taliban government and its al-Qaeda allies, two years of occupation have left Hamid Karzai as more mayor of Kabul than president of Afghanistan. Bloody factional fighting is rife throughout the country.

As yet Karzai does not even trust his safety to Afghan bodyguards. In order to extend his power, U.S. forces are increasingly intervening in local squabbles, bombing contending warlords, for instance. "It's all tribal now," declares Whitney Azoy, a former U.S. diplomat: "The US military is being used for these personal vendettas, and they don't have the experience in this region to realize it."

Yet American action no longer goes unchallenged. With some regularity American soldiers are being ambushed and occasionally killed in southern Afghanistan. There are increasing attacks on aid workers and tourists as well. In October special envoy Zalmay Khalilzad warned that the Taliban "may be planning even larger attacks, more spectacular attacks."

While most Afghans remain pleased at their liberation from Taliban rule, many are chafing at America's continued control: Washington carries out searches and detentions on its own authority and was widely criticized for the war in Iraq. America won no friends when it arrested

Naeem Koochi, an influential tribal leader, on his way to Kabul to meet with government officials, and then transferred him to Guantanamo Bay over the protests of the Karzai government. Public demonstrations greeted the accidental killing of four Afghan soldiers by U.S. forces in Kabul. Continuing accidents, mistakes, and harshness are likely to further wear out America's welcome.

Nor has the West bought dramatic reconstruction progress with the $800 million spent in 2002 by various aid agencies. Observes Scott Baldauf, South Asia bureau chief for the *Christian Science Monitor*: "Despite some positive signs in Afghanistan over the past year—children going to school, homes being rebuilt, wells being dug—there is much about postliberation Afghanistan that hasn't changed during President Hamid Karzai's first months of power. Businessmen complain about harassment by corrupt policemen and thuggish soldiers. All but the bravest women still wear sky-blue burqas, their only protection from the hungry eyes of gunmen. Some villages are so far away from doctors or medical clinics that preventable diseases like polio and measles are making a comeback."

He is not alone in his assessment. Writes Marc Kauffman in the *Washington Post*: "virtually every significant system in the country is broken. The military is splintered by factionalism, the police force is untrained, the justice system is dominated by religious conservatives who have more in common with the Taliban than with Karzai, and tax collection is largely ineffective. Even the driving rules are in disarray."

One cannot help but think of the Soviet experience: Moscow quickly occupied Afghanistan and faced only modest opposition to start. A decade later it withdrew in the midst of disaster. Baldauf worries that "For all the appearances of stability, Afghanistan is tottering at the edge of civil war. It needs only a nudge." His driver proclaims: "The only thing that keeps this country from going back to the Taliban are those B-52s."

None of these experiences mean that nation-building can never work in a non-Western country. But they do suggest that nation-building is an enormously difficult enterprise in anything but the narrowest circumstances—ones, alas, not present in Iraq. Evident Iraqi enthusiasm at the fall of Saddam Hussein created an illusion, in the mind of the Bush administration, at least, of enthusiasm at the pros-

gered change among the Palestinians. Saudi reforms follow the regime's recognition that royalist rule is vulnerable to jihadist violence.

Sparking the "Cedar Revolution" in Lebanon was the horrid assassination of former prime minister Rafiq Hariri. Citizens of Lebanon, which long has held elections, looked more to the nonviolent protests in Georgia and Ukraine than to anything in Iraq. Most Lebanese doubt the contrary claims by opposition leader Walid Jumblatt, until recently busy applauding the killing of Americans and Israelis.

Moreover, the trend towards democratization, though a very welcome side-effect of the Iraq war, does not justify the invasion. The costs remain too high: More than 1500 dead and 11,000 injured Americans. More than 1000 children who lost a parent.

And no end to casualties in sight. Gen. Richard Myers, Chairman of the Joint Chiefs of Staff, observes that insurgencies elsewhere have typically lasted from seven to 12 years.

The war will have cost more than $200 billion by the end of this year. According to congressional estimates, the total over the next decade could run two to three times that. America's freedom values also are risked by the military and security measures necessary to prosecute foreign wars.

Moreover, terrorism threatens even more. "Islamic extremists are exploiting the Iraqi conflict to recruit new anti-U.S. jihadists," CIA Director Porter J. Goss recently warned Congress. The military is suffering enormous strain, finding it increasingly difficult to recruit and retain the personnel necessary to garrison Iraq and guard against other threats. America's international credibility with regard to other dangers, including Iran and North Korea, has suffered severe damage.

Yet the battle between the President's acolytes and antagonists should not obscure the fact that the Mideast's democratic sprouts might turn into regimes that respect the life and dignity of the human person. However the Iraqi experiment turns out, it would be difficult for the result to be worse that Saddam Hussein's dictatorship.

But we still must be concerned about the result. Popular desires for democratic governance and freedom from foreign domination are basic and vital. Unfortunately, they do not guarantee protection of life, liberty, and the pursuit of happiness. And if the early democratic blooms die off, or become deformed, yielding majoritarian tyranny, the result will be a tragic lost opportunity.

Many signs are negative. In Iraq thousands of Christians have fled, most to neighboring Syria, one of the administration's "outposts of tyranny." Iraq's frontrunning Shiite candidate for prime minister, Ibrahim Jaafari, has promised to introduce Islamic sharia law. Paul Marshall of Freedom House worries that "Islam undefined" might become "the constitution behind the constitution" in Iraq. And irrespective of what the constitution ends up saying, the real question is how Iraqis ultimately govern themselves.

On one side in Lebanon is Druze leader Jumblatt, who has blamed the CIA for 9/11 and vilified Israel. Last December he declared: "The killing of U.S. soldiers in Iraq is legitimate and obligatory."

The alternative is Hezbollah, which represents much of the majority Shiite population. Hezbollah has mixed terrorism with public service, and its members criticize the U.S. as virulently as they do Israel.

Hamas did well in Palestinian elections. It has been rapidly gaining on Fatah in the polls and might win upcoming legislative elections.

Jihadists prospered in Saudi Arabia's recent municipal balloting. The radical Muslim Brotherhood could win a free vote in Egypt.

No one can predict what would happen if Washington's ally Pakistan suddenly implemented the President's democratic rhetoric. Nor would any American want to ask the public in any Arab state what it thinks of Washington's occupation of Iraq or support for Israel.

The U.S. should not oppose democracy in response. Doing so put America on the wrong side of history in such diverse countries as Iran and Nicaragua. Indeed, the mullahs likely would not be in power in Tehran today but for Washington's backing for the Shah. However, Americans inside and outside of government must pay as much attention to the development of a vibrant and tolerant civil society as to the holding of elections.

Give President Bush credit—he has been willing to advance what originally seemed like a Quixotic crusade, pushing democracy in the Mideast. But, warns former top Pentagon aide Dov Zakheim, democracy "isn't a short-term enterprise or one that can be won by force of arms."

Our real goal should be liberty. For without liberty, democracy risks becoming just another tool of tyranny, on behalf of a majority rather than a minority.

How to foster liberal, tolerant peoples and societies is far more complicated than detailing election procedures or providing campaign training. Encouraging today's delicate democratic sprouts to flourish and eventually replace the barren tyranny that continues to dominate the Mideast poses an enormous challenge to all of us.

March 2005

Dying for What?

The passage of another Veteran's Day reminds us of the continuing tragic sacrifice of American soldiers. The even greater tragedy, however, is that their continuing sacrifice in Iraq cannot be justified.

For more than two hundred years average men and women have risked life and limb for their country. The politicians who recruited and sometimes conscripted the soldiers routinely painted military service in glorious terms: protecting America and even the entire world.

President George W. Bush continues in this tradition. The Iraq occupation "is vital to the future security of our country," he says.

And not just of America. He told troops at Fort Bragg: "you are making possible the security of free nations."

Alas, it isn't true. In fact, Americans are dying in a conflict that is making the U.S. and the world less rather than more secure.

To speak the truth in no way denigrates their service. In fact, their patriotic loss demands political honesty.

We now know that Baghdad possessed no WMD and was not involved in terrorist attacks on the U.S. Thus, the war was not necessary for American security. It certainly did not make the world more secure.

The occupation is proving to be even worse. The invasion has turned Iraq into a terrorist training ground, creating a cadre of violent jihadists, many of whom are now bleeding back to their home countries.

The longer the occupation, the greater the hostility against America in both Iraq and beyond. And the larger the number of putative terrorists created. Sadly, young Americans are dying in a campaign that actually is making their nation less safe.

This has forced war advocates to emphasize humanitarian goals, contending that U.S. troops are doing good. And getting rid of Saddam Hussein was a positive. But not something worth 2000-plus American lives with so many more likely to follow.

Even granting the humanitarian case for removing a dictator does not justify a lengthy occupation. Hussein is out of power, facing trial. That objective, even if it warranted war, has been achieved.

The argument that America is building democracy is much weaker. Set aside the difficulty of creating a genuinely free society without the civil and political institutions necessary for sustaining a stable political order. Global social engineering, no matter how well-intentioned, does not warrant sacrificing one's countrymen.

The President and others have attempted to justify the war by circling back to U.S. security: our freedom depends on the freedom of others. But there is no reason to believe that regimes grow more pro-American as they become more democratic.

To the contrary, at least in the short-term, democracy in such nations as Egypt, Jordan, Pakistan, and Saudi Arabia would likely unleash greater anti-Americanism. That's no reason to stand against democracy, as the U.S. did during much of the Cold War. However, launching a militarized crusade to force elections in recalcitrant countries is imprudent at best.

What's left is a moral argument for spreading democracy. Democracy is laudable, but merely one aspect of a free society. Authoritarian, demagogic systems which hold occasional elections do not warrant significant effort by Washington, let alone the sacrifice of American lives.

Even the best intentions do not guarantee the best results. In Iraq, for instance, there is no guarantee that the most liberal constitutional provisions will be enforced; what Iraqi politics will look like even a couple years from now is impossible to know. Americans likely are dying today for something far different than U.S.-style political liberty.

This doesn't mean that democracy is not worth promoting, but that it is not worth pursuing through war. To say that the occupation of Iraq is not in America's interest is not to say that the sacrifices made by American servicemen and women are not noble. Rather, it means that their deaths are unnecessary and unjustified.

Indeed, despite the eloquent rhetoric within which conflicts—Somalia, Haiti, Bosnia, Kosovo, Iraq, and more—are routinely packaged, the crusade for democracy possesses an ugly underside. There is more than a little whiff of imperialism in the claim that the U.S. is entitled, unilaterally and coercively, to determine political systems in other nations.

This presumes that Americans have not only the right, but the knowledge, understanding, and sophistication to essentially reorder the world. It is hubris, hubris on a global scale. The point is not that Americans' intentions are not good, but that the consequences of war are usually unpredictable and often counterproductive.

"Power tends to corrupt," intoned British historian Lord Acton, and "absolute power corrupts absolutely." America as sole global superpower is not immune.

For what are Americans dying in Iraq? Nothing that justifies their heroic sacrifice.

We must win, explains President Bush and his allies. In effect, Americans must die to vindicate those who died before pursuing goals since exposed as fraudulent or unrealistic. Political leaders in both parties must not be allowed to hide behind the soldiers whom they have put in harm's way. We must hold accountable the architects of this misbegotten war.

November 2005

CHAPTER FIVE

Asia

Asia—The More Things Change, the More They Stay the Same

After World War II the United States established an extensive forward military presence and fought two wars in East Asia as part of its strategy to contain communism. The Cold War ended a decade ago, but America's defense posture has changed little. The Clinton administration is determined to keep at least 100,000 military personnel in East Asia and the Pacific, apparently forever.

The Pentagon's 1995 assessment of U.S. security policy in East Asia (the so-called Nye Report) made the astonishing assertion that "the end of the Cold War has not diminished" the importance of any of America's regional security commitments. In November 1998 the Defense Department released an updated report, but it reflected the same outdated analysis in reaffirming support for every one of America's treaties and deployments throughout the region. More than a year later U.S. policy remains the same.

The administration's watchword, and that of the leading Republican presidential contenders, is simply more of everything. DOD gives a nod to multilateralism and cooperation among the countries in the region, but it is clear that the United States is to remain East Asia's dominant actor. And that dominance must be demonstrated in military terms.

The administration's commitment to permanent, promiscuous intervention was preordained. Secretary of Defense William Cohen admitted: "When I first took over, I said everything is on the table for review, except we are going to keep 100,000 people in the Asia-Pacific region—that is off the table."

In short, the Pentagon conducted a supposedly searching review that ignored the most important issue. Rather than expand America's military presence in East Asia at a time when security threats against the United States have dramatically diminished, the administration and Congress should together initiate a phased withdrawal of American forces from the region and adopt the role of ultimate balancer rather than constant meddler.

U.S. taxpayers spent roughly $13 trillion (in current dollars) and sacrificed 113,000 lives (mostly in East Asian wars) to win the Cold War. For five decades Washington provided a defense shield behind which noncommunist countries throughout East Asia were able to grow economically (despite their recent setbacks) and democratically. That policy achieved its objective.

Japan is the world's second-ranking economic power; Taiwan's dramatic jump from poverty to prosperity forced the leaders of the communist mainland to undertake fundamental economic reforms. South Korea now dramatically outstrips communist North Korea on virtually every measure of national power. After years of failure the Philippines seems to be on the path to prosperity, while countries like Thailand have grown significantly and will eventually recover from their current economic travails.

At the same time, the threat environment has become more benign. The Soviet Union has disappeared, and a much weaker Russia has neither the capability nor the will for East Asian adventurism. Elsewhere, tough-minded communism has dissolved into a cynical excuse for incumbent office holders to maintain power. A decade after the Tiananmen Square massacre, China is combining support for greater economic liberty with (admittedly inconsistent) respect for greater individual autonomy, if not political freedom. So far Beijing's military renewal has been modest, and China has been assertive rather than aggressive—although its saber-rattling toward Taiwan remains of concern.

Southeast Asia is roiled by economic and political instability, but such problems threaten no one outside the immediate neighborhood. Only North Korea constitutes a current East Asian security threat, but that totalitarian state, though odious, is no replacement for the threat once posed by Soviet Union.

Some analysts privately, and a few publicly, believe that Japan poses a potential threat to regional peace. But Tokyo has gained all of the influence and wealth through peace that it had hoped to attain 60 years ago through war and the Greater East Asia Co-Prosperity Sphere. Moreover, the lesson of World War II remains vivid in Japan.

So far, neither the Clinton administration nor Congress seem to have noticed these many critical changes. Despite the dramatic diminution in security threats and equally dramatic growth in allied capabilities, U.S. policy looks very much as it did during the Cold War. DOD repeatedly emphasizes its allegiance to the status quo. Washington's motto seems to be "what has ever been, must ever be."

The Pentagon's security strategy report envisions an American security interest in virtually every East Asian country. Not only does it laud alliances with Japan and South Korea. It also wants to promote military ties with Laos and Mongolia, countries with no conceivable relevance to U.S. security.

The Pentagon also devotes substantial attention to nonmilitary issues in a report ostensibly devoted to security. The administration explicitly terms drug trafficking, terrorism, and environmental degradation "security interests." Humanitarian operations, contends the administration, "may likewise serve important U.S. security interests and values, including preservation of regional stability, and promotion of democracy and human rights." It is a breathtakingly broad agenda.

DOD says the presence of U.S. troops is necessary only for "the foreseeable future," but it is hard to imagine the circumstances under which they could depart. If the end of the Cold War, the collapse of hegemonic communism, and the dramatic growth in the strength of friendly democratic and quasi-democratic states throughout the region aren't enough to warrant meaningful change, what would be enough?

The vague specter of instability has replaced the demon of communism as America's enemy. States DOD: "In contrast to Cold War-era alliances, [the U.S. commitments] are not directed at any third power but serve the interests of all who benefit from regional stability and security."

But even in the midst of economic crisis, Asia is not ready to plunge in the abyss. And if it were, there is little a few thousand U.S. troops in Okinawa or South Korea could do about it. Political conflict in Malaysia, thuggish rule in Cambodia, separatist campaigns in Indonesia, insurgency in the Philippines: these kind of internal struggles pose the most serious threat to regional stability but are beyond the reach of America, unless Washington is prepared to repeat its Vietnam experience several times over.

As for the threats of real conflict—the two Koreas and China/Taiwan—America's allies are capable of maintaining military forces necessary to deter war. If that is a slightly less certain guarantee of stability, it is a far better one from America's standpoint. Then if deterrence failed, the U.S. will not find itself automatically involved.

The weakness of the administration's case is evident from its reliance on bottom-scraping, kitchen sink arguments that can best be characterized as silly. For instance, the Pentagon contends: "The presence of U.S. military personnel in the region multiplies our diplomatic impact through engagement with counterparts and the demonstration of professional military ethics and conduct in a democratic society." However, U.S. training programs did not prevent abuses by the Indonesian military in support of the brutal Suharto regime—or promote "the spread of democratic norms," as DOD desires. The American military worked closely with a series of ugly, military-dominated regimes in South Korea. Stationing massive numbers of troops in other nations has proved to be a dubious means of strengthening civil societies in those countries.

Even less compelling are DOD's nonsecurity "security" interests. "We must have the capability to ... get American citizens out" of collapsed states and "We must be able to" mount humanitarian operations, declares Secretary Cohen. However, the possibility of expensive troop commitments yielding some ancillary humanitarian benefits is no reason to maintain those commitments in perpetuity. American businessmen and tourists who flood the world have no right to expect a Marine Expeditionary Force always to be stationed nearby.

Instead of enshrining the status quo, the administration and Congress should adjust U.S. commitments and deployments. Washington should develop a comprehensive plan for the phased withdrawal of all forces currently stationed in East Asia and termination of U.S. defense guarantees to allied nations.

To start, Washington should tell Japan and South Korea that it is time for them to defend themselves. Moreover, while the U.S. should sell Taiwan whatever arms it desires, Washington should indicate that it will not intervene in a war between Taiwan and China. America does not have sufficient interests at stake to risk conflict with nuclear-armed China.

Instead of attempting to upgrade defense relationships with nations like Australia and the Philippines, the U.S. should rely on informal consultations and intelligence-sharing. In cases like Laos and Mongolia Washington should focus on cultural and economic links.

The U.S. should encourage its one-time clients, particularly Japan and South Korea, to expand regional security cooperation through the Association of Southeast Asian Nations (ASEAN) and other appropriate institutions. Washington should press such nations to resolve boundary and territorial conflicts through negotiations, including through such multilateral organizations.

The U.S. should view New Delhi, which possesses the world's second largest population and a sizable military, as an important future counterweight to China. India, in combination with a tough-minded Taiwan, somewhat more heavily-armed Japan, and unified Korea with a potent military, would help establish a new regional balance of power that would allow America to further distance itself from incendiary but local disputes.

Washington's basic objective should be to step into the background as local actors take on responsibility for their own security. Washington should help make such a process as smooth as possible. But America's ultimate goal should be to encourage the region's players to construct a security architecture that reflects the new reality—the absence of an overwhelming hegemonic threat combined with the opportunity for allied states to construct a local balance of power sufficient to constrain any potential aggressor.

Of course, most East Asian states want Washington to stay, but the American people should not be expected to surrender more dollars and risk more lives to police East Asia however long friendly states consider it convenient. Although it might be in the interest of other nations for Washington to defend them—what country would not naturally desire that the world's remaining superpower subsidize its defense?—it is not in America's interest to do so.

The world remains a dangerous place, advocates of a perpetual Pax Americana ritualistically intone, and so it is. But it is not terribly dangerous to the United States. Most world problems will never end up on America's doorstep unless Washington voluntarily brings them there. Real leadership entails separating the few issues involving America's vital national interest from the bulk of problems that belong to someone else.

January 2000

Australia—Updating the Alliance for New Era

Australia is one of America's most faithful friends. The two countries share much history and culture. The relationship is especially close today.

The Bush administration appreciates the Howard government's willingness to act against Australia's interest by intervening in Iraq. Canberra's steadfastness, even after terror attacks in Indonesia and jihadist kidnapping in Iraq, offers a welcome contrast to the behavior of the Philippines, for instance.

However, these two governments will eventually pass from the scene and past cooperation is not enough to justify the alliance in the future. Differences between the two sides already are evident and likely will grow. It would be best over time to narrow the scope of the U.S.-Australia relationship, and especially America's responsibilities in the region. Canberra should take on a more significant role as one of Asia's sheriffs rather than as Washington's deputy.

The two countries' military relationship goes back more than a half century, to the Australia-New Zealand-United States (ANZUS) accord. ANZUS never made much sense, since it was directed less at containing the Soviet Union, which had no military presence in the South Pacific, than at preventing renewed aggression by Japan, which had been decisively defeated.

ANZUS went on the critical list in 1984, when New Zealand refused to allow American ships to use port facilities unless Washington certified that the vessels weren't carrying nuclear weapons. The Australia-United States Ministerial Consultations (AUSMIN) is a half-hearted replacement for ANZUS, more an intention to collaborate than a mechanism to act.

A formal alliance, in contrast to a cooperative relationship, looks outmoded for both nations. There's no hegemonic threat to deter, no aggressive power ready to engulf friendly states in Asia, including Australia. Australia enjoys splendid isolation, with no meaningful direct threats to its security. The likelihood of an attack from a serious power—China, India, Japan—is a paranoid fantasy.

Nor does Australia, which is busily upgrading its military capabilities, need defending by America. Prosperous and technologically advanced, Canberra can meet any future security challenges.

For instance, instability in the Solomon Islands is tragic and an Indonesian implosion might spark a refugee flood, but Australia doesn't need to be defended from such contingencies by Washington. Indeed, few local problems are likely to even be of concern to Washington, as Canberra discovered in 1999. For America East Timor was a tragedy to deplore, not a danger to extinguish.

Perhaps the most worrisome threat facing Australia is the same one facing the U.S.: terrorism. But terrorist attacks like those in Bali and New York City, though monstrous, are not typically exogenous threats. Rather, they usually arise in reaction to other policies. In the case of the U.S., everything from sanctions against Iraq, aid to Israel, and support for Saudi Arabia's royal kleptocracy has generated Islamic hostility. For Australia the most obvious trigger is military cooperation with America.

Thus, the raison d'etre for America to extend formal security commitments in East Asia has disappeared. There's no longer any reason to think of alliance relationships in terms of a fixed security threat, whether Japan or the Soviet Union. (Even in the case of North Korea, the Republic of Korea is well able to develop and deploy sufficient military forces for its own defense.) The focus for the U.S. and its friends now should be the many areas of less formal cooperation—sharing intelligence, thwarting terrorists, and promoting nonproliferation, among others.

In these areas the U.S.-Australia relationship remains valuable. For instance, joint intelligence activities go back decades and both countries gain from identifying and assessing potential threats. Australia has unique regional assets for identifying, tracking, and seizing terrorists in Asia; the U.S. is better positioned to challenge threatening groups further afield.

The impact of proliferation, both nuclear and missile, varies widely depending upon the state involved. But cooperation on missile defense will yield benefits to both nations. The U.S. is a more likely target today but an increasingly assertive Australia could find itself vulnerable in the future. Moreover, Canberra, with a robust navy, is an obvious partner to aid the Bush administration's Proliferation Security Initiative.

Increased inter-operability of weapons and forces may be a plus, but it's hard to imagine many occasions for joint combat operations. Iraq looks sui generis. That war reflected an ideological fixation on the part of the Bush administration rather than serious military threats against America or any of its allies.

The misbegotten consequences of the conflict make it unlikely that Washington will again embark upon such a war of choice. Should the U.S. choose to do so in, say, Syria or Iran, Washington undoubtedly would welcome support from Australia. But Canberra would have obvious reason to say no, especially since another long-term commitment by Australia no less than by Washington would reduce its strategic flexibility elsewhere.

Canberra's focus should be stability, if not democracy, in its own neighborhood. (Democracy is a good thing in the abstract, but may yield increased security problems for surrounding states.) East Timor, the Solomons, and Papua New Guinea all illustrate contingencies in what some have described as an "arc of instability," where Australia has an interest and America has none. The principle of self-reliance, embodied in the Nixon administration's so-called Guam Doctrine of 1969, should apply.

The greatest challenge facing the two nations is likely to be China. America's highest priority in the region is likely to become containing Beijing, and particularly defending Taiwan. Confrontation with China is not obviously wise or feasible for America—a better strategy likely would be to accommodate rather than contest the almost inevitable increase in influence of Beijing in a region that is China's backyard but far distant from the U.S.

There is no reason to assume that Washington will choose wisely, however, and if it does not Australia may be forced to make unpleasant choices. Foreign Minister Alexander Downer pointedly observed that a conflict over Taiwan lies outside ANZUS, setting off a flurry of clarifications. Australian support for Washington is by no means certain, given the active flirtation between China and Australia. Indeed, polling Down Under suggests greater popular warmth towards and less fear of Beijing than Washington. There's nothing wrong with Australia balancing relations between the two, but it demonstrates the relationship's limits for America and risks for Australia.

Whither the alliance? The U.S. should end its security guarantees for populous and prosperous states, including Australia. Then Canberra could become even more active in promoting coalitions to respond to mutual threats, such as East Timor in 1999 and the Solomons in 2003. The acquisition of long-range missiles and plan for a "maritime security zone" further demonstrate Australia's seriousness. This is all to the good—for Australia, America, and Asia.

Prime Minister John Howard's vision of "the three great Pacific democracies," America, Australia, and Japan, ensuring regional security is both too broad and too narrow. It should reach further afield, especially to India, while reducing reliance on the U.S. South Korea has begun to look beyond the Korean peninsula. The ASEAN nations also can play a role.

Melding such diverse countries into a coalition won't be easy, but creating a framework for cooperation might be possible. The East Asia Summit planned for December 2005 in Kuala Lumpur is yet another regional forum in which Australia can play a role. On the vast majority of issues Australia should work with its neighbors without expecting Washington to become involved.

There still will be much for the U.S. and Australia to do together. Economic and trade issues will remain important, though that framework has been established through the free trade agreement. Intelligence and military officials should scan the horizon for potential threats and discuss possible responses. Washington should be ready to act if a serious hegemonic threat, such as from China, arises that allied states cannot contain.

But alliances should be created for a purpose, not as permanent organizations constantly seeking a new justification for existence. America's security commitment to Australia has served its purpose; Canberra is now capable of promoting stability throughout the South Pacific. Many shared interests remain, but it's time to adjust both nations' policies and the forms of bilateral cooperation to changing strategic realities.

May 2005

Burma—Forgotten War in a Forgotten Country

LAW THI HTA, BURMA—It wasn't much by Western standards: a clearing in the dense foliage with a half dozen wood and bamboo buildings, covered by thatched roofs. A short walk along the dirt path led to more houses, sitting on stilts and open to rain, animals, and mosquitoes. There was also a small clinic, constructed with American aid. Dense, green jungle growth covered the hills that marched endlessly beyond.

But some 40 people called Law Thi Hta home. Like thousands of other ethnic Karen in Burma, they had been displaced by the Burmese military—the dictatorship styling itself the State Peace and Development Council (SPDC). More than 100,000 Karen now live in refugee camps in Thailand, many just across the narrow Moi River.

Freedom Hospital Number One, as it was called by Christian Freedom International (CFI), a relief group based in Front Royal, Virginia, looked anything but. Electricity was unknown in the village and the only running water was located in the river. Wooden platforms served as beds, operations were performed on bamboo tables, and modern equipment was absent.

Still, it was something in which CFI head Jim Jacobson—whose cargo pants, print shirt, floppy hat, and running shoes made him look more at home in Washington, D.C. than in the Burmese jungle—could take pride. The clinic served children suffering from potentially deadly diarrhea, adults with typhoid, and anyone who stepped on a landmine. Enthused Jacobson, "If the hospital lasts through the dry season, we'll build it up."

Burma, now officially Myanmar, is an international tragedy. Gen. Ne Win seized power in 1962 and, though formally retired, remains the leading power in Rangoon.

Mass protests for democracy in 1988 led to creation of the State Law and Order Restoration Council (SLORC), which crushed dissent with martial law backed by bullets. The leading democratic figure is Aung San Suu Kyi, daughter of Gen. Aung San, a leading nationalist who was assassinated shortly before Burma won independence. SLORC foolishly called elections a decade ago and Suu Kyi's National League for Democracy won more than 80 percent of the votes. SLORC, which has since transmuted into the less-sinister sounding SPDC, annulled the election, put Suu Kyi under house arrest, and arrested many of her followers. Human Rights Watch estimates that 1300 political prisoners languish in prison.

Although international attention has focused on Suu Kyi, the more serious threat to Ne Win and his junta comes from the Karen and other ethnic groups. Britain promised them autonomy, but did little to implement its commitment when Burma became independent in 1948. Moreover, most Burmese are animists or Buddhists, while the Chins and Nagas are primarily Christian. So too are many Kachins and Karens, whose ancestors were converted by missionaries centuries ago. Secession struggles began against Prime Minister U Nu's government in 1949 and intensified after Ne Win's coup.

The insurgencies have waxed and waned over time. During the last decade several groups have come to terms with Rangoon. But the Karen fight on.

In response, the SPDC has expanded its military to some 400,000. Conscripts are simply dragged off the streets. Two years ago, explains fifteen-year-old Yei Shweh, who defected to the KNLA, he took a bus to Rangoon to see the big city: he was arrested by the army when he arrived. Pay is irregular, training sparse, and morale low. But fear keeps most soldiers in the ranks.

The war has no rules. Rangoon maintains numerous bases in eastern Burma, while guerrillas move freely around the camps. Periodically the government strikes at villages suspected of harboring rebels. SPDC forces impress civilians, women as well as men, as porters for months at a time. Yei Shweh and two other Burmese defectors described how food rations are no more regular than the $2 monthly pay: Hungry soldiers take villagers' crops and livestock. Refugees also report frequent beatings, rapes, and murder, stories confirmed by the abashed defectors.

As a result, the Karen fight desperately. One 38-year-old guerrilla, whose long brown hair made him look more like a Bohemian resident of Greenwich Village than a dedicated defender of Burmese villages, figures that he has killed some 200 SPDC soldiers.

The battle is sadly uneven, however. The KNLA fields 4000 to 5000 ill-equipped guerrillas. The troops I met tended to run from teens to thirties. They mix fatigues and boots with ethnic Karen wraparound skirts, flip-flops, and American-language shorts, t-shirts and baseball caps. Soldiers carry a motley assemblage of arms, ranging from antiquated M1 carbines to captured Ma rifles to AK-47s to home-made teak landmines.

War consumes their lives. One 22-year-old said he had been fighting "for many years," perhaps ten. But Gen. Bo Mya, who also serves as vice president of the Karen National Union (KNU), joined the Karen revolution when it started in 1949. Gen. Saw Htey Maung, the 70-year old commander of the Seventh Brigade, described how he started with the Karen Rifles, then part of the British Army, in 1946.

The KNLA usually inflict far more casualties than they suffer—they claim a 20-to-1 kill ratio. Their shared Christian faith gives them hope. "Jesus is with the Karen soldier," says Gen. Htey. But they can rarely stop a determined SPDC offensive.

The KNLA lost its capital of Manerplaw ("victory field") four years ago. The Karen are increasingly pressed against the Thai border. Burmese forces have even launched attacks into Thai territory.

The dry season is known as the "killing season" because steep jungle trails dry out and rushing streams run low. Military action typically ends mid-year, but SPDC troops arrived at Law Thi Hta and Freedom Hospital Number One before the rain. Just six weeks after my visit earlier this year, Burmese forces advanced, capturing some villagers and driving the others away. They burned the hospital and other buildings and sowed the area with landmines, to prevent the residents from returning. A second clinic to the north, along with an entire refugee camp housing 4000 people, was also destroyed.

"This happens every year," observes Jacobson, but this is "one of the worst years." Last year CFI lost only one Freedom Hospital.

Nevertheless, Gen. Htey offers a positive spin; since the Karen rely on "guerrilla tactics, hit-and-run," it looks "to the outside world that we are losing. But every month we can see that the casualties of the SPDC are more than before."

In fact, the Burmese government's victories are usually costly and often temporary. Although some sections of the border are less than 120 miles from Rangoon, the SPDC cannot garrison the rugged and isolated jungles. But it doesn't have to. All it has to do is terrorize and displace the Karen. As Gen. Htey acknowledges, "the SPDC try to fight the grassroots, our backbone, the villages," so the people "don't have the morale to support us with food or anything else." The result is a million internally displaced persons and 200,000 refugees in Bangladesh, China, India, and Thailand.

The latter bears the heaviest burden. Although Bangkok has no love for the SPDC, it also eschews conflict with the numerically larger Burmese army. At the same time, Burma's internal instability and porous border offer profit opportunities: drug smuggling and teak logging have enriched people on both sides of the 1300-mile border. This peaceful coexistence was challenged in January when soldiers from God's Army, a small independent Karen force, and the Vigorous Burmese Student Warriors, a faction of exiled students, briefly seized a Thai hospital in an attempt to win international attention to the Karen's plight. Bangkok responded by killing all of the raiders and shelling territory occupied by God's Army, pushing them deeper into Burma, where SPDC troops overran their camp.

Thailand has reportedly been talking with both Rangoon and the United Nations about moving the refugee camps into Burma. Yet this is impossible so long as war rages. No Burmese pledge of safety could be believed. The KNLA is not strong enough to safeguard the territory.

How to end the conflict? KNU President Saw Ba Thin says that "only a political settlement can make peace last." And, he adds, as independence hero Aung San realized, "Burma must be based on system of federal union." Karen representatives have met with the central government several times, most recently in 1996. But "on all of these occasions it told the KNU to lay down its arms instead of trying to reach an understanding through political discussion."

Earlier this year Jim Jacobson carried a new offer by the KNU to negotiate, at a neutral location outside of Burma, to Tin Winn, Burma's Ambassador to the U.S. Winn rejected it out of hand, suggesting instead that the KNU send representatives to Rangoon. But Jacobson doubts they would return alive. Nor is there any evidence that the SPDC is prepared to end its murderous depredations, let alone offer the autonomy for which the Karen have been fighting for a half century.

Which leaves Suu Kyi and the Karen alike hoping for outside support. In a video smuggled out of Burma earlier this year, Suu Kyi argued that the greater the international backing received by democracy activists, "the sooner we shall achieve our goal." Similarly, stated

Gen. Htey, "If we had a chance we would request that the American people help us to get our freedom state."

But what can be done about a repressive, secretive, and isolated regime like the SPDC? It is supported by China, which covets naval access to Burma's long coastline and began arming and financing Rangoon in 1990. "Without Chinese help, the Burmese would never have taken Manerplaw," complains Gen. Htey.

Western nations have far less clout. The U.S. had only modest economic ties with Burma before banning trade and investment in 1997; the European Union simply denies Rangoon duty-free access to its market. Such restrictions obviously inconvenience the SPDC, but have not shaken its hold on power.

Unfortunately, however, warns Robert Manning of the Council on Foreign Relations, as a result of sanctions Rangoon "has drifted toward Beijing, its major arms supplier." The ASEAN states (Rangoon joined in 1997) similarly complain that U.S. policy has hindered their efforts to counter Chinese influence.

Moreover, economic restrictions impoverish those who languish under SPDC jackboots. Consider the controversial Yadena natural gas pipeline, running from Burma's coast to Thailand. The project has generated jobs and led to construction of roads, wells, schools, and health clinics for local residents. (The investors, including America's Unocal, should be held accountable if, as critics charge, forced labor was used to construct the pipeline, but many outside observers back the companies' denials.)

Some activists contend that stronger multilateral sanctions would bring the regime to terms. KNU President Saw Ba Thin explains that "we'd like to see the U.S. government increase pressure like trade sanctions and diplomatic sanctions, and other pressures." But the 1997 Asian economic crisis actually has had this effect, cutting ASEAN investment in Burma by 70 percent. Rangoon has not repented.

Anyway, most countries are moving in the opposite direction. The Japanese have long chosen to deal with Burma. Australia is considering restarting aid projects. Indeed, at meetings in Seoul earlier this year Asian, European, and U.S. officials met to consider new approaches to Burma. Not that more contact is likely to directly change the SPDC's repressive policies. A reported World Bank/United Nations offer of $1 billion in aid in exchange for democratic reform has fallen on deaf ears.

Some Karen pine for Western military intervention. Last year a top KNU official told a colleague of mine: "do like you did in Kosovo." Saw Ba Thin concurs: "If the American government could do it, it would be helpful." Similarly, Gen. Htey says "The Karen people were waiting for the English government, but never mind if the British don't come and help us. You are from the U.S. You can come and help us."

Of course, that isn't going to happen—and for good reason. America's interest in the Karen's struggle is humanitarian, not strategic, and does not justify risking U.S. lives.

A better alternative to current policy, which has manifestly failed, is probably a mix of diplomatic pressure, which can most effectively be applied by Japan, India, and the ASEAN states, and economic engagement, primarily by private individuals and organizations. Over time broader contact with the West might strengthen internal democratic forces. Indeed, in May the SPDC cracked down on unauthorized international email and telephone services. More investment and trade might help spread such "tools of freedom." But this will be an uncertain and long-term process at best.

The West's most important role may be to help the Karen and other ethnic peoples cope with the SPDC's brutality. That largely means private assistance—like that provided by CFI and similar groups—since neither the U.N. nor Western governments will work in Burma against Rangoon's express wishes.

CFI is currently supporting six "Freedom Hospitals" in Kawthoolei, which typically treat about 600 Karen a month, and will be constructing new facilities to replace the two destroyed earlier this year. It regularly sends teams of CFI-trained medics (usually five, accompanied by several helpers and soldiers), into eastern Burma for up to four months at a time. Three other Americans and I spent three days with one group of such itinerants as they climbed narrow jungle trails, dodged SPDC patrols, and acted as human pack animals to provide basic medical care and distribute drugs, food, Bibles, and hymnals. CFI also sells Karen handicrafts to help provide refugees with a means of support.

Moreover, a shared faith gives CFI an important connection that government agencies and other private groups lack. Jacobson works through local pastors to arrange visits, bring aid, and offer spiritual support. "What is making Rangoon so upset is that we change lives," explains Jacobson.

He can also offer practical advice. Lost limbs from landmines are a result of war. The pervasive diarrhea, dysentery, malaria, measles, tuberculosis, typhoid, utero-infections, and other diseases—malaria alone afflicts up to 60 percent of some village populations—reflect the lack of minimal sanitation. Villages lack outdoor as well as indoor plumbing. Cattle, chickens, and pigs run loose and settle under homes; insects travel from animals to humans through floor slats. People sleep without mosquito nets. Rice baskets are sealed with dried dung. Streams simultaneously act as toilets, wash basins, and water fountains. Other than the plastic water jugs and English-language t-shirts, life is largely unchanged from a century ago.

Years of practice are hard to change, but Jacobson is determined. First, "we're going to try to get them to dig latrines," he says, and then to "pen up the animals." Pastors will spread the message, using the Bible as reinforcement. "Designate a place outside the camp where you can go to relieve yourself," God instructed the Israelites (Deut. 23:13). Such a message seems mundane in the larger geopolitical scheme, but it means lives saved.

Still, the Burmese military will continue to kill. And no matter how hard it works, CFI can only help clean up the carnage that results.

Scores of wars dot the globe. Occasionally one captures newspaper headlines—Kosovo last year, for instance. Most languish in obscurity, like Burma.

The latter tragedy continues to worsen, despite the canting sanctimony of political leaders who routinely invoke the "international community" when pushing their favored causes. Unfortunately, answers are in short supply. "Remember the Karen people. Don't abandon us like the British did," Saw Ba Thin pleads. But most of the world doesn't know enough about the Karen to abandon them. The Karen's only hope lies in groups like CFI, which are helping oppressed peoples survive until the so far illusive political solution is found.

May 2000

China—The Morality of Business

The recent visit of Chinese President Jiang Zemin widened the already significant fault lines over policy towards Beijing. Most office-holders and corporate executives emphasized potential business opportunities in what will some day be the world's largest market. In contrast, some liberals and many social conservatives pressed for trade restrictions to punish Beijing for its human rights abuses.

As a matter of policy, advocates of trade have the better case. President Jiang and his colleagues are committed to maintaining power more than anything else, so even sanctions would not be likely to move them very far on human rights. Moreover, while economic prosperity does not guarantee political democracy, trade with the West has loosed forces that are likely to increasingly unsettle China's sclerotic leadership. The Tiananmen Square massacre continues to stifle political discussion, but China's people enjoy growing freedom in other areas. And, of course, trade creates jobs.

Unfortunately, corporate America seems unable to articulate any argument except the latter. Commerce enhances corporate profits, so nothing else matters, contend business lobbyists. Never mind the opposing arguments—involving human rights, religious freedom, and national security. Nothing, it would seem, is more important than an additional airplane or tractor sale.

Nothing, that is, except a subsidized airplane or tractor sale. Business does not stop at pressing to maintain Most Favored Nation (MFN) status, encouraging relatively free trade between China and the U.S. Corporate America also lobbies for subsidies, particularly through the Export-Import Bank, which backs private exports with taxpayer credits. Many firms also support World Bank loans to the Chinese government for projects on which U.S. firms hope to bid.

This single-minded preoccupation with sales led business to give President Jiang the warmest welcome of his trip. In New York City Jiang rang the bell to open the New York Stock exchange, had breakfast with executives of Goldman Sachs and Salomon Brothers, wandered by IBM's offices on Madison Avenue, and spoke at a dinner hosted by the U.S.-China Business Council and the China Chamber of Commerce. At the latter affair, attended by a Who's Who of the Fortune 500, Jiang announced that "China's market is open to you all" and criticized U.S. trade policy; he received a prolonged standing ovation.

All of which demonstrates business' moral obtuseness. The fact that people are ruled by a murderous government does not mean that firms should not sell products to them and consumers here should not buy goods from them. There are some important exceptions—involving military technology and slave labor, for instance—but in general private trade should not be held hostage to politics.

Nevertheless, as human beings living in a democratic republic, business leaders do have moral responsibilities. In the case of China, the government is ugly. To warmly receive the head of that regime is unseemly, at best. Had he announced Beijing's willingness to respect religious freedom and free political dissidents, then he would have deserved a standing ovation. But why honor him for stating that he was willing to allow firms to invest in China, something in his government's interest?

Moreover, business leaders fail to address moral arguments at their political peril. One corporate lobbyist complained to me about the lack of Export-Import Bank funding for U.S. firms seeking to participate in constructing China's Three Gorges dam. That made no sense since the project would continue anyway, he contended. I explained that I couldn't care less, since I didn't want my tax money supporting the Chinese government. "But that's a moral argument," he sputtered, and offered no response.

Yet Americans respond to moral arguments. Supporters of engagement with China would be more persuasive if they chattered about something in addition to business profits. They should be concerned about the moral implications of dealing with China and tailor their case accordingly.

And there are good moral reasons to let commerce flow. As a matter of personal liberty, Americans should have the right to buy and sell across borders. Moreover, trade is likely to encourage private entrepreneurs and create alternative power centers at the other end, in this case undermining Beijing's political and social controls. It is for the latter reason that many Christian missionary groups in China support MFN.

There is, however, no commensurate argument for conscripting taxpayers' money to underwrite trade with China. Companies that want to reap the gains of commerce should bear the costs of doing so. And business would reduce opposition to MFN if it didn't demand that all Americans subsidize the Chinese government in order to enhance exporters' profits.

International trade benefits people in the U.S. and around the world. That's a good reason to support economic ties with China. But not the best reason—more important is helping to increase human liberty. American business would better advance its cause if it realized that moral arguments matter.

November 1997

China—Trade With China: Business Profits or Human Rights?

Business profits versus human rights. So do critics of trade with China frame the debate. But freer trade is likely to advance human rights as well as boost business profits.

For years, Congress has voted annually on permitting "normal trading relations" with China. Now the Clinton administration is working with administration critics like House majority whip Tom DeLay (R-Tex.) to grant permanent status (PNTR) for Beijing, which would allow China to enter the World Trade Organization (WTO).

Lobbying furiously for a yes vote is American business. Without doubt trade with China, now about $95 billion both ways, is economically beneficial: Some 200,000 Americans are directly employed providing exports to China.

Much more would be possible with a more open economy. Western firms, investors and exporters alike, have found China to be a tough market. Companies cite rising labor costs, market access restrictions, high taxes and customs duties, and corruption.

But PNTR critics don't care about increased profits. Columnist Abe Rosenthal cites "Beijing's human rights crimes." The AFL-CIO denounces Chinese labor practices (while actually worrying most about increased imports).

The Weekly Standard complains about China's "threats to attack Taiwan." Frank Gaffney of the Center for Security Policy worries about Chinese nuclear developments posing "a new threat to this country."

Obviously it would be easier to grant PNTR if China was capitalist and democratic. It is neither. But the most important question is: what policy, economic integration or isolation, is most likely to move China towards capitalism and democracy?

To ask the question is to answer it. Membership in the WTO might not sweep away all of Beijing's economic restrictions, but despite determined internal opposition, the regime has made significant market-opening concessions.

As my Cato Institute colleague Mark Groombridge puts it, "A vote in favor of extending PNTR to China is a vote for reform of the Chinese economy." Indeed, the U.S. has received more than just promises.

Beijing has begun revamping the banking sector. Government officials are planning to relax investment and trade controls, and Chinese companies are maneuvering to better meet anticipated international competition.

Although market reforms do not guarantee greater respect for human rights, economic prosperity brought increased pressure for democracy in such countries as South Korea and Taiwan. In China itself political decentralization and personal autonomy have been expanding. Particularly dramatic has been the growth of private associations and companies.

The communist leadership will undoubtedly resist future democratization; in fact, military and security agencies resolutely opposed the WTO accord. However, the greater people's access to the tools of freedom, such as computers, the larger the number of private power centers, such as businesses, and the increased autonomy of subordinate governments, such as the coastal trading provinces, the greater the pressure for change.

Isolation would merely give the central authorities a pretext to crack down. Notably, religious groups like Ned Graham's East Gates Ministries support continued trade with China.

Finally, while Beijing could end up as an enemy of the U.S., such a result is not preordained. China threatens not America, but America's domination of East Asia. The best response would be to step back and encourage U.S. allies to defend their own interests.

Anyway, since Beijing's future is not predetermined, Washington should adopt policies, such as freer trade, more likely to encourage friendship than hostility. It is for this reason that Taiwan and many of its Capitol Hill allies, like Rep. DeLay, support Beijing's entry in the WTO, despite China's persistent threats.

The silliest argument against PNTR is that Chinese imports would overwhelm U.S. industry. In fact, American workers are far more productive than their Chinese counterparts.

Moreover, Beijing's manufacturing exports to the U.S. remain small—about half the level of those from Mexico. PNTR would create far more export opportunities for American than Chinese concerns. Estimates of the likely increase in U.S. exports range up to $13 billion annually.

There is another issue: The right to trade is a basic human right.

Fundamental to one's humanity is the freedom to peacefully exchange the product of one's labor with others. If Americans want to buy, say, toys, clothes, or Christmas ornaments from Chinese rather than U.S. firms, they have a moral right to do so.

That trade should be free does not mean anything goes. Congress can rightly restrict trade with security implications: Americans need not improve the accuracy of Chinese ICBM's, for instance. And goods produced by forced labor in prison camps do not represent free trade.

Moreover, American officials should challenge Beijing to respect the rights of its citizens. U.S. taxpayers should not be forced to subsidize the Chinese government through the Export-Import Bank, Overseas Private Investment Corporation, and foreign aid agencies.

Everyone wants a freer, more democratic China. Granting PNTR to Beijing would make that more likely.

May 2000

China—Making Beijing Mind Its Own Business

China has an exalted sense of nationhood. Its leaders vilify almost any comment on its political practices as unwarranted outside "interference." Yet Beijing is always ready to lecture America on its policies.

Most recently the People's Republic of China was outraged because last week U.S. officials met with Martin Lee, founder of the party with the most directly elected seats in Hong Kong's legislature. The only proper response from Washington is a not-so-polite directive that Beijing stop interfering in America's internal affairs.

The 1997 reversion of Hong Kong from a colony of Great Britain to a "Special Administrative Region" of the PRC was a sad moment. It was perhaps inevitable, but certainly no cause for celebration by anyone who values human liberty above brutal nationalism.

Still, the city's 6.8 million residents obviously value freedom. Hundreds of thousands rallied last year to oppose proposed "anti-subversion" legislation pushed under Hong Kong's Article 23 by China. Many of them now are advocating free elections and universal suffrage.

In fact, in the 1984 Sino-British Joint Declaration China promised to guarantee Hong Kong's autonomy and various freedoms, including a "legislature constituted by elections." In the 1990 Basic Law, signed by both Britain and China, Beijing pledged to provide an elective legislature and executive by 2008.

However, Beijing has responded to talk of democracy with a vitriolic barrage, denouncing advocates of democracy as "clowns," "dogs," "dreamers," and "traitors," as well as being "unpatriotic" and "traitorous," and for seeking "outside interference" in Hong Kong's affairs. But it should come as no surprise that the unelected Communist leadership in Beijing fears the exercise of democracy any where, and especially in lands peopled by ethnic Chinese.

Consider the PRC's reaction to past and present presidential races in Taiwan, as well as President Chen Shui-bian's use of a popular referendum on relations with China. Equally threatening is the fact that Hong Kong residents, too, can vote, and have favored independent voices over Beijing lackeys. Bai Gang, director of the Centre for Public Policy Research at the Chinese Academy of Social Sciences, complains: "Pro-democracy politicians have serious inadequacies in identification with the country. However, they have the upper hand over the patriotic camp in Hong Kong."

That is, in the PRC's view the wrong folks are winning elections. As a result, Martin Lee has more popular legitimacy than does Chinese President Hu Jiantao. Observes the *Wall Street Journal*: "Mr. Lee is thus a leader of the only elected majority party in China. In free countries that would make him prime minister, not a pariah."

Not in Beijing's opinion, however. Officials are now talking about allowing only "patriots" to participate in Hong Kong's governance. And "patriots" do not include anyone who favors Taiwanese independence, opposes China's Communist government, fought the anti-subversion legislation, or simply doesn't back the Communist Party. Beijing has even threatened to dissolve the Hong Kong legislature should pro-Beijing candidates lose control in elections scheduled for September. "None of the democrats are trustworthy," explained Wen Wei Po, China's spokesman on Hong Kong.

Unfortunately, there is nothing Washington can do to prevent the PRC leadership from engaging in unseemly name-calling when residents of Hong Kong ask China to keep its word. Nor can the U.S. force China to keep its word.

Americans might not be able to enshrine democracy in Hong Kong, but at least they can talk to democrats in Hong Kong.

Sen. Sam Brownback (R-KS) invited Mr. Lee to Washington to testify last Thursday about the situation in Hong Kong. While here, Mr. Lee met with a number of legislators, as well as Secretary of State Colin Powell and NSC Adviser Condoleezza Rice.

Nothing seditious about any of this. Indeed, Mr. Lee stated his faith that China's top leaders would "get it right." He also wryly noted that he would have preferred to make his case in Beijing. But the PRC refuses to let him come.

Nevertheless, Chinese apparatchiks were angry about his trip. Hong Kong Chief Executive Tung Chee-hwa complained, "We will not accept interference from foreign people. Our own people should also not invite foreign people to interfere."

Similar was the reaction of PRC Foreign Minister Li Zhaoxing: "Hong Kong is China's Hong Kong. The Chinese people have the resolve, the ability and the wisdom to maintain the stability and the prosperity of Hong Kong. We do not welcome, nor do we need, any outside intervention in Hong Kong affairs." The Foreign Ministry issued a statement even denouncing "irresponsible comments by outside forces."

It brings to mind China's earlier attempts to browbeat Washington into not allowing Taiwanese Presidents Lee Teng-hui and Chen Shui-bian to visit the U.S., even in a private capacity and to make airline connections to other nations. Shamefully, the squeamish Clinton administration proved ever ready to appease Beijing.

For instance, a decade ago President Lee stopped at a military base in Hawaii on his way to Latin America. The Clinton administration insisted that he not leave the facility. A year later Mr. Lee sought a visa to attend an alumni gathering at Cornell University, his alma mater. Only under congressional pressure did the administration approve his request—and only after insisting that he avoid any "political" activities.

Four years ago President Chen wanted to fly into Los Angeles on his way to Latin America (where a number of small states official recognize Taiwan as an independent nation). Again ever so reluctantly, the Clinton administration allowed the visit, but only if he spent the entire 16-hours at his hotel. He even had to cancel a planned meeting with four congressmen.

Not that Beijing was satisfied. The PRC declared that the Chen visit might "severely" damage Sino-American relations.

China has similarly pressured other nations. Beijing sought to convince Great Britain to prevent President Lee from visiting and Japan to bar former President Lee from receiving medical treatment.

Stipulate that good relations with the PRC are important. Admit that one can disagree over the best strategy to diffuse a potential confrontation in the Taiwan Strait. Acknowledge that there are both costs and benefits of selling weapons to and offering to defend Taipei.

There still can be no compromise over America extending its hospitality to those who share its ideals around the globe. Whether Lee Teng-hui, Chen Shui-bian, or Martin Lee, they should be encouraged, not just allowed, to come for alumni visits, trip layovers, and political discussions. This is an internal affair for the U.S. China has no right to interfere.

It's obvious that Beijing has yet to get the message that it cannot dictate American policy towards visitors. The Bush administration should call in China's ambassador to settle the matter once and for all.

Like Beijing, he should be told, America does not appreciate outside interference in its internal affairs. Thus, Washington will allow whomever to visit whenever it desires.

Martin Lee is hopeful about Hong Kong's future: Chinese leaders "will know ultimately that democracy is not something they should fear." Sadly, the U.S. cannot prevent the PRC from suppressing human rights in China or even in Hong Kong. But America certainly should not suppress human rights in the U.S. at China's behest.

March 2004

Taiwan—A War Waiting to Happen

President Bill Clinton has returned from his trip to China and the House has voted to preserve an open trading regime with Beijing. U.S.-Chinese relations, which for a time dominated newspaper headlines, are receding as a political issue. But the President's bizarre mixture of appeasement of and threats to Beijing risk turning Taiwan into an even greater flashpoint than the Korean peninsula.

The Republic of China (ROC) has long been an anomaly of international politics. Founded on the island of Taiwan after the communist victory on the mainland in 1949, the ROC claimed to be the legitimate government of all China.

In 1972 Richard Nixon opened relations with the People's Republic of China (PRC), leading to the ROC's ouster from the U.N. and loss of diplomatic recognition around the globe. Washington followed suit in 1979. Since then the ROC has existed uneasily at the periphery of global politics—an economic powerhouse but diplomatic midget.

At the same time the ROC steadily moved to democracy. The burgeoning opposition, which actually won more votes than the ruling Kuomintang (KMT) in last year's local elections, supports independence for Taiwan; the KMT has steadily abandoned its unrealistic claim to govern all China. All that separates Taiwan from statehood is a formal declaration of independence.

But doing so could bring war with the PRC. Beijing regards Taiwan as a renegade province, separated from the motherland first by Japanese aggression and then by U.S. intervention. Even many Chinese outside the PRC leadership view Taiwan as the final symbol of a century of humiliation at the hands of assorted Asian and Western powers.

The ROC's increasing behavior like a sovereign state caused the PRC to rattle its sabers—or, more accurately, to test its missiles—in early 1996. Beijing's threats led Washington to respond with a warning of "grave consequences," meaning military intervention, should hostilities erupt between the two Chinas.

Since then tensions cooled and U.S.-PRC relations rebounded. In Beijing the President, despite his protestations to the contrary, unmistakably tilted the PRC's way. Whereas since 1972 Washington ambiguously noted both states' contentions that there was but one China, the President explicitly opposed independence for Taiwan as well as Taipei's entrance into international organizations.

This damages the ROC's bargaining position in any negotiations with Beijing. More serious, however, as my Cato Institute colleague Ted Galen Carpenter observes in a forthcoming study, "Clinton's policy shift presages a reduction and eventual elimination of arms sales to Taiwan," as has already been suggested by several members of the China accommodationist school. That, in turn, "could leave Taiwan highly vulnerable to PRC intimidation or outright military coercion within a decade," warns Carpenter.

Yet, at the same time, the administration apparently maintains its informal policy of threatening a military response to Chinese intimidation or coercion. Thus, the admininistration has sold out the American as well as the Taiwanese people.

Consider the Clinton policy package. The U.S. opposes self-determination by people who have built a highly successful capitalist and democratic society. Washington is simultaneously moving to deny that community the ability to defend itself. Having made conflict more likely, the U.S. promises to intervene if war breaks out.

The danger is increased by Beijing's failure to take American threats seriously. Chinese Gen. Xiong Guangkai reportedly told former ambassador Chas Freeman that Washington would not intervene "because, in the end, you care a lot more about Los Angeles than Taipei." Although the implied threat offended many U.S. policymakers, Guangkai highlighted a critical issue: the status of Taiwan matters a lot more to China than to America. Is Washington really willing to risk a nuclear confrontation to defend the independence of a state which it doesn't recognize diplomatically?

In fact, America shouldn't take that chance. But that doesn't mean it should leave the ROC undefended. Rather, Washington, after making clear that it believes the status of Taiwan, whether reunification or independence, is up to people of Taiwan, should sell the ROC whatever weapons Taipei desires to purchase for its own defense. Among the weapons so far denied the ROC are attack submarines, anti-missile technology, and sophisticated air-to-air and air-to-surface missiles.

Taipei only needs to maintain the capability to exact a sufficiently high price that Beijing will only use peaceful means to achieve reunification. Although U.S. relations with the PRC would suffer from increased arms sales, that would be better than a future nuclear confrontation between the two nations.

Now, before the next crisis, is the time to adjust U.S. policy towards Taiwan. Otherwise the President risks inadvertently encouraging a military confrontation in the Taiwan Straits that would be disastrous for all nations concerned.

July 1998

Taiwan—Meeting the Taiwan Challenge

Chinese Prime Minister Wen Jiabao is visiting the U.S. even as Beijing breathes fiery threats of war against Taiwan. Washington must avoid any conflict. However, the Bush administration should explain to China that it respects Taiwan's independent existence and that Chinese aggression would have catastrophic international consequences.

The island nation of Taiwan, once known as Formosa, has been separate from China for a century. The first 50 years it was ruled by Japan; the second half century it has hosted the nationalist government ousted in the communist revolution of 1949.

Both Chinas long fought to be recognized as the one legitimate Chinese government and the advantage gradually shifted towards Beijing. As part of its strategic opening to the People's Republic of China (PRC) during the Cold War, the Nixon administration allowed the United Nations to toss out Taiwan's Republic of China (ROC) in favor of the PRC. The Carter administration followed by formally recognizing Beijing, though Washington today retains a de facto embassy in Taiwan.

The two Chinas continue to spar on the international stage. Although small in size and with a population of just 23 million, the ROC became a leading trading nation; checkbook diplomacy helped it retain a smattering of diplomatic recognitions, particularly in Latin America. The Pacific island of Kiribati recently became number 27 in recognizing Taiwan, causing the PRC to break relations in turn.

After China moved towards market economics starting in the late 1970s, the mainland became an economic superpower; it now possesses the world's second largest economy, surpassing Japan's. Beijing has become more active on the international stage and is now aggressively pressing Taiwan to accept some form of "one nation, two systems" reunification under the PRC's control.

In early December the official Chinese press quoted Maj. Gen. Peng Guangqian as saying: "Taiwan independence means war" and Taipei's officials had pushed the island toward an "abyss of war." Indeed, added Gen. Peng: "Taiwan leader Chen Shui-bian will be held responsible if a war breaks out across the Straits, and separatists on the island will be treated the same way war criminals are dealt with elsewhere in the world."

Of course, war would "break out" only if the PRC invaded Taiwan. Taipei is not outfitting an expeditionary force to attack the mainland.

China's current excitement stems from passage by the ROC's legislature of a bill allowing a national referendum, which could raise the issue of independence. Beijing, which remains a communist dictatorship, obviously doesn't like the idea of people voting anywhere, and certainly not in Taiwan on the issue of independence. Said Prime Minister Wen in advance of his U.S. visit, "The Chinese people will pay any price to safeguard the unity of the motherland." He added that Washington must explicitly oppose Taiwanese independence.

Formulating a sensible policy regarding the conflicting interests reflected in the Taiwan Strait isn't easy. There is no reason in principle why the Republic of China should not be an independent nation, whether it calls itself the ROC or Taiwan or something else. China may have been victimized when Japan stripped the island of Formosa from its control, but that was a century ago and the people of Taiwan today have built a separate, and free, society.

However, logic has little impact on the importance of Taiwan as a matter of Chinese nationalism. Even many ethnic Chinese residing abroad, who do not subject their own lives to Beijing's tender mercies, believe that Taiwan is a part of China. And in the PRC it is not just communist apparatchiks who are willing to threaten military force against Taiwan.

Involvement in any war across the Taiwan Straits would be disastrous for America. Early in his term, President George W. Bush said that the U.S. had to do "whatever it took" to aid Taiwan's defense. But China is not Grenada or Panama or Serbia or Iraq; China is a nuclear-armed state aspiring to great-power status.

Although the U.S. possesses a far superior military to that of the PRC, mistake or desperation could turn any conflict into a nuclear confrontation. At the same time, Washington likely would find itself bereft of allies in East Asia: neither Japan nor South Korea would likely choose to become a permanent enemy of Beijing by backing the U.S. over Taiwan. Even Australia might hesitate serving as America's "deputy sheriff" in the region.

Moreover, America has much at stake in a peaceful relationship with China. The economic ties are large and already under stress, after the administration restricted Chinese textile imports.

Washington also remains highly concerned about Chinese arms sales around the world. Further, Beijing has the most leverage of any party over North Korea. The PRC's willingness to use that influence to discourage Pyongyang from becoming a nuclear state will be affected by the overall state of China-U.S. relations.

Still, America neither can nor should hand the free people of Taiwan over to Beijing. Avoidance of war does not mean complicity in coercion.

First, Washington should insist that the ROC's future is up to the people of Taiwan. Taipei obviously has an interest in talking with China, but the latter has no automatic claim to the allegiance of the Taiwanese people.

Second, it is not America's place to pronounce its opinion on independence for Taiwan. The U.S. formally recognizes only one China and doesn't expect to change that policy. But Taiwan is governed from Taipei, not Washington. Although prudence suggests that Taiwan not needlessly provoke Beijing, the decision is up to Taiwan.

Third, the U.S. will brook no criticism over who it allows to visit America. The PRC has complained about Taiwan President Chen Shui-bian's October stopover visit in New York, but he met no government officials. The U.S. remains a free country open to Taiwanese as well as Chinese.

Finally, Washington should indicate that it will continue to sell arms to Taiwan. The surest guarantee of peace in the Taiwan Strait is a well-armed ROC. As Ivan Eland of the Independent Institute has pointed out, "Taiwan does not need to be able to win a conflict with a more powerful China; it needs only to inflict unacceptable damage on Chinese forces" to deter an attack.

In fact, Taiwan should understand that the latter offers better security than does a U.S. military commitment. No matter what previous administrations have promised, any U.S. president will—and, in fact, should—hesitate risking Los Angeles to protect Taipei. In any crisis, Taiwan might find itself very alone.

May you live in interesting times, runs the old Chinese curse, and we seem to be doing that. The Chinese themselves, both on the mainland and Taiwan, are helping to make it so.

Although Washington must avoid getting in the middle of any war between China and Taiwan, it must emphasize that any conflict would wreck the PRC's economic and political standing in the world. Nor should the U.S. deny Taiwan the tools to assert itself internationally or defend itself. Beijing must understand that while Washington is sticking with its "one-China" position, Taiwan's future must be decided in Taipei.

December 2003

Japan—Reordering East Asia's Defense

TOKYO—America's military presence in the Far East "is outdated," explains Shunji Taoka of *AERA* magazine. "Japan believes in continuity. America's Pentagon is the same way, resisting any change."

Such a belief in continuity is evident throughout Tokyo's foreign policy establishment. America's "interest is best preserved" through its alliance with Japan, argues former ambassador Hisahiko Okazaki. "All that is necessary is for Japan to be a real partner," he adds, which requires U.S. prodding.

Alas, this sentiment ignores the role of incentives. For years America has been lobbying Tokyo to do more, but as long as the U.S. guarantees Japan's security it has no reason to do so. To the contrary, Tokyo is currently reducing its military budget as a percentage of GDP.

Indeed, while the U.S. is devoting 3.9 percent of its GDP to the military this year, Japan's share is below .9 percent and dropping. Many officials privately blame the coalition government, featuring socialist Prime Minister Tomiichi Murayama, for the fact that Tokyo is, in the words of one, "moving in the wrong direction on military spending."

But socialist influence does not explain why Japan's relative defense effort has been declining since 1988. However much America "prods" Japan, Washington continues to insist on the privilege of defending Tokyo. Japan thus feels no serious pressure to do more.

Even leading Japanese acknowledge this effect. Admits one top Foreign Ministry official: there "is a ring of truth" to the belief of many Americans that the defense relationship "gives Japan breathing space where it can rest and not make an effort to increase its international role."

Of course, some American officials want it this way. Unconcerned about the cost and risk of foreign military commitments, they, too, like continuity—and a world in which a predominant U.S. can order around junior partners. Although they cloak their policies in national interest rhetoric, professional convenience is also at stake: international alliances are, after all, a good excuse to travel, courtesy the taxpayers.

Moreover, Japanese officials like to play on American fears. Would you really want the Imperial Japanese Navy roaming the Pacific, asks one?

The answer, of course, is no, but circumstances are dramatically different today than in the 1930s. It is these differences, not America's military presence, that prevents the reincarnation of the Empire of the Rising Sun. If the enormous social and political changes necessary for such a transformation occurred, they would sweep away the U.S.-Japan security treaty too. Indeed, if Japanese citizens come to believe that America's military presence is more to watch than defend them, the alliance will almost certainly end acrimoniously.

A much better alternative would be to encourage a responsible Japanese military build-up in cooperation with its neighbors. In fact, some Japanese officials are contemplating a larger defense role. "We agree that it is time to rethink and reevaluate the security alliance," explains one high-ranking military officer. Former Ambassador Okazaki, though a supporter of American defense guarantees, envisions an extra $100 billion over a five to ten year period for Theater Missile Defense, AWACS aircraft, Aegis cruisers, and the like. Scholar Toshiyuki Shikata, a former army corps commander, suggests Japanese defense outlays of between 1.5 percent and two percent of GDP.

Such an increase would undoubtedly unnerve some of Japan's neighbors, but any build-up could be tailored defensively—such as air and naval forces to defend sealanes without an oversize army that could conquer and occupy other nations. Moreover, Japan, backed by the U.S., should promote regional security discussions through such organizations as the Asia-Pacific Economic Council (APEC) and the Association of South East Asian Nations (ASEAN).

Many of these countries still would not be pleased, of course, which Japanese officials are quick to point out. But surely Washington should not risk the lives of American soldiers and sailors because Singapore, for one, prefers not to deal with the ghosts of World War II. It is time for East Asia to recognize that Japan does not possess a double-dose of original sin and poses a far smaller threat to regional stability than does, say, China.

"Maybe we have over-relied on the U.S. for security," opines one Japanese defense official. But he still wants Washington to provide a regional security blanket. And who can blame Japan for desiring that the U.S. continue helping to pick up its defense tab? However, World

War II ended 50 years ago and the Cold War is over. Japan needs to become a normal country with a normal military and regional security responsibilities. And it will do so only if Washington ends its enervating defense dole.

August 1995

Japan—Freeing Okinawa

Okinawa, Japan—Prime Minister Keizo Obuchi has visited Washington, offering the usual promises of economic reform and international cooperation. But neither Tokyo nor Washington seem interested in upgrading their relationship to reflect the post-Cold War world.

Although the Diet recently passed legislation to implement the guidelines originally adopted in late 1997, the changes are largely cosmetic. Japan neither intends to do anything on its own nor use its military even in conjunction with that of the U.S.

Moreover, the latest Pentagon strategy report on East Asia, released late last year, makes clear that Washington intends to maintain its dominant role, apparently forever. And that presumably means keeping its forces and facilities in Japan, also apparently forever.

Yet the Japanese consensus in favor of a protracted American protectorate may finally be cracking. The election of novelist Shintaro Ishihara as governor of Tokyo, running on a platform for the return of Yokota Air Base, brings the issue of Washington's presence to Japan's national stage.

Which is where it belongs. Only Tokyo can address the worst injustice stemming from the American-Japanese alliance: Okinawa. Although Gov. Masahide Ota's defeat last year by Keiichi Inamine may have reduced attention to the island's plight, the issue remains no less pressing.

It is hard to go anywhere on Okinawa without running into a U.S. base. Or being run into. Yuki Uema, an Okinawan high school student, died last October after being hit by a U.S. Marine in a hit-and-run accident.

On April 1, 1945 the U.S. invaded the Ryukyu Islands, the last stepping-stone towards mainland Japan. Okinawa remained under U.S. occupation after the war; although Tokyo and Washington signed a peace treaty in 1952, the U.S. retained control of the island, leaving Japan with only "residual sovereignty."

During the Korean War the U.S. began expanding its military operations, seizing land at bayonet point from farmers to make airfields. Many displaced residents were encouraged to emigrate. Washington acted like a colonial overlord.

Only in 1972 did Okinawa revert to Japanese control. However, Washington and Tokyo continued to collude against the island. With three-quarters of U.S. facilities concentrated in the most distant and poorest .6 percent of its land area, Japan was largely unconcerned about Okinawa's plight. Tokyo enjoyed the benefit of defense by America, while Okinawans bore the burden.

Okinawans have grown tired of the cost. Even Gov. Inamine, though a member of the ruling party, favors reducing America's presence.

Over the last quarter century the U.S. returned just 15 percent of the land it occupied in Okinawa, compared to 60 percent of the property it used on the mainland. American facilities currently occupy one-fifth of the island, and are home to some 30,000 servicemen and nearly as many family members. Fences topped with barbed wire line major roads and cut through towns.

U.S. facilities occupy more than half the land area of four communities. Roads, homes, schools, and businesses abut American bases. The U.S. controls 29 sea zones and 15 air zones and runs two of the island's three airports. It is not just the extraordinary incidents—the 1995 rape of a 12-year-old school girl, for instance—but the daily noise, congestion, crowding, and accidents that irritate Okinawans.

However, the rape galvanized Japanese public opinion; in September 1996 89 percent of Okinawans voted in favor of reducing the American presence. The U.S. and Japanese governments created the Special Action Committee on Facilities and Areas in Okinawa (SACO) to ease the burden of America's military presence. But SACO proposed only modest land reversions, most of which remain stalled because of the difficulty in finding alternate facilities. For instance, Tokyo planned to replace Futenma Air Station with a floating heliport off the city of Nago, but in December 1997 municipal voters rejected the proposal.

In any case, SACO does not reach the more fundamental issue: why should the U.S. continue to station a Marine Expeditionary Force and other units on Okinawa? Although Washington doesn't seem to have noticed, with the end of the Cold War the world has changed, and so, too, has East Asia. The threats have diminished—the Soviet Union is no more, North Korea is crumbling, China has discarded Maoism.

Moreover, the region no longer needs America's protection. Japan is the second-ranking economic power on earth, South Korea far outstrips its northern antagonist, and most of the ASEAN states have made dramatic economic progress. Indeed, so complacent are Tokyo and Seoul that both are cutting their defense budgets.

What reasons do U.S. officials give for a policy that could be summarized as what has ever been must always be? China looms large on the horizon, but if Washington and Beijing eventually come to blows, the air force and navy would do the heavy lifting. Another favorite is the maintenance of regional stability, given widespread economic problems, political uncertainty in Indonesia, and so on.

Yet it is time for East Asia to look after its own stability. If one wanted to catalog conflicts in which the U.S. should not intervene, it would be these. What if the Habibie regime in Indonesia totters? Let it fall. What if Filipino and Chinese ships exchange shots over the Spratly Islands? Stay out of the fight. What if Japan and South Korea rattle sabers over the Tokdu/Takeshima Islands? Tell both countries to grow up. These are East Asia's, not America's, problems.

That doesn't mean Washington should be unconcerned about the region. But instead of being meddler of first resort, the U.S. should act as balancer of last resort, intervening only if a hegemonic threat develops that allied states are incapable of containing. America could then sharply reduce existing force levels and redeploy advanced units—like the Third Marine division, currently stationed on Okinawa—back to Guam and Hawaii. Japan, South Korea, and other countries could take on the military role dictated by their economic success.

For a half century Okinawans have borne the brunt of U.S. military deployments in Japan. But the Cold War is over. It is time for Japan to defend itself. And America to give Okinawa back to the Okinawans.

May 1999

Korea—Ending the Anachronistic Korean Commitment

The U.S. has defended South Korea for 50 years. But newly elected ROK President Roh Moo-hyun suggests that his nation might "mediate" in any war between America and the North. Talk about one-way alliances!

The presence of 37,000 troops in South Korea is a Cold War artifact, resulting from the post-World War II division of the peninsula and subsequent Chinese and Soviet support for North Korean aggression. Today the Cold War is over and China and Russia are friendlier with Seoul than Pyongyang.

Moreover, the South has raced ahead of the North, enjoying 40 times the GDP, twice the population, and a vast technological edge. The DPRK's military is large, but decrepit. To the extent that the ROK's military still lags behind that of its northern antagonist, it is a matter of choice, not necessity.

Although no U.S. forces are needed to guard against the bankrupt North, they are ubiquitous in South Korea, with some based in downtown Seoul. Thus occur purposeless violent altercations and tragic traffic deaths.

After the acquittal in military court of two soldiers charged in the accidental deaths of two children, demonstrations erupted. Americans have been barred from restaurants, jeered, and in a few cases physically attacked.

President-elect Roh has called for a more "equal" relationship and promised not to "kowtow" to Washington. Even the U.S. seems prepared to change the status of forces agreement governing the treatment of American servicemen.

But the relationship between the two countries will never be equal as long as South Korea is dependent on Washington for its defense. And that inequality will weigh particularly heavily in dealing with the prospect of a nuclearized North Korea. Washington continues to dominate policy on the peninsula. Yet a misstep towards Pyongyang would be only bothersome for the U.S.; it would be catastrophic for the South.

It is time for Washington to move to the background. First, it should downplay the current crisis—thereby reducing the value of the DPRK's nuclear card—and leave the surrounding states to pressure

Pyongyang to drop its program. More fundamentally, the U.S. should drop its security guarantee for South Korea and withdraw (and demobilize) its troops stationed there. The American protectorate over South Korea has lost its raison d'etre. It's time for an amicable divorce rather than a much more bitter parting in the near future.

Whither Inter-Korean Relations?

Hopes for an end to the Korean cold war raced skyward when ROK President Kim Dae Jung visited Pyongyang in mid-2000. Since then relations have waxed and waned. But this should come as no surprise, since that has long reflected the course of inter-Korean relations.

In 1972 the two Koreas signed a reconciliation agreement and halted hostile propaganda. The accord, which endorsed unification, promised inter-Korean exchanges, and provided for a bilateral telephone hot-line, soon collapsed. A decade later the North Koreans attempted to assassinate South Korean Chun Doo Hwan during a state visit to Rangoon, Burma.

In 1990 the two nations' prime ministers met; soon thereafter they inked weapons disarmament and economic cooperation agreements. The latter was even more detailed than the pledges made by the two Kims in June. But the nuclear crisis soon followed, with the U.S. threatening (and, by some accounts, coming close to inaugurating) war.

In 1994 North Korea's Kim Il Sung and South Korea's Kim Young Sam planned a summit, only to have the former die of a heart attack 17 days before the meeting. Relations rapidly soured, with the North returning to threats and aggressive action.

Since then positive changes have occurred, even though they have been frequently overshadowed—by a naval shoot-out, for instance, and most obviously by the recent nuclear announcement. Yet, argues William Taylor, president of TAI, a Washington D.C. consulting firm, who has traveled extensively to North Korea, the intermittent process reflects the deep suspicions that continue to dominate much of North Korea's leadership and the lack of Western-educated technocrats to respond to the economic and political challenges of an opening to the West.

Moreover, the obstacles to increased trade and investment remain immense. The North has attempted to create a more inviting investment climate, and some North Korean officials evidence surprising knowledge of the outside world. But the DPRK remains an isolated totalitarian country: It lacks a rule of law, convertible currency, productive industry, and transportation network; business customs differ and even many companies which once intended to invest in the North have abandoned their plans.

Most important, the DPRK remains as capable, if perhaps not as willing, to threaten South Korea. Nearly two million soldiers still fill the peninsula. Although Pyongyang has pulled some FROG-7 rocket emplacements back to the rear and reduced naval activities, the bulk of its military remains poised near the border. Argues Karl Swanson, chief historian of U.S. Forces Korea, "Don't think of it as a heavily armed border—think of it as a fighting zone waiting for the attack to be launched." Although the South's qualitatively superior force would likely triumph, Seoul, barely 25 miles south of the Demilitarized Zone, would almost certainly be destroyed in any conflict.

Unresolved Problems

Thus, the past will not soon lift its heavy hand. Observes Robert Gallucci, dean of Georgetown University's School of Foreign Service: "There is a lot of history here—war, terrorism, nuclear ambitions, incidents at sea—that suggests the need for a lot of caution." And even more reason for the U.S. to leave the issues to the surrounding powers which should be most concerned about them.

What the 2000 summit yielded, then, was the first step in a long process of rapprochement. A huge, indeed vital, first step. But a first step nonetheless.

The Clinton administration responded with what Pentagon spokesman Kenneth Bacon called "controlled exuberance," lifting economic sanctions. U.S. companies now can trade and invest in nonstrategic areas without a license and open direct communication and transportation links. One official told the *Los Angeles Times*: "It's not a reward, because we don't know if there's anything to reward yet. It's the U.S. trying to do what it can to support this positive movement by North and South Korea."

This step was long overdue. The 1994 Framework Agreement, negotiated in an attempt to halt the North's nuclear program, also committed Washington to improve bilateral ties. Although misbehavior by the so-called Democratic People's Republic of Korea gave the Clinton administration a convenient excuse to do nothing, Washington had as much as or more than the North to gain from improving relations with Pyongyang. The only downside would have been if such a step aided the North Korean military, but despite charges of food aid diversions, it appears that most assistance has gone to starving civilians.

But upon taking office President George W. Bush almost immediately changed course. Although his skepticism towards foreign aid for the North (in contrast to his enthusiasm for increased assistance everywhere else in the world) was understandable, his refusal to talk with the North was not. He and his advisers seemed to prefer isolation as a policy, even though isolation had failed to transform Pyongyang over the previous 50 years.

It seemed to be an especially foolish policy since along the way there have been little signs of progress. Kim Jong Il and various North Korean officials continue to say that a return visit by Kim to Seoul is certain, though the timing is not. Indeed, in 2001 Pyongyang hosted a marathon, with Western advertising sponsors and some leading international runners. An executive for Italy's Fila Sport SpA told the Asian Wall Street Journal that "We're getting great exposure up there." An even more intriguing sponsor was the British newspaper, the *Financial Times.*

Kim Jong Il traveled to Shanghai and exhibited interest in information technology, another positive sign; Pyongyang claims to plan on opening an information technology center and requested outside investment. The North opened diplomatic relations with a number of Asian and European states and began participating in regional organizations (such as the ASEAN Regional Forum). Moreover, the ROK and Russia have begun working on a rail link, which would dramatically increase the potential benefits of opening the line between North and South. This work continues despite a bitter debate in the ROK over how to respond to the North's ambitions.

Of course, the DPRK is hoping to benefit from the economic investment that will follow a political opening without having to bear the cost of the pressures for political reform that often follow economic growth. Explains Kim Chung Kyun of the Hyundai Research Institute in Seoul: "North Korea has followed a mosquito-net liberalization policy. They're trying to open the window to catch a cool summer breeze without letting in the insects." But the danger created for the North by successful enterprises will be enormous. Increasing contact with the West will almost inevitably have some corrosive political impact.

Alliance Forever?

More important for Washington is the issue of the alliance with the South. Washington naturally denies that anything, even changing dynamics on the peninsula, should have any impact on American troop deployments. P.J. Crowley, spokesman for the Clinton National Security Council, said that "we don't envision any change in the U.S. troops status." Then-Pentagon spokesman Kenneth Bacon observed that the ROK expects the troops to remain "for a long time to come."

Opined Clinton's Secretary of State Madeleine Albright, "our forces, when they are stationed somewhere, provide evidence of America's interest." In Korea, she claimed, they promote "stability." Robert Manning of the Council on Foreign Relations epitomized establishment fears when he worried about not only South Korean "giddiness," but also the "loose talk about the future of the U.S.-South Korean alliance and the U.S. military presence in Korea."

The Bush administration took an even tougher policy. In fact, President Kim found himself badly deflated when he visited the U.S. in March 2001. President Bush was dismissive of the South's efforts to engage the North. Subsequent discussions between Washington and the DPRK were perfunctory at best.

There is much for the two countries to discuss. Especially after the latter's dramatic announcement that it had been pursuing nuclear research despite the Framework Agreement that was to have halted the North's program in return for construction of two nuclear reactors.

But America's policy discussion needs to begin with the ROK. After all, Washington has no intrinsic interest in what goes on in North Korea. An impoverished distant state surrounded by significant powers (China, Japan, Russia), the DPRK has no international impact and little regional influence, and poses a diminishing danger even to South Korea. Put bluntly, it doesn't matter to the U.S.

The only reason America cares is because the South is a U.S. protectorate. It's time for that to change.

In the aftermath of the inter-Korean summit, Pentagon spokesman Kenneth Bacon explained, "we intend to remain a force for stability in that area as long as we are needed." But U.S. forces weren't needed even before the summit.

The South has upwards of forty times the GDP and twice the population of the North. Although the North Korean regime survives, to the surprise of many observers, the economy is thought to have shrunk every year from 1990 to 1998, dropping almost in half. Even Pyongyang, the capital and national showcase, has reportedly suffered power outages. As many as two million people are thought to have died of starvation, with 200,000 or more illegally crossing into China.

Seoul has also won the foreign contest, accumulating the most international recognitions, and effectively breaking the alliance between the North and its onetime communist allies, Beijing and Moscow. Both maintain more significant economic ties with the ROK. Moscow apparently has refused to commit to the large arms package reportedly requested by the DPRK; in contrast, Russia has begun shipping arms to the South to pay off its debts.

Leading Indicators

Curiously, Gen. Thomas Schwartz, commander of U.S. forces in Korea, told Congress in March 2001 that "the threat is more serious today than it was last year." He complained the North has "the world's largest artillery force for such a small nation," and hopes for acquisition of the Crusader howitzer and other artillery systems in response. Deputy Defense Secretary Paul Wolfowitz similarly ranked the DPRK as the most serious threat against the U.S.: "We face enormous conventional threats from North Korea."

But who is "we"? America does not face a conventional threat from Pyongyang. America's ally, the ROK, does. The defense of the South obviously is not—or certainly should not be—as important to Washington as the defense of America.

Moreover, the threat is diminishing and Seoul's ability to defend itself is increasing. For instance, the North's forces are decrepit. The last new weapons arrived in 1990, ancient history in terms of weapons acquisition. There is no money for spare parts, maintenance, or training. The North's air force and navy would disappear within an hour of the commencement of hostilities. The army's mass of men and arms might reach Seoul; it would not get much further, however.

Indeed, South Korea leads the DPRK in every measure of national power other than armed force levels, and the latter is a matter of choice, not an inevitable consequence of geography. Seoul's military is qualitatively better and backed by a larger reserve, a much stronger economic base, and a network of friendly states. The ROK could match its northern neighbor tank for tank if it wished. As South Korea acknowledges in its own defense reports, for years it *chose* to focus on economic development at the expense of military strength, which it could do secure in the protection by the U.S.

Indeed, Seoul has indicated its willingness to respond to North Korean efforts to build uniquely threatening weapons. More than two decades ago only pressure from Washington killed the Park Chung Hee government's incipient nuclear program. And while the North's missile development has created a furor, Seoul has responded with its own missile program, including rockets allegedly intended for a nascent space program. In fact, South Korea has been working to extend the range of its surface-to-surface missiles, which raised American complaints that it was violating the two nations' missile development agreement.

In such a world, there's no need for Washington to defend the South. The U.S. deployment is an anachronism, a Cold War leftover with no present justification. (The units should not just be withdrawn, but disbanded, since their role as well as basing facilities would be eliminated.)

Of course, some people back the U.S. presence in Korea for what Avery Goldstein, Director of the Foreign Policy Research Institute's Asia Program, calls "dual-use" purposes. That is, North Korea provides a convenient pretext to maintain troops actually directed at other purposes—containing China, restraining Japan, and maintaining regional stability. Alas, for supporters of American involvement, Goldstein worries that "Rapprochement on the Korean peninsula will eliminate this line of argument and require the US and its allies, including Japan, to offer new justifications for their post-Cold War military postures." Imagine, peace breaking out and ruining the argument for continued U.S. occupation! Poor Washington.

The "dual-use" arguments are outmoded, however. Whatever the future course of Chinese-U.S. relations, and Beijing is not an inevitable enemy, the forces in Korea (especially the lone Army division) would be of little use since America would hardly be so foolish as to fight a ground war against China. Tokyo needs to be pushed to do more militarily; despite disquieting memories among its neighbors, Japan is not about to embark upon another imperialist rampage. Finally, the greatest threats to regional stability are internal—Muslim insurgency and political chaos in the Philippines, democratic protests and ethnic conflict in Burma, economic, ethnic, nationalistic, and religious division in Indonesia. There is little that U.S. forces stationed in Korea could do to solve any of these problems even if the American people had the slightest interest in Washington getting involved in such irrelevant troubles.

Initiative Grabbing

There were subtle indications that Seoul intended to grab the policy initiative away from Washington even before the recent election. And President Roh almost certainly will chart a more independent course. Official fear over U.S. aggressiveness towards the North mixed with popular anger over American intrusiveness makes a combustible combination. So, too, has Tokyo taken an increasingly active diplomatic role, including a summit with Kim Jong Il in Pyongyang despite Washington's concerns.

Even so, many leading South Koreans advocate an American military presence even after reunification. They all reflexively cite the kitchen sink argument of "stability." President Kim Dae Jung supports retention of the U.S. presence "in order to maintain the balance of power in northeast Asia." Sometimes, though, they are even blunter. Hong Choo Hyun, a former ROK ambassador to America, observes: "The South Korean president added it would be better for the [U.S.] forces to be kept in South Korea to prevent Japan and China from engaging in efforts to gain hegemony in the region."

Curiously, there is some indication that the North is warming to the idea of maintaining U.S. forces in a different role: as peacekeepers. Kim Dae Jung alleges that during his meeting with Kim Jong Il, he argued: "Korea is in a strategic location, surrounded by Russia, China and Japan. Were the Americans to withdraw, the three countries could easily get into a fight over influence." Jong Il allegedly responded: "I know your position and I agree... Yes, we are surrounded by big countries who could get into a fight if the Americans leave." That is, the North is hoping the U.S. will defend Pyongyang from a potentially overpowering South Korea. Thus, Washington should permanently subsidize the ROK's defense, despite its rapid economic development, from the North, and protect the DPRK, with which the U.S. fought a war, from the South.

A New Policy for a New Age

America's overriding goal should be to maintain peace on the peninsula. Policy towards Seoul is simple. Phase out America's troops. Sell the ROK whatever weapons that it desires. And end the defense guarantee. Leave the American and South Korean peoples to trade with one another and expand the abundant cultural ties that already exist, centered on the large Korean community in the U.S.

The North is more complicated. Although prior predictions of imminent collapse have proved false, North Korea seems destined for the great dustbin of history. The only question is whether Pyongyang falls in peacefully.

To encourage that end, the U.S. should end all trade and investment restrictions and initiate diplomatic relations. In the aftermath of Pyongyang's violation of the Framework Agreement, food aid should be left to private groups.

Washington should talk with the North about its demands—a final peace treaty, for instance, but Washington should reverse today's dynamic, under which the North misbehaves in the hope of receiving more benefits. More important, the U.S. should let the surrounding states take the lead. China, Japan, Russia, and South Korea all have more at stake; all have an incentive to discourage a nuclearized North

Korea; all have significant leverage over the DPRK. Washington should follow their policy, not demand them to follow its policy.

These friendly states should give the DPRK increasing benefits when it behaves, not when it misbehaves. Should it revert to its policy of disruptive belligerence, they should retaliate quickly but quietly. Indeed, they should adopt an official attitude of near insouciance—who cares what the North does? It represents a modest bother, not a massive crisis. Then, without public fanfare or threats, which would likely make the North more obdurate, the surrounding states should slow or suspend positive movement on other issues. Such a strategy is even more important in the aftermath of Pyongyang's nuclear announcement.

The goal should be to squeeze the North, but not too hard. Again, the objective is to push the DPRK toward a more positive stance without creating either a potentially violent implosion or causing it to strike out. And to disentangle Washington from Northeast Asia.

Indeed, the ROK should be encouraged to announce America's intended withdrawal, and to challenge the North to respond positively by ending its nuclear effort, demobilizing some army units, and withdrawing some advanced forces from the Demilitarized Zone. The South's private message should be more blunt: negotiate for serious arms reduction, or face a crushing arms race (including missile and even nuclear development) which North Korea cannot win. An obvious place to start would be the 1992 Inter-Korean Basic Agreement, which pledged more transparency, ranging from a military hotline to opening military exercises to each other's observers.

Korea for the Koreans

In any case, their future course, whether together or separate, should be determined by the two Koreas. With the collapse of hegemonic communism and the DPRK's international support system, Washington and Seoul have increasingly diverged in their assessment of the threat posed by the North and the proper course to take towards the North. Understandably, the ROK is far less interested in increasing pressure and thus tensions on the peninsula.

But the South (and surrounding states) have the most at stake and the most to gain. Without the context of the Cold War, Washington's opinion simply doesn't matter. Of course, warmer relations between the two Koreas is likely to lead to less ROK reliance on Washington. That bothers not only American hegemonists who want to dominate the world, but also some Koreans. Complains Jeon Jae Wook, an adviser to the opposition Grand National Party: "This could open up a Pandora's box by triggering a surge of nationalism that could weaken our alliance with the US and Japan." Some fear a tilt toward China, which dominated the peninsula in centuries past.

But today's quasi-imperial relationship is not good for either America or the ROK. The last revision of the Status of Forces Agreement, which treated Seoul with a bit more respect as an independent nation, obviously didn't go nearly far enough. The Korean War in the midst of the Cold War, with the persistent threat of renewed North Korean aggression, resulted in the unnatural tie between Washington and Seoul. However necessary it might have been through the 1970s, since then the South has moved steadily ahead of the DPRK. The ROK has become a serious country; serious countries normally control their own destinies. By, for example, defending themselves.

Reducing America's role will create uncertainties, of course, but a changing defense posture is inevitable in a changing world. There may have been no better moment for such a shift over the last half century. Write Nick Eberstadt of the American Enterprise Institute and Richard Ellings of the National Bureau of Asian Research: "There probably has been no previous period in modern history when animosities between all of the great powers of the Pacific were as attenuated as they are today—or when the international structure of security and economic relations so encouraged national advance through commercial cooperation and international economic integration among them."

Engagement with North Korea is not appeasement; rather, it is a pragmatic strategy to maintain peace on the Korean peninsula until the communist regime disappears. But America's engagement need only be modest, since the South and its neighbors are capable of taking the lead. After a half century of sometimes tempestuous patron-client relations, it is time that the U.S. acknowledges the existence of the North and forges a friendship of equals with the South.

December 2002

Korea—Washington's Stockholm Syndrome

When kidnap victims identify with their captors, we speak of the so-called Stockholm Syndrome. The foreign policy equivalent is the Washington Syndrome, when American policymakers identify with prosperous, populous allies that prefer not to bear the burden of defending themselves.

Executive branch officials, who dominate U.S. foreign policy, have long believed that America's destiny is to defend, subsidize, and coddle any nation desiring Washington's benevolent attention. The U.S. must do everything for other nations, while they need do nothing for America.

Indeed, the State Department has never met an alliance, treaty, or aid program that it doesn't like. Every relationship must be preserved; every subsidy must be increased; every treaty must be expanded; every organization must be strengthened.

As a result, the list of Washington's foreign policy "welfare queens" is long. For decades the Western Europeans preferred to give endless promises rather than practical aid even when confronting the Soviet Union. Never mind the Red Army arrayed across the Iron Curtain: European military spending was always anemic and increases never matched the promises NATO governments made to Washington.

Japan possesses the world's second largest economy, but only recently has begun to take on greater responsibility for its own and its region's security. Even today, much of its effort, such as its contribution to the Iraq garrison, is mostly for show. Japan's "soldiers" actually are prohibited from fighting; the Netherlands and Australia have successively provided real military personnel armed with real weapons to defend the Japanese forces.

Then there is the Republic of Korea.

In 1950 the U.S. rescued South Korea from an invasion from the North. The war involved mainland China and intensified the Cold War. For another decade or two the South remained desperately poor and vulnerable to subversion or invasion by the so-called Democratic People's Republic of Korea, backed by China and the Soviet Union.

By the 1970s the ROK began to dramatically surpass the North. Today Seoul has about 40 times the GDP, twice the population, and a vast technological edge over the DPRK. But the South continues to concentrate on economic investment, leaving its protection to America.

And Washington has allowed it to do so.

Despite serious and multiple differences over how to approach North Korea, after the June summit between Presidents George W. Bush and Roh Moo-hyun, President Bush opined: "we're strategic partners, allies and friends." President Roh responded in kind, claiming that "We are in full and perfect agreement on basic principles. And whatever problems arise in the course of our negotiations and talks, we will be able to work them out through close consultations."

This kind of diplomatic blather is to be expected from flacks for the State Department and Foreign Ministry. Alas, the Washington Syndrome infects Capitol Hill as well as the executive branch. Rep. Dan Burton, vice chairman of the International Relations Committee's Subcommittee on Asia and the Pacific, has fallen victim to the malady. Last month he sent a "Dear Colleague" letter to other House members extolling the alliance.

"Forged in the heat of battle, the U.S.-South Korean bilateral relationship continues to be one of our most vital and vibrant partnerships politically, militarily and economically; and South Korea remains one of America's most important strategic partners in East Asia," Rep. Burton declared. If the U.S.-ROK relationship is one of Washington's most important, one shudders to think of the state of America's least important relationships in the region.

The congressman cited "the continuing contributions made by South Korea to our mutual alliance—some that are all too often forgotten." Actually, they are forgotten because they aren't worth remembering.

For instance, Rep. Burton pointed to trade. But Americans and South Koreans buy and sell goods from each other because it is mutually beneficial for them to do so, not because of the military alliance. Moreover, China has surpassed the U.S. as the ROK's most important trading partner. Japan may soon edge ahead of America as well.

The South "has been a strong ally in the U.S.-led War on Terror, having committed more than 3,270 troops to Iraq," the congressman noted. Actually, Seoul insisted that its forces be placed far away from hostilities in territory that required no occupying garrison. Whoopee.

Another "contribution," in Rep. Burton's view, is the fact that Seoul "has taken positive steps on the question of human rights in North Korea," having accepted 7000 DPRK refugees. But that is no sacrifice: the South's constitution treats North Koreans as citizens and South Koreans have for years proclaimed their commitment to reunification.

Moreover, a refugee flow from North to South would seem to strengthen the ROK. Accepting North Korean refugees is no favor to America.

In any case, Seoul has turned markedly frigid in its attitude towards those fleeing North Korean tyranny. Government ministers have publicly denounced activists who organize mass defections and disclaimed any interest in undermining Pyongyang.

Rep. Burton also contended that "South Korea is a key partner in the Six-Party Talks to resolve North Korea's nuclear issue." Actually, Seoul and Washington view the threat very differently. They disagree even more about possible solutions.

Indeed, ROK Unification Minister Chung Dong-Young says that the North is entitled to have a nuclear program. These days South Korea is closer to China than the U.S. in the six-party talks.

Moreover, the South has been providing substantial economic aid to and financial investment in North Korea, without asking for much of anything in return, even an accounting for upwards of 500 South Koreans kidnapped over the years. The ROK no longer refers to the North as its "main enemy" in its annual defense reports. In the view of one irritated conservative analyst, Seoul has gone from being an appeaser to a collaborator with the North.

More ominously, ROK public opinion increasingly views the U.S. as a greater threat than the DPRK, an unpredictable totalitarian state that is busily developing nuclear weapons. Young people especially express friendlier attitudes towards North Korea than to America. A recent poll of 16-25 year-olds found that two-thirds believed their nation should support the North if war broke out between the U.S. and Pyongyang.

Nevertheless, Rep. Burton wrote, "South Korea is an important military ally with over 33,000 U.S. troops stationed in the country." But there's no justification for maintaining U.S. troops in the ROK.

The South has lost most of its strategic value to America after the Cold War. It is no longer part of a global struggle against aggressive hegemonic communism.

South Korea's security is irrelevant to America. Certainly the ROK's defense is more important to South Korea, which is well able to protect itself, than to the U.S. Yet Washington spends as much to defend the South—which enjoys a GDP that runs as much as 40 times that of North Korea—as the ROK spends to defend itself. Indeed, Seoul recently announced plans to slash its troop strength by one-quarter while continuing to rely on the U.S. military.

The Korean peninsula remains important for the major powers surrounding it, not for America. The U.S. garrison performs no useful regional role.

If Washington ends up at war with China, Washington won't be launching a ground invasion. More important, South Koreans are unlikely to allow the U.S. to use their nation as a launching pad. Even if public attitudes towards Beijing were not warming, why would Seoul want to create a permanent enemy of its powerful neighbor, one with growing national power and a long historical memory?

Earlier this year South Korean President Roh Moo-hyun emphasized that his nation would not get involved in a war in Northeast Asia at America's behest. Indeed, he announced that Washington could not even use its troops based in the ROK without Seoul's permission.

Finally, having become a prosperous democracy, argued Rep. Burton, South Korea is now "an indispensable partner in promoting democracy and free market economy." But the South performs that role naturally, as a trading nation with an expanded global role. South Korea is not doing so to help out America.

And, in fact, Seoul has turned hostile towards accepting North Korean refugees. ROK officials opine that they do not want to undermine the North, an impoverished totalitarian hellhole. They seem more worried about offending DPRK officials doing the oppressing than the millions of people being oppressed.

Rep. Burton closed his letter with a call "to strengthen and grow this important alliance." The ROK's ambassador to the U.S., Hong Seok-hyun cheerfully responded with fulsome praise for Rep. Burton, opining that "it has been a personal mission of mine to ensure that our alliance remains vital and comprehensive."

Vital and comprehensive for what?

There remains much that Americans and Koreans can do together. But maintaining a close military alliance is not one of them.

The U.S.-Korean security relationship is outdated, even antiquated. Yet many U.S. officials like Rep. Burton suffer from the Washington Syndrome, continuing to sing the praises of America's unnecessary defense subsidy for Seoul.

It's time to focus on the interests of America rather than irresponsible "allies" that believe Washington owes them a defense. The U.S. is badly overstretched. America's interests should come first.

September 2005

Korea—A Military Encore in North Korea?

As if the administration wasn't busy enough already, Undersecretary of State John Bolton says that North Korea should "draw the appropriate lesson from Iraq." That follows a comment from President George W. Bush that if Washington's efforts "don't work diplomatically, they'll have to work militarily." A military strike almost certainly means full-scale war on the Korean peninsula.

The North is thought to possess one or two nuclear weapons, or at least has reprocessed enough plutonium to make them. Once confronted by the U.S. last October over its cheating on the 1994 Agreed Framework, it has taken a series of provocative steps, including reopening its mothballed nuclear plant in Yongbyon and preparing to reprocess 8000 spent fuel rods to produce plutonium.

The DPRK probably chose the current path for a mixture of reasons. Its putative nuclear capability is the only reason nations pay any attention to an otherwise bankrupt, irrelevant state. So far the nuclear option also has been useful in eliciting bribes.

Moreover, developing a nuclear arsenal may be the surest route to ensuring that the U.S. does not attack in the future. The experience of Serbia as well as Iraq is that any country might find itself in Uncle Sam's gunsites: having an atomic arsenal likely will cause Washington to avert its gaze.

A decade ago many American policymakers and pundits blithely talked about military options for destroying the nuclear reactor in Yongbyon and other nuclear facilities. Today many people, including, it would seem, the President, are making the same calculations.

For instance, former Gen. John Singlaub and Adm. Thomas Moorer are avidly pushing a military option. Dennis Ross of the Washington Institute for Near East Policy, is slightly more reticent: "The purpose is not to make the military option inevitable but to build the pressure to produce a diplomatic alternative." Columnist Charles Krauthammer believes the U.S. has no choice but to wait till Iraq is finished: "We simply cannot handle two military crises at once." Then "temporary appeasement" should end.

This may be the private position of the President, who previously indicated that "all options are on the table," including military action.

Similar are the unsubtle Pentagon statements that Defense Secretary Donald Rumsfeld is "immersed" in the issue. Rumsfeld also has called North Korea a "terrorist regime," perhaps the most obvious justification for attack, given the administration's over-arching "war against terrorism," which includes a preventive strike against Iraq.

Indeed, it is hard to find anyone who speaks with administration officials off-the-record who believes war is not a real possibility. An unnamed military official told the *New York Times* that military options were being discussed: "We've been talking about a lot of very ugly scenarios that could play out in the next few weeks." Reports the *Far Eastern Economic Review*: "A prominent Asian academic tells the *Review* that not one of the senior administration officials he met with recently would rule out military action to remove North Korea's nuclear threat."

New York Times columnist Nicholas Kristof interviewed numerous policymakers and concluded: "The upshot is a growing possibility that President Bush could reluctantly order such a strike this summer." Similarly, Seymour Hersh quotes an intelligence official: "Bush and Cheney want that guy's head"—Kim Jong Il's—"on a platter. Don't be distracted by all this talk about negotiations. There will be negotiations, but they have a plan, and they are going to get this guy after Iraq. He's their version of Hitler."

It is not surprising that policymakers in Seoul, within easy reach of North Korean artillery and Scud missiles, have a different perspective on the use of force. Officials in Beijing, Moscow, and Tokyo also worry about radioactive fallout, missile attacks, refugee flows, economic turmoil, and regional chaos. There is no constituency anywhere in the region, even among the countries most vulnerable to a North Korea with nuclear weapons, for war.

The ROK is particularly adamant. As then President-elect Roh Moo-hyun explained, "It is impossible not to have differences [with the U.S.], and I cannot agree to attacking North Korea." During a campaign debate, candidate Roh declared: "For Washington, their prime interest lies in getting rid of weapons of mass destruction to restore the world order, but for us it's a matter of survival."

Some advocates of military action say don't worry, that Pyongyang would choose not to retaliate. Apparently the Clinton administration believed so when it was considering military action in 1994.

Today former State Department official Jed Babbin argues: "If the nuclear weapons program continues, we should consider an Osirak-like strike at the Yongbyon plant which is the center of North Korea's program. It's quite possible to do that without beginning a general war." Ralph Cossa, head of the Pacific Forum CSIS, contends that since regime survival is Kim Jong-il's highest goal, he would not risk destruction by retaliating.

Others propose coupling such a military strike with the use or threat to use tactical nuclear weapons against North Korean conventional forces. But under any circumstance to attack and assume the North would not respond would be a wild gamble. First, a military strike might not get all of Pyongyang's nuclear assets; hitting the reprocessing facility and spent fuel rods also could create radioactive fall-out over China, Japan, Russia, or South Korea.

Second, if the Kim Jong-il regime did not respond, its prestige would be gone. Moreover, given the official U.S. policy of preemption, designation of the North as a member of the "axis of evil," and offensive against Iraq for aspiring to build a nuclear weapon, Pyongyang might decide that even a limited military strike was evidence of America's determination to destroy it, the opening phase of a war for regime change. In that case, it would make sense to roll the tanks to begin hostilities at the time of its choosing. This is certainly how the North is threatening to respond to any U.S. strike.

Bill Taylor, formerly of West Point and the Center for Strategic and International Studies, who met with Kim Il-sung and other senior leaders a decade ago, believes: "faced with a major military strike on its territory, the North Korean leadership will respond with everything it has against Americans and our allies who fall within range of their weapons." South Korean Defense Minister Lee Jun said simply: "if America attacks North Korea, war on the Korean peninsula will be unavoidable."

An account by a high-ranking defector, Cho Myung-chul, is particularly sobering. In analyzing Iraq's defeat in the first Gulf War, North Korean military officials concluded that Baghdad was too defensive: "If we're in a war, we'll use everything. And if there's a war, we should attack first, to take the initiative." He estimates the chances of general war at 80 percent in response to even a limited strike on Yongbyon.

Unfortunately, "everything" is a daunting force: in addition to a large army, the North possesses long-range artillery and rocket launchers, deploys up to 600 Scud missiles and additional longer-range No Dong missiles, and has developed a significant number and range of chemical and perhaps biological weapons. Estimates as to the number of likely casualties run one million.

Also possible would be a limited retaliatory strike against America's Yongsan base in the center of Seoul, accompanied by heavy civilian casualties. The Seoul-Inchon metropolis hosts roughly half of the South's population, some 24 million people, is the nation's industrial heartland, and is being developed into a regional hub for East Asia. Pyongyang is thought to be able to fire 300,000 to 500,000 shells an hour into Seoul.

Washington could hardly afford not to respond to an attack on Yongsan, yet retaliation would likely lead to an escalation that would be difficult to halt short of general war. Indeed, after striking the DPRK might announce that it was finished, that it unfortunately had to retaliate against America but that it planned no additional attacks. However, if the U.S. struck anew, the North would respond.

Such a scenario might threaten civilian control of the military in Seoul; it would almost certainly set the South Korean and American governments at odds. The perception that South Koreans died because the U.S. acted against the wishes of the Roh administration would create a divisive, and perhaps decisive, split between Seoul and Washington.

Publicly, at least, President Roh calls claims of a possible American attack "inaccurate and groundless." Unification Minister Jeong Sehyun asks: "How can [Washington] ignore or go against South Korea in its North Korea policy?" Easily, actually, as the Clinton administration proved in planning for war in 1994.

Dealing with North Korea will prove to be one of the most vexing challenges for this and future administrations. But no one should believe that military action offers a simple and safe solution. Any attempt at military preemption in the DPRK almost certainly means a real war of horrific destructiveness.

April 2003

Korea—Giving China a Reason to Keep the Koreas Nuclear-Free

The Bush administration, focused on Iraq, lacks a clear strategy for deterring Pyongyang from an atomic path. Washington is hoping China will pressure the North. Indeed, there was a collective sigh of relief in Washington in April when Beijing brokered three-way talks in Beijing. Another negotiating round is set for September.

But Pyongyang's willingness to sit down with the U.S. in China's presence could be another stalling tactic. There is no reason to believe that the North is ready to agree to dismantle its existing facilities and accept inspections to prevent any future operations.

Achieving that goal will almost certainly require more from Beijing than a push for talks. And the PRC will be tough on the North only if the U.S. demonstrates that doing so advances Chinese interests.

A half century ago the newly-established People's Republic of China saved the DPRK from defeat in the Korean War. Last year the PRC accounted for about 70 percent of the North's oil supplies.

However, the relationship between the two countries has declined over the last decade. Over the North's strenuous objections China recognized the South in 1992 and has since developed multi-billion dollar economic ties with South Korea.

Over the same period, the PRC cut aid levels to the DPRK. Tensions flared between the two governments last fall when Beijing arrested the Chinese businessman tapped by Pyongyang to head the North's new economic development zone.

Nevertheless, Beijing could play an important role in dissuading North Korea from its nuclear course. And Washington is seeking the PRC's help.

Without great success so far, however. After his visit to the PRC earlier this year, Secretary of State Colin Powell delicately observed that the Chinese "prefer to play their role quietly"—very quietly, it would seem.

Although Beijing has not likely, as some claim, fomented the current crisis, it has done little to resolve the controversy. Yet it should come as no surprise that Beijing is disinclined to solve what it sees as primarily America's problem.

China obviously has little to fear directly from a nuclear DPRK. Moreover, the PRC, like South Korea, fears a North Korean collapse: millions of refugees swarming north, civil and military strife flowing over its borders, American influence extending to the Yalu.

Although China could apply significant economic pressure, it lacks the North's full trust. Coercion probably would permanently poison the PRC's relationship with Pyongyang.

Most important, China is suspicious of Washington's apparent determination to remain the dominant power along its borders and promote, in fact if not name, a policy of containment. North Korea's brinkmanship has embarrassed Washington and caused tensions with its Asian allies.

Why, then, should Beijing aid Washington?

It will do so only if the U.S. convinces the PRC that it is in China's interest to do so. One tactic would be to tell the Chinese "that by failing to support us they put their relations with us at risk," writes Stephen Sestanovich of the Council on Foreign Relations. That might or might not work, but only at great cost, given the many other issues, ranging from nonproliferation to Taiwan also at stake in the relationship.

Better would be to point out the adverse consequences to the PRC as well as America if Pyongyang does not desist. For instance, it is not in China's interest for North Korea to destabilize the peninsula, risking economic ties with the South and inviting U.S. military action.

Moreover, the U.S. should indicate to the North, within hearing of Beijing, that if Pyongyang develops an atomic arsenal, Washington would be disinclined to dissuade neighboring states from following suit. Even if that threat was insufficient to deter the North, it would have a salutary effect on China, which does not want to see nuclear weapons spread, especially to Japan and Taiwan.

Obviously, such a step would be controversial for all concerned. Yet the threat, combined with an appropriate package of carrots and sticks, might yield a peaceful, verifiable end to the North Korean program.

If not, it still would be better for Washington's democratic friends to develop the means to deter the DPRK rather than expect America to remain entangled in such a dangerous region. If China can be trusted with nuclear weapons, why not democratic Seoul, Taipei, and Tokyo?

Indeed, such a course might merely accelerate reality. In coming years Washington is likely to grow more uncomfortable shielding its allies from an increasingly assertive China. The U.S. will fear being drawn into unnecessary wars; Japan, South Korea, and Taiwan will fear America refusing to be drawn in.

A spread of nuclear weapons might encourage a Chinese nuclear build-up, but even worse would be a power vacuum in which everyone is forced to rely on America in any dispute with a nuclear-armed China. What is more chilling for America than having to risk Los Angeles to protect Seoul, Taipei, or Tokyo?

There is no easy answer to the problem of North Korea. Winning the assistance of China—serious, sustained pressure on Pyongyang—is critical to ending the North's nuclear pretensions. But that will require more than begging or threatening Beijing. And resolving the crisis is important to China as well as Washington.

July 2003

CHAPTER SIX

The Balkans

Better to Be Lucky

Seldom have events more dramatically demonstrated that it is better to be lucky than smart. The popular uprising that ousted Yugoslav President Slobodan Milosevic happened despite, not because, of Clinton administration policy. A foreign policy based on humility, as suggested by GOP presidential contender George W. Bush, rather than on hubris, as pushed by Vice President Al Gore, would promote a safer and more stable world.

The Balkans has long been in turmoil; the dissolution of the Ottoman and Austro-Hungarian empires at the end of World War I left a Serbian-dominated Yugoslavia. Italian and German occupation in World War II exacerbated nationalist divisions, which the post-war Tito regime sought to dampen by creating artificial internal boundaries and encouraging population shifts.

After Tito's death and the collapse of the threat of Soviet intervention, Milosevic used Serb nationalism to catapult into power. Never a full dictator, he maintained control through domination of the media, manipulation of the electoral system, and exploitation of a divided opposition.

And by playing on nationalistic sentiments. In this he was not alone: his Croatian counterpart, Franjo Tudjman, was an equally murderous nationalist.

Once Yugoslavia started to split apart, the West encouraged its dissolution, recognizing Slovenia, Croatia, and Bosnia. Yet when Serbs sought to secede from the latter two nationalist enclaves, the West demurred, calling their efforts "aggression." The U.S., which itself refused to allow secession in 1861 at the ultimate cost of 630,000 lives, criticized Belgrade for doing the same.

Rather than promote a peaceful resolution, through, for instance, the so-called Lisbon Accord early in the conflict, Washington fomented war. It encouraged Croatia to conduct the region's largest campaign of ethnic cleansing—kicking hundreds of thousands of Serbs out of ancestral land in the Krajina region.

Then the U.S. began bombing Serb insurgents in Bosnia to compel them to accept the bizarre Dayton Agreement, which purports to preserve a multi-ethnic Bosnia. This artificial state survives only through a Western military occupation and has achieved little other than record corruption—at least a $1 billion stolen as the West was pouring in $5 billion in aid.

Then NATO decided to intervene in Kosovo, internal strife of modest proportions compared to a score around the world, including that conducted by NATO member Turkey against the Kurds. The administration attempted to impose the Rambouillet agreement on the Serbs; it required Yugoslavia to allow Western forces free access throughout the entire country, as if it was conquered territory. No nation, and certainly not America, would have accepted such terms.

Rebuffed by Belgrade, the West launched a war of aggression against a state that had neither attacked nor threatened the U.S.; the President began bombing without congressional or UN authorization. Emerging "victorious" against a third-rate military power, the West then presided over the ethnic cleansing of a quarter million Serbs, Jews, Gypsies, and non-Albanian Muslims. Only continued military occupation will preserve the bizarre status quo in what has become a gangster haven—autonomy within Serbia, which neither Albanians nor Serbs accept.

Washington, along with the Europeans, also intermittently imposed economic sanctions. Yet President Milosevic and his allies enriched themselves on the black market.

In contrast, the middle class was devastated. Zoran Djindjic, head of the Democratic Party and adviser to newly elected president

Vojislav Kostunica, complained to me two years ago that "sanctions lead to centralization of the management of the economy." He said his followers couldn't even afford gasoline to drive to a rally.

The devastation wreaked by the war worsened the problem. Milosevic effectively shifted the blame to the West—and the Western-backed opposition. Observed Mr. Kostunica: "Western policy, above all the American policy" has been "more helpful to Slobodan Milosevic than to his opponents."

In short, Washington fomented the break-up of Yugoslavia, hypocritically denied the same secessionist right to Serbs, intervened in foreign conflicts in which it had no interest, entangled the U.S. in irrelevant foreign strife, and weakened the opposition in Yugoslavia. Some success.

Nor is Mr. Kostunica any friend of Washington. He is a staunch nationalist who criticized Dayton as a sell-out. He opposes relinquishing Serb sovereignty over Kosovo.

He denounced NATO for its aggression, which he termed a "criminal act" and "America's private war." That intervention, he wrote, "caused the humanitarian catastrophe."

He criticized the West for "flagrant interference" in Yugoslavia's affairs by subsidizing Milosevic's opponents. And he refuses to turn over Milosevic or others to NATO's lap-dog, the Hague War Crimes Tribunal.

In short, he won because the elite believed they could deal with him and the public recognized he was no Western lackey.

He is likely to be a far more formidable opponent of the West. He will be more popular with his people and more difficult to demonize abroad. When he demands that the West live up to its promises in Kosovo, allied hypocrisy will be harder to ignore. Moreover, Russia will have to swallow less hard to back him up.

Seldom have American presidents made a greater mess than has the Clinton-Gore administration in the Balkans. Chaos and war have been their trademark. Democracy has come to Yugoslavia through the efforts of millions of common Serbs, not Western policymakers.

October 2000

The Debris of War

KRAJINA, CROATIA—One of the most important priorities for the incoming Bush administration will be freeing itself from the Balkans tar baby created by its predecessor. That means standing aloof from any new sad but irrelevant conflicts.

In sharp contrast was the policy of the Clinton administration, which claimed to be the guardian of humanitarian values. For one brief moment last year President Clinton declared his willingness to stop ethnic cleansing anywhere in the world. But a short visit to the Balkan nation of Croatia quickly dispels the illusion that Washington had adopted anything but cynicism as its policy.

Along the back roads of this Balkans nation, which now hopes to join NATO, remains the debris of war. Abandoned homes, with broken walls and absent roofs, dot the rolling countryside.

For miles at a stretch not a single soul appears. It is ghost territory—and the direct result of Clinton administration policy.

When Yugoslavia began to split apart in 1991, Germany raced to recognize as new nations Slovenia and Croatia. The Europeans and U.S. followed suit.

Yet just as Croatians wanted to secede from Serb-dominated Yugoslavia, Serbs, who made up a bit more than ten percent of the population, wanted to escape their new Croatian-dominated state. Seven months of fighting ensued, with an uneasy ceasefire patrolled by U.N. forces.

The Serb position was hardly unreasonable. If Croats deserved their own state, then why not Serbs?

The boundaries of the Yugoslav republic of Croatia were arbitrary, created by Tito's Communist regime. Croats allied with the Nazis killed hundreds of thousands of Serbs in World War II. The newly independent Croatia was headed by Franjo Tudjman, an anti-Semitic thug unwilling to guarantee any protection for the Serb minority.

Serbs had lived in the Krajina for 500 years. They had as much right to decide their political allegiances, in light of changing circumstances, as did Croats who no longer desired to be part of Yugoslavia.

For three years the Krajina Serbs enjoyed an uneasy existence. Rejected by the rest of the world—the West did not recognize their independence aspirations—and unaffiliated with the nation of Serbia.

In the meantime, the Clinton administration, supposedly committed to peace, helped retrain the Croatian military. It didn't take a genius to guess where Zagreb would employ those troops.

In August 1995 Croatia launched Operation Storm. Although the U.S. Ambassador to Croatia urged President Tudjman to negotiate, Washington winked at the attack, lauding its possible benefits. NATO aircraft attacked Serb radar sites.

The assault spanned a 725-mile front and quickly overwhelmed the Serb defenders. The Croatian military used artillery against Serb towns and refugee columns.

The Croats triumphed in less than five days. Virtually the entire Serb population, estimated at 250,000, fled. Croatian mobs attacked columns of refugees.

Who could blame Serbs for leaving? Those who remained behind were treated like, well, the Serbs have been accused of treating other people. According to Amnesty International:

> A wide range of human rights violations were perpetrated during and in the wake of Operation Storm. These include gross abuses such as extrajudicial executions and disappearances; torture, including rape; a massive programme of systematic house destruction; attempts at forcible expulsions and numerous incidents of ill treatment. ... While the majority of incidents were reported in the days and weeks immediately following the operation, these human rights violations continued to be perpetrated for several months afterwards, and Amnesty International documented killings, acts of violence and intimidation well into 1996, and they have not been completely eliminated as of 1998.

These abuses—war crimes, really—do not, of course, justify Serb misbehavior. But they demonstrate that all parties in the region's successive conflicts have committed atrocities.

They also demonstrate the bankruptcy of Western policy. Demand that Serbs always and everywhere remain at the tender mercies of their enemies. Do nothing when Serbs are murdered. Blame Serbs for every problem everywhere.

Happily Croatia is changing. Tudjman is dead and has been replaced by a more liberal, Western-oriented government. It has begun to cooperate in the prosecution of Croatian war criminals and encourage Serb refugees to return home.

But many wounds in the Krajina have yet to heal. Abandoned Orthodox churches sit as silent sentinels in villages that retain scars from the 1995 fighting. Wrecked homes litter the landscape.

As Amnesty observes, "The widespread and deliberate destruction of houses and other buildings throughout the Krajina is the most visible evidence remaining of the gross human rights violations committed after Operation Storm." It also remains the most visible evidence of an American foreign policy that was both criminal and foolish, stoking the fires of hatred and conflict.

December 2000

Kosovo—Staying Out of the Next Balkans War

GRABOVAC, KOSOVO—We sat nervously in our taxi at the side of the dirt road near the Kosovan village of Grabovac surrounded by members of the Kosovo Liberation Army (KLA). Just ten kilometers (or about six miles) east of the provincial capital of Pristina Serbian government authority has vanished. With even the use of massive military force, it is hard to believe that Belgrade can win the rapidly burgeoning conflict.

In Pristina life seemingly proceeds normally. Children play in the streets, friends drink in sidewalk cafes, and pedestrians stroll by open shops. But the major roads to Pec in the west and Prizren in the southwest have been blocked by KLA roadblocks and fighting ("temporarily jeopardized by terrorists," as Col. Bozidar Filic of the Serbian Ministry of Internal Affairs puts it). Even the main road north to Belgrade is absolutely safe only during the day. "The situation is not good there, for travel at night," one Serbian government official told me.

In fact, the situation isn't good anywhere. At the KLA checkpoint we sat for 45 minutes in the open as the KLA members decided what to do about the photo that one of my colleagues took shortly before we hit the checkpoint. The KLA soldiers demonstrated no fear of discovery as local inhabitants drove by into what our KLA guards called "the free zone." In the end, the KLA seized the offending film—apologizing as they did so—and turned us around.

Government representatives attempt to put the best face on the situation. Goran Matic, the federal Yugoslavian Minister of Information, told me that "in the largest towns the situation is completely normal." There is admittedly fighting but, explains Gen. Nbojsa Pavkovic, commander of the Kosovo garrison, "these are settlements of pure Albanian population. They've been in this territory for the last 70 years. So we are not talking about 'liberated' territory, but territory that they live in." Even these villages, says Aleksandar Vucic, Serbian Minister of Information, "aren't necessarily under the control of terrorist organizations."

Maybe not, but they certainly aren't loyal to Belgrade. According to one American diplomat, last fall "no one believed in the KLA much." It occasionally killed a Serb cop, but little more. However, the collapse of the Albanian government last year made a lot of cheap weapons available to discontented Kosovars. KLA activity increased, sparking police escalation, further inflaming the Albanian community and greatly increasing KLA recruiting

The KLA is now thought to control 30 to 40 percent of the countryside; it has reportedly begun organizing in several larger cities, and the capital, Pristina, is an inevitable target. Several university students told me they knew people who had joined the guerrillas and another said "there may be a time when we shall go and fight."

At the same time, Belgrade is finding resistance at home: some 600 policemen have reportedly refused to accept duty in Kosovo. The parliament of Montenegro (along with Serbia one of Yugoslavia's two federal republics) has voted not to allow Montenegran soldiers to serve in Kosovo. Moreover, Serbian mothers have begun protesting the deployment of their sons to Kosovo.

Belgrade's last resort is the military, the JNA. But Gen. Pavkovic points to constitutional limitations on the employment of the military for anything other than border defense. Moreover, he and other soldiers were quick to distance themselves from police activities. Of one village virtually destroyed during a police assault, Gen. Pavkovic said: "We bear no responsibility for the things that happened there."

The failure to act so far "doesn't mean we aren't capable of solving the problem," Gen. Pavkovic hastily adds. In fact, however, the JNA is probably incapable of solving the problem. Minister Vucic confidently asserts that "we have adequate power to protect our territory." A competent, well-equipped force, the JNA could roll through the KLA barricade that stopped us, manned as it was by a motley collection of guerrillas with weapons reaching back to World War I vintage Lee Enfields.

However, some of the younger soldiers carried modern Kalashnikov assault rifles and the KLA has reportedly been obtaining anti-tank and anti-aircraft weapons. Moreover, ethnic Albanians who once served in the German, Swiss, and even Yugoslavian militaries, along with veterans of the Bosnian war (we encountered one at the checkpoint), including some Mujahadeen, are joining the KLA. "The KLA is way ahead of the Bosnians with arms, determination, and organization" says one U.S. observer.

Moreover, Belgrade has lost the vital fight for the "hearts and minds" of Kosovars. Roughly nine of ten are Albanian (there is some dispute over numbers), and it is hard to find one who acquiesces in, let alone supports, Serbian rule. Most Albanians probably still prefer a peaceful solution, and many resent coercive KLA recruitment tactics. But caught between the KLA and Serbian government there is little doubt where most will fall. And some forthrightly see violence as the only solution. When I asked a 27 year-old refugee who fled fighting in her village what the solution is, she responded: "The radical one. War."

The rise of the guerrillas has effected a tectonic shift in the attitudes of Albanian leaders. "Rational Albanians might have accepted cultural autonomy a year ago," says one U.S. diplomat, "but we've moved beyond that now." Ibrahim Rugova, head of the Democratic League of Kosova (LDK), has increasingly come under attack as a "defeatist." So he now unequivocally supports independence; the LDK backs the establishment of local village militias against the Serb police. Dr. Alush Gashi, a Rugova adviser, even praises KLA guerrillas who are "willing to give their lives" for the Albanian people. He admitted to me that "the democratic forces in Kosovo, unless we produce results, we will lose support."

To achieve independence virtually all ethnic Albanians, from LDK leaders to helpless refugees, hope for NATO intervention. Many have almost mystical faith in NATO's power: "The only hope to solve the problem in Kosovo is NATO," said Dr. Abdullah Zejnullahv, dean of civil engineering and architecture at an Albanian university in Pristina. Another Kosovar told me: "if NATO comes in quick, it will be solved." But speedy intervention requires good press. Explains Gashi, "it depends on how we look on CNN. People need to see victims in their living rooms."

It is easy to sympathize with the Albanians, who have suffered under particularly brutal and repressive rule since 1989, when the central government stripped Kosovo of the autonomy that it until then enjoyed. In its place Belgrade substituted central administration backed by the special paramilitary police. Belgrade also used its political control to fire thousands of ethnic Albanians—bankers, doctors, lawyers, teachers—from government positions.

Although ethnic Albanians responded by creating small businesses and a parallel system of governments, schools, and charities, the economic restrictions continue to fuel the military insurgency that now threatens Yugoslav control of the province. Students at a Pristina university voice frustration over the lack of potential employment, heightening their desire for a political revolution. "First we will become independent," said one. Then "we will get a job." The threat of war looms large. Explained one: "Maybe next year instead of a pencil in our hands we will have something else."

Serbs respond that Albanians earlier abused their autonomy by discriminating against ethnic Serbs. They further complain that the Serb population was artificially limited and that of Albanians artificially inflated (through immigration) by Marshal Tito, who hoped to use Kosovo to coax communist Albania into an anti-Soviet Balkans coalition.

Not that the exact figures are that important, argues Minister Matic: "Albanians have rights much greater than the rights guaranteed by European human rights conventions." Similarly, Ivan Sedlak, the Serbian Minister without portfolio with responsibility for minority affairs, says that Serbia contains "26 different national ethnic communities," 25 of which "are very satisfied with their rights." Of the ethnic Albanians, he argues: "If they made use of their right to have local government, they would have the government over the area."

Serb complaints of past Albanian abuses are undoubtedly true to some degree—few peoples in the Balkans have entirely clean hands—but that doesn't justify the police brutality that has been a constant of Serb rule. In response rose the KLA: Even ethnic Albanians admit that for the last year or two the organization targeted Serb policemen and other government employees, Serbs viewed as abusing Kosovars, as well as Albanian "collaborators," which has included postal workers and forest rangers. "If you're a Serb, hell yes the KLA is a terrorist organization," explains one U.S. embassy staffer. Each cycle of violence has spawned another one.

Both sides now call for negotiation, and talk about introducing NATO personnel as peacekeepers, but the parties take irreconcilable positions. Belgrade firmly rejects Kosovar demands for independence. This region is viewed as the cultural birthplace of Serbs, the home of important churches and monasteries and the site of a famous though losing battle against the Ottoman Empire in 1389. Thus, explains Minister Vucic, "We are not asking for anything that isn't ours, like California. We simply want what's inside of our state for decades and centuries to remain in our state."

He argues less about history, which he admits "won't interest you," and instead points to "the international law principle that state borders are unchangeable and untouchable." With Serbs already victimized by the violation of these principles during the break-up of the old Yugoslavia, they won't let it happen again. "All the international law principles were violated," he complains. There is also domestic politics to consider: "There is no chance that we are going to give up Kosovo, no matter what pressure is applied. This is the basis on which this government was formed."

Serb officials in a variety of positions indicate their willingness to discuss autonomy, "but not autonomy that is bigger than what is guaranteed by the constitution," explains Vucic, meaning no separate status as a republic. The reason for that is the fear that the Kosovars would remain committed to independence. Then they, like Bosnia, Croatia, Macedonia, and Slovenia, would use republic status to push for independence. Matic calls it "secession in several steps." On this point it is hard to blame the Serbs, since the West helped dismantle their nation while denying their co-nationals from Bosnia and Croatia the right to federate with them. As Matic puts it, "we had very bitter experiences of secession from Yugoslavia."

Unfortunately, it is hard to find an ethnic Albanian willing to contemplate less than independence. I came across only one, and he still strongly advocated independence. This position is reflected in the position of Kosovo political leadership. Emphasizes Dr. Gashi: "Independence is inevitable."

Even if it thought autonomy was a good compromise, the LDK, Kosovo's leading political force, has little room to maneuver. A medical student told me: "Rugova has to be for independence. If he was for autonomy, the Albanian people would blow him away." These kinds of sentiments are widespread. "Every single person wants to be independent of Serbia," acknowledges one American diplomat.

Some Albanians reject the idea of even living with Serbs. When asked if it is possible once independence is achieved, one student proclaimed an emphatic "no." A refugee responded to the same question: "can you imagine trying to live with them after what they've done"?

Most Kosovars still proclaim their desire for a multi-ethnic society, but they routinely exclude Serbs "with blood on their hands," "collaborationist"

Albanians, and others. One student allowed that "maybe someone will get his revenge, no one can stop him." Dean Zejnullahv offers a more chilling prediction: NATO intervention is necessary because even "if the Serbs withdraw the KLA would be after them to kill them." Although leading ethnic Albanians like Gashi promise "whatever protection Serbs want, in the constitution, or international guarantees," a newly empowered revolutionary government would not likely spend much time protecting its recently vanquished enemies.

If the LDK nevertheless did accept less than complete independence, only military force, either Yugoslav or NATO, could maintain the semblance of Serbian authority implied by autonomy. After all, the KLA is presently fighting against Serb authority of all sorts. "Imagine going to explain [a compromise accord] to someone whose sons were shot fighting for independence," complained one Albanian.

Nor is an independent Kosovo the only goal of many ethnic Albanians. KLA spokesman Jakup Krasniqi says his organization "is fighting for the liberation of all occupied Albanian territories," including the western section of Macedonia, whose population is one-forth Albanian, "and their unification with Albania." And that seems to be the perspective shared by those funding the guerrillas. One U.S. diplomat says: "The diaspora obviously wants one Albania." Moderate Kosovars disclaim such ambitions, but the prospect of a much wider Balkan war frightens NATO countries.

With no apparent room for compromise, a rising tide of bloodshed seems inevitable. But intervention, either by NATO or a U.S.-led international coalition, offers no solution.

Even the Clinton administration has backed away from its earlier belligerence once it began to assess the likely consequences. Particularly embarrassing is the fact that the West backs Belgrade's position that Kosovo should be part of Yugoslavia. As Gen. Pavkovic put it: We are "performing the honorable task that all countries do, that is, defending the state." State Department spokesman Jamie Rubin has intoned that Kosovars who desire independence are "deluding themselves."

Yet in the name of ending violence, White House Press Secretary Michael McCurry says that Belgrade "must immediately withdraw security units involved in civilian repression without linkage to" the end of KLA operations. Doing so would eliminate Serb authority overnight. It is a demand for preemptive surrender by Belgrade and de facto independence for Kosovo.

Washington's partisan stance has, not surprisingly, encouraged the ethnic Albanians to toughen their position. Statements like that of McCurry, says one U.S. diplomat in the region, "obviously plays into the perception that the U.S. is here to help the Albanians." When Gashi told me that NATO ground forces should "stop the fighting so that negotiations can go on," he meant negotiations over details, like safeguards for Serb cultural landmarks, not over basic issues, such as independence.

Even liberal Serbs, like Vesna Pesic, president of the Serbian Civic Alliance, resent the fact that there is "pressure only on the Serb side." At the same time, Western criticism tends to cause Yugoslavs to rally around their government by, in Pesic's words, "always raising the political temperature" and "frightening people." Zoran Djindjic, head of the Democratic Party, also complained to me that the West's position threatened to enable Albanians to "create a greater Albania, a very radical state in the Balkans."

The West has already tried economic sanctions—a freeze on Belgrade's assets abroad, ban on new investment in Yugoslavia, and denial of landing rights for the national airline—in order to induce it to negotiate and limit military operations. But Yugoslavia demonstrates the limits of sanctions. Western nations isolated the Serbian-dominated state during the lengthy Bosnian civil war without effect. Only exhaustion, backed by threatened Western military intervention on behalf of the Muslims, led to the Dayton Accord and its support for a united Bosnia hated by all three resident ethnic groups.

Sanctions were not just ineffective. Opposition political figures and independent journalists in Belgrade unanimously believe that Western economic controls benefited the oppressive regime of Slobodan Milosevic.

Sanctions enriched those in power and strengthened government economic control. This reinforced dependence on the regime which, in turn crippled the opposition. Complains Zoran Djindjic, head of the Democratic Party, "our only support is from people who are independent in their businesses" since they are least subject to government pressure. However, the West's economic war eliminated this democratic base.

Finally, sanctions gave Milosevic a convenient scapegoat for his policies. "Whatever the problem—health, education, etc.—his response was that it resulted from the undeserved sanctions," explains Vesna Pesic, In fact, throughout the Bosnian civil war, sanctions helped Milosevic rally support. "It seemed unpatriotic to attack Milosevic," explains one American diplomat in Belgrade. Now, he adds, there is again "this feeling that he's defending Yugoslavia against outside pressure."

Many in the West advocate military intervention. But this would mean attacking a sovereign state, inflicting potentially significant civilian casualties on Albanians and Serbs alike, and getting involved in the midst of a burgeoning guerrilla war. NATO could obviously destroy Yugoslavian mlitary forces in a war, but doing so would take an alliance once dedicated to defense against the long-gone Soviet Union and use it to launch a war of, well, aggression against another state that had in no way threatened any NATO member.

If the Serbs actually agreed to NATO "peacekeeping" intervention, and the West continued to insist on only autonomy for Kosovo, NATO forces might well find themselves fighting Albanian Kosovars who desired independence as well as Albanian nationals hoping to unite the nation of Albania with Kosovo and perhaps Albanian Macedonians also hoping to secede. Of course, the West could intervene and sanction independence. But if in Kosovo, why not in Chiapas in Mexico, the Basque region in Spain, Nagorno-Karabagh in Azerbaijan, the Tamil areas of Sri Lanka, and on behalf of any number of other separatist movements around the world? NATO's concern over the fate of the Kosovars is touching, but there are many far more brutal conflicts around the world.

The most reasonable solution to Kosovo is a negotiated settlement recognizing Albanian freedom aspirations and Serbian historic ties. But that requires an as yet invisible willingness to compromise. Says one American diplomat stationed in Yugoslavia: "Something in the water makes all sides myopic. For both sides the idea of compromise and real negotiation is hard to come by. Both sides want to dictate their position and call it negotiation."

Gashi, a moderate advising a moderate, says emphatically: "any transition plan that does not lead to independence is not a matter of discussion." The growing number of guerrillas overrunning the countryside certainly aren't interested in compromise. And Belgrade is unintentionally doing "all it can to build support for Kosovo independence," complains one American diplomat. "If the police keep killing people and burning houses, it isn't helpful to anyone."

At the same time, no one in the Milosevic government will consider independence. The present system may make violence inevitable. Observes Vesna Pesic, "we don't have an institutional means of resolving" the issue. Yugoslavs "still live in a half totalitarian, authoritarian system. So all the government can do is use the police."

However, even strong Serbian critics of Milosevic want Kosovo to remain part of Yugoslavia. Pesic—called a figure of conscience by American diplomats—explains that her party "has always defended Yugoslavia's territorial borders," though it has also been concerned about treatment of minorities. Zoran Djindjic says that "no one is eager to die for Kosovo. But it logical for people to believe that they have a right to Kosovo as their own territory."

Absent a willingness for compromise, there is only "the radical solution," as the one Kosovar put it: war. How much are the respective sides willing to pay? If Belgrade looses the JNA the price of independence will be quite high. But the Kosovars are almost certainly willing to pay more than will the Serbs. Belgrade has little enthusiasm for war; for most people, Kosovo's rich cultural patrimony is not worth the lives of their families and friends. Serb journalist Bosko Savkovic told me "I don't need it, it's just a bit of history." Philip David argues that the notion that Serbs care about Kosovo as the "cradle of Serbian culture" is just a "stereotype"—in fact, "for average people Kosovo means nothing special." When it comes to fighting, he observes, "it is not easy to find anyone who wants to go or who wants their children to go."

However, Minister Vucic claims this is an urban phenomenon—most of those who live outside of downtown Belgrade "would not give Kosovo up for any cost. These people feel it belongs to them." Maybe. But might a steady stream of body bags might change their attitude. Argues Gashi: "For the first time in a 100 years Serbs are dying. It is something the Serbs can't afford."

Kosovo is a human tragedy. "We've slipped into a situation where a lot of people will die," concludes one American diplomat. Unfortunately, there is no right solution for the West to impose, let alone to do so at acceptable risk to its own citizens. The only sensible U.S. position is to stay out. One American on the scene suggests that we simply "seal the border and let them go at it."

In the end, Washington should not risk the lives of its soldiers unless their own political community has a serious interest at stake. As tragic as are the ongoing deaths of Albanians and Serbs, it would be worse to add to them American deaths.

July 1998

Kosovo—Closing the Books on Kosovo

Ethnic Albanians in the Serbian province of Kosovo want independence, but even the Europeans don't believe they've earned it. Javier Solana, the European Union's foreign policy head, has returned from Kosovo's capital of Pristina criticizing the Albanians's refusal to move forward on democratization and minority rights.

Six years ago President Bill Clinton launched an unprovoked war of aggression against Yugoslavia, which had attacked neither the U.S. nor any American ally. The "liberated" Yugoslav (now Serbian) province of Kosovo remains in limbo.

The status quo satisfies no one, especially the ethnic Albanians who dominate Kosovo. Nicholas Burns, Undersecretary of State for Political Affairs, recently told Congress: "The status quo of Kosovo's undefined status is no longer sustainable, desirable or acceptable."

So UN Secretary General Kofi Annan has appointed a special envoy, Kai Eide, Norway's ambassador to NATO, to assess the province's compliance with democratic and human rights standards, with an eye to starting international negotiations on Kosovo's final status in the fall. But the process is dependent on Kosovo's good behavior, which Solana found to be lacking.

The fact that Kosovo remains an issue demonstrates the Clinton administration's hubris and surreal view of the Balkans combatants in 1999. The belief that it could impose a mutually acceptable arrangement, one that enshrined minority rights within a multi-ethnic framework, always was a fantasy.

The hatreds on the ground were too strong. America's intervention—taking the world's greatest military alliance into war against a destitute state suffering through a series of civil wars—irrevocably changed the geopolitical environment.

Stopping the bitter guerrilla conflict was an obvious benefit, but little good has occurred since the bloodletting ended. America's allies, the Albanian majority, conducted ethnic cleansing on a grand scale, kicking out most Serbs, Jews, Roma, and non-Albanian Muslims.

UN rule has done little to prevent endemic violence, crime, and instability, including brutal anti-Serb riots last year. Rep. Chris Smith (R-NJ) says simply: "the human rights situation in Kosovo is still not a good one, particularly for minority communities who live in enclaves and for the displaced."

At a congressional hearing in May, Charles English of the State Department reported that "Discrimination remains a serious problem. Access to public services is uneven. Incidents of harassment still occur. Freedom of movement is limited. And too many minorities still feel unsafe in Kosovo."

At the same time, the local population is dissatisfied with its indeterminate status: still formally part of Serbia, officially ruled by Western occupiers, with effective local control but no final resolution in sight.

Now, at least, the UN, with prodding by the Bush administration, is attempting to move forward. There is likely to be some assessment whether Kosovo is meeting a number of democratic "standards" along with the creation of some forum for discussing the province's ultimate status.

All that can be said is, the sooner the better. The current situation benefits no one. Most obviously it is a source of discord and instability in Kosovo.

The prospect of an international fight over Kosovo also provokes nationalist antagonism in Serbia, where political parties hostile to the West have done well of late. Other nations, too, worry: almost all of Serbia's neighbors harbor ethnic Albanian populations and worry about the impact of border changes.

Unfortunately, it will be easier to start the process than to deliver a good result.

The only hope for finding some solution is to abandon the illusions that long have tainted American policy in the Balkans. First, consent of all of the parties is impossible.

There is no agreement that will satisfy everyone. After seeing other parts of the former Yugoslavia secede, why would Albanian Kosovars accept less than independence? But why would Serbia accept dismemberment at the hands of numerous countries—America, Britain, and Turkey, to start—that have ruthlessly suppressed their own secessionist movements?

Why would an artificial neighboring state like Bosnia back partition of Kosovo between competing ethnic groups, creating a principle that could be applied to it? But why would Greece, Macedonia, or Montenegro support an Albanian minority of another nation in winning independence? Why should the nation of Albania forswear the possibility of union with Kosovo and creation of a greater Albania?

Western nations also should abandon the embarrassingly naive illusion that they can forcibly engineer a federal state that protects minority rights. The bitter serial break-up of Yugoslavia should have ended this fantasy.

If that wasn't a large enough dose of reality, then any belief in a multi-ethnic Kosovo should have disappeared when ethnic Albanians kicked out a quarter million of their neighbors after NATO intervened on their behalf. Whatever final delusions might have remained should have disappeared in last year's spurt of anti-Serb violence by ethnic Albanians.

Understandably, no Albanian Kosovar cares to trust his future to Serb governance. But no Serb, Jew, Roma, or anyone else would want to trust his future to ethnic Albanian governance, irrespective of the promises made by whomever.

It also is important to abandon expectation of a "just" settlement. Since the West cheerfully backed creation of a series of new states out of Yugoslavia, there's no intrinsic reason to say no to Kosovo.

At the same time, the NATO countries denied Serbs the right to secede from the new nations of Bosnia and Croatia. So what principle justifies giving the Albanians more rights than were accorded the Serbs? On the other hand, if Albanians have a right to secede from Serbia, there's no logical reason to deny Serbs the right to secede from Kosovo.

In short, there are no generally applicable principles here. The U.S. and its European allies support the sovereignty of nation states in the face of ethnic pressures—except when they support groups that wish to secede and establish ethnically-based states.

In the case of the Balkans, the only principle that seemed to apply was that everyone got to secede from Serb-dominated territories and Serbs were never allowed to secede from territories dominated by other groups. This might be consistent policy, but it should not be confused with a principled moral stand.

None of the proposed solutions is pretty. Independence would be in keeping with the wishes of Kosovo's ethnic Albanian majority, but would leave the few remaining Serbs vulnerable, inflame nationalism in Serbia, unsettle neighboring states, and create a statelet likely to become the regional fount of crime, instability, and perhaps even terrorism.

Leaving Kosovo with Serbia, whatever the form of autonomy, would satisfy Serbia and other nations with sizable ethnic Albanian populations, but has no support among Kosovo's Albanians. Serbian brutality during the guerrilla conflict and six years of de facto autonomy after allied intervention have eliminated this as a realistic option.

Moreover, this approach would place Serbia's democratic future in doubt, creating a hostile voting bloc accounting for roughly 20 percent of the population. (With a youthful population, ethnic Albanians could constitute 30 percent of army recruits.) Finally, this "solution" would be inherently unstable, creating a sense of unfinished business, seeming ethnic Albanians to be a mere way station on the way to independence.

Independence with partition—really big partition minus little partition—would come closer to satisfying ethnic Albanians, by giving them a country, and Serbs, by leaving most of them in Serbia. Such a system would be difficult to negotiate with Albanians, leave some Albanians in Serb territory, and would unnerve surrounding nations by encouraging further partitions.

Nevertheless, it would come closest to reflecting the desires of residents and applying just principles. Separation would be the means to discourage future conflict. Certainly it should not be ruled out by the West, as the Bush administration has attempted to do, effectively prejudging any "negotiations."

Although Clinton administration officials who did so much to unnecessarily entangle America in the Balkans have demanded continued U.S. "leadership," solving the region's problems always should have been Europe's rather than America's problem. Unfortunately, the U.S. now bears significant responsibility for the outcome due to its foolish intervention in 1999. But Europe retains both a greater interest in Kosovo's final status and ability to influence Balkans governments than does America.

Thus, Washington should baptize the beginning of an international process for resolving Kosovo's status and then step back, withdrawing its last 1800 troops from the region. Europe then could wield its various tools of influence—a willingness to maintain military garrisons, the prospect of joining the European Union, and the offer of economic opportunities and aid. If the Europeans choose a different strategy than preferred by Washington, so be it. And if a continuing troop presence is necessary, as many analysts argue, it should be provided by Europe.

The Kosovo war is over, but the peaceful resolution has barely begun. In the West's search for a solution, no one should unduly worry about respecting international juridical principles or seeking regional consensus. NATO abandoned any pretense of principle when it launched its unprovoked war against Serbia.

The allies should indicate that precedent is irrelevant. Every case, whether Kosovo or Bosnia or Croatia or Macedonia, is unique. International solutions will depend on particular circumstances and won't be determined by any other settlement.

There are lessons to be learned. The U.S., with or without NATO, should say never again. Never again will Washington substitute ideological fantasies for practical realities when implementing its foreign policy. Never again will Washington intervene in a distant civil war of no geopolitical concern to America. Never again will America attack another nation that poses no threat to the U.S. The world is filled with tragedy, and the Balkans—let alone Iraq—demonstrates how difficult it is for outsiders to resolve ancient and intractable conflicts.

Who can and should govern Kosovo, and can they do it fairly and effectively? No one really knows. But it's time to give the local inhabitants a chance to try. And to let them deal with the consequences if they fail.

July 2005

CHAPTER SEVEN

Europe

Uncle Sam, International Nanny

The Cold War may have ended, but Washington policymakers haven't noticed. The U.S. Senate has overwhelmingly approved the addition of three more countries to NATO. And efforts are already underway to expand the alliance, directed against no one, according to its supporters, to all of Central and Eastern Europe.

Indeed, America, facing no serious security threats, accounts for more than a third of the globe's military spending. U.S. expenditures outpace those of Russia by three or more to one; America spends roughly twice as much as Britain, France, Germany, and Japan combined. The U.S. and its friends account for an incredible 80 percent of the world's military spending.

What for? During the Cold War the doctrine of containment provided a coherent rationale for a large military in advanced outposts around the globe. That justification has obviously vanished, so today policymakers are busy concocting new "vital" missions to replace that of resisting communism.

Most NATO supporters speak of preserving peace throughout Europe. But many intend far more. Republican pundit William Kristol wants the U.S. to impose "benevolent hegemony" around the globe. Similarly, Family Research Council head Gary Bauer calls for us to "go forth into the world wherever we are needed, helping our brothers, relieving the afflicted, protecting the powerless, and waging the cause of democracy and freedom." Unfortunately, it is the average working people supposedly represented by people like Bauer who will ultimately pay the price for such grandiose schemes.

The U.S. has no vital interest that warrants guaranteeing the borders of Poland, Hungary, Romania, the Baltic States, Ukraine, and whoever else ends up on a NATO wish list. These nations obviously matter more to Western Europe, but that means Western Europe should defend them. It is time for a European-organized, -funded, and -manned defense of the East.

But lack of national interest is obviously no bar to U.S. military intervention. Although Europe looks secure, NATO officials peer south as well as east, and see only trouble.

Former NATO Secretary-General Willy Claes, for instance, charged that Islam poses as great a threat today as communism did in the past. Although he later recanted that statement, other European officials have warned that North Africa's population is growing much faster than that of Europe, threatening the West. Similarly, explains Adm. T. Joseph Lopez, commander of NATO's Southern Command (AFSOUTH): "if you take a macro-look at our theater, it's literally filled with instability and pockets of unrest." Examples include Albania, Algeria, Armenia, Azerbaijan, Bulgaria, Greece and Turkey, Libya, the Mideast, Syria, and Zaire. "With the end of the Cold War, the new enemy is instability," he argues.

AFSOUTH is also advocating a "Mediterranean Initiative" that promotes military contacts with Egypt, Jordan, Mauritania, Morocco, and Tunisia. But NATO officials, including Adm. Lopez, want more, much more—to expand the so-called Partnership for Peace, the precursor to NATO expansion into Central Europe, to such nations. One NATO official anonymously called for military involvement in Morocco and Tunisia: "you could have a preventive deployment of forces on the requests of those governments." And the Sixth Fleet has been conducting training exercises throughout West Africa. "I believe there's a need to make new friends," says Lopez, "so that NATO and the United States are viewed in a positive, rather than threatening, way." In other words, NATO will become kind of a big Peace Corps, only with nuclear weapons.

Of course, acknowledges Adm. Lopez, "instability is a difficult enemy to deal with." As Washington is discovering in Bosnia. The U.S. is already deeply enmeshed in the Balkans, a region with no serious link to U.S. security. Nevertheless, Washington is using its military to force three contending ethnic groups to remain in a unitary state that all oppose, and to support one nationalist politician over another in Serbian Bosnia. It turns out the kind of democracy Washington is intent on bringing to the Balkans—seizing television and radio stations when it disapproves of their broadcasts and transferring control of police stations to factions it views as more pliant—is more representative of Boss Tweed than George Washington.

Unfortunately, meddling in Bosnia isn't enough. Violent unrest in Kosovo, a Yugoslav province largely populated by ethnic Albanians, has generated calls for intervention there. The U.S. is "not going to stand by and watch" Yugoslavia crush political freedom in Kosovo, thundered Secretary of State Madeleine Albright. Albright pushed for economic sanctions and an arms embargo. Others advocate NATO military intervention.

Then there are proposals to move east. For example, George Melloan of the *Wall Street Journal*, wants to "extend NATO's protection to Georgia and Azerbaijan." That isn't far-fetched: the U.S. is now aiding the militaries of Kazakstan, Kyrgyzstan, and Uzbekistan, areas never before thought to be of great strategic interest, and the latter desires formal links to NATO. Moreover, last fall the U.S. conducted military exercises in the region. Explained Marine Gen. Jack Sheehan, commander of the U.S. Atlantic Command, "there is no nation on the face of the earth that we cannot get to." He did not explain, however, why the U.S. would want to get to such distant, impoverished nations, which border on Afghanistan, China, and Russia.

Is there any country with which America is unwilling to go to war? The answer, unfortunately, appears to be no. NATO officials suggest that "out-of-area" actions may become alliance's primary focus in the future. For what conceivable purpose? Capt. Ken Golden, commander of an Amphibious Readiness Group attached to the Sixth Fleet, says "While a lot of Americans back home seem to think we don't have enemies anymore, I can tell you there's a lot of hatred out there.." Yes, but our enemies—such as Cuba and North Korea—are pathetic. And most of the hatred would not be directed at the U.S. if Washington did not meddle in all sorts of faraway, irrelevant conflicts.

NATO expansion was never really about Europe. Rather, it is about promoting a new imperialism, in which U.S. soldiers are pawns in a global chess game played by policymakers in Washington. Unfortunately, even when they win, the rest of us will lose.

Must America remain at war even when the world is at peace? The U.S. Senate, by voting to expand NATO, says yes. The American people will now pay the price, in higher taxes, lost lives, and less freedom.

May 1998

A European Defense?

It's always dangerous to ask for something, goes the old adage. You might get it. So it is with America's desire that the Europeans do more on defense.

Despite significant disquiet in Washington, the Europeans are talking seriously about developing an independent, "autonomous" interventionist capability. Under the European Security and Defense Identity (ESDI) members of the European Union (EU) would significantly improve their military capabilities in such areas as command and control, intelligence, and strategic lift.

In particular, the EU has proposed development of a European rapid reaction force of 60,000. Although it will be some time before such a unit takes to the field—2003 under current plans—the EU is conducting a war-gaming exercise in February without the U.S.

There's no doubt that Europe's military capabilities could and should be enhanced. Despite possessing a smaller GDP and population than the EU, America spends more than 40 percent extra on the military.

By almost every measure—total outlays, percent of GDP, spending per capita—Europe lags far behind the U.S. The performance of some European nations, such as Germany, is pathetic. But then, Europe's defense anemia existed throughout the Cold War, even though Europe always faced greater security threats than did America.

U.S. dominance was inevitable when NATO was created in 1949, given Europe's post-war weakness. But some American officials warned against excessive European dependence on the U.S. "Permanent troop establishments abroad," observed Dwight Eisenhower in 1961, will "discourage the development of the necessary military strength Western European countries should provide for themselves."

This phenomenon was evident throughout the 1980s when the Europeans routinely failed to honor their promises to increase defense spending. If anything, the gap between U.S. and European military contributions has grown after the fall of the Berlin Wall, because Europe has been cutting outlays faster than has America. Moreover, Europe's industrial base continues to lag far behind that of the U.S.

Even more dramatic is the disparity between the effectiveness of U.S. and European military power. A recent audit by the Western European

Union (WEU), Europe's formal defense organization, concluded that Europe's militaries were largely ill-equipped, outmoded, and unable to fulfill post-Cold War missions. One estimate is that Europe has just one-tenth America's practical military capabilities.

This was evident in the Kosovo war. The U.S. provided virtually all precision-guided missiles, intelligence, and airlift resources and 80 percent of aircraft. Three months of bloodless (on the allied side) bombing was possible only because of sophisticated U.S. military technology, funded by Washington's disproportionate defense R&D outlays.

Indeed, one hesitates to call NATO an alliance. Former National Security Adviser Zbigniew Brzezinski more accurately termed Western Europe "largely an American protectorate, with its allied states reminiscent of ancient vassals and tributaries." Yet despite periodic U.S. complaints about burden-sharing, this arrangement long satisfied both sides.

Perhaps no longer, however. After the war against Serbia, Deputy Secretary of State Strobe Talbott chided an English audience, "Many Americans are saying: Never again should the United States have to fly the lion's share of the risky missions in a NATO operation and foot by far the biggest bill." In early February Defense Secretary William Cohen criticized the Europeans for failing to modernize and relying too heavily on America. Presidential candidate and Texas Gov. George W. Bush has cited "Europe's need to invest more in defense capabilities."

The Europeans, too, seem appalled by their pitiful performance. It's one thing to enjoy having America carry the overwhelming burden. It's quite another to have no choice but to have America carry the overwhelming burden. Explains Javier Solana, who last October shifted from NATO to WEU secretary-general: "To have a good and solid partnership, it has to be more among equals."

Publicly the administration professes itself to be pleased with Europe's greater interest in building effective military forces. One U.S. official told the *Financial Times* that "This is burden-sharing, big time."

However, American support depends on Europe's plans as being "not revolution" but "evolution," as explained by Solana. In October the U.S. Senate passed a resolution advocating that the EU undertake an "autonomous" intervention "only after NATO had declined to take on that mission." Secretary Cohen has made the same point, advocating that NATO have "first option" on any proposed military action.

Washington's oft expressed fear is that the EU initiative will develop parallel to NATO. At best it will distract attention from the Western alliance. At worst it will lead Europe to end its military reliance on America.

The Europeans naturally say there is nothing to fear. French President Jacques Chirac explains that Europe's initiatives "reinforce NATO, in reality." British Prime Minister Tony Blair adds, "It is not an attempt in any shape or form to supplant or compete with NATO."

Although European embarrassment over its relative weakness is real, it is still not clear that Europe is willing to spend what it will take. For instance, Germany has only half the number of soldiers under arms today as in 1991. It would cost Berlin an extra $2 billion a year to fulfill the new EU mandate. Yet Chancellor Gerhard Schroeder has proposed to cut more than $1 billion, or four percent, this year, and almost $10 billion more over the next four years in military outlays. An independent defense panel has proposed cutting German troop strength by more than a third.

In early December Defense Secretary William Cohen complained that Berlin's miserly military efforts were sending a bad message to the new NATO members. In fact, recent initiates like Hungary say they can't afford to fulfill their commitments to modernize their forces and achieve interoperability.

Although France's 2000 budget is also down from last year, Paris, at least, recognizes the conflict between ends and means. Observes French Gen. (ret.) Pierre Gallois, "You can't want a European military organization that can get along without the Americans and reduce military budgets." Similarly, French Defense Minister Allain Richard says: "I think it's not realistic to say we are spending enough and that all we need to do is create more synergy and achieve more efficient cooperation."

So Europe must obviously ask a tough question: how much is pride worth?

In fact, it should be worth a lot, given the likelihood that America might eventually tire of solving overwhelmingly European problems. Already the U.S. has demonstrated in East Timor that its willingness to intervene is not infinite. Australia found that it had to take the lead in the UN peacekeeping force to defend what were overwhelmingly

Australian interests. Canberra is now discussing bolstering its military lest it face similar contingencies in the future.

Washington may continue today to look more favorably upon intervention in Europe. But that is eventually likely to change, especially if NATO's Balkan adventures turn sour. Bosnia offers little argument for a repeat experience: only Western military occupation holds together an artificial state where corruption dramatically outpaces reconciliation. Kosovo could become even worse—U.S. forces were recently stoned by a crowd in the town of Mitrovica, and French and German troops have also come under attack—if NATO is serious about preserving a multiethnic society under formal Serbian authority. Attempting to do so ensures a permanent occupation and risks a new war, this time against the Kosovo Liberation Army.

A serious European force would allow the EU to act if the U.S. said no thanks the next time Europe called. It would also enable the Europeans to defend security interests of less concern to Washington: for instance, European officials are whining that America's proposed missile defense would not cover their continent.

But Europe could do much more with its own military. Chancellor Schroeder argues that "The Europe of the future must be able to defend its interests and values effectively worldwide." With such a capability to intervene, explains French President Jacques Chirac, the EU now "will have at its disposal all the true means of a foreign policy." The outlines of such an independent European stance were evident when European Commission President Romano Prodi announced in February that "any attack or aggression against an EU member nation would be an attack or aggression against the whole EU."

Which is precisely what bothers Washington. Despite its public protestations of good will, the administration has set tough conditions for its support: no decoupling of America and Europe, duplication of NATO capabilities, and discrimination against nonparticipating NATO members, said Secretary of State Madeleine Albright last December. Moreover, American officials have been privately lobbying against the European initiative. ESDI advocates complain that heavy-handed U.S. pressure has been counterproductive.

Washington's position, that Europe should do more while following U.S. dictates, is unlikely to prove popular in European capitals. "We know the Americans," one anonymous EU official told the *Los Angeles Times*: "They want the Europeans to do more in matters of defense, but on the other hand, they're worried about something being done behind their backs."

However, with money and power comes responsibility. In fact, the devolution of additional defense responsibility on Europe seems inevitable because Europe no longer needs America. The threat that gave rise to NATO is dead. Amazingly, the British and French each now spend more than Russia on the military; Germany's outlays are roughly equal. Europe has a combined GDP of about nine times that of Russia. Italy alone has a bigger economy than Russia.

Still, Geoffrey Hoon, Britain's Secretary of State for Defense, argues that "Of course we can never provide the same level of resources and the same power as the United States." But Europe needn't do so, since it lacks America's global interests. More important, Europe could do so if it chose to do so. Lack of will, not capabilities, hobbles the Europeans.

If the EU moves ahead on creating a rapid reaction force, it is hard to imagine the Europeans forever remaining satisfied acting as America's assistants. In June 1999 Guenter Verheugen, Germany's EU ambassador and minister of state for foreign affairs, explained: the purpose of the ESDI "is to engage in active crisis management in Europe with its own resources and under its own responsibility." If Europe acquires the ability to "engage in active crisis management in Europe" and perhaps beyond, what role is there for America?

Geoffrey Van Orden, the British Conservative Party's spokesman on foreign affairs and defense, warns that having the Europeans take first crack at European problems "will inevitably have a negative impact on NATO's viability" and fears "the weakening of trans-Atlantic bonds." Former U.S. Assistant Secretary of State John Bolton contends that if Washington does not stem the creation of European military forces outside of NATO, in a few years "We might well face the prospect that it is the WEU that is the real alliance, and NATO the appendage, rather than the other way around." More bluntly, Defense Secretary William Cohen warns against allowing the Europeans to "simply fend for themselves."

Yet why is that such a bad idea? It obviously isn't likely to occur soon, at least not without American encouragement. Nevertheless, why shouldn't Europe take responsibility for its own affairs?

America's vital interest is to prevent any hegemonic power from controlling the European continent. Such a threat no longer exists. Russia can barely defeat Chechnya. Germany possesses neither the will nor ability to threaten its neighbors (imagine an attack on nuclear-armed France). Milosevic's Serbia is impoverished and pitiful. Terrorists may lurk along the North Africa coast, but America's military presence in Europe only makes the continent a more attractive target.

Whatever intra-European rivalries might eventually emerge, none are remotely likely to turn violent. The world of the EU, Euro, and pan-European cooperation is a different world from that which gave rise to two world wars earlier this century.

What is left is the messy, unfinished business of the Cold War, particularly in the Balkans. More distant are a potpourri of conflicts in the Caucasus. Yet none of these seem particularly important for the security of Europe, let alone America. And modest improvements in European military capabilities would allow the EU states to handle further instability should they believe the price of doing so to be worthwhile. Washington could begin by letting the five-nation Eurocorps take over manning, as well as command, of occupation forces in Kosovo, for instance.

Secretary Cohen has argued, "A stronger Europe means a stronger Alliance, and a stronger Alliance is able to deter the threats and maintain peace and stability." But this applies as much to an alliance run by Europe as one run by America. Although Secretary Cohen contends that "'more Europe' does not mean 'less America'," it should mean less America.

The alternative to a U.S.-dominated NATO is not an isolationist America, but a watchful, wary America ready to play the distant balancer should Europe again be threatened. Even if the Russian Humpty Dumpty reconstitutes itself, it would not easily recreate a threat to Europe. If it did so, Washington could then react, taking appropriate steps, rather than today maintaining its domination of the Cold War NATO alliance largely unchanged.

Europe's new defense initiative should spark a serious debate about fundamentals. Those who believe that it remains in America's interest to continue defending Europe and dominating NATO should bear the burden of proof.

After all, when the world and the resulting threat environment change, so should alliances like NATO. Everyone seems to agree that the Europeans should do more militarily. Now it's time to ask: what, if any, should be America's role?

March 2000

Europe: Friend or Foe?

The U.S. and Europe have grown apart and no presidential visit to the continent will change that. Rather than dwell on past disagreements, Washington should concentrate on resolving a handful of current controversies.

It would be nice, for instance, if Europe offered to supplement the U.S. led garrison in Iraq. That's not going to happen.

But Washington might be able to convince Europe not to raise its ban on arms sales to China. The U.S. "has very specific concerns about lifting the embargo," observes Secretary of State Condoleezza Rice.

There's much about European behavior that irritates Washington. However, the fact that the interests of sovereign nations, even ones so closely tied in the past, sometimes diverge shouldn't surprise anyone on either side of the Atlantic. America's liberation of Europe 60 years ago does not entitle Washington to Europe's unthinking support today.

Nevertheless, the U.S. and Europe share a number of interests. Perhaps most fundamental is preserving their generally free and prosperous societies.

There may be disagreements about how to do achieve certain ends—prevent Iran from developing nuclear weapons, for instance. But no American or European wants to see the rise of a global hegemonic authoritarian power.

Like China.

There's much good that has happened to the People's Republic of China (PRC) over the last three decades. Virulent, murderous Maoism is gone. Beijing has moved dramatically towards free markets, lifting hundreds of millions of people out of poverty.

The political system remains sclerotic, but personal autonomy and religious liberty are expanding. Over the long term, it will be increasingly hard for the nominally Communist Party—more fascist in practice—to preserve its control.

However, further liberalization is by no means guaranteed. And even a more democratic PRC might be aggressively and dangerously nationalistic.

That wouldn't be so important if the country was, say, Burma or Zimbabwe, two other states under an EU arms embargo. But Beijing, which is likely to eventually marry the world's largest population with the largest economy, is a potential peer competitor to America.

Even that alone isn't necessarily frightening. After all, there were sometimes significant tensions between a rising U.S. and declining Britain, but they ultimately forged one of the closest international relationships extant.

With China, however, the differences are more significant—and could conceivably lead to war. That would be horrific, obviously, and should be avoided at almost all cost. But there are flashpoints, such as Taiwan, and if war would come, it would be in the interest of both the U.S. and Europe for America to prevail.

The European Union implemented an arms embargo after the Chinese regime's slaughter of demonstrators in Tiananmen Square. But a number of European companies and governments see potential profits from servicing Beijing's arms needs; PRC defense spending has been growing around ten or so percent annually and now stands at a respectable $150 billion a year.

Some Europeans also hope to become a counterweight to America and believe a relationship with China will aid that effort. A French foreign ministry figure was quoted: "Of course we are in favor of lifting the embargo. It no longer corresponds to the reality of the Euro-Chinese strategic partnership."

There is pressure on the EU to drop the prohibition at its June meeting in Brussels.

Human rights concerns about Beijing remain valid, but that's not the most important point. International security is the issue.

If Europe itself planned on becoming a military counterweight to China, Washington could say go ahead. But for all of the European talk of establishing an independent foreign policy, even leading nations like Germany have no intention of spending the money necessary to develop serious military capabilities. The obligation for real war-fighting will remain America's.

Unfortunately, Beijing is thinking about war. It has been buying advanced Russian weapons, including long-range missiles, aircraft, guided-missile destroyers, and submarines.

Explains Shi Yinhong, professor of international relations at Beijing's People's University: "China really wants to have another source for modernizing its military, especially for the possibility of military confrontation with Taiwan." And confrontation with Taiwan could easily lead to confrontation with the U.S.

Which means high-tech weapons sold by Europe could be used against America. Some EU officials point to Israeli weapons transfers to Beijing, but that is no less an unfriendly act.

Others say don't worry, we will limit the sort of weapons we sell. But that won't be much solace should conflict occur.

Another argument, articulated by French Defense Minister Michele Alliot-Marie, is that European sales might slow Chinese development of its own capabilities. "So maybe if we can sell them the arms, they will not make them. And in five years' time, they will not have the technology to make them."

Actually, even European businessmen worry that China wants to appropriate technology as much as acquire weapons. It's hard to believe that any "code of conduct," especially a voluntary one subject to individual national interpretation, would be enforceable.

The best case has been made by British diplomats, who contend that the existing ban is ineffective. They suggest creating a more limited but transparent export control regime.

It's true that Europeans weapons exports to the PRC have been rising. Beijing already has been able to purchase dual-use micro and nanosatellite technology, jet fan blades, helicopter design assistance, naval engines, and trucks, according to Richard Fisher of the Jamestown Foundation. Unfortunately, the British seem to be about the only ones who are talking about selling less rather than more.

If Europe ignores America's concerns, the administration's options are limited. The U.S. could deny export licenses for sensitive defense sales to companies and nations that sell to China. Beyond that would be the threat of a full-scale trade war. Which would be in no one's interest.

Hopefully a less ostentatiously arrogant Bush administration can forge a more cooperative relationship with Europe. Secretary Rice has called for a "new chapter" in relations and Washington should acknowledge the legitimacy of EU disagreements with American policy and the wisdom of rethinking outmoded institutions, such as NATO.

Most important, the U.S. must recognize the commercial sacrifice it is asking of the Europeans, while convincing them to look beyond to a future in which China's positive role is by no means assured. Washington needs to make the argument to individual governments as well as the European Commission. Indeed, the European public seems to be on Washington's side on this issue, with the European Parliament passing resolutions supporting the ban.

Engagement is a better strategy than isolation for encouraging the development of a free China. However, engagement need not mean strengthening the PRC's military.

China offers enormous economic opportunities and poses serious military threats. Luxembourg's ambassador to America, Arlette Conzemius, says that "the EU wants to show that it is a global partner of the U.S., as it grows stronger." Here's Europe's chance to do so.

Beijing will become a significant military power with or without European arms sales. In today's uncertain world there's no need to hurry the process along.

February 2005

Preserving Freedom in Europe

The great European unity project has stalled. No one was surprised at determined opposition to the proposed constitution among the always distant British. But the solid "non" in France, a leader for five decades in promoting European integration, and overwhelming no in the Netherlands, has left the plan to build a continental colossus in ruins.

That's all to the good, for both Europe and America.

European attitudes towards America have been chilly of late. France, a member of the UN Security Council, led the effort to block the Bush administration's war against Iraq. Although the political struggle focused on Iraq, Paris had far bigger goals in mind: preventing the globe's "hyper-power" from running roughshod over everyone else.

Germany's Chancellor Gerhard Schroeder joined Chirac. Indeed, the German leader won reelection in 2002 by vowing not to cooperate with Washington. Although the friendly Italian government under Prime Minister Silvio Berlusconi continues to hang on under pressure, last year Spanish voters ejected the Bush-friendly Spanish Prime Minister Jose Maria Aznar's Popular Party from power. Since then other European nations have been bringing home their limited forces from Iraq.

Nor can America rely on the influence of "new Europe," the former Soviet-dominated states which now are entering the European Union. Even the Polish government, which ignored its population's wishes in supporting Washington in Iraq, has edged away from the U.S. However supportive of America such nations as Hungary and Slovenia may be, they lack the significant economic and military wherewithal necessary to back up their commitments.

America's most steadfast European friend is Great Britain. Yet backing the U.S. in Iraq cost Prime Minister Tony Blair's government much of its massive majority in Britain's recent election. Although that nation is closer than continental Europe to America in culture and history, even many Conservative Party politicians bridle at Bush administration policies. British referenda on joining the Euro monetary zone and ratifying the European constitution looked to be watershed decisions on with whom—America or Europe—the island nation would most closely tie its future fortunes.

That decision has just gotten easier with the European constitution moribund.

Nine European countries have ratified the constitution and Luxembourg's Prime Minister, Jean-Claude Juncker, who currently holds the EU's rotating presidency, argued that "The ratification procedure must be pursued in other countries." The French and Dutch governments could ratify anyway, despite the popular rejections. Or the two nations could vote again. Indeed, in the past continental elites have responded to popular opposition by holding as many ballots as necessary to get the desired result. But French and Dutch officials have little political choice now but to respect the referendum results, which means the ratification process is over.

The European Union remains, but it may no longer be quite so ready to keep marching eastward, and especially to Turkey. Moreover, the campaign to turn Europe into a superstate, something like a country with a common defense and foreign policy as well as relatively uniform economic market, has become a train to nowhere.

Although European integration has deepened more quickly than most people imagined two or three decades ago, significant national differences obviously remain. No amount of wishful thinking in Brussels can change that reality.

Europeans almost certainly will benefit because a less unitary Europe is likely to be a freer Europe. The U.S. will benefit since a more federal Europe is likely to less consciously see itself as a rival of America.

Continental Europe has never been a bastion of economic freedom. France was a great mercantilist power; Bismarck's Germany created social insurance. The Nordic nations pioneered the concept of the suffocating welfare state.

Yet creation of a "common market" and later the European Union, supplemented by the Euro as a common currency, helped open some of the most socialized and least competitive economies. The continental market reduced national protection for politically influential domestic industries.

European budget and financial rules encouraged economic transparency and discouraged fiscal irresponsibility, especially among the poorer states that have joined most recently. Pressure for political reforms also aided the latter's move towards democracy.

However, the EU and euro impose a complex regulatory overlay enforced by an unelected bureaucracy in Brussels. Unfortunately, writes British historian Paul Johnson, "European societies have become a paradise for bureaucrats, trade unionists, centrist politicians and those businessmen who prefer to work under government protection."

Moreover, the Euro, which binds together 12 very different economies, has come unhinged at a time of slow economic growth. Official Europe worried about compliance by smaller nations such as Greece and Portugal, which were thought to be more irresponsible and thus more likely to violate the three percent deficit ceiling. But then France and Germany brazenly violated the rules. Rather than hold such large states accountable, the Eurozone members changed the regulations.

Formalizing European integration through the proposed monster of a constitution—448 articles in 450 pages—would do more to increase economic micromanagement than openness. Which is precisely what Europe does not need.

Existing EU rules are costly enough. Observes leading Tory MP Liam Fox: "Bureaucracy will be the end of us. That is the special relationship with Europe." American Enterprise Institute scholar Kevin Hassett calls it a "Red-tape Curtain," combining sclerotic regulation and bloated social welfare programs.

Over the last 40 years Europe's spending as a share of GDP has jumped 50 percent while unemployment has trebled. As Brian Carney of the *Wall Street Journal Europe* recently observed, "these two phenomena are related; in a country with generous welfare benefits, rising unemployment increases government spending rapidly." In turn, he points out, rising outlays require higher taxes. The costs of hiring a worker jumps, so total employment falls.

The proposed constitution has even more obvious political overtones. For instance, French Foreign Minister Pierre Moscovici observed: "We don't agree with the Americanization of the world ... we are saying that together we can build a new superpower ... and its name will be Europe." European Commissioner for Regional Policy, Michael Barnier, pushed the same theme: "The choice is between an independent Europe and a Europe under American influence."

Even some British officials want to move closer to Europe and away from the "special relationship" with America. Former Labor defense minister Peter Kilfoyle complained that "Britain ends up as America's handrag."

The European constitution was intended to reduce dependence on Washington. Argued France's Socialist Party, the document would allow Europe to be "strong in the face of the United States." The new phase of European integration, in contrast to the old, is overtly anti-American.

Of course, the desire to counter-balance Washington does not automatically bring with it the means to do so. And few Europeans nations, whether "old" or "new," have demonstrated the willingness to invest in their militaries, which would be necessary to turn the continent into a genuine independent force.

Nor would a united Europe be free of bitter divisions within. Creating a European foreign minister is easier than creating a European foreign policy. Still, it is hard to see how further centralizing continental policy would benefit America.

Where Europe goes from here is unclear. And Washington should say little. Europe's future is, after all, Europe's decision.

But the U.S. can provide options to individual countries that decide they want out, or at least a better alternative. For instance, John Hulsman of the Heritage Foundation has suggested expanding the North American Free Trade Association (NAFTA) to any interested European countries.

They could try to renegotiate the Treaty of Rome, allowing them to join NAFTA. Failing that, they could shift from the EU to the European Free Trade Area and European Economic Area (which include Iceland, Liechtenstein, and Norway), and sign up with NAFTA. Creating a broader free trade association also would offer nations now seeking to join the EU a better, freer alternative.

Or the U.S. could unilaterally lower trade barriers against select European nations—most obviously Britain, but others that indicated an interest in pursuing extensive economic liberalization irrespective of the state of Europe. That would benefit Americans by expanding commerce while encouraging stronger bilateral links.

The U.S. might be today's hyper-power, but future challenges can be seen on the horizon. China is the most obvious eventual peer competitor to America. India could follow. A united Europe conceivably still could become another.

Although Washington can do little to prevent any of these future rivalries, it could offer expanded economic ties to help discourage development of a centralized, monolithic Europe arrayed against America. That might be the most important lesson for Washington to draw from the French and Dutch votes against the European constitution.

June 2005

CHAPTER EIGHT

The Mideast

Israel—Ethnic Cleansing on the Jordan?

Despite its continued backing of Israel, the Bush administration's patience apparently is not endless. Should Ariel Sharon's government continue to construct a security fence effectively annexing Palestinian areas to Israel, Washington has threatened to withhold some of the $9 billion in planned loan guarantees.

Israelis are not pleased. "It's none of their business," complained Zitrin Eliezer, an Israeli settler in the West Bank. "Let them give California and Texas back to the Mexicans and then they can come and tell us what to do."

In fact, Mr. Eliezer is correct: Israel's policies aren't America's business. At least, they wouldn't be if Washington wasn't backing Israel against all comers, providing billions in aid annually, arming its distant ally, and offering diplomatic cover for Israel. The price of dependence on America is meddling by Washington.

And the U.S. has no choice but to demand, pressure, and whine. As September 11 dramatically demonstrated, America pays a price for being identified with Israel's repressive policies in the Gaza Strip and West Bank.

Obviously, terrorism against the U.S. reflects complex causes and circumstances. And the slaughter of innocents, whether Americans or Israelis, can never be justified. Retaliation against those who kill is inevitable and justified.

But anger over U.S. support for Israel permeates Arabic and Muslim nations. Even pro-American liberals in the most pro-American Mideast Muslim state, Kuwait, uniformly criticize Washington when they see Israeli tanks confront Palestinian children. Dr. Steve Gilliland of Brigham Young University spent eight months in Jerusalem; he complains of "the assault on human rights, the incessant harassment, and the humiliation and violence the Palestinians suffer at the hands of the Israeli government."

Alas, the situation is only likely to get worse. Every killing encourages more killing: the young woman who set off the deadly bomb in Haifa apparently acted in retaliation for the killing of her brother and cousin in Jenin in the West Bank four months before. Her murder of 19 virtually forced an Israeli response. And on it goes, a tragedy without end.

Indeed, Israeli officials, including Vice Prime Minister Ehud Olmert, publicly talked of assassinating (or expelling or jailing) Palestinian leader Yassir Arafat. No great loss: The man is a blood-stained thug. But for Israel to kill an elected quasi-head of state would make it, and its chief ally, America, appear to be international rogues.

Even worse is talk of "solving" the conflict through ethnic cleansing. An extremist segment of Israeli opinion has long pushed such an option; expulsion is the implicit if not explicit goal of most settlers. Understandable frustration over murderous suicide bombings has increased popular support for this brutal option.

It's not just frustrated Israelis who are prepared to treat Arabs as animals. Columnist Ben Shapiro writes: "If you believe that the Jewish state has a right to exist, then you must allow Israel to transfer the Palestinians and the Israeli-Arabs from Judea, Samaria, Baza and Israel proper. It's an ugly solution, but it is the only solution."

The euphemisms roll off of his tongue. "It's not genocide; it's transfer." Czechoslovakia and Poland did it to Germans after World War II; Winston Churchill thought it was a good idea. Indeed, "expelling a hostile population is a commonly used and generally effective way of preventing violent entanglements." So expel nearly five million people from their homes: it's okay, says Mr. Shapiro, because "Jews are not Nazis."

But he is advocating forced ethnic cleansing, not voluntary transfer. And that means inflicting mass hardship and death on the population being "transferred." After all, the victims aren't likely to obey an Israeli decree to willy-nilly abandon all. They will have to be forced to do so. And that means destroying their homes. Wiping out their villages. And killing at least some of them. No wonder Mr. Shapiro concludes: "It's time to stop being squeamish."

Indeed.

Look at the World War II experience, which Mr. Shapiro endorses. An estimated nine to 15 million Germans were forced from ancestral lands in Czechoslovakia, Hungary, Poland, Romania, and Yugoslavia. R.J. Rummel, author of *Death By Government*, estimates the casualty toll at between 500,000 and 3.7 million, most likely about 1.9 million, similar to the numbers offered by other analysts. Some ethnic Germans were killed before their expulsion; many died while fleeing; some died later as a result of their treatment. So horrific was the "transfer" process lauded by Mr. Shapiro that Rummel places Poland "among the megamurderers" of history.

But then, in an earlier column Mr. Shapiro wrote: "I am getting really sick of people who whine about 'civilian casualties'." For instance, the Palestinian town of Jenin, he argued, should have been leveled by air attack rather than searched by ground forces: "Civilian casualties? So be it. That might have struck a note of fear into the Palestinians."

One thing about which Mr. Shapiro is correct: ethnic cleansing is distressingly common. Large numbers of Greeks, Hungarians, and Turks were expelled in the aftermath of World War I. Nazi Germany forced out 100,000 French and one million Poles from territory that it conquered early in World War II. Various nations "transferred" Hungarians, Lithuanians, and Russians. Some 700,000 Palestinians are refugees from the Arab-Israeli conflict of 1948 (today survivors and descendents number about 4.5 million). Over the last decade Albanians, Croats, and Serbs all engaged in the practice during the Yugoslavian civil war. But as common as the practice might be, it now is uniformly condemned—except by Mr. Shapiro. In fact, the U.S.

intervened in Kosovo at least in part to stop the mistreatment of ethnic Albanians.

Still, forget the grotesque immorality of kicking roughly five million people out of their homes. And the inevitable thousands, or tens of thousands, of casualties.

In principle, separation seems the best answer. Whatever the theoretical long-term value of diverse peoples living together in harmony, it's not going to happen soon in the Mideast. Daily contact between Israeli and Palestinian only seems to provide further opportunities for the former to oppress the latter and the latter to murder the former. Better to stop the killing than to foolishly hold onto some hopeless multicultural ideal.

For this reason, a security fence makes sense. A security fence which actually separates Jew from Arab.

Unfortunately, the one being constructed by Israel mixes Jew and Arab and separates Arab from Arab. For Israel is attempting to protect a number of disparate settlements erected in the midst of Palestinian communities. The more settlers Israel includes, the more Arabs it also gains. And the less continuity there is among Palestinian lands.

Indeed, by one estimate, so far the fence is set to include 13 villages containing 12,000 Palestinians, 75 acres of greenhouses, 23 miles of irrigation pipes, and 100,000 olive and citrus trees. Those numbers could grow substantially, depending upon the path ultimately taken by the fence.

But separation will work only if it really is separation. The more Palestinians who end up on the Israeli side, the more seeds for continuing and future conflict will be sown. So long as Palestinian territory is fragmented, Arabs will live under a system of de facto Apartheid; the anger and hatred that helps give rise to suicide bombing will continue to fester. Peace will remain as distant as ever.

The basic question posed by separation on Israel's terms is: Why should the Arabs go? Israel may have taken the land through conquest, but after 36 years of occupation the land remains almost exclusively Arab. The Jewish presence is largely the result of a conscious policy of colonization.

Were the land empty to start, there would be little cause to complain. But it was not. When Israel triumphed in the 1967 six-day war, Gaza was part of Egypt and the West Bank was part of Jordan. There were essentially no Jews.

In 1978, when the Camp David accords were midwifed with the help of President Jimmy Carter, there were only about 4,000 Jewish settlers in the occupied lands. And everyone agreed that Israeli settlers had to leave the Sinai, which was returned to Egypt, to reach an agreement.

But during the 1980s the number of settlers increased six-fold. Since then the total has trebled again. With subsidies approaching $1 billion a year the number of settlers has reached about 230,000. (Most are in the West Bank, but inexplicably 6500 live in Gaza.) And it is the settlements that require a pervasive and humiliating Israeli military occupation, under which Palestinians essentially live in South African-style Bantustan "homelands." Writes Avraham Burg, former speaker of Israel's Knesset:

> It is very comfortable to be a Zionist in West Bank settlements such as Beit El and Ofra. The biblical landscape is charming. You can gaze through the geraniums and bougainvilleas and not see the occupation. Traveling on the fast highway that skirts barely a half-mile west of the Palestinian roadblocks, it's hard to comprehend the humiliating experience of the Arab who must creep for hours along the pocked, blockaded roads assigned to him. One road for the occupier, one road for the occupied.
>
> This cannot work. Even if the Arabs lower their heads and swallow their shame and anger forever, it won't work. A structure built on human callousness will inevitably collapse in on itself.

In fact, at stake is the future of Israeli democracy. Burg argues: "The prime minister should present the choices forthrightly: Jewish racism or democracy." A single state requires nearly universal willingness to live and work together. Moreover, demographics creates an ever-advancing crisis. There are roughly 5.3 million Jews in Israel and a couple hundred thousand in the occupied territories. There are 1.3 million Arabs in Israel and about 3.4 million in the Gaza and West Bank. Given respective birthrates, there soon will be more Arabs than Jews in the combined territory between the Mediterranean Sea and Jordan River. Arabs are likely to account for 60 percent of that population and nearly one-third of Israel's citizens by 2020. Notes Uri Dromi of the Israel Democracy Institute, "Either we give the Palestinians equal rights, in which case Israel ceases to be Jewish, or we don't, in which case Israel ceases to be democratic. The only way for Israel to remain both Jewish and democratic is for it to pull out of the territories." Israeli academic Shlomo Avineri makes the same point. Separation is "a counsel of despair," but "the current situation is awful. We remain in a neocolonial relationship with the Palestinians, which forces us to do things that are incompatible with being a democracy."

The conflict between Israelis and Palestinians is intractable. The murderous bombing in Haifa and the retaliation that followed seem almost routine. But there is hope. Because, as Mr. Shapiro notes, Jews are not Nazis. Israel is a humane, democratic state that stands apart from its neighbors. As a result—and to its great credit—Israel is incapable of conducting Mr. Shapiro's plan of ethnic cleansing.

Instead, the most obvious solution is separation. Not ethnic cleansing. Not expulsion. Not assassination. But separation requires dismantling Israelis settlements that dot Gaza and the West Bank. And as long as Washington backs Israel financially and politically, the future of the settlements is America's business.

October 2003

Israel—Misguided Theology Makes Bad Foreign Policy

Victorious in Iraq, President George W. Bush is now pushing for peace between Israel and the Palestinians. But even some of his own allies oppose the increasingly tattered roadmap. Lectured Gary Bauer, one-time presidential candidate and head of American Values: "The land of Israel was originally owned by God. Since He was the owner, only He could give it away. And He gave it to the Jewish people."

Actually, God still owns the land of Israel. And of America. But that isn't a reason to oppose the Bush administration's peace plan.

Interest groups have long played an important role in making American foreign policy. Rarely, however, has foreign policy rested on theology.

Even the vast majority of American Jews who support Israel do so more on cultural and ethnic than on religious grounds. But now some American Christians are attempting to turn the U.S. government into an arm of the church.

Developing an intelligent solution to the current conflict is insanely difficult. Sympathy towards Israel is understandable: there is no excuse for suicide bombings that slaughter and maim.

But Washington needs to develop a policy in the Mideast that advances America's national interests—basically staying out. Not one that advances a peculiar interpretation of Christian theology.

For instance, columnist Maggie Gallagher writes: "my support is based on an inchoate sense that if put into words would be something like this: As Christians, we just cannot sit by and let Islamic nations exterminate the Jewish people." Not that the Arabs have the capability to do so, but never mind.

Former Christian Coalition head and Georgia Republican Party state chairman Ralph Reed wrote: "there is an undeniable and powerful spiritual connection between Israel and the Christian faith. It is where Jesus was born and where he conducted his ministry."

True, but so what? This has nothing to do with the formulation of foreign policy for the secular nation of America, which represents non-Christians as well as Christians.

Another contention is that the U.S. should back whatever the Israeli government wants to do because God gave Israel to the Jews.

As Bauer explains: "The Bible is pretty clear that the land is what is called covenant land, that God made a covenant with the Jews that that would be their land forever."

Even more fervent is activist Ed McAteer: "I believe without any reservation whatsoever that every grain of sand on that piece of property called Israel belongs to the Jewish people. It's not because I happen to think that. It's not because history gives a picture of them being in and out of there. It's because God gave it to them."

Yet the premise of Christianity is that God's covenantal promises were voided by disobedience and disbelief, and thus now run to the body of Christian believers (as distinct from cultural Christians). Why assume that the nonreligious Jews who have set up a secular state in the Mideast are entitled to the same land once held by religious Jews following in the line of Moses? As Marvin Olasky, editor of *World* Magazine notes, "A biblical case can certainly be made that Israelis who are atheists have tossed away their inheritance just as Esau did."

Moreover, if the land were to belong to Jews forever, why did they lose control of it? Why assume they are supposed to get it back at this moment? And with Washington's help? It seems strange to suggest that God requires the assistance of the secular nation state of America to give the land back to the Jews.

Finally, to how much are Jews entitled? In Genesis 15 God says to Abraham: "I will give your descendents the land east of the Shihor River on the border of Egypt as far as the Euphrates River." Which suggests ownership of Jordan and chunks of Iraq, Saudi Arabia, and Syria. Perhaps Washington should simply hand over a conquered Iraq to Israel.

Another group of Christians, primarily Protestants, back Israel because they hold a dispensationalist eschatology, or end times theology. This minority view presumes a gathering of the Jewish people in the Mideast, conveniently achieved by the state of Israel, who will then be attacked by enemies; the battle of Armageddon and Christ's Second Coming eventually will follow.

In short, backing the government of Ariel Sharon, or whoever happens to be Prime Minister, is supposed to accelerate Christ's return. Says activist Ed McAteer: "When the nations gather against Israel, I believe at that time the Scriptures will be fulfilled."

Arguments over eschatology rapidly become tedious, since there is no way to prove what God actually intends. But the dispensationalist case is particularly strained. For example, for years some arm-chair prophets claimed that the old European Common Market was going to yield up the Antichrist when it hit ten countries. Current candidates for the Antichrist include the Pope, European Union President Roman Prodi, and England's Prince Charles.

In fact, the book of Revelation is best understood in the context of the Roman Empire, when it was written. Its predictions foreshadow an apocalyptic end of mankind; they do not provide an exact timeline of events.

Equally bad, this view arrogantly suggests that God needs man's help to achieve his ends. The God who reconciled mankind through the sacrifice of his son requires the assistance of Washington to get the end right?

Some people take this philosophy to truly wacky ends. In 1996 fundamentalist Christians set up a cattle breeding program in the hopes of siring a red heifer, which must be sacrificed before Jews can rebuild the third temple. They did this to encourage religious Jews to destroy the Dome of the Rock shrine and al Aqsa mosque, Islam's third most holy site, on Jerusalem's Temple Mount.

Such actions certainly would trigger all sorts of, er, interesting events, including, some Christians hope, a Biblical Armageddon. Yet how can Christians believe they are able to accelerate God's timing? Indeed, a number of Orthodox Jews are hostile to Zionism precisely because they view it as hubris for man to try to supplant God's timetable in reestablishing a Jewish state.

Another argument is that only by supporting Israel will America be blessed and protected from terrorism. For example, McAteer cites the promise that "I will bless them who bless you and curse them who curse you." Two decades ago the Rev. Jerry Falwell declared that God had been kind to America only because "America has been kind to the Jews."

Alas, it isn't easy to find the Biblical verse that explains that to bless the Jewish people or to be kind to them means to do whatever the secular government of a largely nonreligious people wants several thousand years later. This is junk theology at its worst.

Or almost worst. Sen. James Inhofe (R-Ok.) said in a speech after September 11 that "One of the reasons I believe the spiritual door was opened for an attack against the United States of America is that the policy of our government has been to ask the Israelis, and demand it with pressure, not to retaliate in a significant way against the terrorist strikes that have been launched against them."

Eh? God is punishing the American people because their government, which has long supported Israel more firmly than any other, is insufficiently pro-Israel?

Trying to speak for the creator of the universe is always a dicey proposition and I won't try. But presuming that an injunction to "bless" the Jewish people requires a secular state run by nominal Christians to offer a blank check to a secular state run by ethnic Jews is simply bizarre.

There are lots of perfectly sensible arguments to be made for supporting Israel, and Christian leaders like Olasky and Reed do so. But there is still reason to exercise judgment and balance.

Friendship does not require blind support. Indeed, the best way to bless Jews in Israel today would be to help them find a way to peace with the Palestinians—some of whom are, in fact, Christians.

Warns a statement organized by faculty members of the Knox Theological Seminary, an evangelical Christian institution:

> Lamentably, bad Christian theology is today attributing to secular Israel a divine mandate to conquer and hold Palestine, with the consequence that the Palestinian people are marginalized and regarded as virtual "Canaanites." This doctrine is both contrary to the teaching of the New Testament and a violation of the Gospel mandate. In addition, this theology puts those Christian who are urging the violent seizure and occupation of Palestinian land in moral jeopardy of their own bloodguiltiness. Are we as Christians not called to pray for and work for peace, warning both parties to this conflict that those who live by the sword will die by the sword? Only the Gospel of Jesus Christ can bring both temporal reconciliation and the hope of an eternal and heavenly inheritance to the Israeli and

> the Palestinian. Only through Jesus Christ can anyone know peace on earth.

American Christians should be concerned about American foreign policy as should all citizens. But crackpot theology is no substitute for thoughtful analysis in developing foreign policy.

September 2003

Religious Freedom in the Gulf

KUWAIT CITY, KUWAIT—The outdoor souk, or market, offered a little of everything, from cosmetics to electronics to sandals. Hanging prominently was a prayer rug picturing the Christian nativity scene. The Christ child smiled down upon Kuwaiti traders as the Muslim call to prayer blared in the background.

Americans sometimes forget how other nations restrict religious worship. In Saudi Arabia, for instance, evangelism earns a foreigner jail time; apostasy results in death for a Christian convert. Last year 14 Ethiopian and Indian Christians were imprisoned and then expelled for privately worshipping in their homes.

A welcome exception to such Muslim intolerance is Kuwait. Barely a block from my hotel on a major street sat a Catholic and a Coptic (the Egyptian branch of Orthodoxy) church. Another long block away was an evangelical church, the meeting point for several independent congregations.

Christian churches were evident in the Gulf as early as the 5th century A.D. During Ottoman times the British, Dutch, and Portuguese plied the trade routes and practiced their faiths.

In 1909 American Dr. Arthur Bennett took up residence in Kuwait, beginning a medical practice that led to construction of a hospital and church. Although the American Mission in Kuwait no longer exists, the Christian presence is bigger today, growing out of some 1.4 million foreign workers compared to just 800,000 native Kuwaitis.

There is a "very big Christian community" here, says Msgr. Francis Micallef, a Carmelite Bishop, who presides over the Catholic church. Estimates of the number of practicing Christians run upwards of a quarter million. Most are Asian, Filipinos and Indians, along with some Lebanese. "Before the war there was a large community of Palestinians and Jordanians," he adds, but "because of what happened they had to leave and have not yet come back."

Micallef figures there are between 60,000 and 80,000 Catholics. The first Carmelite arrived in 1947, to minister to foreign workers of the Kuwait Oil Company. The present church, the Holy Family Cathedral in the Desert, is a large compound combining offices and worship space, and was constructed in 1961.

During services the block surrounding the church is alive, with cars circling and parishioners streaming through the grounds. "We are free to have all our activities within the church and the church compound," says Micallef. And there's no mistaking the church: three large crosses are imbedded in the building, visible to all who drive or walk by.

There are even three private schools, run by nuns and priests but "not church schools as such." Micallef is from Malta; his eight fellow priests include Filipinos, Lebanese, and Indians.

The adjoining St. Mark Coptic church is smaller, but still busy. The sanctuary holds up to 1000, forcing Theophane Anba Bishoy and two other priests to run multiple services to meet the needs of an estimated 60,000 Coptics.

Offices and living quarters are upstairs. "It's a small space, so we try to use it as effectively as we can," Bishoy explains. His church's activities also extend beyond church grounds: during a recent festival one evening 10,000 to 12,000 people attended outside events.

Nearby sits the National Evangelical Church, the heir to the American Mission chapel. The sprawling complex hosts several brick and stucco buildings, with a parking lot across the street.

It is the most diverse religious community, made up of 15 different ethnic groups, ranging from English to Nepalese to Korean to Arabian. The church operates as an "umbrella to every congregation," explains Rev. Rafik Farouk, an Egyptian associate pastor. There is even an English-language Anglican minister.

What evangelical church could exist without peddling Christian kitsch? The Bible Society in the Gulf runs a bookstore within the compound. Mixed in with the Bibles, study guides, and devotional tapes are key chains, pens, mugs, baseball caps, and "Left Behind" videos. Business was brisk when I stopped by.

Some problems are international and universal. One poster warns members to be alert for terrorism and to "maintain a low profile as much as possible."

There are also more mundane concerns. States one note on the bulletin board: "Please switch off your mobile phone/pager before entering the sanctuary. Thank you. And God bless you."

Kuwait remains a Muslim country, of course. Some blocks host two mosques and the Grand Mosque alone covers a square block.

Kuwaiti cleric Sulaiman Abu Ghaith turned up as a spokesman for Osama bin Laden.

But Ghaith's activities were so shocking precisely because his case is so extreme. Moreover, as in the U.S., much of the dominant worship is formalistic, not social. Business trumped devotion as deal-making continued at the souk while the call to prayer wafted across the city.

When four women swathed in black burqas walked by, a Kuwaiti companion commented acerbically to me on the "group of batmans." It was not unusual to see women in this most conservative dress shopping at a cosmetics stall in the market or a fashionable clothing store in the mall. The conservative dress often reflected cultural, not religious, values, I was told.

Islamist influence in parliament—higher education has just been segregated by sex—is of concern to liberal Kuwaitis as well as Christians, but most of the former with whom I talked attributed it more to the government's weakness than extremists' influence.

Despite the significant influence of Islamist and tribalist members in parliament, so far Christians have not been targeted, as they have been in other Muslim societies. "We have very good relations with the authorities," says Micallef. "We feel that we are respected and not only respected, but also welcomed."

Bishoy confirms that judgment: we have "no problem" with the government. Only three or four of the seven churches have official permission to operate, "but there is no problem for the others," he says.

Indeed, while the Coptic church might have to move due to a new road project, the government has promised "to find a solution." His office sported photos of the Emir and other Kuwaiti officials; Farouk's wall hosted a photo of an ecumenical delegation meeting with a cabinet minister.

As a minority, Christian leaders work together. "We have an ecumenical spirit and we meet regularly," Micallef explains. "We try to be supportive of one another." Observes Farouk: his church "works with every congregation in Kuwait, and not just Kuwait only, but in the entire Gulf."

"Everything is free here," he says. At the church you "see lots of people over here, many nationalities, many ethnic groups."

There is one significant limit, however. The churches minister to Christian believers; they do not proselytize, that is, seek out new converts.

"No, no, we don't even think of doing that," says Micallef. "We respect Muslim sensitivities and we don't want to give the sense of being missionaries." Lest there be any misunderstanding, Micallef adds: "We are here to cater to the spiritual needs of Christians here. If there were no Christians here, we wouldn't be here."

Bishoy echoes these sentiments. "We prefer not to go out to Muslims, to make problems for us." It is enough, he says, "just to try to serve our own people."

For a church built on Christ's admonition to make disciples of all the nations, and which grew through evangelism, this is no small concession.

The restriction on spreading the Good News seems to bother the National Evangelical Church the most. We are to minister to "Christian people only," says Farouk, "But any man can come here to ask, and we will respond." And many Kuwaitis have come to ask questions, he adds.

The church's sentiments are obvious from the back of its welcome sign, seen only by those leaving the compound. It cites Mark 16:15: "Go into all the world and preach the Gospel to every creature."

It's an irritating restriction. But it is rare to find a Muslim country where Christians are not routinely discriminated against, oppressed, and even killed. Kuwait is a relative oasis of freedom compared to some of its neighbors.

October 2002

A version of this article was originally published in the Wall Street Journal, *August 16, 2002.*

The Lure of Lebanese Quicksand

Two decades ago Ronald Reagan committed his greatest foreign policy blunder: intervening in Lebanon's civil war. After Muslim opponents of the bedraggled Lebanese government targeted U.S. diplomats and Marines to deadly effect, President Reagan "redeployed" American military forces to ships offshore and sailed away. Now the Bush administration risks sliding back into the Lebanese imbroglio.

The bloody bombing murder of former prime minister Rafiq Hariri has led to calls for the U.S. to force Damascus, which retains paramount influence in its smaller neighbor, to withdraw its 14,000 occupying troops. Some Syrian exiles are even circulating a petition calling for regime change, which in practice would require an American invasion.

The President's rhetoric has been measured, but the administration has withdrawn the U.S. ambassador, Margaret Scobey, and is threatening to expand sanctions beyond those embodied in last year's Syrian Accountability Act. Limiting the movement of Syrian diplomats, freezing Syrian assets, and banning investment and trade are possibilities.

Lebanon turned from a tolerant commercial oasis of stability into a fulcrum of hellish conflict when it descended into civil war in 1975 after the carefully crafted Christian-Muslim power-sharing arrangement collapsed. The conflict was complicated by Syrian intervention with as many as 42,000 soldiers over the years, the Israeli invasion in response to Palestinian terrorism, and the slaughter of Palestinian refugees by Lebanese falangists allied with Israel.

The U.S. entered Lebanon in 1982 along with France and Italy, nominally as a peace-keeper. In fact, however, Washington acted as an ally of the minority Christian government that ruled little more than Beirut. And Washington became an active combatant—before the bombings of the U.S. embassy and Marine Corps barracks.

Washington then sharply stepped up military operations. On February 18, 1984 the Washington Post headlined an article "Pentagon Keeps Details on Shelling Secret." It reported on "the heaviest U.S. naval bombardment since the Vietnam war" and widespread concern about civilian deaths. A Pentagon spokesman acknowledged that "there may have been some [civilian casualties] and that would be unfortunate."

Who was right in the underlying civil war didn't matter at that stage. Nor did America's professed good intentions. Violent antagonism towards the U.S. was inevitable.

There was no compelling reason for Washington to have intervened. The U.S. had no serious security interests in Lebanon; America's political concerns were mostly indirect, through Israel. The civil conflict was tragic, but beyond Washington's control.

Yet the U.S. became an active combatant in the bitter fight. Thus, the barracks bombing, which killed 241 Marines, cannot be considered an act of terrorism, in contrast to the World Trade Center attack.

Rather, it was an assault on military forces of what was seen as an enemy power that had wreaked devastation on local Druze and Muslim communities. The horrific bombings demonstrated that America can't go to war and then claim immunity from retaliation on the battlefield.

In one of his finest moments, President Reagan retreated. He never admitted how badly he had blundered, but he obviously recognized his mistake. Although he talked tough, he soon brought U.S. forces home.

The Lebanese civil war eventually burned out in 1990. Since then the country has enjoyed a substantial renaissance, much of it presided over by former premier Hariri. Once friendly to Syria, he broke with Damascus last year and was expected to do well in upcoming parliamentary elections. His murder has stoked fears of renewed conflict.

What should the U.S. do?

Reagan's decision to pull out of Lebanon was widely applauded at home, but derided by some as immoral abandonment of a suffering people and appeasement of Islamic terrorists. And it has become part of the litany of supposed examples of weakness that encouraged Osama Bin Laden to attack the U.S.

For instance, Michael Young, opinion editor of Beirut's Daily Star newspaper, denounced Reagan for having "abandoned the Lebanese to a long night of Syrian hegemony, to an extended period of militia rule, and to six more years of civil war." Former CIA Director James Woolsey complains that Washington "ran" after the barracks bombing, which, along with incidents such as not aiding the Kurds and Shiites against Saddam Hussein and leaving Somalia after the killing of 18

Army Rangers in Mogadishu, created a perception of cowardice that encouraged anti-American terrorists.

Apparently both Young and Woolsey believe the U.S. should have escalated its military involvement, crushed opposing Muslim and Druze forces, occupied the entire country, sorted out the complicated interests of competing factions, reordered the political system, and engaged in good old-fashioned nation-building. The mind boggles.

At least in Iraq most of population is pleased to have been freed from Saddam Hussein's rule. The majority of Lebanese would have not have welcomed a U.S. invasion, and many would have violently opposed an American occupation. Indeed, many Lebanese Druze and Muslims who had suffered from the depredations of Palestinian guerrillas quickly turned against Israeli forces after originally welcoming them.

Thus, Lebanese would have not have been spared six more years of war. Rather, the conflict simply would have taken a different turn, with America involved. U.S. soldiers and Marines would have died for nothing that any family member would have recognized as an important, let alone vital, American interest.

And ultimately Washington would have been faced with the same issue as in 1984: how to get out without losing face? Given the lack of any reasonable hope that an American invasion and occupation could have fixed Lebanon, let alone done so at acceptable cost, the "abandonment" and "appeasement" would only have been postponed.

Twenty years later Washington's options look little better. Diplomatic and economic pressure might moderate Syria's behavior, but today the U.S. should be most concerned with choking off any support for Iraqi insurgents operating from Syrian territory.

Moreover, Damascus obviously has long viewed Lebanon as a key security interest. It won't abandon its dominant position lightly.

Nor is regime change going to come through any combination of carrots and sticks, short of military action. The dubious experience of the Iraqi National Congress demonstrates how difficult it is for Washington to create an effective opposition movement, no matter how lavish the subsidies.

War would be a bad option at any time, but especially when U.S. forces are badly stretched by the brutal and apparently still growing insurgency in Iraq. Americans are patriotic, but there likely is a limit on how many wars they will volunteer to fight. Indeed, Gen. Richard Myers, Chairman of the Joint Chiefs of Staff, has warned that even now the U.S. would have trouble quickly responding to an emergency in Iran or North Korea.

And at least Baghdad looked like it might pose a threat to the U.S. Syria does not. Asks Martin Indyk of the Brookings Institution: "Are we ready to have people die for the sake of Lebanon's freedom from Syria?"

Moreover, acting against Damascus would likely worsen the problem of terrorism. Serious analysts warned the Bush administration that military action against Iraq would inflame antagonism towards America. Now CIA Director Porter J. Goss tells the Senate Select Committee on Intelligence that "Islamic extremists are exploiting the Iraqi conflict to recruit new anti-U.S. jihadists." War with Syria would do more of the same.

Damascus is an ugly regime, though it probably does not quite meet "Axis of Evil" standards. And that is the case whether or not it had anything to do with the assassination of Rafiq Hariri.

In any case, thugs the Baathist rulers in Damascus may be, but threats to America they are not. Washington should confront Syria, but over the activities of Iraqi insurgents, not the presence of Syrian troops in Lebanon. The Lebanese tragedy never seems to end, but the U.S. already has enough wars to fight.

February 2005

Saudi Arabia—Befriending Saudi Princes: A High Price for a Dubious Alliance

For a time last year rumors circulated in Washington that Saudi Arabia might ask America to withdraw its troops from the Gulf kingdom. Naturally, both Washington and Riyadh quickly affirmed their commitment to the relationship. Similar stories arose earlier this year, as Washington prepared for war against Iraq. Again the denials came quickly. But Saudi Arabia has always been among Washington's more dubious allies. Once Saddam Hussein is removed from power Washington should remove its forces from and close its bases in Saudi Arabia.

The House of Saud has long leaned towards the West. King Abdul Al Aziz Al Saud, who fathered 44 sons, is the fount of today's royal family, including King Fahd bin Abdul Aziz. King Fahd suffered a series of strokes beginning in 1995, however, and his half-brother, Crown Prince Abdullah bin Abdul Aziz, now largely runs the government.

Saudi Arabia would be unimportant but for the massive oil deposits sitting beneath its seemingly endless deserts. There have been tensions with the West, especially at the time of the oil boycott against the West in 1973 and 1974. However, most attention has focused on defending the Gulf from other potential invaders.

To contain Saddam Hussein's Iraq, America backed its military units in Turkey and carrier forces in the Persian Gulf with about 5000 air force personnel in Saudi Arabia as part of the Southern Watch command, comprising aircraft ranging from F-15s and F-16s to C-130s and KC-135s. Another 1300 military personnel and civilian contractors work with Saudi National Guard. No temporary response to Saddam Hussein's aggression, America's presence has a "permanent feel," as Howard Schneider of the *Washington Post* put it.

Although the relationship between Riyadh and Washington is close, it has rarely been easy. For American administrations that loudly promote democracy in such diverse nations as Burma, China, Cuba, Iraq, and Zimbabwe, the alliance with Saudi Arabia has been a deep embarrassment.

Saudi Arabia is an absolute monarchy, an almost medieval theocracy, with power concentrated in the hands of senior royalty and wealth spread amongst some 7000 Al Saud princes (some analysts number the royals at 30,000). Political opposition and even criticism are forbidden. In practice there are few procedural protections for anyone arrested or charged by the government; the semi-autonomous religious police, or Mutawaa'in, also intimidate and detain citizens and foreigners alike. The government may invade homes and violate privacy whenever it chooses; travel is limited. Women are covered, cloistered, and confined, much like they were in the Taliban's Afghanistan.

Most ugly, though, is the religious totalitarianism enforced by Riyadh. Non-Muslim worship as well as proselytizing is prohibited for citizens and foreigners alike. Conversion means apostasy, which is punishable by death. Yet in its most recent report on religious persecution, the State Department declined to censure Riyadh, preferring cooperate with Saudi authorities—this after Saudi Defense Minister Prince Sultan said that the outcry of "fanatics" would not alter his country's persecution of other faiths.

Moreover, up to 100 American women and children have been essentially held captive in Saudi Arabia, denied their husband's or father's permission to travel. Some of the victims have been kidnapped despite valid U.S. custody orders granted while both parents were residing in America. Riyadh responds that this is a matter of Islamic, not civil, law, so there is nothing it can do. Washington's efforts to aid its own citizens have been anemic at best, dependent upon the initiative of individual ambassadors and often undercut by the State Department. So these U.S. citizens continue to suffer often brutal Saudi hospitality.

Thuggish behavior alone is rarely enough to preclude diplomatic relations, but it should discourage Washington from affirmatively embracing the Saudi regime, even in the name of stability. Moreover, U.S. policies have identified Washington with the Saudi kleptocracy. As Richard Perle of the American Enterprise Institute observes: "We are associated with regimes that are corrupt and illegitimate." Americans are now paying for that association, which has helped make the U.S. a target of terrorists. A desire to end America's support for the corrupt regime in Riyadh and expel U.S. forces from the Gulf appears to be one of Osama bin Laden's main goals.

The Saudi ruling elite is also paying for its repression and links to Washington. With 70 percent of government revenues (and 40 percent of GDP) derived from oil sales, the long-term drop in energy prices has caused economic pain in Saudi Arabia; unemployment is now estimated to be at least 15 percent overall, and 20 percent for those under 30. (The median age is 17.) That has helped generate unrest, but the discontented feel helpless to initiate political change.

Soaring dissatisfaction with the regime due to slumping revenues and a slowing economy has merged with criticism of America. Many Saudis are angry with U.S. support for the House of Saud; many students irrationally blame America for their economic problems. Additional irritants are Washington's support of Israel, attacks on Iraq, and air strikes in Afghanistan. Admiration for Saudi terrorist Osama bin Laden is evident even among those who dislike his austere Islamic vision. Worries Richard Murphy, a one-time U.S. ambassador to Saudi Arabia now with the Council on Foreign Relations: "we've worn out our welcome on the popular level, though not with the leadership."

With no political outlet to voice discontent, criticism tends to be expressed through religious leaders. Radical free-lancers have developed a widespread following: 15 of the 19 hijackers of September 11 were from Saudi Arabia. One Saudi businessman told the *Wall Street Journal*: "Many young people are disgruntled and disenchanted with our society's openness to the West and U.S. foreign policy."

But that leadership has proved wary of aiding the U.S. despite direct attacks on Americans. The 1996 bomb attack on the Khobar Towers barracks in Dharan killed 19 Americans and wounded another 372. However, U.S. efforts to investigate the bombing were hamstrung by the Saudis, who refused to turn over relevant information and or to extradite any of the 13 Saudis indicted by an American grand jury.

In the same year, the Saudis refused, despite U.S. urging, to take custody of bin Laden from Sudan. In 1998 bin Laden and several other extremist Muslim leaders issued a manifesto calling for a holy war to drive the U.S. from Islamic lands. Even so, U.S. officials were unable "to get anything at all from King Fahd" to challenge bin Laden's financial network, charged John O'Neill, a former FBI official involved with counter-terrorism who died in the 9/11 attack on the World Trade Center, where he was security chief.

Riyadh's reluctance to risk popular displeasure by identifying with Washington continued even after the deaths of three thousand Americans on September 11. Despite public protestations that all is well between the two governments, Bush administration officials privately acknowledged that Riyadh was not as cooperative as hoped. Saudi Arabia refused to run "traces," involving background investigations, of its citizens who committed the atrocities of September 11 and supply passenger lists of those on flights to America. Riyadh resisted blocking terrorist funds flowing through supposed charities (if the money goes awry, the regime explains, it does so outside of Saudi Arabia).

The Saudis have, it is true, allowed use of the operations center at Prince Sultan Air Base, near Riyadh, in the Iraqi war, but Saudi Arabia joined its neighbors in ostentatiously announcing that no foreign troops would use Saudi facilities to stage attacks. Moreover, the regime does everything possible to hide the presence of Americans from its own citizens: U.S. soldiers are not even allowed to take photos on base that reveal the photos were taken on base, lest a Saudi see evidence of America's military presence. Unfortunately, the refusal to defend cooperation with the West encourages the growth of extremist sentiments.

Still, the lack of a public endorsement pales in comparison to Riyadh's support for the very Islamic fundamentalism that threatens to consume the regime in Riyadh as well as to murder more Americans in future terrorist attacks.

Riyadh's strategy has been to buy off everyone. It long subsidized Arab governments and guerrilla movements at war with Israel, and opposed the 1979 peace treaty between Egypt and Israel. The regime was, along with Pakistan, the primary financial backer of the Taliban in Afghanistan, which provided sanctuary for bin Laden and his training camps. It is widely believed that Saudi businessmen have made contributions to bin Laden in an attempt to purchase protection. There are serious charges of financial support from some of the Saudi royal family for bin Laden's al Qaeda network.

Even today it is not clear how much has changed. Riyadh has issued new rules governing Saudi banks and charities, but the nub is effective enforcement. Moreover, al-Qaeda documents seized last year were recently released in Washington. They noted the role of so-called charities in Saudi Arabia in moving terrorist money and listed 20 Saudi members of "the Golden Chain," major financial backers of the terrorist organization. The families deny any connection.

Such disclosures might encourage more lawsuits from September 11 victims against Riyadh. And the Saudis now know that their extensive U.S. investments, $60 billion in New York banks alone, are potentially at risk. In early March a lawsuit against the Saudi royal family for helping spirit a husband and his money out of America to avoid paying a divorce settlement resulted in a $216 million judgment against the House of Saud.

America's problems with Riyadh run even deeper. The Saudi state, run by royals who often flaunt their libertinism, enforces the extreme Wahhabi form of Islam at home and subsidizes its practice abroad. Wahhabism is thought to dominate as many as 80 percent of the mosques in America. Within this sect, hostile to modernity and the West, political extremism and support for terrorism have flourished. The threat now reaches beyond the Middle East to Indonesia, Malaysia, and even the Philippines. If past patterns repeat themselves, Riyadh will soon be funding fundamentalist madrassahs in Iraq. Despite some reassuring English-language promises from Saudi officials regarding educational reform, Steven Stalinsky of the Middle East Media Research Institute notes that "There have been many more recent statements from high-ranking Saudi government officials explaining in Arabic that thay have no intention of changing their curriculum."

In short, "these are SOBs who are barely even *our* SOBs," complains *National Review* editor Rich Lowry. By any normal assessment, Americans should care little if the House of Saud fell, as have other illegitimate monarchies, such as Iran's Peacock throne. Except for one thing. Saudi Arabia has oil.

Riyadh naturally presents itself as a benefactor to the West, willing to stabilize supply in times of crisis. It has been pumping an extra two million barrels daily over its official OPEC quota and indicated its willingness to go higher, depending upon the extent of damage to the Iraqi fields and related supply disruptions. However, Saudi Arabia is the primary beneficiary of doing so: the government is expected to collect an extra $28 billion this year, a nice windfall which will wipe out the budgeted $10 billion deficit. One will look far and wide to find evidence that Riyadh has ever sacrificed its interest to benefit the U.S.

As for using the oil weapon to hurt America, Riyadh would do far more damage to itself than the U.S. Saudi Arabia is ill-equipped to do much more than inconvenience the West.

Saudi Arabia has the world's largest proven reserves, but only accounts for roughly ten percent of global production. It could have a dramatic impact on prices only if the other Gulf states joined with it, an unlikely prospect, especially once Iraqi oil again comes on line.

Nor would the overthrow of the monarchy likely limit Saudi sales. After all, only oil gives Riyadh influence, something that would be equally obvious to a fundamentalist regime. Indeed, Iran's mullahs have increased production since seizing power. Further, targeted boycotts are impossible with a uniform product in a global market. The celebrated embargo of 1973-1974 actually had little impact on production.

To the extent the existing or a new regime pumped less oil in order to raise prices, other producers would reap most of the benefits. And any price hike would accelerate the discovery and development of new petroleum fields, ranging from West Africa to Russia to the Caspian Basin. Sharply higher prices would bring forth new supplies in America as well: abundant oil is likely lying beneath a small section of the Arctic National Wildlife Reserve on America's outer continental shelf. In fact, total proven world oil reserves have risen steadily over the last two decades, even as prices have dropped, because of man's improved ability to find and develop existing supplies.

In short, Saudi Arabia needs America more than America needs Saudi Arabia.

To mention Saudi Arabia's shortcomings or suggest that the regime's survival is not vital to the U.S. makes policymakers in Washington and Riyadh nervous. In particular, the House of Saud doesn't take criticism well.

However, the U.S. should reassess the current Washington-Riyadh axis. The American commitment to the Saudi royal family is a moral blemish and a practical danger. Overthrowing Saddam Hussein ends the threat of Iraqi aggression, and Iran is unlikely to act, bedeviled by a growing opposition at home and an enhanced American presence in Iraq. Moreover, the prospect of American disengagement would, like a hanging, help greatly concentrate the mind. Such a possibility would also increase pressure on the Gulf states to forge defensive relationships with surrounding powers, most notably Egypt and Turkey, and to inaugurate serious political reform to generate a popular willingness to defend the incumbent regimes.

Proposals for political reform recently have received at least modest encouragement from Crown Prince Abdullah. But, in practice, not much has changed, and a U.S. military presence in which American servicemen are largely locked on base does nothing to encourage liberalization. If anything, the security tie works the wrong way, inflaming anti-Western sentiments by tying the guardians of Mecca and Medina to the U.S.

Indeed, as the war against Iraq approached, the State Department warned American travelers to be careful visiting the Kingdom and to consider leaving, unusual guidance for visiting a supposed solid friend. And popular hostility towards America rose during the conflict. For this reason, Riyadh continues to distance itself from Washington. It even bizarrely suggested a ceasefire as U.S. forces approached Baghdad.

Moreover, at least some members of the royal family are looking forward to putting some distance between the two countries. Saudi Deputy Defense minister Prince Khaled bin Sultan observes: America's troops "are there for a purpose, and in accordance with U.N. resolutions." He adds: "Once the Iraqi problem is solved, and the destruction of the weapons of mass destruction is completed, then I'm sure that the restructuring of the presence and the numbers will be discussed."

Washington shouldn't wait for Riyadh to act, however. There were many causes to September 11, but a contributing factor was America's willingness to make common cause with the morally decrepit, theocratic monarchy in Riyadh. Observed Deputy Defense Secretary Paul Wolfowitz, the price of the commitment has been "far more than money." America's presence "in the holy land of Saudi Arabia" along with the bombing of Iraq were "part of the containment policy that has been Osama bin Laden's principal recruiting device, even more than the other grievances he cites." It is time to disable this recruiting tool. Once the firing in Iraq has stopped, the troops in Saudi Arabia should come home. Eliminating Iraq as a threat to regional stability allows Washington to adjust its objectives and presence elsewhere. There no longer will be cause to support illegitimate and unpopular regimes such as that in Saudi Arabia.

April 2003

Turkey—Democracy for Whom?

With the peace in Iraq proving to be as messy as the war, the Bush administration has spent a year desperately trying to get other countries to send troops for occupation duty. Brazil, Egypt, and India said no; Japan temporized, before sending in 550 soldiers for "humanitarian" duty. The kidnapping of one Filipino truck driver caused the Philippines to withdraw 56 soldiers in a rush. In August Thailand began pulling out its small contingent.

Notably, no Muslim nation—outside of minuscule Albania, which sent in forces with no equipment—has sent troops to patrol Iraq. Pakistan, with jihadists active in its western provinces and multiple assassination attacks on President Pervez Musharraf, said no. A Saudi initiative went no where. And Turkey, with one of the largest and perhaps the most competent military in the region, outside of Israel, is a source of contract trucking services, nothing more.

None of this should come as a surprise. What is surprising is how an administration supposedly full of "adults" has proved to be so ineffective in enlisting allied support. It is bad enough to jump into an unnecessary war. But to bungle the peace at every turn is almost criminal.

Last fall Secretary of State Colin Powell went calling in Turkey. After much hemming and hawing, and Washington's approval of $8.5 billion in loans in September 2003, the Erdogan government recommended dispatch of as many as 10,000 soldiers. Parliament then said yes, despite strong popular opposition, avoiding a repeat of the body's surprise refusal to allow U.S. military action against Iraq from Turkish territory. Then came difficult negotiations on turning Ankara's promise into boots on the ground. In the end, Iraqi opposition derailed the plan.

The Bush administration's bid for Ankara's help reflected quite a change from just a few months before, when Deputy Defense Secretary Paul Wolfowitz dismissed potential Turkish contributions to the occupation. "I wouldn't rule out a role for Turkey, but I think right now we are looking to those people who were with us in the coalition to build a core of the peacekeeping function." Indeed, he added, "My experience is if you talk to Iraqis, almost every one of their neighbors, including Turkey, is viewed from a historical perspective that is not always positive."

But that was when the administration was talking about cutting its occupation forces to 30,000 by the end of the year. Talk about hysterically high hopes. Just a few months later Bush administration officials, if not the president himself, were debating the need to increase the U.S. garrison in the face of continuing guerrilla activity and urban terrorism. And that meant pushing even Turkey to contribute troops.

So much for relying on original members of the coalition. So much for caring about what the Iraqis think.

Alas, Washington found that it had to pay a high price for Turkish help. Ankara has a keen sense of Turkish national interests. That is why it long has treated its Kurds with brutality approaching that used by Saddam Hussein in Iraq. In fact, after Washington's victory Turkey dispatched special forces to the city of Kirkut in U.S.-occupied Iraq to assassinate the Kurdish interim governor. Turkey denied the plot after Washington captured (and eventually released) 11 Turkish soldiers.

But the Bush administration reportedly promised to suppress the Kurdistan Workers Party, today known as KADEK, which has long fought for ethnic autonomy. In Turkey's view that means military action, if necessary. Which would mean involving Washington in a guerrilla war that has cost nearly 40,000 lives over the last two decades. And involving the U.S. on the opposite side from its position backing Kurdish autonomy under Saddam Hussein.

In short, Turkey, no less than, say, France, wanted to constrain America's options. The Turks just weren't as obvious about doing so.

Moreover, it was not clear that Turkish troops would actually have helped stabilize Iraq. The American-appointed Iraqi Governing Council objected to the plan and Kurdish leaders threatened to fight if Turkish soldiers are lodged in the north. In turn, Ankara threatened to respond sharply to any attacks on its forces, which would further inflame hostility—Kurds understandably see little difference between oppressive Turkish and Iraqi rule.

That Washington did not make sure everyone was in agreement before publicly pushing for the Turkish deployment is evidence of incredible ignorance or incompetence or both. But better the initiative was stillborn than that Iraq was plunged into a Kurdish-Turkish war.

The issue also brought into sharp relief the tension surrounding U.S. support for democracy around the world. The interim Iraqi Governing

Council opposed the presence of Turkish troops. What if the future permanent elected government rejects the presence of American forces and bases?

The Bush administration's rhetoric suggests that it should live with that result. But in practice Washington seems much less enthusiastic about the results of democracy.

Like in Turkey.

In 2002 Deputy Defense Secretary Paul Wolfowitz cited Turkey as "a model for the Muslim world's aspirations for democratic progress and prosperity." He went on to add: "What is fundamental is Turkey's democratic character."

Yet the U.S. has been less happy with the results of Turkish democracy. Negotiations between America and Turkey over aid in the war against Iraq took on the appearance of haggling over a carpet at Istanbul's Grand Bazaar. Turkey demanded lots of cash to let America open a second front against Iraq. Washington demanded a discount before saying yes.

Then the unexpected happened. Turkey's ruling party split while the opposition stood firm against. In parliament the measure won a majority of those voting, but not the required absolute majority.

As a proponent of democracy, Washington should have been understanding. Instead, for a moment Turkey joined France on America's least liked list. Congress threatened to cut off aid; the Bush administration complained because civilians made the decision.

Indeed, Deputy Secretary Wolfowitz made the rather astounding assertion that the military did not play "a leadership role" on the issue. The fact that the vast majority of the Turkish population opposed the war didn't matter. In the same interview, with CNN Turkey, Wolfowitz proclaimed that "we believe in democracy" and that Ankara should "look into its democratic soul." But, he said shortly after the vote, the government "didn't quite know what it was doing." The result was a "big, big mistake."

The problem, in Wolfowitz's view, was that the military should have said that "it was in Turkey's interest to support the United States" in Iraq. But members of parliament were hardly unaware of the stakes. They knew that billions in ill-disguised bribes hung in the balance.

Wolfowitz stated: "I'm not suggesting that you [the military] get involved in politics at all." But what else could have been the implications of his remarks for a country where the military has formally overthrown and more often maneuvered to pressure and overthrow democratically elected governments and dismantle popular political parties? In January 2003 there was a public spat between Prime Minister Abdullah Gul and the chief of the Turkish General Staff, General Hilmi Ozkok, over the expulsion of seven soldiers for "fundamentalist activities." Although purges for Islamic activism are not new, these soldiers were allowed no right of appeal.

In fact, Turkey's military has long played a leadership role in that nation. Unfortunately.

While the Bush administration wants the military to play a larger role in making Turkish policy, last year Turkey's parliament approved a measure reducing the military's control of the National Security Council, which influences most domestic as well as foreign policy decisions. The NSC will have a reduced role, and the body's secretary general will be nominated by the Prime Minister rather than the chief of the Turkish General Staff; in fact, Ankara recently installed the first civilian in that position. Moreover, legislators will be able to review the defense budget, once the military's exclusive prerogative. The reforms are necessary if Ankara hopes to join the European Union, but they also are likely to transform Turkish politics.

Thus, Washington should step carefully. Warns Omer Taspinar, a Visiting Fellow at the Saban Center for Middle East Policy, "the current mood in Turkey is still very anti-American." Appearing to range itself against the democratization of Turkish life could only worsen Washington's image.

The Bush administration's ambivalence towards democracy is evident in its attitude towards other U.S. allies. For instance, Pakistan's Musharraf took power in a coup and conducted a set of fixed elections to provide a veneer of respectability. But the absence there of the sort of democracy that Washington is attempting to build in Iraq is not viewed as a problem.

Musharraf, Wolfowitz told the New York Times in 2002, has "shown an impressive level of fortitude in facing" down Muslim extremism. Indeed, "No leader has taken greater risks in the struggle against terrorism," Wolfowitz later added. Musharraf's willingness to ignore popular sentiments was "good for him and his country as well as for us and our country."

That might be the case. But obviously Pakistan is a country where the U.S. does not value democracy, and especially "popular sentiments." As a result, "The Pakistanis are doing everything they can" to cooperate against Islamic terrorism, said Wolfowitz.

In fact, that's not obviously true. Musharraf seems to be playing both sides of the street. However, Karachi is certainly more helpful today than it was before September 11.

There's nothing wrong in emphasizing Musharraf's willingness to cooperate. But it does come at a cost, undercutting those democratic values that Wolfowitz and the rest of the administration claim to value.

Does Washington like democracy abroad? Turkey "is a model for the Muslim world's aspirations for democratic progress," Wolfowitz proclaimed in 2002. "What is fundamental is Turkey's democratic character: It changes its leaders at the ballot box."

That is how a moderate Islamic government came to power and a democratically elected Islamic parliament came to reject America's request for military aid in the war against Iraq. And how the same body could have refused the government's proposal to augment America's occupation. Which is why the Bush administration's push for the Turkish military to play "a leadership role" risked damaging a democracy that is supposed to be "a model for the Muslim" world.

Throughout the Mideast, and especially in Iraq, Washington must decide whether it values indigenous democracy or geopolitical support more. The choice isn't easy to make, but America's experience with countries ranging from Egypt to Pakistan and especially Turkey demonstrates that it is a choice that, unfortunately, often must be made.

August 2004

CHAPTER NINE

Iraq

Bombing Without End

"We bomb, therefore we bomb," seems to be Washington's policy towards Iraq. Ten years of sanctions and military strikes have failed to tame or oust Saddam Hussein. Yet the Bush administration thinks only of doing more of the same.

U.S. policy in the Persian Gulf has long been a pernicious muddle. A half century ago Washington helped install the Shah of Iran, whose thuggery eventually spawned an Islamic revolution which treated America as the "Great Satan."

After the humiliating seizure of the U.S. embassy, Washington was happy to aid Iraq's Saddam Hussein when he struck at his seemingly disorganized neighbor. Iran and Iraq essentially fought to a draw after years of horrific combat. Then Iraq did what Washington was afraid Iran was going to do—move on its Gulf neighbors. Saddam swallowed Kuwait and eyed Saudi Arabia.

The Gulf monarchies are ugly bastions of privilege in which antiquated royal families leech off their poor subjects. Saudi Arabia doesn't enjoy even the hint of liberalism evident in Kuwait: Riyadh is essentially a totalitarian dictatorship which enforces Islam in order to preempt political change.

But the various sheikdoms and emirates have oil, so the U.S. intervened to make the region safe for monarchy. Washington, aided by allied states, restored the Emir's regime and wrecked the Iraqi military.

Yet an enfeebled Iraq raised the worrisome prospect of a resurgent Iran—which is why Washington previously had backed Iraq. So President George Bush and many of the officials who now people his son's administration left Iraq unconquered.

Washington established economic sanctions, created an inspections regime to forestall development of weapons of mass destruction, and imposed a "no-fly" zone throughout much of Iraq to inhibit military action against Shiite and Kurdish rebels. The U.S. also backed a motley assemblage of Iraqi dissidents while hoping for a coup.

A decade later, American policy has failed.

Sanctions have killed hundreds of thousands of Iraqi civilians but proved to be only a minor inconvenience to Saddam. Iraq has ended U.N. inspections.

The U.S. (backed by Great Britain) continues to regularly bomb Iraq, yet America's attempt to protect Iraqi Kurds contrasts with America's support for brutal Turkish suppression of Kurds in that country. And factional infighting has doomed Kurdish resistance, irrespective of the no-fly zone.

Washington's support for other opponents of the regime—Congress voted $97 million for the London-based Iraqi National Congress three years ago—has been even less successful. Saddam has hung many an alleged coup plotter from the nearest Baghdad lamp post.

The lack of results has sapped support from allied states. France and Russia have tired of the ineffectual containment game, and hope to profit from renewed commerce. Even some Mideast states, including Egypt and Turkey, have begun a wary dance with Iraq. They rained criticism down upon the U.S. even as Secretary of State Colin Powell was preparing to visit the region in February.

So now what? Explained President George W. Bush: "We will continue to enforce the no-fly zones. The no-fly zones are enforced on a daily basis. It is a part of a strategy, and until that strategy is changed, if it is changed at all, we will continue to enforce the no-fly zone."

That's really helpful. The administration has a strategy. The strategy has manifestly failed. But the administration will continue to pursue that strategy unless it changes that strategy.

Curiously, the Washington Post argued that the latest strikes "present a welcome reinvigoration of an existing policy that had been allowed to slide." The administration should formulate a new policy, the paper opined, but at least "the Bush administration is paying attention" to the threat, which is "a good start."

Unfortunately, such a reassessment seems likely to only reinforce past policy. One Bush official told the Washington Post that he favored "an exponential escalation."

Doing more of the same doesn't deserve to be called a strategy. Even many of those serving Saddam would probably like to see him overthrown. But congressional resolutions and presidential proclamations won't make it happen.

Anthony Cordesman of the Center for Strategic and International Studies was reduced to endorsing the attacks because "America cannot afford to show any weakness in dealing with Mr. Hussein." Iraq must be contained militarily, and that, apparently, means haphazardly bombing forces and installations that in no way threaten Iraq's neighbors.

After all, "If Mr. Hussein created a successful military sanctuary in the no-fly zones, this would be seen as a symbol of his growing strength. If he then succeeded in shooting down an American or British plane, it would be seen as an Iraqi triumph."

Yet lifting the no-fly zone would not create any sort of "sanctuary": the Iraqi military is far weaker today than it was a decade ago and a continuing arms embargo would keep it that way. If a U.S. or British plane is downed, it will be because it is buzzing Iraqi territory, not because Iraq is invading another nation. So much for the Pentagon's claim that the strike was in "self-defense."

Were Washington policymakers not wedded to failure, they would try something different. First, drop the no-fly zone. No purpose is served in preventing Iraq's air force from flying throughout Iraq.

Second, recognize the limits of U.S. power. Washington can't force a change in Baghdad.

It certainly won't do so by funding groups like the Iraqi National Congress. The INC has spent $3 million so far to set up offices, hold a conference, and generate publicity. Reports Betsy Pisik of the Washington Times: "As resistance groups go, the INC leadership is noticeably upscale, with many of its visible members operating successful businesses in London."

Just a guess, but Saddam, one of the nastiest brutes to control a country, probably isn't scared. Instead of tossing more good money after bad, the West should plan to out-wait a much-weakened Iraq, just as the West ultimately outlasted a variety of communist states.

Third, negotiate to drop sanctions in exchange for an inspections and import control regime that limits Baghdad's access to the tools necessary to make weapons of mass destruction. The effectiveness of such a system would be limited, but with sanctions fraying daily and inspectors barred by Iraq since 1998, almost anything would be an improvement.

Fourth, expect friendly nations to develop militaries—and build popular support—to contain Iraq. The U.S., with security dependents strewn about the globe, shouldn't pick up another set of permanent wards. Yet Patrick Cronin of the U.S. Institute of Peace lauds the latest attack for sending a message that other Arab regimes "are not left alone at the time of the 10th anniversary of the Gulf victory."

But only the prospect of them being alone will move them to cooperate against Saddam. And to adopt the sort of political reforms that would make them less vulnerable. The obvious illegitimacy of regimes like that in Saudi Arabia poses as great a danger to stable oil supplies as does anything being concocted by Saddam.

Washington has tried and failed in its attempt to transform Iraq. It's time to instead transform U.S. policy towards Iraq.

February 2001

Don't Start the Second Gulf War

President George W. Bush says that he hasn't made up his mind about "any of our policies in regard to Iraq," but he obviously has. To not attack after spending months talking about the need for regime change is inconceivable. Unfortunately, war is not likely to be the simple and certain procedure that he and many others seem to think.

Lots of arguments have been offered on behalf of striking Baghdad that are not reasons at all. For instance, that Saddam Hussein is an evil man who has brutalized his own people.

Certainly true. But the world is full of brutal regimes that have murdered their own people. Indeed, Washington ally Turkey's treatment of its Kurds is scarcely more gentle than Iraq's Kurdish policies.

Moreover, the U.S. warmly supports the royal kleptocracy next door in Saudi Arabia, fully as totalitarian, if not quite as violent, as Saddam's government. Any non-Muslim and most women would probably prefer living in Iraq.

Also cited is Baghdad's conquest of Kuwait a dozen years ago. It is a bit late to drag that out as a justification for invading Iraq and overthrowing Saddam. He is far weaker today and has remained firmly contained.

Richard Butler, former head of the UN Commission on Iraq, complained to the Senate Foreign Relations that Iraq had violated international law by tossing out arms inspectors. In fact, there are often as many reasons to flout as to obey UN rules. Washington shouldn't go to war in some abstract pursuit of "international law."

Slightly more plausible, at least, is the argument that creating a democratic system in Iraq would provide a useful model for the rest of the Mideast. But that presupposes democracy can be easily planted, and that it can survive once the U.S. departs.

Iraq suffers from significant internal stresses. Convenient professions of unity in pursuit of democracy from an opposition once dismissed by Mideast special envoy and retired Gen. Anthony Zinni as "silk-suited, Rolex-wearing guys in London" offer little comfort and are likely to last no longer than have similar promises in Afghanistan.

Also problematic are Kurdish demands for autonomy and Shiite Muslim resistance to the central government. One defense official told the *Washington Post*: "I think it is almost a certainty that we'd wind up doing a campaign against the Kurds and Shiites." Wouldn't that be pretty?

There are external threats as well. Particularly worrisome would be covert and possibly overt action by Iran, with which Baghdad fought a decade-long war and which might see intervention against a weakened Iraq as an antidote to serious political unrest at home.

Indeed, the U.S. backed Baghdad in its conflict with Iran and decided not to depose Saddam in 1991, in part out of fear of Iranian aggression throughout the Gulf should Iraq no longer provide a blocking role. Keeping the Iraqi Humpty Dumpty together after a war might not be easy.

Moreover, while Americans might see America's war on Iraq as a war for democracy, most Arabs would likely see it as a war for Washington. If the U.S. deposes Saddam, but leaves in place friendly but despotic regimes elsewhere—such as Egypt, Pakistan, and Saudi Arabia—few Arabs would take America's democracy rhetoric seriously. Nor should they. Yet to go to war against everyone, including presumably Iran, Syria, and maybe others, would have incalculable consequences.

Saddam's complicity in September 11 would present a good argument for devastating retaliation for an act of war, but there's no evidence that he was involved. All that exists is a disputed meeting, which might not have occurred, in the Czech Republic between hijacker Mohammed Atta and an Iraqi official.

Certainly Saddam shed no tears over the thousands who died on that tragic day, but he has never been known to promote groups which he does not control. In contrast to Osama bin Laden, Saddam Hussein is no Muslim fanatic looking forward to his heavenly rewards; moreover, he heads a government and nation against which retaliation is simple.

Probably the best, at least the most fearsome, argument for overthrowing Saddam is the prospect of Baghdad developing weapons of mass destruction. Yet if nonproliferation should be enforced by war, Washington will be very busy in the coming years.

The problem is not just countries like Iran and North Korea, which seem to have or have had serious interest in developing atomic weapons. It is China, which could use them in any conflict with the U.S. over, say, Taiwan. And India, Pakistan, and Russia, which face unpredictable nationalist and theological currents, enjoy governments of varying instability, and offer uncertain security over technical know-how as well as weapons.

Potentially most dangerous is Pakistan's arsenal. The government of Pervez Musharraf is none too steady; Islamabad long supported the Taliban and its military and intelligence forces almost certainly contain al-Qaeda sympathizers. It is easy to imagine nuclear technology falling into terrorist hands.

An Iraqi nuclear capability seems less frightening in comparison. Saddam would not use them against America, since to do so would guarantee his incineration. Israel possesses a similarly overbearing deterrent.

Would Baghdad turn atomic weapons over to al-Qaeda or similarly-motivated terrorists? Not likely.

First, it would be extraordinary for Saddam to give up a technology purchased at such a high price. Second, Baghdad would be the immediate suspect and likely target of retaliation should any terrorist deploy nuclear weapons, and Saddam knows this.

Third, Saddam would be risking his own life. Al-Qaeda holds secular Arab dictators in contempt and would not be above attempting to destroy them as well as America.

Of course, the world would be a better place without Saddam's dictatorship. But there are a lot of regimes that should, and eventually will, end up in history's dustbin. That's not a good reason to initiate war against a state which poses no direct, ongoing threat.

Especially since war often creates unpredictable consequences. Without domestic opposition military forces to do America's dirty work, Washington will have to bear most of the burden. The task will be more difficult and expensive without European support and Saudi staging grounds.

If Iraq's forces don't quickly crumble, the U.S. might find itself involved in urban conflict that will be costly in human and political terms. If Baghdad possesses any weapons of mass destruction, Saddam will have an incentive to use them—against America, Israel, Kuwait, and Saudi Arabia—since Washington would be dedicated to his overthrow.

Further, the U.S. would be sloshing gasoline over a combustible political situation in friendly but undemocratic Arab regimes stretching from North Africa to Southeast Asia. Israelis and Palestinians are at war, America continues to fight Taliban and al-Qaeda forces in Afghanistan as the pro-western government teeters on chaos, fundamentalist Muslims rule western Pakistan, and Muslim extremists are active a dozen other countries. Yet the administration wants to invade Iraq. Riots in Egypt, a fundamentalist rising in Pakistan, a spurt of sectarian violence in Indonesia, and who knows what else could pose a high price for any success in Iraq.

War is a serious business. Making war on a country which does not threaten the U.S. is particularly serious. Even if the optimists who think a campaign against Iraq would be easy are right, and we can only hope they are, war should be a last resort. As House Majority Leader Richard Armey warned, an unprovoked attack "would not be consistent with what we have been as a nation or what we should be as a nation."

There's certainly no hurry to go to war. Nothing is different today from September 10, 2001, or any time since Iraq was ousted from Kuwait. Observes Jim Cornette, formerly an expert in biological warfare with the Air Force: "We've bottled [Saddam] up for 11 years, so we're doing okay."

There are times when Washington has no choice but to fight. Iraq is not such a place and now is not such a time.

August 2002

Defending a Constitutional Republic

There was a time when conservatives fought passionately to preserve America as a constitutional republic. That was, in fact, the essence of conservatism. It's one reason why Franklin Delano Roosevelt's vast expansion of government through the New Deal aroused such bitter opposition on the right.

But many conservative activists seem to have lost that philosophical commitment. They now advocate autocratic executive rule, largely unconstrained by constitutional procedures or popular opinions.

This curious attitude is evident in the conservative response to the gnawing question: Where are Saddam Hussein's weapons of mass destruction? So what? respond a surprising number of conservatives. He must have had them. Maybe he gave them away. And, anyway, Saddam was a bad guy.

In their view, even to ask the question is to mount a partisan attack on President George W. Bush. Why, to ask is downright unpatriotic. Liberals, we don't care about the WMD, forthrightly declares pundit Anne Coulter.

It always seemed likely that Baghdad possessed WMD. Not only did Iraq once maintain a WMD program, but how else to explain the regime's obstructionist behavior during the inspections process?

Yet it made equal sense to assume that a desperate Saddam Hussein would use any WMD to defend his regime. And that serious elements of Baghdad's arsenal would be quickly found.

There may be a logical explanation for the fact that WMD were neither used nor have been located; significant WMD stockpiles might eventually turn up. But the daisy chain is long: they were buried deep to hide them; Hussein and his leadership were effectively decapitated/isolated, preventing authorization of their use; everyone who knows their whereabouts has evaded capture or remained silent.

Moreover, it's hard to imagine the administration simply concocting its WMD claims. The President, though a practiced politician, is not the type to lie so blatantly. Whatever the faults of his lieutenants, none seem likely to advance a falsehood that would be so hard to maintain.

But the longer we go without any discoveries, the more questionable the pre-war claims appear to have been. The allies have checked all of the sites originally targeted for inspection, arrested leading Baath Party members, offered substantial rewards for information, and created powerful incentives for cooperation. Even in Saddam Hussein's centralized regime, more than a few people must know where any WMD stocks were hidden or transferred.

Which means it is entirely fair to ask the administration, where are the WMD? The answer matters for the simplest practical reasons. Possible intelligence failures need to be corrected. Washington's loss of credibility—saying "trust me" will be much harder for this president in the future or a future president—should be addressed.

Stonewalling the issue poses an even more dangerous threat to our principles of government. It matters whether or not the President lied to the American people. Political fibs are common, not just about with whom presidents have had sex, but also to advance foreign policy goals. Remember the Tonkin Gulf incident, inaccurate claims of Iraqi troop movements against Saudi Arabia before the first Gulf war, and repetition of false atrocity claims from ethnic Albanian guerrillas during the Kosovo war.

Perhaps the administration manipulated the evidence, carefully choosing the information that backed its view, turning assumptions into certainties, and hyping equivocal materials. That too would hardly be unusual. But no President should take the U.S. into war under false pretenses. There is no more important decision: the American people deserve to hear official doubts as well as certitudes.

The point is not that the administration is necessarily guilty of misbehavior. But it should be forced to defend its decision-making process. Who cares, ask the president's critics? Anyone who advocates limited republican governance should care.

Pointing to substitute justifications for the war just won't do. Deputy Defense Secretary Paul Wolfowitz notes that the alleged al-Qaeda connection divided the administration internally and humanitarian concerns did not warrant risking American lives. Only fear over Iraqi possession of WMD unified the administration, won the support of allies, particularly Great Britain, and served as the centerpiece of the administration's case. If the WMD didn't exist, or weren't worth using, Washington's professed case for war collapses.

Conservative disinterest in the WMD question takes an even more ominous turn when combined with general support for presidential war-making. Republicans—think President Dwight D. Eisenhower, for instance—once took seriously the requirement that Congress declare war. These days, however, Republican presidents and legislators, backed by conservative intellectuals, routinely argue that the chief executive can unilaterally take America into war.

Thus, in their view, once someone is elected president, he or she faces no legal or political constraint. The president doesn't need congressional authority; Washington doesn't need UN authority. Allied support is irrelevant. The president needn't offer the American public a justification for going to war that holds up after the conflict ends. The president may not even be questioned about the legitimacy of his professed justification. Accept his word and let him do whatever he wants, irrespective of circumstances.

This is not the government created by the founders. This is not the government that any believer in liberty should favor.

It is foolish to turn the Iraq war, a prudential political question, into a philosophical test for conservatism. It is even worse to demand unthinking support for President Bush. He should be pressed on the issue of WMD—by conservatives. Fidelity to the Constitution and republican government demands no less.

June 2003

Winning Votes, Avoiding Responsibility

"Once we have victory in Baghdad, all the critics will look like fools," Vice President Richard Cheney reportedly declared in 2002. Alas, a year after invading Iraq those looking like fools are concentrated in the administration, which apparently took America into war based on a lie. "We were all wrong," says David Kay, who spent several fruitless months searching for weapons of mass destruction in Iraq. It is time for President George W. Bush to admit that he, too, was wrong.

But the President has proved as unwilling as Bill Clinton to admit to a mistake: "There is no doubt in my mind that Saddam Hussein was a grave and gathering threat to America and the world" maintained President Bush, even as he bowed to pressure and promised an investigation into erroneous U.S. intelligence claims. In his most recent State of the Union speech he smoothly switched terms to cite Iraq's "weapons of mass destruction-related program activities" as justifying the war.

And Vice President Cheney continues to claim that two trailers discovered after the war are part of a biological weapons program, despite rebuttals by both Kay and the CIA. He also says that the administration has yet to give up hope of finding WMD: "We still don't know the whole extent of what they did have." Similarly, Defense Secretary Donald Rumsfeld says that WMD might still turn up. Maybe, but the possibility seems increasingly slight. Kay calls such hopes the same as holding out "for a Hail-Mary pass," even though "I believe we have enough evidence now to say that the intelligence process, and the policy process that used that information, did not work at the level of effectiveness that we require in the age that we live in." So some conservative commentators now call Saddam Hussein himself a WMD.

It is difficult to overestimate the importance of the administration's failure to find weapons of mass destruction and, equally important, to acknowledge the error. The signature issue for the Bush presidency has been the war on terrorism, and the most important aspect of that campaign has been the war in Iraq. Yet far from basking in glory while its opponents looked like fools, the administration now finds its and America's credibility ruined.

At home, a majority of Americans say that they believe the President deliberately exaggerated, or lied about, evidence on Iraq's alleged possession of WMD. The percentage of Americans who see Bush as "honest and trustworthy" has fallen from a high of 71 percent in mid-2002 to 52 percent in February 2004. A Pew survey found the most common description of Bush was "liar." For the first time since the war was won a majority of people declared that it was not worth fighting.

Equally significant is the impact on U.S. credibility overseas. "The foreign policy blow-back is pretty serious," says Kenneth Adelman, a member of the Pentagon's Defense Advisory Board who famously predicted that the war would be a "cakewalk." Governments of "Old Europe" feel vindicated in their opposition to the U.S. Former NSC adviser Zbigniew Brzezinski writes that "There is manifest resentment of recent American conduct and a pervasive distrust of America's leaders, even in countries that have participated in the coalition in Iraq." U.N. Secretary General Kofi Annan notes "damage" to U.S. credibility: people "are going to be very suspicious when we try to use intelligence to justify certain actions."

Unfortunately, this isn't the first time that Washington demonstrated that being a superpower means never having to say it's sorry. In 1998 the U.S. blew up a nondescript Sudanese pharmaceutical plant in the name of punishing Osama bin Laden, an action now widely viewed as a serious error. Yet CIA Director George Tenet steadfastly defended that strike and the Clinton administration never conceded its mistake.

The loss of credibility from the WMD fiasco was inevitable. A president faces no more important decision than going to war. And George W. Bush could not have made the case without pointing to Iraq's alleged WMD program.

Until the administration decided on war, it proudly proclaimed that Iraq had been contained. In July 2001 NSC Adviser Condoleezza Rice argued that "We are able to keep arms from [Hussein]. His military forces have not been rebuilt." In September of that year Vice President Cheney declared: "Saddam Hussein is bottled up."

In February 2001 Secretary of State Colin Powell declared that sanctions had worked. Saddam Hussein "has not developed any significant capability with respect to weapons of mass destruction. He is unable to project conventional power against his neighbors."

Similarly, Secretary Powell testified before Congress:

> The Iraqi regime militarily remains fairly weak. It does not have the capacity it had 10 or 12 years ago. It has been contained, and even though we have no doubt in our mind that the Iraqi regime is pursuing programs to develop weapons of mass destruction, chemical, biological, and nuclear, I think the best intelligence estimate suggests that they have not been terribly successful.
>
> There is no question that they have some stockpiles of some of these sorts of weapons still under their control. But they have not been able to break out, they have not been able to come out with a capability to deliver these kinds of systems, or to actually have these kinds of systems. That is much beyond where they were 10 years ago. So containment using this arms control sanctions regime I think has been reasonably successful.

But that was when facts still mattered to the administration. Once it decided upon war, its position changed. For instance, President Bush used last year's State of the Union speech to paint Iraq as a dire and imminent threat to America.

War was necessary, he explained, since "our nation and the world" could "not allow an even greater threat [than North Korea] to rise up in Iraq." Hussein, said Mr. Bush, could develop enough anthrax "to kill several million people."

Iraq had botulinum toxin that could "subject millions of people to death." Moreover, the Hussein regime "had the materials to produce as much as 500 tons of sarin, mustard and VX nerve agent," which could "kill untold thousands."

Baghdad possessed chemical munitions. Mobile biological weapons labs. And, of course, an earlier nuclear program, along with alleged attempts to buy "significant quantities of uranium from Africa."

In a speech delivered in Cincinnati in October 2002, President Bush went further. He claimed: "surveillance photos reveal that the regime is rebuilding facilities that it had used to produce chemical and biological weapons." Iraq had ballistic missiles "with a likely range of hundreds of miles."

The President warned that not only might Saddam Hussein use such weapons on his neighbors, but he might transfer them to terrorists. Indeed, in Cincinnati he proclaimed: "Iraq could decide on any given day to provide a biological or chemical weapon to a terrorist group or individual terrorists." Thus, he concluded, "The threat from Iraq stands alone—because it gathers the most serious dangers of our age in one place."

Finally, in his televised ultimatum when he demanded that Hussein leave Iraq within 48 hours, he asserted: "Intelligence gathered by this and other governments leaves no doubt that the Iraq regime continues to possess and conceal some of the most lethal weapons ever devised." Thus, "The danger is clear: using chemical, biological or, one day, nuclear weapons, obtained with the help of Iraq, the terrorists could fulfill their stated ambitions and kill thousands or hundreds of thousands of innocent people in our country or any other."

These charges were regularly repeated by other administration officials. Three days before the U.S. invaded Iraq, Vice President Cheney declared: "We believe he has, in fact, reconstituted nuclear weapons."

Secretary of State Powell provided a lengthy bill of particulars in his celebrated presentation to the UN Security Council. "Saddam Hussein could have produced 25,000 liters" of anthrax and had accounted for none of it. "Saddam Hussein has never accounted for vast amounts of chemical weaponry: 550 artillery shells with mustard [gas], 30,000 empty munitions and enough precursors to increase his stockpile to as much as 500 tons of chemical agents."

Added Secretary Powell, Washington estimated that Iraq had stockpiled "between 100 and 500 tons of chemical weapons agent. That is enough agent to fill 16,000 battlefield rockets." Secretary Powell calmly asserted: "Saddam Hussein has chemical weapons."

Secretary Powell also cited unmanned aerial vehicles, or drones, which "are well suited for dispensing chemical and biological weapons." In fact, Sen. Bill Nelson (D-Fl.) and Rep. Paul E. Kanjorski (D-PA) said that the administration claimed in a classified briefing that Iraq could target American cities with UAVs.

Similarly, Defense Secretary Rumsfeld argued that Iraq had "large, unaccounted-for stockpiles of chemical and biological weapons—

including VX, sarin, cyclosarin and mustard gas; anthrax, botulism, and possibly smallpox." On and on it went.

Moreover, the threat allegedly was immediate. Not that administration officials had good memories: on Face the Nation in March, Secretary Rumsfeld claimed that "you [Bob Schieffer] and a few other critics are the only people I've heard use the phrase 'immediate threat.' I didn't. The president didn't. And it's become kind of folklore that that's what happened."

Unfortunately for Rumsfeld, Schieffer and co-interrogator Thomas Friedman were prepared with examples of just such administration claims. In fact, the administration chorus was overwhelming: No delay was possible. In his Cincinnati speech, explained Bush, "America must not ignore the threat gathering against us."

Indeed, the President added, "The danger is already significant, and it only grows worse with time. If we know Saddam Hussein has dangerous weapons today—and we do—does it make any sense for the world to wait to confront him?" To the contrary, "we have an urgent duty to prevent the worst from occurring." Vice President Cheney simply said: "There is no doubt that he is amassing them to use them against our friends, against our allies and against us."

When asked in May 2003 whether the U.S. went to war because Iraq's WMD "were a direct and imminent threat to the United States," Presidential spokesman Ari Fleischer responded, "Absolutely." Direct and imminent. A year ago Fleischer's deputy (and current press secretary) Scott McClellan argued that NATO should follow the administration because "this is about imminent threat."

Various officials, from the President on down, declared that the Hussein regime was "a threat," "a significant threat," "the most dangerous threat of our time," a "threat to the region and the world," "a threat to the security of free nations," "a serious threat to our country, to our friends and to our allies," a "unique and urgent threat," and "a serious and mounting threat." Indeed, said Defense Secretary Rumsfeld, "No terrorist state poses a greater or more immediate threat to the security of our people and the stability of the world."

Even in March 2004 NSC Adviser Condoleezza Rice claimed that the Hussein regime was "the most dangerous regime in the world's most dangerous region," and thus a greater threat than North Korea. When pressed by Tim Russert on Meet the Press about the administration's many obviously false claims of imminent danger, Rice responded: "we cannot wait until it becomes imminent" and she continued to claim that despite everything "it is an urgent threat and I believe to this day that it was an urgent threat."

Powerful rhetoric. Too bad that none of it was true. None of it.

So far, the U.S. has found not one WMD warhead, not one thimbleful of WMD materials. There were no reconstituted nuclear weapons, no uranium purchases from Africa. The much-cited aluminum tubes purchased by Iraq were almost certainly intended for use by conventional missiles.

Reported David Kay, who ran America's Iraq Survey Group: "information found to date suggests that Iraq's large-scale capability to develop, produce, and fill new CW munitions was reduced—if not entirely destroyed—during Operations Desert Storm and Desert Fox, 13 years of U.N. sanctions, and U.N. inspections." He added, "We have not yet been able to corroborate the existence of a mobile biological weapons production effort." Indeed, "Technical limitations would prevent any of these processes from being ideally suited to these trailers." Nor have any ocean-spanning UAVs turned up.

Indeed, Kay's search discovered some "contemporary documents" proving that Iraq had destroyed weapons. His final assessment: "I don't think they [Iraqi WMDs] existed." He added, "What everyone was talking about is stockpiles produced after the end of the last [1991] Gulf War, and I don't think there was a large-scale production program in the '90s."

The newly-released Carnegie Endowment's report, "WMD in Iraq: Evidence and Implications," found that Baghdad's nuclear program had been dismantled and nerve agents "had lost most of their lethality *as early as* 1991." Any threat from biological weapons would be in the future, not the present. The only active program seemed to involve longer-range missiles—but still not capable of reaching America.

As for the President's convenient switch of his emphasis from actual weapons to "program-related activities," Vincent Cannistraro, former head of the CIA counter-terrorism unit, says the latter claim is "not as flatly wrong, but it is misleading," since "having the capability of doing this requires the acquisition of a lot of component parts you don't have." Similarly, notes Jonathan Tucker, a former UN weapons inspector in Iraq: "It would be inaccurate to say they had a rapid breakout capability."

Not only were there no WMD, but "there was no evidence to support the claim that Iraq would have transferred WMD to al Qaeda and much evidence to counter it." Concluded Carnegie, Iraq's WMD efforts did not "pose an immediate threat."

In short, nothing that the President said was true. Nothing. Which means that Iraq posed no threat, especially not an immediate one.

But then, posing a threat to America was not why the administration went to war. Ray McGovern, who chaired the National Intelligence Estimates during his 27-year federal career, notes that "the Bush administration's decision for war against Iraq came well before any intelligence estimate."

Instead, intelligence was gathered to support a prior decision. As former Treasury Secretary Paul O'Neill pointed out, "From the very beginning, there was a conviction that Saddam Hussein was a bad person and that he needed to go." Another official backed up O'Neill's account, telling ABC News that at NSC meetings in early 2001 President Bush "told his Pentagon officials to explore the military options, including use of ground forces," to oust Hussein. This should come as no surprise, however; nearly a dozen top Bush staffers had signed a 1998 letter for the Project for the New American Century urging President Bill Clinton to overthrow Hussein. September 11 provided the opportunity and claims of WMD yielded the most persuasive argument.

And this argument was crucial in generating public support for war. Although David Kay supported the war for humanitarian reasons, he admits that on the basis of WMD "clearly it was not" worth it. Consider also then-House Majority Leader Richard Armey, who initially doubted the legitimacy of attacking Iraq. After intensive administration lobbying, he voted for war, explaining: "If you're going to conduct a war on terrorism then you must stop that person who is most likely and most able to arm the terrorists with the things that will frighten us the most." But if that person doesn't possess any of the weapons that frighten us the most, he obviously couldn't arm any terrorists, even if he wanted to do so.

The failure to find any WMD has created widespread concern about the sacrifice of U.S. credibility in pursuit of the administration's ideological agenda. Even conservative columnist Jonah Goldberg, whose enthusiasm for the war remains undiminished, believes that President Bush should have admitted his error. Conservative TV personality Bill O'Reilly admits "I was wrong," and plans to be "much more skeptical about the Bush administration now."

Ramesh Ponnuru, an editor at *National Review*, acknowledges that "the argument for [the war's] urgency—the argument that time was not on our side—has lost a lot of its force." Columnist and Fox News commentator Morton Kondracke admitted that the argument which had "convinced people in Congress" and him to go war had turned out to be false. Hollywood conservative Mel Gibson proclaimed himself to be a Bush fan until recently, but "I am having doubts, of late. It mainly has to do with the weapons claims."

The most important disaffected hawk might be Secretary of State Powell. In a February interview with the *Washington Post*, he was asked if he would have recommended an invasion if he had known that Iraq possessed no WMD. "I don't know, because it was the stockpile that presented the final little piece that made it more of a real and present danger and threat to the region and to the world," he responded. The "absence of a stockpile changes the political calculus; it changes the answer you get."

Unsurprisingly, that answer did not go over well elsewhere in the administration. A day later Powell loyally declared: "The President made the right decision." Of course.

Some conservatives who don't seem bothered in principle about America going to war because of false administration claims nevertheless worry about the political fall-out, since the American people seem to care. Observes Tod Lindberg of the Hoover Institution: "If Mr. Bush does lose in November, I think that underlying it will be a sense of unease about a leader who has taken the country to war on the basis of a mistaken or misstated casus belli."

How could so many supposedly bright people have gotten it so wrong? Not surprising is the fact that administration officials picked the intelligence claims that most suited their preferences and ignored the rest. Far more disturbing is their apparent willingness to manipulate the intelligence process to their own ends.

In fact, we were not "all wrong," as David Kay said. John B. Judis and Spencer Ackerman of the *New Republic* point out that "Unbeknownst to the public, the administration faced equally serious opposition within its own intelligence agencies." First, the CIA inappropriately turned incomplete information into specific warnings, focusing on worst-case scenarios, in the view of the Senate Intelligence Committee. Said Chairman Pat Roberts (R-KS): "The picture in regards to intelligence is not very flattering."

Even so, at the CIA many analysts and officials were skeptical that Iraq posed an imminent threat." Greg Thielmann, formerly head of the State Department's intelligence bureau, explained that "I think it [Iraq] didn't even constitute an imminent threat to its neighbors at the time we went to war." The Defense Intelligence Agency, Department of Energy, U.S. Air Force, and International Atomic Energy Agency also criticized particular administration claims. The top secret version of the National Intelligence Estimate concerning Iraq continued some 40 caveats and dissenting views—which were left out of the public release. Perhaps most significant was the conclusion of the UN inspectors, on the ground in Iraq, who found no WMD.

Such contrary conclusions, and many more like them, were not what the President and his war-minded aides wanted to hear. So they found many ways, large and small, including repeated visits to the CIA, to pressure the intelligence services to offer an appropriate rationale for attacking Iraq. Observed Thielmann, "The main problem was that the senior administration officials have what I call faith-based intelligence. They knew what they wanted the intelligence to show." And they claimed that it showed it.

Says Lt. Col. (ret.) Karen Kwiatkowski, the Pentagon's Office of Special Plans was dedicated to manufacturing a case for war: "It wasn't intelligence—it was propaganda." The result was "a narrow and deeply flawed policy favored by some executive appointees in the Pentagon used to manipulate and pressurize the traditional relationship between policymakers in the Pentagon and U.S. intelligence agencies." She adds, "They'd take a little bit of intelligence, cherry-pick it, make it sound much more exciting, usually by taking it out of context, often by juxtaposition of two pieces of information that don't belong together." Max Boot of the Council on Foreign Relations responds that Kwiatkowski and other administration critics "have flaky views" that undermine their credibility.

But top officials certainly made their preferences clear. As Spencer Ackerman and Franklin Foer write, administration claims "were not pieces of objective evidence that the administration relied on to formulate its Iraq policy. Rather, they were products of an intelligence process that the administration—and the Office of the Vice President, in particular—had already politicized in order to justify its Iraq policy." Officials were simply more inclined to believe evidence that suggested Iraq was a threat than evidence running the other way.

The insistence on believing what they wanted to believe may be most obvious in the administration's reliance on Ahmad Chalabi, the Iraqi exile convicted of bank fraud who was once favored by administration neoconservatives to run occupied Iraq. Now a member of the Iraqi Governing Council, Chalabi made light of his consistently erroneous claims in early February: America was now in Baghdad, and little else mattered. "We are heroes in error," he joked. (Amazingly, the Pentagon has budgeted $3 million to $4 million this year for continued payments to Chalabi's Iraqi National Congress for its so-called Information Collection Program.)

Finally, the President and his aides were highly selective in their claims. Not only did they "dismantle the existing filtering process that for fifty years had been preventing the policymakers from getting bad information," writes Kenneth Pollack, a member of the Clinton NSC staff who favored war with Iraq. But "the administration was only telling part of the truth to the American people because it was trying to justify a war in 2003." The most obvious way to demonstrate alleged imminence of a threat was an al Qaeda connection and possession of nuclear weapons, "and the administration was grossly distorting the intelligence on both things," said Thielmann.

Once the truth came out, the President could have responded as a serious person. He could have taken responsibility for his claims and acknowledged that he'd been wrong.

Still, he could have added, the administration relied on the best evidence that it had. He could have pointed out that other countries believed that Iraq had WMD. He might have promised to investigate what went wrong with U.S. intelligence-gathering. In short, he could have acted like the steadfast chief executive his supporters acclaim him to be, a president who regretted that he'd taken the nation into war on a falsehood.

But no. As Joseph Circincione, director of the nonproliferation program at the Carnegie Endowment for International Peace, observed, the President "shirked any responsibility for misjudging the Iraqi WMD programs."

In the State of the Union speech, George W. Bush talked about liberating Iraq. He cited the challenge of the occupation. But he devoted just two sentences to WMD, noting the presence of "dozens of weapons of mass destruction-related program activities."

No weapons. No weapons close to production. No weapons stockpiles. No weapons of mass destruction programs. But "weapons of mass destruction-related program activities."

When pressed by ABC's Diane Sawyer on the issue, Bush responded that there was a "possibility" Hussein could have acquired them. "So what's the difference," asked Bush? A lot. As surely the President knows.

CIA Director George Tenet knows. He implicitly admitted to the Senate Armed Services Committee that administration officials have misstated the evidence. "If there are areas where I thought someone said something they shouldn't say, I talked to them about it," he explained. Although he wouldn't give specifics, "When I believed someone was misconstruing intelligence, I stood up and said something about it."

And surely the American people know. WMD deceptions are a major reason that the percentage of people believing Bush to be honest and trustworthy has fallen to 52 percent, down seven points from October. A majority of those polled believed that the administration intentionally exaggerated the evidence regarding WMD.

And they have less reason to trust any president, and especially this one, in the future. When challenged by Tim Russert for having believed that Hussein possessed WMD, former Vermont Gov. Howard Dean responded: "I did, because the president told us. And I'm inclined to believe presidents in most circumstances. I think most Americans, Democrats or Republicans, ought to believe the president of the United States when he does something as serious as send us to war."

They ought to do so. But they obviously can't do so any longer, at least with this president.

Nevertheless, if only President Bush were suffering, then one could feel satisfied that he was simply receiving just recompense. Alas, the U.S., too, has paid a huge price for the administration's error. Observes Pollack: "when the United States and its coalition partners invaded Iraq, the American public and much of the rest of the world believed that after Saddam Hussein's regime sank, a vast flotsam of weapons of mass destruction would bob to the surface." When they did not, both the administration and U.S., as noted earlier, lost much of their credibility.

Indeed, the surprise defeat of Spain's conservative party is more easily explained as a reaction against the incumbent government's discredited decision to back the Bush administration in Iraq than as an attempt to "appease" terrorists. So, too, the new government's intention to remove its 1300 troops from Iraq. Stated Prime Minister-elect Jose Luis Rodriguez Zapatero: "The war has been a disaster; the occupation continues to be a great disaster. It hasn't generated anything but more violence and hate."

He would not likely have spoken this way had the Bush administration discovered massive WMD stockpiles. After all, observed Zapatero, the war "divided more than it united, there were no reasons for it, time has shown that the arguments for it lacked credibility, and the occupation has been poorly managed." Even more blunt was his pronouncement: "you can't organize a war with lies." Now another former steadfast ally, Poland, is complaining about being misled as well. It says it might withdraw its occupation forces ahead of schedule.

And administration credibility is suffering far beyond Europe. Regarding North Korea, for instance, China is questioning U.S. claims that Pyongyang has a highly enriched uranium program. Whispers of doubts also are being heard in Japan and South Korea. Even if Washington is correct, it is ill-positioned to persuade anyone that is the case.

Moreover, imagine the Bush administration trying to create another international coalition based on American intelligence. Imagine Washington claiming that Syria or Iran or another country possessed a dangerous WMD capability. Imagine the U.S. arguing that another destitute, isolated state posed a direct and immediate security threat. Imagine an American campaign to win global support for another preventive war. Imagine the resulting chorus of laughter around the world, even if the administration wasn't crying wolf.

Indeed, that is the great tragedy: Washington will find it harder to lead even if its leadership is critically required in that instance. Asks Michael Ignatieff of the Kennedy School of Government: "What if the example of Iraq leads electorates and politicians to respond too slowly to the next tyrant or terrorist?" Thank the Bush administration.

Only by fessing up can Washington begin to repair the damage. Writes Pollack, "The only way that we can regain the world's trust is to demonstrate that we understand our mistakes and have changed our ways." That is, for the President to take responsibility and acknowledge that he was wrong.

But there's an even more important issue. Conservatives, in particular, once fought passionately to preserve America as a limited, constitutional republic.

Which means that they should take the lead in demanding that the administration be held accountable. The President's attempt to change the subject, dismiss his critics, and otherwise avoid responsibility is an affront to our democratic principles of government.

It matters if the President lied to the American people. It matters if the administration manipulated the evidence. It matters if U.S. intelligence operations are flawed. It matters if officials pressured intelligence analysts. It matters if America went to war based on a lie.

An intelligence failure doesn't necessarily mean that the administration is guilty of misbehavior. But Americans should demand that the President defend his decision.

The failure to find WMD doesn't take "away from the merit of the case" for war, says Secretary Powell. No, it destroys it. Along with the President's and America's credibility.

Republicans rightly criticized Bill Clinton for constantly portraying himself as a victim, refusing to take responsibility for his manifold failings. President George W. Bush is taking the same path. It appears that he was wrong on WMD. If he cares about American credibility and democracy, he should admit the truth, and thus "come clean with the American people," as David Kay puts it.

March 2004

Kabuki Theater, Iraqi-Style

The Bush administration continues to move inexorably towards war as it and its critics debate the relative success of Hans Blix and his inspectors. But the inspection process is a sideshow, irrelevant to Washington's decision whether or not to attack Iraq. The real issue is whether an invasion is necessary to protect America.

While the inspectors have used the threat of war in an attempt to improve Iraqi cooperation, the Bush administration has always viewed inspections as an impediment to be overcome in developing a pretext for war. After all, before going along with the UN vote on inspections, Undersecretary of State for Arms Control and International Security John Bolton declared: "Our policy at the same time insists on regime change in Baghdad and that policy will not be altered whether inspectors go in or not."

Assume that Iraq has not genuinely disarmed in response to the UN's demands. The real question is not what do the inspectors find?, but is war the only way to deal with Baghdad?

The answer is no.

Sometimes the advocates of preemption appear to have forgotten which country is the overwhelming superpower and which is the impoverished third world wreck. They should relax: the U.S. is well able to defend itself without going to war.

Obviously, Saddam Hussein is not the world's only brutal dictator. Nor is his the only ugly regime to possess deadly weapons and to desire to develop even deadlier ones. A dozen states have nuclear weapons programs; at least 16 are thought to possess chemical weapons. Even more have ballistic missiles.

Nor is Iraq the only nation to have threatened its neighbors. Saddam is not a crackpot megalomaniac, but a cautious if violent predator.

Consider his wars. For years he has battled Shiite and Kurdish separatists. In this he is no different from neighboring Turkey, which destroyed 3000 villages and displaced as many as two million people before defeating that nation's Kurdish insurgency.

In 1980 Saddam attacked Iran, which had been applying pressure on an Iraq under both the Shah and the mullahs. He rightly figured that the West would back him. In fact, Washington was all too willing to help him, murderous aggressor that he was, in that venture, figuring that the enemy of its enemy was its friend.

One does not justify his war to note that Saddam started with only limited aims. Explain John Mearsheimer and Stephen Walt, of the University of Chicago and Harvard, respectively: "it was an opportunistic response to a significant threat."

Baghdad invaded Kuwait in 1990 in the mistaken belief that the first Bush administration would acquiesce. After all, U.S. Ambassador April Glaspie told Saddam that Washington had "no opinion" in his border dispute with his smaller neighbor. Indeed, the State Department emphasized that the U.S. had no treaty commitment with Kuwait.

Since then, with his military and nation ravaged by war and sanctions, he has done nothing. Obviously that's not because he has chosen a new path of righteousness.

But he understands the correlation of forces and is not interested in certain defeat. More than most outlaw states, Iraq has been weakened, constrained, and contained. There's no reason to believe that the restraints will soon disappear.

Deterrence works equally well against use of weapons of mass destruction. Saddam has employed chemical weapons against the Kurds and Iranians, but neither had a means to retaliate. He would face nuclear obliteration if he used those or nuclear weapons, which no one believes that he presently has, against the U.S.

Indeed, deterrence worked against Joseph Stalin and Mao Zedong, the two greatest mass murderers in human history. And it worked against Hussein, who did not use biological or chemical agents against U.S. forces even as bombs were raining down upon him during the Gulf War.

It will work in the future. Except if the administration seeks forcible regime change. After all, if Washington is determined to depose Saddam, he has no reason not to unleash whatever chemical and biological weapons that he has, at U.S. forces, Israeli civilians, and America's Arab allies.

September 11 raised the issue of terrorism, but the leading Bush administration hawks advocated war with Iraq long before this president was inaugurated. Were there serious evidence linking Hussein to al-Qaeda—secular dictators and religious fanatics rarely mix—President

George W. Bush undoubtedly would have made the case. That he has not done so means that he cannot do so.

Saddam has aided Hamas and Hezbollah, but support for terrorists who murder others is not the same as support for terrorists who attack America. After all, there are many brutal terrorists in the world. Indeed, the bloodiest force which has most commonly relied on suicide bombings is the Tamil Tigers in Sri Lanka. They are all evil. However, they are not all enemies of America.

As for the future, Hussein is unlikely to cooperate with a group that detests him and cannot be controlled, let alone give away the nuclear crown jewels after spending decades to develop them. Indeed, he would risk devastating retaliation if such ties were ever discovered, especially in the aftermath of another terrorist attack. Baghdad is the first place any U.S. government would look.

War also creates a far greater risk of proliferation to terrorist groups. The ambassador of a friendly nation privately worries: assume American troops are nearing Baghdad. Saddam disperses a couple of dozen canisters of Anthrax to loyal military and intelligence officers, telling them to do as much damage as possible. Or simply hands them over to al-Qaeda agents directly.

War against Iraq is unnecessary. While the world would be a better place without Saddam Hussein, the cost of getting rid of him is likely to be considerable.

Especially considering the collateral consequences of any war. In the short term there may be little the U.S. can do to reduce Islamic hatred. But attacking Iraq is sure to inflame fundamentalist sentiments, offering yet another grievance for recruiting terrorists.

Moreover, it could set off populist waves that might swamp already fragile regimes, such as that of Pakistan's Pervez Musharraf. Islamabad has helped North Korea with its nuclear program; imagine a nuclear-armed fundamentalist Islamic government in Pakistan.

In Iran, in contrast to elsewhere in the Islamic world, events are moving America's way, with a pro-American democracy movement threatening the mullahs' rule. War with Iraq is as likely to interrupt as accelerate that process, however.

Further, war will divert attention and resources from the ongoing battle against al-Qaeda. Yes, it has been said, America fought in both

Europe and the Pacific in World War II. But that was the same kind of war, only conducted in different theaters. The war against terrorism is not the same as a war against Iraq; so far Baghdad has been AWOL on the Islamic side and the battles are very different.

The war on terrorism requires more detailed attention to diffuse and diverse threats as well as international cooperation to prosecute. The Taliban may be gone, but terrorist attacks continue across the globe, with bombings in Kenya, off the coast of Yemen, and in Indonesia.

American soldiers are being shot even in Kuwait, America's closest Gulf ally. And war continues to rage in the hills of Afghanistan, where U.S. soldiers are being ambushed by opponents who escape into Pakistan. One most recent attacker was a Pakistani border guard.

Yet Islamabad plays both sides of the street, offering cooperation when pressed by Washington but avoiding confrontation with Islamic radicals when possible. A U.S. attack on Iraq will reduce America's leverage to demand assistance and Pakistan's incentive to accede to such requests. Relations with a host of other nations necessary to battle international terrorist networks—Egypt, Indonesia, Malaysia, Saudi Arabia—will be similarly strained.

Then there's the aftermath of any war. American troops continue to occupy the artificial state of Bosnia, six years after President Bill Clinton promised that they would be home.

Dealing with Kurds, Shiites, tribal leaders, Baathist elements, and returning émigrés while juggling demands from Iran and Turkey will be explosive as well as expensive. Even the dissidents in exile are demanding that Washington hand over power and then go home. And any attempt to run the oil industry for America's benefit will generate an international firestorm of criticism and vindicate the gaggle of critics who have termed any conflict a "war for oil."

"We do not think that war is inevitable," says Hans Blix. It isn't, but not because of the inspections. Watching intrepid UN investigators search the far corners of Iraq may capture public attention, but their efforts are irrelevant.

War is not inevitable because George W. Bush can say no. Iraq has not attacked the U.S. or a U.S. ally. Iraq is not threatening any other nation, the traditional justification for preemption.

Baghdad can continue to be contained, as it has been contained for the last decade. And contained in a manner that does not maximize the likelihood of the use and proliferation of weapons of mass destruction, in contrast to the administration's preferred instrument of war.

In short, war is not inevitable, but not because the inspectors are likely to succeed, with or without Saddam's cooperation. War is not inevitable because it does not serve America's national interest.

February 2003

The Dishonest Pursuit of War

President George W. Bush's latest attempt to generate public support for his Iraq policy comes even as more evidence emerges that the invasion of Iraq was a war of choice. His argument that we must persevere because Iraq has become "a central front in the war on terror" sounds like the man who kills his parents and then throws himself on the mercy of the court for being an orphan.

It has long been evident that leading administration officials desired war against Iraq well before September 11. Vice President Richard Cheney, Deputy Defense Secretary Paul Wolfowitz, and others had pressed the Clinton administration for regime change. In 2002 then NSC adviser Condoleezza Rice told Richard Haass, the State Department's policy chief: "that decision's been made." A CIA analyst concerned about the unreliability of the defector code-named Curveball was told by his supervisor that "the powers that be probably aren't terribly interested in whether Curveball knows what he's talking about."

Thus, the year-long debate in the U.S. and at the UN was mere Kabuki theater, irrelevant to the preordained result. The war never was in doubt.

This makes the administration's lack of preparedness for the consequences of war particularly shocking. Having a year to plan the invasion, why didn't the President's aides do a better job preparing for the aftermath?

Although the administration's determination to go to war irrespective of Saddam Hussein's actual weapons capabilities has long been evident, any remaining doubt was eliminated by the so-called Downing Street memo and related documents, which document both British attitudes and American policies.

Although Iraq was not involved in the terrorist attacks of 9/11, that became the excuse to turn preexisting desires into policy. Noted British Foreign Secretary Jack Straw in a memo dated March 25, 2002, "If 11 September had not happened, it is doubtful that the US would now be considering military action against Iraq."

On July 23, 2002 foreign policy aide Matthew Rycroft wrote a memo for the British cabinet summarizing a briefing by Richard Dearlove, then head of MI-6, Britain's CIA, for Prime Minister Tony

Blair and other officials. Rycroft observed that "It seemed clear that Bush had made up his mind to take military action, even if the timing was not yet decided." At another point Rycroft allowed: "Military action was now seen as inevitable."

Public debate obviously was pure pretense, since, Rycroft explained, "The NSC had no patience with the UN route, and no enthusiasm for publishing material on the Iraqi regime's record."

Indeed, he added, Geoff Hoon, Britain's Defence Secretary, reported "that the US had already begun 'spikes of activity' to put pressure on the regime." That was probably an understatement. The London Times recently reported that "The RAF and US aircraft doubled the rate at which they were dropping bombs on Iraq in 2002 in an attempt to provoke Saddam Hussein into giving the allies an excuse for war." In November 2002 Rear Adm. David Gove, then deputy director of global operations for America's Joint Chiefs of Staff, said that pilots of both nations were "essentially flying combat missions."

Alas, observed Rycroft, enthusiasm for war was not enough: "The Attorney-General said that the desire for regime change was not a legal base for military action." A Cabinet Office paper entitled "Conditions for Military Action," prepared on July 21, 2002, acknowledged: "Regime change per se is not a proper basis for military action under international law." Foreign Secretary Straw similarly wrote that "regime change per se is no justification for military action."

A separate options paper developed by the Overseas and Defence Secretariat on March 8, 2002 noted that no legal justification for war "currently exists. This makes moving quickly to invade legally very difficult."

Washington, observed the anonymous memo writer, believed a legal justification to exist. But what?

Concluded the options paper, "there is no justification for action against Iraq based on action in self-defence." To the contrary, observed Peter Ricketts, then political director of the Foreign Office, in a memo dated March 22, 2002, "It sounds like a grudge match between Bush and Saddam."

Reported Rycroft, the U.S. believed the goal of removing Hussein from power was "justified by the conjunction of terrorism and WMD." But frankly: "The case was thin. Saddam was not threatening his neighbours, and his WMD capability was less than that of Libya, North Korea or Iran."

On March 18, 2002 Britain's ambassador Christopher Meyer lunched with Paul Wolfowitz, who, he reported to London, "thought it indispensable to spell out in detail Saddam's barbarism." But Meyer noted that was not enough for war.

Moreover, explained Meyer, Wolfowitz thought "it was absurd to deny the link between terrorism and Saddam." Yet Wolfowitz himself seemed to repudiate that position the following year when he allowed that even the Bush administration was divided over the issue.

Further, noted the options paper, "Saddam has not succeeded in seriously threatening his neighbours." And, it added, "there is no recent evidence of Iraq complicity with international terrorism."

Ricketts made similar points: the "US scrambling to establish a link between Iraq and Al Qaida is so far frankly unconvincing." Moreover, "the pace of Saddam Hussein's WMD programmes" had not changed since September 11. Nor, said the options paper, was there any "greater threat now that he [Hussein] will use WMD than there has been in recent years, so continuing containment is an option."

Still, observed Ricketts, it was "necessary to create the conditions" that would make an invasion legal. So Washington came up with an ingenious solution. Explained Rycroft: "the intelligence and facts were being fixed around the policy."

This was eight months before the U.S., aided primarily by Great Britain, invaded Iraq.

Several strategies were invoked. Push to reintroduce UN weapons inspectors to provide a pretext for war. The Cabinet Office paper observed that "an ultimatum for the return of UN weapons inspectors to Iraq" might help create "the conditions necessary to justify government military action." Indeed, the writer later noted, "It is just possible that an ultimatum could be cast in terms which Saddam would reject." Foreign Secretary Straw noted: "I believe that a demand for the unfettered readmission of weapons inspectors is essential, in terms of public explanation, and in terms of legal sanction for any subsequent military action."

Yet the legal minded British worried that the Bush administration might carelessly provoke Baghdad into war. Noted the Cabinet Office memo, military action could be "precipitated in an unplanned way by, for example, an incident in the No Fly Zones," in which Washington had been aggressively bombing—the "spikes of activity" noted earlier.

The significance of the Rycroft (Downing Street) memo has been dismissed by some, including Michael Kinsley of the Los Angeles Times and Tim Cavanaugh of Reason. After all, much of its contents are hearsay and it only tells us what we already knew. The Bush administration has largely ignored its existence, while Prime Minister Tony Blair pointed to the fact that Washington ultimately went to the United Nations—even though the Bush administration always indicated that it would act irrespective of what the United Nation Security Council decided.

But taken together the memos paint a far different picture than that presented by George W. Bush to the American public and foreign peoples. The documents discredit the President's disingenuous claim that military action would be a last resort. Indeed, in his speech before invading the President said: "We are doing everything we can to avoid war in Iraq," which was a blatant, shameful falsehood. The administration's elaborate show, put on with great fanfare at home and before the UN in early 2003, alleging Baghdad's terrorist connections and WMD programs, was only for show. (Prime Minister Tony Blair looks no more honest: "all the way through that period of time, we were trying to look for a way of managing to resolve this without conflict," he responded when asked about the Downing Street memo: "The decision was not already taken.")

In fact, the Iraq war was a matter of choice, not necessity. And the Bush administration's goal never was disarmament. It intended to overthrow Hussein irrespective of any diplomatic initiative, the reintroduction of UN inspectors, or compliance with any UN resolutions.

Perhaps most tragically, the memos foretold the catastrophic mismanagement of the so-called peace. Rycroft noted that "There was little discussion in Washington of the aftermath after military action." David Manning, then Blair's chief foreign policy aide, wrote the Prime Minister on March 14, 2002, advocating that the latter should "not budge either in your insistence that, if we pursued regime change, it must be very carefully done and produce the right result."

The options paper stated that "The greater investment of Western forces, the greater our control over Iraq's future, but the greater the cost and the longer we would need to stay." Foreign Secretary Straw worried that the U.S. had not answered "how there can be any certainty that the replacement regime will be better." After all, he added, "Iraq has had NO history of democracy so no-one has this habit or experience."

White House spokesman David Almacy has tartly responded to the memos, asserting that "There was significant post war planning." But that claim, if true, is even more damning, given the actual consequences. But evidence of serious planning is in short supply. After looting swept occupied Baghdad, Defense Secretary Donald Rumsfeld said simply: "stuff happens."

However mistaken the U.S. government's decision to invade, finding an acceptable exit will be difficult. When it came to Bill Clinton's war in Kosovo, then-candidate George W. Bush observed that "Victory means exit strategy." Now, however, he believes that America must remain entangled for years. What Press Secretary Scott McClellan calls the administration's "strategy for success" just looks like more of the same.

But as the administration calls upon the rest of us for support, it is paying a price for its prior deceits. By an amazing 49 to 44 percent plurality, Americans blame Bush more than Hussein for the war. And 60 percent of Americans want to withdraw at least some U.S. troops—with only a third willing to wait until a stable government is formed. Unfortunately, there is ample reason to distrust the President. Whatever promises he or his officials make in the future will be no easier to believe.

July 2005

The Faithless Coalition

The U.S. is the strongest nation on earth. But it has discovered that power doesn't buy love. The U.S. should make clear that from now on real friendship must run both ways.

Over Washington's objections, the Philippines withdrew its minuscule military contingent from Iraq to save a captive Filipino truck driver kidnapped by Islamic terrorists. After the Madrid bombing earlier this year, the new Spanish government brought home its 1300 troops from Iraq.

The Dominican Republic and Honduras pulled out their small detachments shortly thereafter. In early July Norway withdrew 140 of 155 troops; Moldova and Singapore also have brought home most of their few score personnel. New Zealand and Thailand plan to get out in September.

Estonia says its troops will be coming home soon. The Netherlands and Poland are expected to exit by spring or summer 2005.

What has always been a coalition more in name than reality threatens to disintegrate. It will be the U.S., Britain, and a few others—Japanese who won't fight, South Koreans sent to where they won't have to fight, Ukrainians who retreated when they had to fight.

Even the contributions from serious nations, other than that from Great Britain, are too small to make other than a psychological difference. And the stalwarts eventually may falter. Should Australia's Labor Party win the upcoming election, that nation's contingent will be gone by Christmas; only a narrow parliamentary majority recently extended Italy's deployment.

Hostage crises have generated significant popular opposition in Japan and South Korea to their participation. With more than 50 foreigners kidnapped so far and allied forces evidently unable to provide security, there will be more macabre terrorist beheadings. Even countries with no troops on station—Egypt, India, Jordan, and Kenya—have had citizens kidnapped, with the terrorists demanding that civilian workers "transporting goods, weapons and military equipment" for the U.S. go home.

Pleading by the provisional Iraqi government and pressure from the Bush Administration—on Hungarian television Secretary of State Colin

Powell recently warned America's allies to "not get weak in the knees"—has proved to be of no avail. Few friendly governments ever believed in Washington's policy or trusted the Bush administration's management. When involvement in Iraq proved to be far more costly than expected, many of America's so-called friends began running for the exit.

That resulted in predictable name-calling in Washington. "Appeasers" was the most predictable and common insult. But it was not the only one.

"Cowardly," "weasels," "craven," and even "milksops" are others applied to the Philippines. Manila "caved in" and "stabbed America in the back."

In fact, Washington recalled its ambassador for "consultations." Secretary Powell said the Bush administration was "seriously disappointed" in the Arroyo government's action.

Yet in one sense Washington has little cause for complaint. Even countries that have withdrawn their forces did contribute. It wasn't their fault that the Iraqi occupation proved to be far bloodier than Washington predicted. As both Spain and the Philippines have tartly noted, they are entitled to make policies based on their nations's best interests.

So is the U.S., however.

There is nothing to be gained from juvenile insults. There is much to be gained from letting countries know that if they can't be bothered to help America in its time of need, Washington might not help them when they call for assistance.

With the collapse of the Soviet Union and end of the Warsaw Pact, there really isn't much that the Europeans require from America. That's why 50 years of an American-dominated NATO is enough. Irrespective of France's, Germany's, or Spain's policies towards Iraq, the U.S. should leave Europe's problems, such as the Balkans, to Europe.

In Asia allied countries are even more insistent that the U.S. remain not just engaged, but on the military frontline. Washington should start asking them the simple question: what have you done for America lately?

For instance, U.S. forces have been defending South Korea for 54 years. Seoul's planned dispatch of 3600 soldiers to Iraq in return is a bit paltry, though better than nothing.

But sending them to the north in peaceful Kurdish territory—after explicitly refusing to patrol fractious Kirkuk—is not much better than nothing. The Bush administration's plan to withdraw 12,500 soldiers from the ROK for possible redeployment to Iraq should become the start of full disengagement.

Japan's Iraq garrison is of even less value. Tokyo, also the beneficiary of decades of American military protection, has sent in 600 troops for humanitarian duties only. They have been instructed not to aid allied forces in battle but would undoubtedly call for help from the same troops if they came under attack.

True, Tokyo still is working to overcome the unnatural constraints lingering from World War II and the American-imposed pacifist constitution. But the U.S. can help Japan come to terms with history by indicating that the world's second-ranking economic power can no longer stand idly by while America diverts personnel to guard Japanese sea lanes, backstop Japanese territorial disputes, and safeguard Japanese security.

Still, at least Seoul and Tokyo remained firm when confronted by terrorist kidnappers. The Philippines surrendered, pulling home its 51 soldiers. Filipino President Gloria Arroyo proclaimed that it was "a time of triumph," a truly singular judgment.

Washington should respond with the pointed message: don't call us, we'll call you.

The Philippines teeters on the edge of failure: inefficient, corrupt, poor, dysfunctional, semi-democratic. It has grand pretensions, but rarely delivers. "We are with you in your leadership against terrorism, wherever it may be found," Arroyo once claimed.

Yet Manila cheerfully deploys an air force that doesn't fly and a navy that doesn't float, in the words of one former defense minister. So the Philippines relies on the U.S. for aid in defeating domestic Islamic guerrillas and fending off China's territorial claims over the Spratly Islands.

"We will consider the United States as our big brother in the security arena," says presidential spokesman Ignacio Bunye: "Our longstanding and maturing relations with the United States will survive this hostage crisis."

Friendly relations should survive, but American military guardianship should not. Washington is not looking "to punish the Philippines in any way," said America's Charge d'Affaires, Joseph Mussomeli, in Manila. Fair enough.

The issue is not that countries are either "with us or against us" in the fight against terrorism, as President George W. Bush once put it. The issue is that sacrifice must be a two-way street.

The U.S. has sent thousands of troops to train Filipino forces fighting Islamic guerrillas. Several Americans have died in joint exercises. And U.S. taxpayers have contributed billions in aid to the Philippines over the years.

It is time to say, no more.

Washington faces a world full of unfinished business. It must set priorities.

It should cut off onetime clients that are unimportant strategically and faithless morally. America has more important things to do than subsidize and defend them.

"Every life is important," said President Arroyo. Absolutely. That includes the lives of American service men and women presently stationed around the world, protecting scores of friends and allies.

For most of the Cold War the U.S. gave a lot and asked for little. Now America needs help. When asked by supposedly friendly countries for aid, Washington should respond: What have you done for the U.S. lately?

July 2004

They Are Coming, Mr. President

"BRING 'EM ON," said President George W. Bush

"Close-Up Shot At Campus Kills a Soldier," *New York Times* headline

"In Postwar Iraq, the Battle Widens," *Washington Post* headline

"U.S. Soldier Shot and Killed in Baghdad," *Associated Press* headline

"Attacks Kill 3 U.S. Soldiers in Baghdad," *Associated Press* headline

"Iraqi Attacks Wound Seven U.S. Soldiers," *Associated Press* headline

President George W. Bush's earthy simplicity was a strength after September 11. He helped rally a wounded nation and forge a strategy that targeted terrorists who had targeted America.

But today that earthy simplicity seems out-of-touch with foreign realities. Of Islamic militants he says, "bring 'em on." He added, "there are some who feel like that conditions are such that they can attack us there," but "we have the force necessary to deal with the situation."

The President, cosseted by a White House staff and Secret Service guard, might not have noticed, but America's enemies are bringing it on, killing and wounding American soldiers every day. Washington's assumption about the ease of rebuilding Iraqi society belongs in history's ashheap along with Saddam Hussein's monstrous regime.

The situation is alarming, far more serious than the administration admits. The problem is not that Saddam Hussein, if he is alive, is capable of driving out American forces and reestablishing his dictatorship. Hatred of the Baathists is too widespread to allow them any popular victory.

The problem is that violent opposition to American rule will make it far more difficult promote the widespread civil institutions that undergird a free society. It will be harder to create an independent, representative government. And the occupation will require ever harsher tactics that will inflame further resentment around the world against America.

Attacks on U.S. military convoys demonstrate surprising organization and capability among the opposition. Murders of opportunity—of soldiers shopping in Baghdad, for instance—demonstrate the equally worrisome vulnerability of U.S. forces to anonymous freelancers. We are involved in a multi-front war.

Of course, at some level President Bush is right when he argued: "We have the force necessary to deal with the situation." The U.S. deploys the finest military on the planet. With 1.4 million men and women under arms, supplemented by substantial reserve call-ups, America theoretically can withstand a couple of casualties a day, the going rate.

But already half of the Army's ten divisions are committed to Iraq. Washington also is garrisoning wealthy allied states in East Asia and Europe, policing cold peaces in Bosnia and Kosovo, fighting Islamist remnants and protecting an unstable government in Afghanistan, and perhaps reconstructing Liberia.

Even enlisting the Marines in garrison duty won't yield the troops necessary to maintain all of these commitments and give soldiers sufficient time back in America with their families. Few GIs volunteer in hopes of never seeing their nation's shores again; keeping 150,000 to 200,000 troops in Iraq for years will put an intolerable strain on those expected to maintain what increasingly looks like a little empire.

Nor can the problem be solved by calling up the reserves. They offer an important surge capacity in case of an emergency, not a ready supply for constant deployment. Overseas service is even harder on reservists, since they must leave job as well as family.

In the short-term, of course, the administration can order and soldiers will obey. But in the longer-term, troops simply won't re-up. And civilians won't join.

Already troops in Iraq, who thought they were going over to liberate, not garrison, that country, are angrily demanding to go home. Their families are even more insistent. And the frustrations of America's finest will only grow.

A few years ago the Pentagon found it more difficult to retain skilled personnel, such as pilots, and attract new recruits; surveys and focus groups found resistance to promiscuous deployments for frivolous purposes by the Clinton administration. The problem will be even greater if continued service means participating in a shooting war in Iraq.

And it will.

Dismissing all resistance as tied to the old regime is too easy. Baathists are but one source of dissatisfaction with the U.S. occupation.

Sunni elites used to governing Iraq fear lost privileges; fundamentalist Shiites most resent an occupation by Western Christians allied with Israel. Independent Islamic terrorists along with agents from Iran and Syria are looking for targets.

Any attempt to reestablish central control over Kurdish areas will anger groups that had been America's strongest allies. Imagine an uncoordinated Baathist insurgency, Shiite civilian intifada, and Kurdish resistance coming together against U.S. forces.

Washington's assumption that the U.S. would be treated as a liberator was always too simplistic. No surprise, most Iraqis were glad to be rid of Saddam Hussein.

But equally no surprise, most Iraqis share the general antipathy towards the American government evident throughout the Mideast and Islamic worlds. Moreover, like all peoples everywhere, Iraqis want to run their own affairs.

The U.S. proclaimed liberation but has done little to convince Iraqis that they will soon become masters of their own fate. Increasingly tough military operations against suspected guerrillas only makes the problem worse. One U.S. sergeant told the *Economist* magazine: "You promise freedom. They get martial law." And they don't like it.

Every time American troops arrest, bind, and blindfold an Iraqi they create another Iraqi ready to demand Washington's ouster. Every time American troops wound or kill an Iraqi, they push family members and friends towards a violent response.

Indeed, U.S. forces have increasingly been criticized for shooting first and asking questions later. Perhaps the worst incident was in April, when Americans came under fire and shot killed 15 Iraqis in two days of protests in Fallujah. The atmosphere has been ugly and dangerous ever since.

Even the British forces, suffering their own troubles with angry Shiite residents, have been appalled by some American practices. After learning that U.S. troops had arrested three innocent Iraqis—whose families came to the British for help—British Col. Steve Cox termed the Americans "idiot" and "stupid."

The fault is not that of U.S. soldiers. They are trained to be warriors, to destroy an opposing military, not to be governors, to balance amongst competing political factions.

If occupation forces were able to target only terrorists or guerrillas, Washington might avoid expanding hostility and resentment. But it hasn't been able to do so so far and seems unlikely to do so in the future.

The result will not necessarily be direct support for those killing Americans. But a refusal to oppose them could make U.S. control untenable.

At Baghdad University an American civil affairs soldiers was gunned down in the cafeteria and the culprit disappeared unscathed, despite a campus full of witnesses. If Americans increasingly are murdered without recourse, who will want to toss in his or her lot with the U.S., working in a pro-American government? Seven Iraqi police recruits were recently murdered, and many more "collaborators" will undoubtedly die.

The longer Washington temporizes, the more difficult the situation becomes. Most important, it must enlist local Iraqi factions in the governing process, so they understand that they have a stake in rebuffing any attempt by the Baathists to return to power.

The U.S. must quickly withdraw from issues of day-to-day governance while preparing a decentralized government structure with some hope of surviving America's departure. It should swallow its pride and request allied assistance—which requires allied participation in decision-making. And Washington must create a rough timetable for pulling out, indicating that the U.S. is prepared to live with any government that neither aids terrorists or develops weapons of mass destruction.

Once committed, it is hard to leave. Indeed, some argue that it is vital that America get Iraq right.

But it will take years to get Iraq right, if that goal is even possible. Along the way Washington is likely to face an increasingly costly guerrilla war guaranteed to increase hostility towards America throughout Iraq and the Islamic world. It may be too late to win the peace; now Washington can only hope not to lose it.

July 2003

Iraq: Whither the U.S.

Concerned about declining confidence in administration policy in Iraq—and, equally important, falling support for his reelection campaign—President George W. Bush gave the first of several planned speeches on Iraq to an audience at the Army War College. Alas, he offered the usual platitudes about giving to Iraq "a free, representative government" and occupying that nation only for "as long as necessary." He promised that "Iraqis will govern their own affairs," except, apparently, peripheral matters such as changing occupation rules, blocking U.S. military action, and holding Saddam Hussein.

Moreover, U.S. forces won't be going home any time soon. Deputy Defense Secretary Paul Wolfowitz recently told Congress: "I think it's entirely possible that U.S. troops could be stationed in Iraq for years." At best, "we will be able to let [the Iraqis] be in the front lines and us be in a supporting position." Yet the Pentagon has developed contingency plans for inserting another 25,000 soldiers should the security situation deteriorate. Unfortunately, the President's warning that "Terrorists are likely to become more active and more brutal" is about his only prediction that has proved to be accurate.

Nor are suicide bombings the only barrier to progress. Consider the problems leading up to the creation of the provisional Iraqi government. One-time administration ally Ahmed Chalabi, a member of the Iraqi Governing Council, was accused of being a corrupt Iranian spy. The head of the Iraqi Governing Council was assassinated. The Abu Ghraib prison abuses sapped already declining Iraqi support for the U.S. Reconstruction work lagged because of violence and insecurity. Fighting continued in the holy Shiite cities of Karbala and Najaf; the U.S. retreated from its promise to arrest radical cleric Moktada al-Sadr. American, Italian, and South Korean hostages were beheaded before a global audience.

Until Iraq possesses a government seen as legitimate by Iraqis, unlikely until free elections are held, nationalists will continue to make common cause with Baathists and terrorists against American and allied forces. (Even moderate Ayatollah Ali al-Sistani says the interim regime, though a step forward, lacks "electoral legitimacy.") Unfortunately, the death toll will continue to rise. There will be more dancing Iraqis celebrating the killing of more coalition soldiers and civilians.

How to respond? The tough-minded advocate using whatever force is necessary, no matter how many Iraqis die, to maintain order. We should have leveled Fallujah, a city of 300,000, for instance. Michael Rubin of the American Enterprise Institute says we still should do so, despite the nominal return of sovereignty to Iraq. But we can't. It's not what America is about. Especially if the professed goal is to promote liberty and democracy in Iraq.

But the fact that we can't do "what it takes" provides yet more proof, as if more proof was needed, that sticking around in an attempt to forcibly create an Iraq in America's image, "a free, representative government that serves its people and fights on their behalf," as President Bush put it, is not just foolish, but dangerously foolish. We cannot leave tomorrow. But we must leave.

Iraq's apparent lack of either WMD stockpiles or operational ties to al-Qaeda have embarrassed an administration that looks careless, deceptive, and arrogant. Still, however flawed the justification for the war, America is now stuck with the aftermath.

Nevertheless, Washington can choose what the aftermath entails. The Bush administration has embarked upon a reconstruction program breathtaking in its ambitions: true social engineering on an international scale.

The goal, a democratic, humane, Western-oriented Iraq, is surely worthy. It also likely is an illusion.

George Downs and Bruce Bueno de Mesquita of New York University looked at 35 cases and concluded that in only one did a "full-fledged, stable democracy ... emerge within 10 years" after U.S. intervention. The oft-celebrated cases of Germany and Japan differ dramatically from Iraq; both were real countries, with a sense of nationhood, relatively homogenous populations, and democratic experience.

That doesn't mean Iraq cannot become a democracy. It may become such a nation one day, but Washington is unlikely to achieve that end through force of arms on its terms. Iraq will succeed only in its own time, through the development of domestic civil institutions, and not at the point of an American gun.

Of course, it has long been the mantra of the administration and its supporters that there is a lot of good news in Iraq that is not being reported. For instance, the harbors are being cleaned, said columnist Mark Steyn in one piece celebrating administration policy. The occupation authority put out a cheery fact a day—the issuance of grants to promote women in leadership, the inauguration of new economic regulatory bodies, and more.

Indeed, there is genuine good news. The end of the Hussein regime is a blessing. Iraqis have a chance for freedom and prosperity.

But there is little good news for Washington. House-to-house fighting in Fallujah and multiple risings in Shiite cities in April constituted a violent leap well beyond improvised explosive devices and snipings. Iraq today is a different Iraq than that right after liberation.

Don't worry, proclaims columnist Jack Kelly, "If we stand firm, victory is all but certain." If so, it seems to be a victory that Iraqis don't want.

A Gallup poll conducted in March and April found that while Iraqis were gratified by Saddam Hussein's ouster, 57 percent of them wanted American forces to leave immediately and an astonishing 52 percent believed that attacks on U.S. soldiers are at least "sometimes" justified. A plurality said that the U.S. had "done more harm than good." Strip out the small Kurdish population, almost unanimous in its backing of America, and the numbers were far worse. "Go home" said 61 percent of Shiites, 65 percent of Sunnis, and 75 percent of Baghdad residents.

And the poll was conducted before the extended violence in Fallujah and Najaf and the scandal at Abu Ghraib prison, which undoubtedly have driven America's negatives even higher. A May Reuters poll found more than nine of ten Iraqis viewing themselves as occupied. Subsequent polls yielded similar dismal results.

Alas, the Bush administration's options are shrinking. It has continually breathed fire regarding deadly insurgents and terrorists, only to retreat each time after achieving little more than bad publicity. For instance, occupation officials long threatened the Sunni insurgency with destruction, to no obvious effect. "This will not be tolerated," said occupation head Paul Bremer of al-Sadr—who, months later, remained at large with his militia members still battling U.S. forces. A deal emerged for his forces to stop fighting, but al-Sadr avoided arrest while winning a two-thirds approval rating from Iraqis. After promising to retaliate for the killing of four contract security personnel in Fallujah, the U.S. besieged the city, then temporized for weeks, and finally pulled back in favor of onetime Baathist generals. Can anyone spell appeasement?

The U.S. is desperately enlisting Iraqi security forces, but insurgents are targeting them too. Nor are the very men trained and paid by Washington trustworthy; a quarter of police ran off or joined the rioters during the civil uprisings. In Fallujah civil defense personnel may have led the four American contractors into a trap, while the police stayed in their walled compound as the Americans were being murdered and their bodies were being desecrated. The new Iraqi army simply refused to fight in Fallujah. Iraqi forces have proved to be no more reliable in battles since then.

The transition to Iraqi sovereignty has proved to be equally difficult. Bremer's occupation authority changed strategies month-by-month. President Bush was left to hope for success through a UN-orchestrated rescue. Yet confused charges and denials about who would be appointed interim president and prime minister left it unclear if anyone was in charge. The leaders ultimately selected by the U.S.-UN process were respectable, but lacked popular authority.

The constitution, largely developed by the U.S., is a worthwhile document. But it is unlikely to ever be put into practice. Representatives of the majority Shiites on the U.S.-appointed Iraqi Governing Council evidently agreed to the constitution only to speed elections, after which, if the Shiites take control as expected, they will revise it. Sharp disagreements between Kurds and other Iraqis over promised Kurdish autonomy were barely papered over.

Americans limits on the sovereignty of the interim Iraqi government combined with contradictory statements about whether Baghdad could send U.S. forces home—after Washington had expressed its expectation of maintaining more than 100,000 troops in Iraq through at least 2006—undercut the perceived authority of the new Iraqi government. Under pressure from British Prime Minister Tony Blair, among others, President Bush publicly promised that Baghdad would possess "full sovereignty," but U.S. officials have indicated that everything from security to oil will be beyond the new government's authority. Plans for a huge American embassy suggest that the Bush administration expects Baghdad to be little more than a puppet regime.

Which ensures that indigenous insurgents and outside terrorists will continue to have an excuse, however cynical, to ply their deadly trade. And that enough Iraqis will back them to spread the violence.

Hostile attitudes are especially likely to grow if the U.S. leaves forces in Iraq for years, as suggested by Deputy Secretary Wolfowitz, and especially if Washington does "whatever it takes," as some hawkish analysts advocate, to preserve U.S. control. Brutal suppression of Iraqis might deter additional brutal murder of Americans. But it more likely would encourage further attacks. The U.S. has raided homes, arrested suspects, and encircled entire cities in barbed wire. The resistance never ebbed. The assault on Fallujah united some Shiites and Sunnis, an ominous development. A recent poll cited by Iraqi blogger Juan Cole found that two-thirds of Iraqis supported or somewhat supported al-Sadr as he resisted U.S. forces.

Perhaps America has not been ruthless enough. After all, the Marine Corp's assault on Fallujah paled in comparison to, say, the Nazi destruction of the Czech village of Lidice in World War II. But even the latter did not quell resistance. More important, it is not in America's character to be that brutal. Especially in a campaign presented as advancing democracy.

Ruthlessness inevitably afflicts the innocent as well as guilty, creating yet more anger. A year ago U.S. forces killed and wounded some 80 demonstrators in Fallujah. American troops killed nine Iraqi policemen chasing a suspect towards a U.S. checkpoint in Fallujah later last year. These and others might be inevitable accidents of war, but they should leave no one surprised that hostility towards Washington reaches well beyond disaffected former Baathists.

The consequences of the occupation do not stop at Iraq's borders. Unfortunately, even as al-Qaeda has been badly damaged by allied military and security operations over the last two years, a host of smaller groups around the world have been created or rejuvenated. And Iraq has become a potent recruiting vehicle for them. Concluded the International Institute for Strategic Studies in a new report, "Galvanized by Iraq if compromised by Afghanistan, al Qaeda remains a viable and effective network of networks." Indeed, adds the IISS, "over 18,000 potential terrorists are at large with recruitment accelerating on account of Iraq." The President may be right to describe Iraq as "the central front" in the war on terrorism, but it is so only because the U.S. invasion and occupation have made it so.

A recent Pew Research Center poll found that "A year after the war in Iraq, discontent with America and its policies has intensified rather than diminished" around the globe. For instance, large majorities of Jordanians, Moroccans, and Pakistanis, whose governments support the U.S., view America unfavorably. Huge majorities believe Washington to be insincere in its war on terrorism.

In European as well as Islamic countries sometimes large majorities of people say that the war in Iraq has caused them to doubt America's commitment to democracy and have less confidence that America is trustworthy. Indeed, many of the Muslims polled endorse suicide operations against coalition forces in Iraq; an incredible third of respondents do so even in Turkey, long thought to be a firm American friend. Because of the Abu Ghraib prison abuse allied governments helped block efforts to exempt U.S. forces from liability under the International Criminal Court.

Last year Defense Secretary Donald Rumsfeld presciently asked whether the U.S. was killing terrorists faster than it was creating them. When it comes to Iraq, at least, the answer seems to be no.

Which means that Washington must develop an exit strategy. Not a closet strategy, now advanced by Paul Wolfowitz, to hide U.S. forces on bases behind high walls once more Iraqi cops are on the streets. But a genuine exit strategy.

Of course, even after multiple terror bombings Washington cannot pull out precipitously no matter how much it would like to do so. And America has an interest in making the hand-off to Iraqis as smooth as possible.

But the U.S. needs to clearly understand what is essential for American security and what is not. An Iraq in which the harbors have been dredged is not. An Iraq in which more schools have opened is not. Even an Iraq with Western-style elections and liberties is not.

All are desirable. None is essential. Nor necessarily attainable at acceptable cost in terms of lives and resources, burden on the military, and other deleterious consequences—most notably, encouraging more terrorism.

Rather, the criterion of success is simple: Is America made more secure? It is if an Iraqi government comes to power that cooperates in identifying, fighting, and eliminating al-Qaeda forces. And that helps dampen Islamic jihadist sentiments.

America is not safer if Baghdad trafficks with terrorists. It is not more secure if Iraq offers sanctuary to al-Qaeda operatives and facilities. It is not better off if Baghdad creates weapons of mass destruction.

Ironically, making Iraq more democratic will not necessarily make America more secure. Democratic governments representing those hostile majorities in Jordan, Morocco, and Pakistan would endanger America. Democracy in Egypt, Saudi Arabia, and elsewhere also likely would bring to power regimes wishing the U.S. ill. So too, perhaps, in Iraq.

Washington should work with Iraqis to develop a firm, accelerated timeline for elections, full restoration of Iraqi sovereignty, promulgation of a permanent constitution, and complete U.S. troop withdrawal. The timing is somewhat arbitrary, but the process cannot be allowed to drag on. Washington should begin drawing down its military presence now, after handing over sovereignty, with an objective of removing all of its occupation forces—in contrast to any advisers or liaison officers necessary to aid in dealing with al-Qaeda—by mid-2005 at the latest.

Could Iraq hurtle toward a bloody breakdown? Perhaps, but that threatens even with an American presence. Indeed, U.S. garrisons and patrols risk inflaming conflict. Should widespread civil, religious, or ethnic strife impend, it would be better for Washington to be out of rather than in it.

Could radical Shiites attempt to establish a theocratic state? Perhaps, though most Iraqis, Shiite, Sunni, and Kurd, appear to favor a more secular system. And as occupier the U.S. could ill-afford to reject a duly elected government. Better to set only the truly essential bottom line: no terrorist connections and no WMD.

Could jihadists claim a moral victory from an American departure? Perhaps, but they will achieve a clear strategic victory if America stays. With Iraq the U.S. has created an entirely new battlefield, but one against forces, Baathist remnants and Iraqi nationalists, that otherwise would ignore America. As for al-Qaeda and related groups which focus on the U.S., the Iraqi occupation has created yet another terrorist excuse and recruitment aid.

President George W. Bush says that he plans to "finish the work of the fallen," apparently however long that might take. Even presumptive Democratic presidential nominee John Kerry takes the "we cannot fail" position, proclaiming: "No matter who is elected president in November, we will persevere" in helping "Iraqis build a stable, peaceful and pluralistic society." And a number of outside analysts still talk of an occupation for years, decades, or even longer.

But many of the latter predicted that resistance would cease first with the fall of Saddam Hussein, and next with his capture. And that Iraqi oil would pay for Iraqi reconstruction.

They are the people who promised that most U.S. forces would come home last summer. And who suggested that democracy would sweep the Mideast following America's invasion. Claims that an extended U.S. occupation, if only a little tougher and longer, will succeed are no more credible.

America must not cut and run, it is routinely said, and that's true. But the alternative must not be to reinforce failure, accepting ever-increasing costs that make a future policy change even more difficult. It is in America's interest to get out; Washington must develop a plan to get out on its own terms, before it is forced out.

June 2004

The Tragic Meaning of London

London can be thankful that not all terrorist bombers are competent. But even before the dramatic televised threats from Ayman Zawahiri, al-Qaeda's number two leader, the second attack within two weeks in Britain's capital clearly answered the question: has the Iraq war reduced the terrorist threat? No.

Unfortunately, it's hard to speak honestly about such horrid events because so many war advocates tar any critic as disloyal. But policy must be grounded in reality, not fantasy, no matter how politically painful the assessment.

Too many Americans and Iraqis already have died based on false claims of Saddam Hussein's supposed possession of WMDs and connection to 9/11. No one should die now under the illusion that we are fighting terrorists in Baghdad and Fallujah instead of in New York and London. To the contrary, we are helping to create terrorists around the world as we fight in Iraq.

To state what should be obvious in no way justifies what amounts to mass murder. Those who kill and maim should themselves be killed or captured.

That is as true in Baghdad as in London. Whatever one thinks of the war and occupation, simple justice dictates supporting Iraqi authorities as they attempt to track down those who remorselessly murder, targeting even children lined up to collect candy.

Still, U.S. policy must be based on the unfortunate fact that has been evident for months: the war in Iraq has spawned new terrorist threats. We are less safe because of President George W. Bush's unnecessary war.

The administration initially responded to 9/11 by confronting the anti-American terrorists who attacked the U.S. The coordinated international search for members and money seriously damaged al-Qaeda and associated groups. The overthrow of the Taliban in Afghanistan removed the organization's national sponsors.

Of course, even these steps angered some jihadists. But most Muslims and Arab governments backed or at least accepted the U.S. response. It was measured, proportional, and effective.

And, if resolutely pursued, this strategy promised to greatly diminish the ability of those who wish us ill to act. Alas, the threat would never disappear completely so long as the "root causes" remain. Explaining terrorism does not justify it. But explaining it does help us more effectively respond to it.

In general, terrorism is a violent tool in a political struggle, where one side is overmatched in conventional terms. Robert Pape, author of the new book, Dying to Win: The Strategic Logic of Suicide Terrorism, reviewed 315 bombing attacks between 1983 and 2003 and found that virtually all of them had "a specific secular and strategic goal: to compel democracies to withdraw military forces from the terrorists' national homeland."

There presumably are some jihadists who simply hate America and its freedoms. And a few others might have wild ideas about reestablishing Islamic glory over Western lands. But most of the antagonism springs from hatred of U.S. (and allied) government policies.

Polls have long found surprisingly widespread appreciation for American values (and products) among both Muslims and Arabs. Hostility was concentrated on the U.S. government over its support for the Israeli occupation over Palestinians, maintenance of sanctions against Iraq, despoilation of Islamic holy lands in Saudi Arabia, and support for assorted dictatorships.

Although the attack on Iraq incidentally eliminated the second and third grievances, the war and occupation added an even more powerful new one. Set aside Ayman Zawahiri's demand, undoubtedly shaped to maximize its PR value, for the West's "withdrawal from our land." Polling by John Zogby has found a sharp rise in anger against Washington after the U.S.-led invasion. It should surprise no one that this upsurge spawned new terrorists destined to attack America and its allies.

The President prefers ideology to reality. "We fight today because terrorists want to attack our country and kill our citizens, and Iraq is where they are making their stand." Actually, Iraq is making more of them, terrorists who would not be taking a stand except for the invasion of Iraq.

And that has been recognized by most everyone outside of the President's own political appointees. Although terrorists and their sympathizers tend to accumulate grievances, Iraq stands out as the one pushing many of them to take up arms and bombs.

For instance, before the London bombings an assessment by British intelligence services that "events in Iraq are continuing to act as motivation and a focus of a range of terrorist-related activity" leaked to the press. In a new report Britain's Chatham House, formerly the Royal Institute of International Affairs, observed that "the situation over Iraq has imposed particular difficulties for the UK" because it has given "a boost to the al-Qaeda network's propaganda, recruitment and fund-raising." Nearly two-thirds of Britons acknowledged after the London bombings that Iraq had been a factor.

The Israeli Global Research in International Affairs Center published a report earlier this year which found that Iraq "has turned into a magnet for jihadi volunteers." But not established terrorists. Rather, explains Center director and report author Reuven Paz, "the vast majority of Arabs killed in Iraq have never taken part in any terrorist activity prior to their arrival in Iraq," whether Afghanistan, Bosnia, or Chechnya.

Larry Johnson, who served with both the CIA and the State Department's counterterrorism office, observes that "You now in Iraq have a recruiting ground in which jihadists, people who previously were not willing to go out and embrace the vision of bin Laden" are "now aligning themselves with elements that have declared allegiance to him."

The British government has compiled an extensive report entitled "Young Muslims and Extremism," warning that British-U.S. foreign policy is alienating many Muslims who see "the war on terror, and in Iraq and Afghanistan ... as having been acts against Islam." Analysts informed the prime minister that the Iraq war is acting as a "recruiting sergeant" for extremism. Although the U.S. is the primary target of jihadist fervor, Chatham House reports that "The UK is at particular risk because it is the closest ally of the United States" and has been involved in several American-led military operations.

The CIA has warned that Iraq has become what Afghanistan was, a national training ground for terrorists. Chatham House reports that the war has provided "an ideal targeting and training area" for terrorists.

Similarly, warns Reuven Paz: "The battle experience that Jihadists gain in Iraq, a campaign that, unlike in Afghanistan, Bosnia, or

Chechnya, is plagued more by acts of terrorism than by guerrilla warfare, supplies the Islamist adherents of the Global Jihad culture with a wealth of first hand field experience, in spite of the absence of organized training camps." Larry Johnson worries that Iraqi insurgents are learning how to build bombs and run military operations.

Even more menacingly, after being trained in the ways of urban warfare these terrorists are "bleeding out" across the world, from the Mideast to Europe. An investigative article in Germany's *Der Spiegel* magazine reports that scores of Muslim extremists have returned to Europe from Iraq, and all "are equipped with fresh combat experience and filled with ideological indoctrination. It is these men who are considered particularly dangerous."

Improvised explosive devices—the main killer of U.S. soldiers in Iraq—have spread to Afghanistan. Iraq has overtaken Sri Lanka as the locus of the most suicide bombings. Suicide bombers now seem to be the terrorist tool of choice in London.

Thus, when the President says that the terrorists "want us to retreat from the world so they can spread their ideology of hate," he's got it entirely wrong. They already are spreading their ideology of hate. Alas, America's intervention has made more people listen more closely.

The terrorists and their sympathizers want us to retreat so we are no longer—in their professed view—at war with them. Ayman Zawahiri denounced "aggression against Muslims," such as occupation of Afghanistan and Iraq, theft of oil and wealth, and support for corrupt regimes. Osama bin Laden's earlier phrasing was: "If you bomb our cities, we will bomb yours." Although condemning the London attacks, Mahmoud al-Zahar, a senior leader of Hamas, contended that Muslims have suffered "too much from the American aggression." Other jihadists have expressed similar sentiments.

The point is not that their assessments are accurate or American policies are unjustified. But terrorists are blowing up innocent people because they want to change allied government policies, not because they want to shut down MTV or bankrupt Disneyland.

Obviously, neither London nor Washington can precipitously retreat from Iraq, allowing terrorist acts to determine national policy. Moreover, officials might decide that some objectives are important enough to pay the cost.

But policymakers must recognize the risk. Intervention is more likely to foster than suppress terrorism. For this reason, both countries should accelerate their exit from Iraq. Equally important, they should abandon the illusion that invading and occupying Middle Eastern states is a remedy for terrorism.

Observed Robert Pape: "Since suicide terrorism is mainly a response to foreign occupation and not Islamic fundamentalism, the use of heavy military force to transform Muslim societies over there, if you would, is only likely to increase the number of suicide terrorists coming at us." Unfortunately, despite the President's optimistic assumptions, we aren't likely to be able to kill them all. Noted Pape, "suicide terrorism is not a supply-limited phenomenon where there are just a few hundred around the world willing to do it because they are religious fanatics. It is a demand-driven phenomenon."

The London bombings offer further proof that Iraq war supporters are deluding themselves if they believe that the conflict has provided a killing field for terrorists otherwise bound for America. Rather, it is providing an opportunity for extremists to kill U.S. troops while learning skills that may eventually be employed in Western lands. The Bush administration's misguided policies have made America and the world a more dangerous place.

August 2005

A version of this article was originally published in the Reason, *August 22, 2005.*

Democracy or Liberty?

For some, the Iraq constitution-writing process called to mind America's founding. But whether any Iraqi constitution will deliver liberty as well as democracy to their people remains tragically uncertain.

The failure of Washington to find WMDs in Iraq or link Baghdad to anti-U.S. terrorism forced Bush administration officials to find an alternate justification for the war. The President and many of his supporters therefore fastened on democracy promotion, effectively stealing Woodrow Wilson's disastrous legacy from the Democratic Party.

No where has the democratic process been watched more closely than in Iraq. Lebanese elections have dampened Syrian influence, but at the cost of moving anti-American politicians center-stage.

Small Saudi Arabian reform moves have aided fundamentalists more than liberals. The leaders of Eqypt and Pakistan do little more than mouth democratic platitudes, but real elections would likely aid anti-American jihadists.

Iraq, however, is Washington's showcase—liberated, occupied, and recreated by U.S. troops. If coercive nation-building can succeed anywhere, it should be in Iraq.

Elections for a transitional government began the process. Alas, Washington's candidate, interim prime minister Iyad Allawi, developed no serious popular following. Despite complaints in Washington about ungrateful clients, the Iraqis chose other leaders.

Still, the constitution remained to be written. Would-be nation-builders, from administration staffers to media heavyweights, were free with advice. The constitution should enshrine women's rights and protect religious liberties. It should create a federal structure and separate law from Islam.

American activists protested and Washington officials cajoled. As the original August 15 deadline—desperately extended in the attempt to win Sunni agreement—for the constitution approached, Preeta D. Bansal and Nina Shea, members of the U.S Commission on International Religious Freedom, wrote "Now is not the time for the international community to take a hands-off approach, which it may be tempted to do by a false sense of cultural relativism and a misguided 'respect' for a flawed 'democratic' process that could, ultimately, lead to undemocratic results."

Similarly, demanded the New Republic: "The administration must bring to bear all the leverage that billions in reconstruction funding and the presence of the 138,000 American troops stationed in Iraq can provide." Some Iraqis also urged U.S. pressure. Basma Fakri, president of the Women's Alliance for a Democratic Iraq, said Washington should let the constitution writers know "that Iraq should be free."

American Ambassador Zalmay Khalilzad actively intervened in Baghdad, proclaiming Washington's support for equal rights, for instance. "There can be no compromise" he declared.

U.S. pressure seems to have some effect, though sections of the draft document still disappointed. Thus Sunnis denounced the proposal, which went to Iraqi voters in October.

Alas, the actual result probably never mattered much.

Obviously, constitutions are important. But only if they are enforced. And that requires a particular civic culture, political discourse, and legal regime. At the moment, Iraq appears to lack all of these.

Nor can the U.S. provide the necessary means of enforcement. Today American military occupation does not guarantee basic security. It is even less capable of ensuring equal rights.

Thus, a constitutional provision guaranteeing equal treatment will do Iraqi women no good if ignored by political authorities. Promises of fair treatment for Christians and others are of no avail if the Iraqi government cannot or will not protect religious minorities from attacks by Islamic fundamentalists.

Even formal democratic governance will mean little if authoritarian elements abuse their power. After all, the Soviet Union was notable for the professed liberality of its constitution—and complete irrelevance of that document. Similar is the experience of dozens of smaller hellholes dotting the globe, many of which officially modeled their governments after the American or British system.

If the Iraqi constitution ends up as a liberal document in an illiberal society, it would not be completely valueless. Such a blueprint would offer idealistic goals and provide a legal basis for real reform if the political culture changed.

However, the most pressing objective for those in the West who hope for a better future for Iraq is to promote within Iraqi society a greater appreciation of the importance of liberty. Democracy is a worthy means, but it is only a means. The objective is a free society.

And this is what makes America's present challenge in Iraq so great. "The idea that 1,800 American troops died so Iraqi women can enjoy the full blessings of religious medievalism ought to disturb the Bush administration and the American public," editorialized the New Republic. Absolutely.

"No American blood should be spilt for the creation of a sharia rule state," said Nina Shea. Very true.

But it is far easier to teach the efficient forms of political democracy than the civil forms of political discourse. Without a tolerant civic culture, real democracy is unlikely to flourish. And given the violent resistance against U.S. occupation forces even two years after the ouster of Saddam Hussein, Washington has neither the time and nor the ability to so educate the Iraqi people.

In fact, Washington's best policy is to do less. The U.S. government should begin withdrawing its troops while emphasizing its intention to expeditiously pull out all of its forces. Moreover, Washington should publicly disclaim any interest in acquiring permanent bases. Iraq's destiny will be in the hands of Iraqis.

More helpful may be the efforts of private groups. Without Washington's obvious political agenda, they can develop personal ties, model civil behavior, and teach liberty's meaning.

Iraq's constitutional negotiations should be seen as a start, not an end. They have opened the first political discussions in decades. They have highlighted the importance of a vibrant legal and political process. But whether that process eventually develops is unknowable.

Necessary, but yet to be built, is the foundation of a truly liberal society: a belief in freedom and a willingness to accept adverse political outcomes. Unfortunately, creating such a democratic ethic almost certainly lies beyond Washington's best efforts.

September 2005

Destroying the U.S. Military

Rep. Charles Rangel (D-NY) is reintroducing legislation for a draft. He first pushed his bill in 2003 in an attempt to slow the Bush administration's rush to war. Now he's advancing conscription to provide the bodies necessary to prosecute the Bush administration's unnecessary war.

Returning to a draft would ruin the world's dominant armed forces, filling its ranks with people who don't want to serve and turning military service into a divisive political issue. Yet Rangel's proposal reflects an ugly reality: the Bush administration's disastrous intervention in Iraq—dubious social engineering on a global scale—already is wrecking the U.S. military. As Rangel points out, "the entire volunteer system is in danger of collapse under the weight of the burden being placed on those who are serving."

Recruiting and retention are suffering. The active forces have joined the reserves on the manpower critical list, with both the Army and Marines failing to meet their recruiting goals for months.

Reservists are being treated as regular substitutes rather than emergency complements for the active forces. Many are serving one, two, or more years, losing jobs and businesses. Active duty personnel are spending successive tours overseas.

Only Pentagon "stop-loss" orders, which bar personnel from leaving when their terms expire, are holding many servicemen and women in uniform. A desperate Department of Defense has even called up members of the Individual Ready Reserve, former active duty personnel who serve in no units and receive no benefits.

The Army still hopes to make its year-end recruit objective, but only by lowering its standards. There is no simple answer, however. The problem is neither inadequate benefits nor lack of patriotism.

Rather, many young men and women, often influenced by their parents (only 25 percent now would recommend a military career, compared to 42 percent in 2003), are not enthused about risking life and limb for an increasingly dubious cause. It's one thing to go to war to preempt, or believe that one is preempting, a dangerous state seeking nuclear weapons. (Of course, the administration's manipulation of evidence against Iraq will make this case much harder to make in the future.)

It's quite another thing to fight to promote "democracy," whatever that means, in a nation that has not yet developed the civil and social institutions so important for the emergence of a genuine liberal society. The U.S. has achieved the obvious goals of ousting Saddam Hussein and organizing elections. Now young Americans are dying as Iraqi politicians squabble over governmental positions and constitutional provisions.

Of course, the mere fact that attacking Iraq was a mistake—a war based on lamentably false claims about Baghdad's possession of WMDs and criminally optimistic promises as to the ease of occupation—does not mean that America should quickly leave. But at a time when few military leaders share the President's optimism of freedom marching forward, decisions cannot be based on more simplistic rhetoric from those who sold the war with simplistic rhetoric.

For instance, Clifford May, head of the Foundation for the Defense of Democracies, says that "Failure is not an option." Of course, no one wants to see failure. But an administration that has been building fantasies in the sky should start thinking realistically about Iraq.

The first issue is the standard of success. Is it creation of a Jeffersonian democracy, meeting Western standards of political participation, protection of human rights, and government accountability?

Or is success development of a somewhat democratic, but often authoritarian state which mistreats minorities, and particularly religious minorities? Or is success establishing a stable regime run by a house-broken Saddam Hussein, who uses force to suppress dissenting ethnic, political, and religious factions?

There's no doubt that number one is preferable, but it also is the most difficult to achieve. Number two is more likely to occur and might allow Washington to avoid too much criticism for sacrificing democratic values in its supposed war for democracy. The last would be an ugly outcome, but might be the most likely outcome whenever the U.S. leaves.

Question number two is at what cost? Of course Americans should prefer a free, democratic, and capitalist Iraq over an unfree, authoritarian, and statist Iraq.

However, how much treasure should be spent and lives sacrificed to reach Washington's stated goal? Failure is not an option unless failure cannot be avoided at acceptable cost.

For instance, envision the lion lying down with the lamb in Baghdad and people throwing flowers at American visitors, like was supposed to happen in 2003 after the U.S. invaded. Unfortunately, assume it will take, say, a 50-year occupation, 25,000 American deaths, a quarter million maimed and wounded military personnel, and $3 trillion in outlays to "succeed" in this way. Would it be worth it?

Moreover, what if the continuing occupation intensified anti-American passions overseas, further encouraged terrorist recruitment, and spawned an entire generation of terrorists who knew how to defeat urban security measures, construct car bombs, escape government surveillance, and infiltrate security forces? And what if some of them decided to employ those skills outside of Iraq? What if hundreds or thousands of Westerners in general and Americans in particular ended up dying as a result?

Maybe the Iraq optimists who have been so wrong so often will be right this time. Maybe the insurgency is in its "last throes," as Vice President Richard Cheney claims. Maybe.

But there have been many supposed turning points—the killing of Hussein's two sons, Hussein's capture, the transfer of sovereignty, the elections. Unfortunately, notes David Phillips, a State Department consultant who worked in Iraq before quitting in frustration: "at no point have any of these milestones proven to be breakthroughs."

The number of daily insurgent attacks is up over 2004. U.S. commanders say they need more troops and warn that the number of reliable Iraqi forces lags far behind official estimates.

After two years the U.S. still can't protect the six-mile road between Baghdad airport and the capital. The city of Basra has fallen under sectarian militia control. Western Iraq is ungoverned and perhaps ungovernable.

Thousands of Christians have fled to Syria. American employees, such as interpreters, are leaving due to threats against them and their families. Much of the country is unsafe for any foreigner. The vast majority of both Shiites and Sunnis want the U.S. forces to leave.

But maybe this time the wild optimists will be right.

If they are not, however, Americans have to be prepared to make some tough decisions regarding Iraq. The U.S. can't leave tomorrow. It must begin planning to leave, however, and sooner rather than later.

First, Washington must define "success" in Iraq as a political regime that respects vital American interests, not one that represents a utopia seen only in college political science textbooks. We want to see and should encourage development of a liberal political order in Iraq. But we should not make it the essential baseline of our foreign policy.

Second, the U.S. must weigh both costs and benefits. The primary benefit of the war with Iraq has been achieved: eliminating Saddam Hussein's regime. Improving the operation of Iraqi democracy is a laudable but not essential objective.

The costs, in contrast, continue to mount. Iraq may well be the most important recruiting tool for terrorists abroad. U.S. officials talk about the "bleed out" of terrorists active in Iraq back to their home countries, where it will be even harder to identify them.

American casualties continue to mount. Patriotic young men and women are being killed, maimed, and wounded daily. The Iraqi election has proved to be yet another false dawn. We almost certainly have months or years of more fighting and killing ahead.

(Iraqis are dying too. Nearly 300 Iraqi security personnel were killed in May, the most ever. Another 600 died from January to April 2005, half the toll from the preceding 18 months. An incredible 800 Iraqi civilians were murdered in bombings and shootings in May alone.)

The U.S. is spending $5 billion a month on the war. Attention and effort, too, are being channeled into an unproductive guerrilla war rather than planning to meet future challenges and to transform the U.S. military.

Moreover, the armed services are stretched badly, with recruitment and retention veering towards disaster. Today America would be ill-equipped to deal with a second crisis—say Iran or North Korea, let alone China. It has taken Washington three decades to shape a military that can quickly and decisively defeat any antagonist on earth. It has taken the Bush administration just two years to endanger the same force. And legislators like Rep. Rangel want to complete the wrecking job by returning to a draft.

There are no good policy options in Iraq. But the administration must abandon the fantasies that have been driving it so far. Otherwise America will suffer a series of ever-worsening nightmares, including the possibility of conscription.

July 2005

Time for Apologies All Around

In the wake of the London bombings, President George W. Bush continues to rally public support for his policies in Iraq. Instead, he should apologize to Americans for those policies.

Republicans have been demanding a lot of apologies recently. They pushed Sen. Richard Durbin (D-Ill.) to recant his ill-considered comparison of Guantanamo jailors to Nazis. The GOP demanded that Democratic National Committee Chairman Howard Dean repent of his virulent attacks on Republicans. But it is the Republican President who should do most of the apologizing.

Not that the Democrats don't have much to apologize for. But this President is no conservative, at least as that philosophy was traditionally understood. He should acknowledge responsibility—and apologize—for grievous failures that dramatically overshadow those of his political adversaries.

President Bush took the U.S. into war based on a falsehood. His appointees talked about mushroom clouds, stockpiles of biological and chemical weapons, and unmanned aerial vehicles that could hit America.

The Vice President claimed that Saddam Hussein was involved in September 11. Various officials, from the President on down, declared that the Hussein regime was "a threat," "a significant threat," "the most dangerous threat of our time," a "threat to the region and the world," "a threat to the security of free nations," "a serious threat to our country, to our friends and to our allies," a "unique and urgent threat," and "a serious and mounting threat."

None of these claims was true. The President should apologize.

Although President Bush apparently believed what he was saying, he and his appointees chose to believe what they wanted to believe. John B. Judis and Spencer Ackerman of the *New Republic* pointed out that "Unbeknownst to the public, the administration faced equally serious opposition within its own intelligence agencies." The CIA, State Department's intelligence bureau, Defense Intelligence Agency, Department of Energy, Air Force, and International Atomic Energy Agency all criticized particular administration claims.

If the President's insistence on believing what he wanted to believe had only cost America $200 billion, it would be bad enough. But more than 1700 servicemen and women have been killed, nearly 14,000 have been wounded, many of them maimed, and even President Bush admits that Iraq has become a vortex of international terrorism.

He should apologize.

The failings of U.S. intelligence—the assumption that Iraq possessed a wide variety of threatening weapons when it in fact had none—were manifold. The Senate Intelligence Committee report noted that "most of the major key judgments" in the October 2002 National Intelligence Estimate were "either overstated, or were not supported by, the underlying intelligence reporting."

Yet the President didn't address the issue until the 9/11 commission prepared to announce its findings as the 2004 election approached. And he has yet to hold anyone accountable for anything, other than in the few cases when people told him what he didn't want to hear.

Once the truth came out, the President could have taken responsibility and acknowledged that he'd been wrong. Instead, in his 2004 State of the Union speech, George W. Bush devoted just two sentences to WMD, noting the presence of "dozens of weapons of mass destruction-related program activities." The administration mantra became never mind, check out at the mass graves.

The administration's loss of domestic credibility and America's loss of international credibility have been huge. The President should apologize.

Although the administration evidently made its decision months before it actually invaded Iraq, it failed to prepare for the inevitable consequences of loosing the dogs of war. Most incredibly, it failed to contemplate the possibility of sustained opposition—the sort of resistance routinely engendered by foreign occupations—with officials from the Vice President on down dismissing the prospects of a violent insurgency. The administration deployed inadequate forces to suppress violent criminals and insurgents alike, neglected to secure sensitive sites after Hussein was overthrown, and provided too little body armor and too few armored vehicles to protect U.S. forces.

Even now, two years later, the latter problem continues. The Boston Globe reports that Marines in Western Iraq lack not only armored vehicles, but also heavy machine guns and communications equipment. And concern over Washington's ultimate intentions makes a bad situation worse. Army Lt. Gen. John R. Vines, commander of the Multinational Corps in Iraq, observes that "Part of the recruitment for this insurgency is fueled by the perception that we are an occupying power and have no intention of leaving."

All Americans, and particularly the troops in the field, are paying a very high price for this shameful irresponsibility. The President should apologize.

Even as the occupation turned violent, senior officials refused to level with the American people. Turning points and new dawns were constantly said to beckon: the deaths of Uday and Qusay Hussein, Saddam Hussein's capture, the transfer of sovereignty, the election, and the formation of a government.

New assaults are now routinely claimed to have broken the back of the guerrillas. On the eve of the President's speech attempting to rally American support for his policies, Dick Cheney opined that the insurgency was in its "last throes."

The administration similarly makes extravagant claims about the readiness of Iraqis to take over their own security. He's "pleased with the progress," says the President.

But military officials are far more circumspect. Gen. Jon Abizaid, the commander in the Persian Gulf, says the insurgency appears to be the same strength as six months ago. The head of the Defense Intelligence Agency testified before Congress in April that "The insurgency has grown in size and complexity over the last year." The U.S. military's spokesman in Iraq, Brig. Gen. Donald Alston, says that "military options or military operations" aren't going to solve the problem of terrorism in Iraq: "It's going to be settled in the political process."

Soldiers doing the fighting say much the same. Lt. Col. Frederick P. Wellman, who helps train Iraqi security personnel, explains "We can't kill them all. When I kill one I create three." Nor will loyal Iraqi security forces quickly solve the problem. "I know the party line," observes Lt. Kenrick Cato of Long Island, "But on the ground, I can say with certainty they won't be ready before I leave. And I know I'll be back in Iraq, probably in three or four years. And I don't think they'll be ready then."

The President should apologize.

Finding it tough to justify the invasion and occupation of Iraq on its own terms, administration officials constantly point to 9/11. "I will not leave the American people at the mercy of the Iraqi dictator and his weapons," said the President just days before he ordered an invasion. He went on to cite Hussein's "terrorist connections." The Vice President long linked Iraq to 9/11 even after the claim had been discredited everywhere else. The bipartisan 9/11 Commission concluded that there was "no collaborative relationship" between Iraq and al-Qaeda.

In his recent speech President Bush made the only slightly less misleading argument that "We fight today because terrorists want to attack our country and kill our citizens, and Iraq is where they are making their stand." In a mid-June radio address he opined: "We went to war because we were attacked, and we are at war today because there are still people out there who want to harm our country and hurt our citizens." Indeed, he added, "Our troops are fighting these terrorists in Iraq so you will not have to face them here at home."

But we were not attacked by Iraq. And jihadists are making their stand in Iraq only because U.S. forces are in Iraq. No former Baathist would think of flying to the U.S. to kill Americans, and most of foreign fighters could never make it to America, whatever their personal inclinations. Even worse, the Iraq conflict is creating terrorists—and creating them faster than coalition forces so far have been able to kill them.

The President should apologize.

The result of the administration's war of choice has been to make America far less secure. The President has involved the U.S. in a conflict that Defense Secretary Donald Rumsfeld now warns could run a dozen years.

The military is badly stretched, with no relief in sight. The reserves are breaking and recruiting is off even for the active forces: "We are getting toward the end of our capacity," warns retired Gen. Barry McCaffrey. It is hard to imagine the volunteer military surviving many years more of this war.

Iraq has been turned into the central front of terrorism, preparing killers who may eventually find targets elsewhere around the world, including in America. The CIA warns that Iraq may prove to be more important than was Afghanistan in training deadly militants. Reports the National Intelligence Council: "The "dispersion of the experienced survivors of the conflict in Iraq" to other nations will create new threats in the form of mutations off of the al-Qaeda network. Jihadists already have begun returning to their home countries, including in Europe.

The President should apologize.

Unfortunately, George W. Bush gives no evidence of recognizing his mistakes, let alone admitting his responsibility. The Republican-controlled Congress is unwilling to hold him accountable. Even long-time conservative activists have been largely quiet. Other than a few courageous souls at small publications such as the American Conservative and Chronicles, most conservatives say nothing publicly. They apparently hate the Democrats too much or fear the loss of power too greatly to break ranks.

But as Republican activists busily demand public repentance from their adversaries, they should look in the mirror. They should apologize. And the President should apologize.

July 2005

A version of this article was originally published in Salon, *August 1, 2005.*

CHAPTER TEN

Religious Freedom

Islam: Africa's Religion of War

If there is one characteristic that seems to define Christian societies across the globe, it is tolerance. In Western Europe, home of the Papacy and Reformation, Europeans hesitate to even refer to their Christian heritage. In America organs of liberal power, especially the courts, attempt to empty the public square of any mention of religion.

Dramatically different is the Muslim world, however. There are, or at least long were, a few outposts of relative religious liberty: until recently Turkey ruthlessly suppressed the slightest hint of political Islam. Middle Eastern states such as Bahrain, Kuwait, and Oman allow Christian worship, though evangelism is not encouraged.

Far more Muslim countries persecute non-Muslims. Saudi Arabia is essentially a totalitarian state. Iran is little different, though younger Iranians are straining against rigid religious law. (Ironically, there was far greater religious freedom in Iraq than in either of these two countries, the first a close U.S. ally.) Pakistan imprisons those who blaspheme the Prophet and disables non-Muslims in other ways; private violence, unconstrained by the state, also is common.

More surprising, perhaps, is Africa. Muslims make up at least half of the population in 25 of Africa's 56 nations. North Africa is no surprise, but large, and sometimes overwhelming majorities in Chad, Comoros, Djibouti, Gambia, Guinea, Mali, Mauritania, Nigeria, and

Senegal are Muslim. "Africa has been a confluence of" three civilizations—the West, Islam, and indigenous Africa—writes Ali Mazrui of the State University of New York at Binghamton.

In the parts of Africa dominated by animists and Christians religion usually plays only a small role in the violence that so tragically afflicts that continent. In Muslim states, however, religious violence is common or persistently threatens. Islam might be a religion of peace to some, but that's certainly not evident in many cases.

Some of the worst violence occurs largely within the Muslim community. In Algeria, for instance, the military's 1992 suspension of elections for the National Assembly because of the victory of a militant Islamic party inaugurated a civil conflict that is estimated to have generated 100,000 casualties over the following eight years. Islamic radicals assassinated Egypt's President Anwar Sadat and employed terrorism against tourists to undermine the nation's economy. Extremist forces are active, though of less influence, in nations such as Morocco.

Many Islamic societies also are likely to persecute Christians. The problem of Islamic political activism extends to terrorism. Although Africa is a minor front in so-called war on terror, two U.S. embassies were attacked by al-Qaeda. Reports Ted Dagne in a detailed report for the Congressional Research Service: "For over a decade, Sudan has been a safehaven for a number of terrorist organizations, including Al-Qaeda, Islamic Group, Hezbollah, and Palestinian Islamic Jihad. ... Terror groups from the Middle East have established a presence in Somalia, Kenya, South Africa, Tanzania, and Uganda."

Even deadlier has been routine violence by African Muslims against African Christians. Mobs can and do kill more people than bombs. Problems are worst where religions "reinforce pre-existing divisions of other kinds," writes Mazrui, such as tribal identity in Nigeria. The link often is complex, but its malicious effect is clear.

Ethiopia. Although the home of the storied Coptic church, Ethiopia often is not a hospitable home for Christians. At least part of the cause of the three decades long conflict between largely Ethiopia and Eritrea was religion, with a strong Islamic influence in the former.

Problems have been more sporadic than systemic. The group International Christian Concern reports: "While there are no established extremist groups perpetrating acts of violence, there are incidents of harassment. These incidents are often as racially motivated as religiously. Tensions have erupted into harassment, intimidation, and violence between Muslims and Christians in the Oromiya and Somali regions."

The September 11 attacks and Washington's response have exacerbated tensions between the two faiths. For instance, mobs have destroyed churches and beaten converts from Islam. In 2002 Fikru Zeleke, Evangelism and Missions Secretary of the Meserete Kristos Church, worried about escalating violence: "Muslims in this country have targeted the evangelicals as number one enemy." More recently have come complaints of government discrimination against groups seeking land for cemeteries and churches, bans on religious-oriented parties, and restrictions against the entry of religious workers. Alas, there also have been intra-Christian incidents between Orthodox and Pentecostals.

Local governments often are inattentive or ineffective in protecting lives and property from violence generated by whatever source. Of particular concern is the presence of some Muslim fundamentalists. Reports the State Department: "Leaders of the Ethiopian Islamic Affairs Supreme Council struggled with Wahhabist fundamentalism within their ranks." The Council was concerned about "the growing influence of radical elements within Islamic communities in the country, aided by funding from Saudi Arabia and other Gulf states for mosque construction and social services."

Eritrea. Once part of Ethiopia, Eritrea successfully won its independence in 1993 after decades of conflict. The United States Commission on International Religious Freedom reports that "The government of Eritrea engages in particularly severe violations of freedom of religion and belief."

However, the issues have generally not been Muslim versus Christian. Undifferentiated oppression is more the norm. Explains the Commission: "Beset by internal political problems and violent confrontations with neighboring Ethiopia and Sudan, the ruling Popular Front for Democracy and Justice (PFDJ) has become increasingly repressive, targeting political opponents and members of religious groups undermining national unity." That has meant registering religious groups, discriminating against evangelical and Pentecostal churches, and restricting Christian activities among members of the armed forces.

Somalia. Problems are limited in scope but real. Happily, the lack of an effective national government prevents serious official discrimination. But popular antagonism towards the U.S. government remains a serious problem. For instance, shortly after the U.S. attacked Afghanistan, mobs in the town of Argessa destroyed church buildings and the government arrested three church leaders.

Nigeria. The populous state of Nigeria has become one of the continent's most bitter battlegrounds. Reports the United States Commission on International Religious Freedom:

> the response of the Nigerian government to the country's religious freedom problems remains inadequate and ineffectual. These problems include an ongoing series of communal conflicts along religious lines that have claimed the lives of thousands in the last five years; the controversy over the expansion of sharia (Islamic law) into the criminal codes of several northern Nigerian states; and the persistent reports of official discrimination against Christians or Muslims in areas of Nigeria where either group is in the minority. Furthermore, there are increasing reports of foreign sources of funding and support for Islamic extremist activities in northern Nigeria, activities that threaten to fracture already fragile relations between the two main religious groups.

Nigeria long has suffered radical Islamic movements. Extremist sentiments were fueled by the illegal immigration of many Nigerians to Saudi Arabia and their subsequent expulsion in the 1970s and 1980s. A new round of anti-American sentiment growing out of the aftermath of September 11 have fueled some local groups, though they are "not mobilized on the scale of the Muslim Brotherhoods of Egypt or Uzbekistan, or the popular Islamist parties of Algeria or Pakistan," observes Peter M. Lewis of CSIS.

In 1986 the Muslim military regime upgraded Nigeria's status within the Organization of Islamic Countries to that of a permanent member. That raised substantial controversy and heightened religious tensions.

Large-scale riots occurred in northern Nigeria in 1987. A Christian general attempted a coup in 1990, in part to contain Islamic influences. Violence among Muslims and between Muslims and Christians flared in succeeding years.

Today the nation embraces democracy, but that, ironically, has only made the problem of religious strife worse. Some 10,000 people are thought to have died in communal violence since President Olusegun Obasanjo was elected in 1999 (a more recent estimate puts that toll at over 50,000).

The worst of the violence began after the newly elected governor of the northern state of Zamfara announced his intention to impose sharia. Other states followed. Although the original proposals did not purport to cover Christians, sharia often was advanced as part of a larger hostile campaign against Christianity.

State governments discriminated against Christians in broadcast access, church-building, education, government employment, and land use. Explains the Commission on International Religious Freedom: "Calls for violence against non-Muslims has sometimes accompanied sharia implementation. In April 2004, press reports quoted the governor of Zamfara state, in northwestern Nigeria, as saying that he intends to implement the second phase of his plan to institute sharia by ordering the destruction of all Christian churches and non-Islamic places of worship, in accordance with what he believes is his 'duty to subjugate infidels'."

So far the governor has not attempted to implement this program. Nevertheless, Sulayman Nyang of Howard University warns: "The issue remains a very divisive one for many Nigerians and thus entails serious potential for violence."

Unfortunately, the national government has ineffectively relied primarily on mediation: "Senior leaders have also been unable or unwilling to ensure that government security forces can maintain order with discipline and restraint," reports Peter M. Lewis. Ethnic clashes, largely between Christians and Muslims, killed an estimated 2000 people in both 2000 and 2001. Hundreds died the following year, many in riots directed against the Miss World beauty contest held in Lagos. Islamic militants also target individual Christians.

Another danger was demonstrated in September 2004 when the Al Sunna wal Jamma group, which had been inspired by the Taliban, attacked police stations in northeastern Nigeria. According to Berhane Habtemariam writing in Dehai Africa, "Political analysts saw the emergence of Al Sunna wal Jamma as a sign that violent, extremist groups may be gaining a significant foothold in religiously and ethnically divided Nigeria. They expressed fears that they could make the country a theatre for acts of terrorism and worse sectarian violence than it has seen in recent years."

Admittedly, the killing has not been only one-way. In early 2004 hundreds of Christians and Muslims were killed in attacks and counter-attacks in Plateau state. Some 30,000 Christians and 27,000 Muslims fled their homes following the worst of the sectarian violence.

Sudan. Most in the news of late has been Sudan. Of Sudan, observes Baroness Caroline Cox, a member of Britain's House of Lords, "the present National Islamic Front regime took power by military coup and immediately declared a militaristic jihad against all who oppose it; that includes many moderate Muslims as well as Christians and traditional believers." Full-scale civil war began in 1983, when Khartoum abandoned regional autonomy and imposed sharia law on the entire nation. By some estimates, since 1989 two million people have died—many of them due to war-induced famine—and another four to five million have become refugees, constituting the world's largest population of internally displaced people.

Sudan's governments have varied in ruthlessness. But discrimination is embedded within the system: For instance, as is common for Islamic governments, Sudan prosecutes apostates. Christian converts face arrest and possible death. Attempts also have been made to forcibly convert Christians to Muslims and impose sharia on Christians.

The Voice of America reports that "Many non-Muslims in Sudan say they are treated as second-class citizens and discriminated against in government jobs and contracts." Registration of religious groups is required. The government has destroyed churches and denied building permits to non-Muslims. All told, reports the United States Commission on International Religious Freedom: "The government of Sudan continues severely and systematically to commit violations of freedom of religion or belief, particularly against Christians, disfavored Muslims, and followers of traditional African religions."

Of even greater concern is the long-term military conflict. The fight is not strictly Muslim versus Christian, but Christians and animists in the south are the most common victims of a seemingly endless civil war involving the Muslim government.

Atrocities by government forces and government-backed militias have been common. The most publicized crisis today is occurring in Darfur. Some 70,000 people are thought to have died and another 1.5 million people there are homeless.

Columbia University's Mahmood Mamdani explains that "The major change in the political map of Darfur over the past decade was the growth of the Islamist movement." As a result, "Darfur became 'Islamist,' not 'Arab'." In 1990 the government organized local militias to battle the Sudan People's Liberation Army (SPLA). Adds Mamdani, "Neither monolithic nor centrally controlled, many were purged when the Islamists split in 1999." Although the government may not have intended today's promiscuous killing, Khartoum set the fire.

Africa is a continent of tragedy. The causes of violence are many, but Christians are often the victims of Muslim depredations. Alas, the drive to politicize Islam in Africa, writes Sulayman Nyang, has "deep historic, ethnic, cultural, political, and economic roots." Moreover, events even in secular Muslim societies such as Indonesia and Turkey demonstrate how Islamic extremists can build upon both jihadist theology and political antagonism towards the United States to foment religious violence.

Some day Islam may turn into a genuine religion of peace. Until then, African Christians are likely to remain victims of Muslim-inspired pogroms across the continent.

December 2004

Indonesia—Modern Religious Wars

AMBON, INDONESIA—The weathered boatman peered at the three Westerners as we climbed into a small water taxi to cross the bay from the city of Ambon to the airport. "You're from America? Send us arms. The Muslims are bad." He used his hands to indicate a rifle as we pulled away from shore.

Muslim terrorists are active, and not only in Afghanistan. So too in Southeast Asia, particularly the globe's most populous Islamic nation, Indonesia.

Ambon, the provincial capital of the Moluccas, or Spice Islands, is now largely quiet. The city is blanketed with police and military units, which have suppressed most inter-communal violence.

The remains of war are omnipresent, however. A few blocks from our hotel street barricades separate Christian and Muslim sections of town.

One ventures into enemy territory at one's peril. While returning from Muslim territory our interpreter, a Christian hotel manager named Theny Barlola, allowed that it was the first time he had been in that area in three years. He initially hesitated to accompany us, because we would have to change into a Muslim cab at the city divide. "If I go, they will kill me, they will take me away," he exclaimed. But he relented when the Muslim authorities sent a van for us.

The sight of the three of us—me, a newspaper reporter, and Jim Jacobson, head of the relief group Christian Freedom International (CFI)—wandering the city garnered endless stares. It also generated an instant entourage: a newspaper hawker, who spoke English, a few fascinated kids, and a couple of bemused residents. Our informal guide chattered away while leading us through the labyrinthine ruins. But he stopped short at the street leading into Muslim territory, where several toughs glowered at us. We chose a different route, which led to a street with multiple army strongpoints.

Between the sections lie several blocks of no man's land, ruined buildings which once housed Christians and Muslims, as well as a thriving Chinese business district. Today the remains of gutted two- and three-story buildings stand as silent sentinels.

Little remains of most smaller buildings. Bits of wall surround the debris of war: rusty corrugated roofing, dented dishes, skeletons of sewing machines, burned motor bikes, bent bed frames, weathered chairs, shattered bricks.

Many people, especially in outlying villages, have ended up in refugee camps. They are relying on outside assistance for help—Jacobson's CFI has been providing construction tools and fishing equipment, for instance. Others have come back to live in neighboring homes that were only damaged.

A few businesses have reopened. Small, dilapidated stalls line the streets. A small supermarket has taken over the first floor of a nightclub that was targeted by Muslim mobs—drapes wave through broken windows above, and bullet holes mark the facade. But the large bank building at the corner sits vacant. A makeshift wooden cross marks the spot where a church once sat, now between the two camps.

Although the city is now generally quiet, the terror of mob murder hangs in the shadows. Barlola, a bright, well-dressed 35-year-old who demonstrates initiative unusual in a city marked by languid passivity, describes the mood last year as one of "panic." For a time, he considered heading to the mountains.

So did C.J. Boehm, a Dutch missionary who has spent more than 30 years in Indonesia. He works at the Crisis Centre Diocese of Amboina, which sits next to a Catholic church on a busy street in the Christian section of town. When violence engulfed the city last June, Boehm and 235 frightened parishioners had packed bags and were ready to flee. "There was only one escape route," he said, a narrow road up into the hills. Luckily they didn't have to use it: in this case the police and military did their jobs and the Muslim warriors never came.

Today security strong-points litter the city, especially along the dividing line between the communities. Soldiers use anything handy for their barricades: Oil drums, sandbags, concrete blocks, rubble, and even household debris, such as metal chair frames.

With an estimated 5000 to 8000 people dead and as many as 500,000 refugees since January 1999, war-weariness pervades the Moluccas. Both sides speak of reconciliation. But the two communities remain far apart.

Economic stagnation hangs over the city. At 80, Haddi Soulisa retired long ago from Indonesia's education bureaucracy. He has spent 42 years with the mosque and maintains contacts among Christians. He complains: There is "no school, no work, people are hungry in their belly. How do you then do reconciliation?"

Poverty is obvious: people scavenge for food in garbage piled on the street, and Barlola, a hotel manager, was grateful for even $20—which would buy his family rice for a month, he said.

Yet economic development was a casualty of, not spark for, the conflict. Muslim mobs targeted shops owned by ethnic Chinese. In the Chinese section of Ambon buildings are gutted and shops are shuttered. "All of the big shops are burned down, all are gone," says Boehm." Small shacks fill city sidewalks but are an inadequate replacement. "Most of the traders here were Chinese," says Boehm: "Almost all have left."

Haddi Soulisa also argues that fighting in the Moluccas is linked to that in Aceh, Java, and elsewhere. "It is the same. It comes from separatism." The Christians, he says, want to secede, while "we want Indonesia." A break-up "is impossible because we are one Indonesia." The Laskar Jihad Muslim militia also justifies its involvement as necessary to oppose Christian separatism.

However, "Christians have no intent to separate," says Boehm. There once was a Christian-dominated secessionist movement, but it sputtered out long ago. Ruthless rule under successive dictators Sukarno and Suharto smothered what independence sentiments persisted. When the latter was ousted three years ago, separatist sentiments flared elsewhere—most obviously in East Timor, which is now independent, and currently troubled provinces like Aceh—but not the Moluccas.

Christians express obvious frustration and anger at their government. Barlola observes "many Christians don't like Indonesia now. It's our country, but it can't protect us." Nevertheless, I found no one who supported an independent Moluccas. To the contrary, Barlola says "I'm afraid Indonesia is going to be like Yugoslavia, with so many conflicts." Anyway, even if the charge was true, observes Boehm, "the proper response is from the government. It is not for the Muslims to do."

Violence is pandemic throughout the polyglot nation made up of 6000 inhabited islands and 300 ethnic groups. Early in 2001 came gruesome killings in the province of Central Kalimantan on Borneo, highlighted by beheadings by the ethnic Dayaks, onetime headhunters, of Madurese settlers.

What set the Moluccan fighting apart is that it grew out of Muslim-Christian tensions that continue to pervade Indonesia. As military spokesman Graito Usodo, a Rear Air Marshall, explains, "the case in Maluku is far different from those in other parts of the country since it involves religious matters." There is growing Muslim-on-Christian violence throughout the island of Java. Several churches were attacked around Christmas 2000 throughout Indonesia. They have been burned and bombed even in the seemingly cosmopolitan capital of Jakarta.

None of these incidents compared with the Moluccas, however. There long were tensions. Lobulisa Leo, a retired general who served under Suharto, told me that "They would start fighting, and then normally two or three days later settle it. This was a normal happening." The first round of the latest Moluccan violence grew out of a spat in January 1999 between a bus driver and passenger.

Many who lived on the islands quickly lost their taste for killing. But the fighting then took on a larger, and more ominous, dimension. Upwards of 4500 fighters of the Laskar Jihad, or "Holy Warrior Troops," flocked to the island. Said Lobulisa, "Ambonese, Christians and Muslims of Moluccan origin, were fed up." But the Muslims "must follow the provocateurs, or they will be killed."

Some Muslim leaders still contend that religion is not important. Jusuf Ely, chairman of the Jaziratul Muluk Muslim organization in Ambon, said religion was used "to blow up the conflict" and that "the conflict involves Muslim and Christian Protestants only." But the Crisis Centre Diocese of Amboina emphasizes that Christians of all stripes have been attacked; with only five percent of the Christian population, Catholics lost half as many buildings as have Protestants. As a result, Catholics and Protestants cooperate "very well," says Boehm.

In fact, in January 2000 more than 80,000 Muslims marched in Jakarta to demand a Jihad, or holy war, against Christians; parliament speaker Amien Rais, a member of the governing coalition before helping to oust moderate Muslim cleric Abdurrahman Wahid from the presidency, appeared at the rally, announcing that "Our patience has limits." The Moluccas become a cause for Muslims; fighters were identified from Afghanistan, Moro Islands (the Philippines), Saudi Arabia, and Yemen. The Laskar Jihad played a particularly important role.

As a result, religious sites have been targeted for attack, with some 400 churches destroyed. Human casualties include not only dead and wounded, but also forced conversions, principally to Islam. Such pressure has been particularly intense on the islands of Bacan, Buru and Seram; residents of the island of Kesui report forced male and female circumcision, a particularly painful process for women. For many flight has been the only alternative. Moreover, Jaffar Umar Thalib, head of the Jihad forces, has formally called for the imposition of "Syariat Islam" or Islamic law, at least in areas cleared of Christians. Although Christians are not without blame in the fighting, they have rarely attempted to impose conversion.

Religion also split the security forces. Muslim attacks on Christians in the Moluccas coincided with the collapse of the central government's authority. In 1997 and 1998 500 to 600 Christian churches were destroyed or damaged throughout Indonesia, but "not one in the Moluccas," says Boehm. That reflects the relative population parity, now roughly 45 percent Christian. "If Muslims here had tried to burn down a church, ten mosques would have been burned."

The Suharto government collapsed more than three years ago, and with it Indonesia's tenuous peace. Even after violence erupted in the Moluccas, however, in the beginning Christians were able to defend themselves, Christian leaders point out. But then the Muslims gained the backing of not only the Laskar Jihad forces, but also many soldiers.

"There were certain units that were very clearly neutral" and tried to stop the killing, says Boehm. However, "in most cases individuals and in some cases whole units, because they were afraid, or cowards, did nothing." Some simply stood by while Jihad forces arrived. "The military hasn't done anything," complained one Christian leader, who insisted on anonymity, in an interview last year. The Jihad couldn't have arrived without the military's complicity in the view of him and several others. Other soldiers turned over their weapons to Muslims. Finally, "some were among the attackers," says Boehm.

Although Muslims appeared to be the chief beneficiaries of outside intervention, some police, who tend to be drawn locally, were more inclined to help the Christians; there were even clashes between military and police. And some Christian military officers have been willing to help; militia leader Agus admitted to acquiring ammunition from a Christian officer.

Gradually the security forces moved back to neutrality. When we flew out of Ambon members of different services mingled at the airport without incident; at one point the lobby hosted five different uniforms. An inter-service military unit has proved to be an effective strike force against those inclined towards violence.

Indeed, today both communities speak more respectfully of the military. Haddi Soulisa says "they are now neutral." Before, "some were pro-Muslim, some were pro-Christian." The police, he says, "were the same." Agus said that if the military had not intervened last year, "the Muslims would have killed all of the Christians."

Unfortunately, sporadic fighting continues. In January 2001 some 500 Islamic militants attacked the Christian village of Hatu Alang. They burned down scores of homes, as well as churches and schools. More than 800 residents fled into surrounding jungles, and were later evacuated by boat.

Indeed, killing could flare up at any time. For almost any reason. The potential sparks are many.

Both sides continue to prepare for war. Although the violence has receded, the Laskar Jihad, blamed by most Christians for stoking the violence, remains one of the most important stumbling blocks. "Last year they are coming to Ambon for war, coming to help the Muslims," said Agus. And they remain. "They are still around, but how many, where they are, we don't know," says Boehm.

They were likely involved in an attack in late February on the western part of the island of Seram, in which a Christian village was sacked for the third time. "There was hardly anything left to be burned, but they did so," observes Boehm. Naturally, Christians demand the Jihad's removal. "Without Laskar Jihad we can have reconciliation," argued Agus. But not otherwise. "They must leave, go back to Indonesia. It is very important."

In contrast, Haddi Soulisa defends the Jihad: "There is no problem with the Laskar Jihad." They "come to help Muslims," he said, and "not only for war." They bring doctors, help repair burned houses, and more. And they "are still helping."

His response is disingenuous, but no matter. It reflects genuine fear within the Muslim community.

Even Agus understood the Muslim reluctance to do without the Jihad: "The Muslims fear that if the Laskar Jihad goes back to Jakarta, who will protect them?" Before the worst of the fighting Agus, a 54-year-old education bureaucrat, promoted reconciliation among young Christian and Muslim men. When the Christians went to meet at the border, Muslim militants attacked some of them. He disclaimed any notions of revenge, but blamed the Muslim fundamentalists for their "bad propaganda," which says the Christians are lying when they say they want reconciliation, and that they will kill Muslims if the group leaves.

And Agus, a Baptist in a long line of Baptists, saw no reason to trust the other side. "Christians and Muslims are talking about reconciliation. Okay, but the Muslims fight and shoot Christians. Until today, we don't believe they mean it." Indeed, he says he had received a sign from God "that Muslims would attack again, and that Christians must be ready."

There is no Christian equivalent of the Jihad, "no people from outside," says Boehm. Instead, "in matter of war there are Christian militias," which are "only local, organized spontaneously to resist." Their presence is obvious; they have a well-fortified camp down the road from a military base and the Pertamina headquarters. There is also a manned roadblock on the road up into the Christian neighborhood in which Agus lived.

Agus, one of the most important militia leaders, looked like an aging biker: slight of build, his dark features deepened by dark black mustache and hair pulled back in a ponytail. When we met he sported an Adidas t-shirt and Nike baseball cap. A touch of gray in his hair hinted at his 54 years, but his wiry body moved quickly and confidently.

During the worst of the conflict he fought Muslims every day. Even in February 2001 he said that he continued to battle Muslims. His fighters went by speedboat to nearby islands if the Muslims attacked. He claimed to act—around Ambon and on nearby islands such as Seram—only when Christians were under attack. "We don't have desire for war with Muslims, but only to protect our area. If Muslims come for war, we will fight." But "we don't want to fight again. Ambonese

Muslims and Ambonese Christians are brother and sister. It is a brotherhood. Without the Laskar Jihad we can have reconciliation."

His militia relies primarily on homemade weapons, supplemented by purchases when possible. In fact, he solicited funds from his three visitors to help him buy guns. "Only to protect Christians. Not to go to war. We must be ready. We need help, money."

Muslims understandably have a different view of his activities, and there have been Christian as well as Muslim atrocities. But the bulk of the blame seems to fall on the Muslim side. While Boehm doesn't claim all Christians have been in the right, he argues: "Christians haven't done any attacking over the last half year. Only the Muslims. The Christians say they have had enough."

Another problem is that the communities "are quite divided themselves," explains Pastor Boehm. Muslim factions have squabbled violently. Some favor reconciliation, some don't. Thus, it is "hard to make peace with the Muslims, since one agrees, but one says no," says Boehm.

Haddi Soulisa admitted the divisions, but contends that it is "the same, Christian and Muslim, all the same. Many, many want to make reconciliation. Many groups say no reconciliation because there has been conflict for a long time, with too much damage done." However, he admits that some Muslims believe they can gain materially from war. Haddi Soulisa says that upper- and middle-class Muslims tend to favor reconciliation. Not the lower-classes, however: "many of them want conflict. Because of conflict, they take something, they loot," he says.

Muslims "in general very much want to come to reconciliation," argues Boehm, but the local Jihad leader says the Muslims "must stop Christian separatists." Agus complained that the Jihad "comes to Ambon and says, don't believe Christians, the Christians are lying. If you follow reconciliation, they will kill you." Indeed, another leading Muslim, Malik Selang, general secretary of the Indonesian Muslim Council in Ambon, advocates formal partition: "What the Christians already have and what the Muslims have should be their areas," he told the *Los Angeles Times*. There appears to be nothing comparable to the Laskar Jihad on the Christian side.

Few Christians or Muslims credit the central government. Haddi Soulisa is dismissive: the central government "does nothing. Nothing," he spits out. The authorities are corrupt and dishonest, there is no rule of law. Agus doesn't believe Jakarta can or will solve the problem. "We need peacekeeping from the UN to come to Ambon to promote real reconciliation."

Few had put much hope in President Wahid before his ouster. "I think we can trust Gus Dur [Wahid] to have good intentions," said Boehm. "But there are those in the military who regret that they lost control of the government. Cronies of Suharto want to hide things and tend to want to divert attention of the government. And some fundamentalists want Indonesia to become an Islamic state like Malaysia." Although one resident expressed hope that newly inaugurated President Megawati Sukarnoputri will surround herself with good people, she has been a greater nationalist than Wahid and has been closely linked to authoritarian military elites.

Indeed, common among Christians is the belief that a variety of forces are using religious tensions to undermine the central government and promote Islamic rule. It was one of the pervasive fears articulated at a meeting last year with Christian educators, journalists, and clergy. One senses that after Wahid, like France's King Louis XVI, is "le deluge."

Many Christians want the army to leave the Moluccas, and no wonder: they remember its intervention on behalf of Muslims. They, like Agus, disclaim any desire for revenge. Yet Barlola allows that talk sometimes turns toward retaliation when they drink, but "only when drunken." And when asked if Christians would go on a rampage without the military present, Father Boehm replied: "I don't know. I don't think so. I think Christians have sincere aspirations to come to peace. But I don't know what the grassroots think after so much suffering."

Yet that is the key. Agus said he doesn't "believe in reconciliation from the government. If it comes from the grassroots, then it will be okay."

Is there hope at the grassroots? Despite sporadic outbursts, "the situation has calmed down. Refugees have started to come back," says Boehm. A returning doctor and his wife and toddler shared my flight into Ambon.

Theny Barlola seemed moved by his time with Haddi Soulisa, as well as the Muslim driver who shepherded us through the Muslim section of town. During our meeting Soulisa pointed at Barlola: "there is reconciliation here."

True enough, but the street barricades still stand. There is no pedestrian flow between sections: we lost our spontaneous entourage when we crossed the line. Our newspaper vendor friend sent the kids away as we neared the border and he refused to venture past a desolate no man's land into the Muslim section. We could see scowls mixed with amusement from residents as we went by. "If a Christian goes into a Muslim neighborhood, he will get beat up," contended Boehm. Most cabs, particularly the plentiful pedicabs, stick to their own section of town. Speedboats are the preferred mode of transportation for many people to avoid hostile sections of town.

What of American policy? Barlola notes that last year the Christian community was busy signing petitions and mailing letters asking for outside help. Most Christians wanted foreign peacekeepers or, failing that, evacuation. Indeed, my meeting with Christian leaders last July was filled with demands that the international community in general and the U.S. in particular do something, though there was little agreement on what. Most at least wanted Washington to pressure the central government to discipline military forces that were backing the Muslims.

Jakarta resisted any outside involvement, just as it did more recently in Borneo. Muslims are even less enthused. Activists "tell stories that Western military aid is used by Christians," says Boehm. Individual Westerners with aid organizations are seen as partisans, aiding Christians: Muslims have said that workers with Doctors Without Borders, one of best international humanitarian groups, are "spies for Christians," says Boehm. Washington's reputation is far worse. Agus made the same point: "they say you all come to Ambon to protect Christians. From Australia, from other countries, you come only to protect Christians, not Muslims. "

Haddi Soulisa was polite but blunt when it came to the U.S. No, he didn't believe any outside government could help Ambon: "The U.S. shouldn't police the world. I don't agree with Clinton. Bush is okay. I don't like Americans' claim to make themselves policemen of the world. Give us time for Indonesia to make it by ourselves. Democracy, Indonesian democracy, not by any country imposing it on Indonesia."

But Indonesian democracy may not survive. The political system is nearing collapse; the country is slowly disintegrating. A messy explosion would be bad enough for the average Muslim. It could be catastrophic for Christians, who are "only tolerated," worries Boehm: As only ten percent of the population, they can't defend themselves."

And there's all too much reason to fear that the current respite in Ambon is only temporary. "Now we are in round 5 or maybe round 6. We finish one, have reconciliation, then it starts again," observes Barlola. The next bout could come at any time—perhaps with the opening of roads within the contending communities, perhaps with something else. And then there will be more deaths, more destruction, more refugees, more promises from Jakarta, and more hand-wringing from abroad.

"Don't forget us," pleaded Agus. "We are a brotherhood. Go back to America, and tell Christians that they must help us here." But any help will be too late for Agus, who was shot and killed barely three weeks after I interviewed him. And there's precious little America can do for anyone else. The U.S. government can't invade; American Christians can't run guns. Which leaves relief groups like CFI to try to help clean up the mess.

November 2001

Laotian Communism: Sleepy Repression

VIENTIANE, LAOS—The flight from Bangkok to Laos was full of tourists. It was less difficult to clear customs there than when arriving back in the U.S. I didn't see a cop on the street until the evening. Sandwiched amidst Vietnam, Cambodia, and Thailand, Laos has a Third World, not communist, feel.

Behind the gentle facade lurks a mailed fist, however. The State Department's new report on religious liberty notes restrictions on the right to worship in Laos. Naturally, the Laotian government rejected Washington's criticism, claiming that the charges "contradict the reality of religious freedom" in Laos. However, one doesn't have to travel far in Laos to see the persecution of minority faiths, and particularly of Christians.

There are numerous Christians in this largely Buddhist country of 5.4 million. But their ability to practice their religion varies by village and changes over time. What was once permitted often ends up prohibited.

A concerted assault on religious liberty began with the communist takeover in 1975, which yielded what one local Christian termed, with profound understatement, a "new government." Even greater hostility towards Christianity became evident during the early 1990s; Hmong believers were a particular target given that tribal people's long resistance to the communist regime and past cooperation with America.

Persecution, confirmed by Amnesty International and Christian groups, as well as the State Department, has grown more intense over the last two years, earning Laos a number two ranking on the Open Doors International Persecution list. Since 2000 an estimated 60 churches and other religious institutions have been closed; several church buildings have been confiscated. More than 250 Christian pastors and church leaders are thought to have been arrested, though no one knows for sure. Estimates of the number who remain in custody ranged up to 100 earlier this year, according the Maranatha Christian News Service.

Believers are reported to have been coerced into signing declarations renouncing their "foreign religion"; there are stories, which my group wasn't able to confirm directly, of believers in some villages being forced to partake of pagan rituals. Believers even in the freer areas that we visited feared that at least some Laotian officials desired to eliminate the church.

Yet my visit to Laos also found some signs of hope. Before the most recent round of persecutions, an estimated 1100 churches were operating. Even today, the church exists above ground. For instance, there are three or four large churches, with hundreds of members each, in the capital of Vientiane; we drove by the Lao Evangelical Church, with its sign proudly standing in front. However, they must register, explained one underground activist, and operate under the watchful eye of the government.

Moreover, Vientiane has indicated its willingness to allow foreign Christian organizations to operate, so long as their activities were "arranged through the government," the worker explained. "People were helping the church secretly," which "the authorities didn't like." So the government is trying to pull religious activities to the surface.

This comes as no surprise. The government, through its Department of Religious Affairs, has long attempted to ensure that Buddhism is practiced in conformity with communist principles. The Department forbids Christians from proselytizing or distributing religious materials. One young professional, who organizes activities in the capital, warned: "if you work with the government, they will send someone to work with you," with the goal of preventing evangelism. It appears to be the Chinese solution, observed an American who has aided some underground churches: "I'm not surprised that Laos has caught on."

Despite the ban, several professionals in Vientiane use their jobs to promote church growth. They move about freely and are rarely bothered; even our small group of Westerners didn't generate any apparent interest from the authorities. Joining the local activists, we attempted to reach both the church and share the Gospel with those outside by distributing medicine.

But any unusual activity risks unwanted attention. One Christian wanted us to provide educational materials for rural schools. He allowed, however, that "I'd be scared if I received too much," since the authorities would notice. The Vientiane organizer said that he is often under surveillance. The "government is very suspicious" of meetings, especially those with foreigners, he observed. If Vientiane suspected that a church or organization was being subsidized from abroad, it would "put a cop in front of a person's house every day."

Religious life generally becomes more difficult as one moves further away from Vientiane. Much depends on the whims of local officials. We visited a small house church close to the capital. "In this village we have no problems with the government," one of the local church leaders told me. The official view was that Christianity taught "everyone to be a good person," which was fine.

Roughly ten percent of the villagers are Christians—higher than the national average—and many of their neighbors join them to celebrate Christmas, one told me. Moreover, the village head, who is not a believer, stopped by and invited us to return any time. His friendly attitude was probably enhanced by the fact that our Christian host gave packages of medicine to non-Christian families, including the official's.

Although this home group is not registered with the government, it works with one of the Vientiane churches. Thus, its activities, though not monitored in detail, are known. Still, observed one of the church leaders, "it's like a small business, not a big business, so we can operate without government interference."

When we went another couple dozen miles outside of the capital, we encountered a more difficult situation. A group of worshippers received local permission to construct a simple church, which they used for months without incident. A couple of years ago, however, "someone in the village told the government in Vientiane," explained a woman active in the local congregation.

The central authorities ordered local officials to stop the practice. They did, but the village head, an unbeliever but a friend of her husband, suggested that they meet in her home. They continue to do so today.

When our Western team moved further into rural Laos the situation worsened notably. The most virulent examples of persecution have been carried out by distant authorities, who often take the lead in suppressing Christian worship. The Vientiane activist who has sometimes found himself spied upon warned us against venturing into unknown villages. As white Westerners, we would be immediately suspect.

It came as no surprise, then, when our Christian host would not let us leave our vehicle, its windows conveniently tinted to prevent easy identification, in some areas. In these communities, local believers are closely monitored, and the arrival of foreigners, he explained, would "mean big trouble" for everyone. Local officials are more likely to be promoted the more they report, including the activities of Christians.

Particularly frustrating is the fact that even Laotian Christians are not sure about the real position of the local and central governments. Last year the authorities "persecuted Christian people a lot," complained my host. For example, he figures that local officials closed down 26 of 30 above ground churches in southern Laos. Some Laotians with whom we spoke thought that Vientiane was secretly encouraging the campaign and reports to that effect have circulated through groups such as the international Christian group Jubilee Campaign.

Yet our host wasn't sure that was the case. He worked with many of the closed churches and said it appears that the Vientiane government was "concerned about appearances overseas" and therefore opposed the crackdown. "Local officials and the government were fighting," he explained, with the national authorities preferring to "leave the churches alone."

The American's take was similar: "Vientiane is show and tell time. But it looks like the further away you go from Vientiane, the tougher it is."

Despite the hardships, things "are better for Christians now," opined my host, who continues to visit underground churches. "But we still have to be careful." Nevertheless, the worshippers—many of them farmers and laborers who possess little in this world—in the churches that we visited were not discouraged. "Every family helps each other," one told me.

And if freedom ever comes, the Laotian believers are ready. The woman whose church was closed at Vientiane's insistence told us that the owner of the building, now unused and decrepit, has promised them the land for a new church. "If the government gives permission to build, we're ready," she said. And she obviously looked forward to that day with emotion.

There are no easy solutions. Laotian Christians are free to worship openly in some places. They aren't free to do so in others. Says one American who has followed religious persecution: "it's like China—everything they say is true somewhere."

Western Christians can help. We can do whatever is possible with the government's consent to aid legal congregations. We can use Laos' relative openness to tourists to work informally with house churches, bringing in Bibles, distributing aid, and encouraging believers.

We can embarrass the communist government by being salt and light to Laotians, providing medical assistance, for instance, to believer and nonbeliever alike. One Christian health care worker told us that a communist delegation which recently visited Thailand was angry on seeing Christian hospitals better than those constructed by the Lao government.

Western Christians can labor mightily to publicize abuses and pressure on the regime to liberalize. We know that international attention criticism: even the isolated communist regime in Vientiane worries about its reputation.

And Christians can pray.

Aggressive ideological communism may be dead, but detritus from that disastrous social experiment continues to clutter the globe. As in Laos, where a languid style of life cannot hide the vicious repression, especially of Christians.

October 2002

Dubious Allies

Lahore, Pakistan—"We love our children, but we need food," said Masih Saddiq, a 50-year-old brickmaker, explaining why none of his 13 children were in school. They range in age from one and a half to 25; all seem destined to spend their entire lives making bricks, as have their parents.

The brickyard sits outside central Lahore, Pakistan's second most populous city. Owned by a Muslim, it employs several Christian families, all of whom live on his land in a makeshift brick village. The homes are crammed together, with head-high outer walls creating a narrow alley. Most homes consist of two rooms, with a small enclosed courtyard. Even the make-shift toilets, such as they are, are enclosed by bricks. Occasional mats or rugs cannot hide the dirt floors; dust hangs in the air. There is neither electricity nor running water.

Families usually work together, typically 12 hours a day, six days a week. Each group stakes a plot of land: about a dozen families covered a half dozen football fields. One person digs up the clay and wets it; another fills a cart to move it. Two or three others pack the clay into molds.

The bricks are then left to dry before being fired through burial on top of an enormous furnace. A furnace into which brickmakers have occasionally fallen when the roof has given way. Finished bricks are then stacked, row after row, for the owner's representative to count.

Average production is 2500 to 3000 bricks a day, at a price of 140 rupees per thousand. Which means that families are earning $6 or $7 a day.

Life is hard. And the work is interminable. "We have no other choice, no other job," said one worker. Saddiq's family, with eight sons and five daughters, has labored in this brickyard for 15 years. Most of these families are effectively indentured servants. It is "like slavery," explains Rev. Emanuel S. Khokha, the 41-year-old pastor of a Methodist church in Lahore. Most of the families have borrowed heavily from the brickyard owner—20,000 or 30,000 rupees for a dowry, for instance. And they must work off the debt, which never seems to end.

Nor is there any escape for the children. "There is no school," Saddiq explains. And even if there was, he could not afford to send his children. All except the very youngest work to make bricks.

Some residents are even more vulnerable. Two orphaned girls, seven and ten, live with their grandparents. They work in the fields making bricks. Dependency extends to the end of life as well. One 95-year-old widow recently lost her husband. Unable to work, she lives with her children, who now struggle with one fewer pair of hands.

Yet their faith lives. Said Saddiq, "I have a strong faith in Jesus Christ. We're happy in this situation also."

Not all brickmakers are Christians. But Christians, who account for just two percent of the population, account for a disproportionate share. For they are uniquely vulnerable to abuse in a society where discrimination is pervasive.

Persecution of Christians is hardly unusual, but noteworthy is how thoroughly America's chief ally in the War on Terrorism oppresses those most favorably inclined towards the U.S. Khokha expresses his faith boldly—meeting us at the airport dressed in his collar and sporting a fish pin. Even before September 11 Christians were seen a believing in an alien god. "They blame us because Christians are linked to America," explains Khokha. "They blame us for Israel and the problem with the Palestinians. And they blame us because we are Christians." Some Muslims have claimed that Pepsi stands for "pay every penny, support Israel."

Life has gotten much worse since last fall. "In the Afghan war one mosque was destroyed by bombing, and Muslim scholars preached, we will destroy the churches in Pakistan," observed Khokha. "Why," he asks? "We are Pakistanis and this church belongs to Pakistan. But they say, they are Christians and you are Christians." Nevertheless, he does not despair. Explained Khokha: "Praise the Lord. He is using us to testify in our country. Christians here have a strong faith." He added later: "We are serving the Lord with gladness. We are happy in God's plans."

Pakistan is a series of dual societies. The economic stratification is obvious.

The capital of Islamabad sports wide, tree-lined boulevards, fine government buildings, and a sold-out luxury Marriott Hotel. But the "economy is very low" now, says Rev. Khokha, and far more people are suffering, especially after the start of the war in Afghanistan. And Christians, in particular, "tend to live in slum areas," says Khokha. Down a nearby ravine sits a tent city of 66 Christian families, whose mud-homes were washed away a couple years ago. Blankets serve as doors; canvas occasionally acts as a floor. Makeshift latrines drain into a ditch.

Luxury exists only in the midst of danger. There are armed guards in front of fine hotels, gas stations, and even McDonalds. Lahore's Pizzeria Uno, a meeting place for wealthy Pakistanis as well as Westerners, deployed four armed guards. The doorman held the door in his left hand and a shotgun in his right hand.

The political divide is almost as broad. Pakistan has long alternated between dictatorial and democratic rule. Today the military, in the person of Pervez Musharraf, is in charge.

Democracy remains the professed goal of most people, including Musharraf. But Nawaz Sharif, the ousted prime minister, is in exile and his predecessor, Benazir Bhutto, has seen her husband jailed on corruption charges. Moreover, many Westerners fear that elections might bring Islamic radicals to power.

Asked to compare Musharraf, Sharif, and Bhutto, Shagufta Irene Samuel, general manager of the Technical Services Association (TSA), a Christian rehabilitation organization, said that Musharraf "is the best. I think he is very democratic." We had "large expectations" for his elected predecessors, she allowed, but they were not met. "The politicians are ruining the whole country." Still, on many day-to-day issues, when it comes to treating Christians, Khokha complains that "it doesn't matter which government. They are all the same."

Religious tensions are equally obvious. Pakistan is formally an "Islamic Republic," in which the word of Mohammed is law. Mosques abound and copies of the Koran replace the Gideon Bible in hotels.

For many this is only a matter of appearances, however. A nattily-dressed elite wears Western clothes; teens wear jeans and cargo pants (but never shorts or short-sleeve shirts. These Pakistanis ignore the call to prayer as it wafts across their neighborhoods, and travel overseas to most any destination except on a Hajj. They join Americans in dining at restaurants like Pizzeria Uno.

This is the Pakistan that supports Pervez Musharraf in his quest for a more secular state. But there is another Pakistan evident even in

Islamabad, and especially in a city like Peshawar, on the border with Afghanistan. Bearded men wear a uniform of baggy pants and shirt rather than suit; women navigate crowded streets while wearing a burqa.

Although in many foreign countries Americans stand out, rarely does their conspicuousness seem so dangerous. There are angry stares even on the capital's streets and in leading airports. In more distant locations hatred fills the eyes. Not that you can always see the eyes—or need to. In Peshawar a woman in a burqa shouted at me and two other Westerners as we walked towards her neighborhood: "They are not Muslims, they are bad people. The Americans are not good. They are hurting our people in Afghanistan." Khokha literally pushed us back into our van at that point: "they are dangerous people, angry people," he explained. Even in capital of Islamabad stand police signs, in English, announcing an "emergency service for foreigners."

Indeed, the one constant of this divided society is persecution of Christians, who make up barely two percent of the population. "Discrimination is everywhere," the resident of one poor neighborhood told me. It begins with children and extends through school, work, government, and the rest of life.

For instance, kids "don't want to be friends with Christians," one 12-year-old told me. Even when allowed to attend school, they are isolated and ignored. Sometimes teachers will tell them "you are not good," complained one family. "So school teachers will fail them. There is great discrimination." In local sports, such as cricket competition, a Christian team is less likely to be chosen to advance.

Employment for everyone in this poor society is tenuous, but especially so for Christians. Jobs and opportunities are offered to Muslims first. One young resident of a poor neighborhood, where her salary of $200 a month was a princely sum, was fired by her Muslim supervisor, who disliked her faith. She now wiles away her days in a two room hovel, surrounded by others who also long for work.

Charity would help, but Pakistan is not a wealthy society in which private aid abounds. Moreover, what little assistance is offered tends to be restricted to Muslims. "If Christians ask for help, the Muslims say that the tithe is not for non-Muslims," Khokha explained. I met a Christian who worked for a hospital administrator; even at his facility, built in part with U.S. aid, charity care was limited to Muslims.

Impoverished Christians, who because of pervasive social and political disabilities tend to languish at the economic bottom, are often pressured to convert. Says Khokha: "When crisis comes, some poor Christians become Muslims, as Muslims say then we will help you."

When Christians stay firm, they must rely on themselves. "We have been living together. Everyone knows they are poor," noted the resident of a poor Lahore neighborhood. And they help each other. Or they rely on outside groups, such as Christian Freedom International (www.christianfreedom.org), with which I traveled.

The 66 Christian families in Islamabad live in tents because their homes were destroyed by flooding a couple of years ago. Few of them work and they can't afford new homes. And the government won't allow them to build where they are. So relief agencies have given them tents. A local Catholic church supports them sometimes. But "we get nothing from the government," one man told me. To the contrary, "sometimes high officials and police come and destroy our tents, and tell them to go somewhere else." For they are embarrassingly close a government building and a mosque.

Foreign aid is no answer, since even more debilitating is pervasive government bias which leads Islamabad to similarly skew foreign aid. This means directing even supposedly humanitarian assistance, and the resulting jobs and services, towards Muslims. Says Khokha: "If an international agency comes and gives support door-to-door, we can survive. But international agencies give to the government. They don't give it to us." Whatever jobs result are parceled out politically: "overseas agencies need people for labor, but no one calls us Christians. If there are jobs available, they are not calling us," says Khokha. Even money meant for private aid groups goes elsewhere. Observes Samuel: the state "doesn't help us. There is a lot of money from elsewhere, for the government and NGOs. But they never give us any clue how to get that funding. They won't even give us the forms to get it."

Discrimination pervades the political system. That begins with an electorate long divided between Muslim and non-Muslim, for instance. Musharraf plans to change that, but little else is likely to change in what is systemic discrimination.

Islamabad has never been noted for its responsiveness to its citizens; Christians have especially low expectations: "if a Christian wants a service in a government office, he can't get it because he is a Christian," complains Khokha. The impoverished status of the Pakistani state intensifies discrimination. "Our government is also poor, so it doesn't supply Christian people," one Christian complained to me.

Some slights are small. Others greatly affect living standards. For instance, Pakistan's poor enjoy little security of land tenure. Most at risk are Christians.

I visited one community of about 60 families in Lahore, which has spent 35 years in makeshift homes on army land. Made of brick or stucco, with tin roofs, mud walls outside, and dirt courtyards, these homes often hold two large families. Five or more people are frequently packed into small rooms, of 100 square feet or less. Of his one-room home, joked one: "This is the bedroom. And the dining room. And the TV room." Others sleep outside: "there is no privacy," observed one. Sometimes rugs are used as doors to the outside.

Some residents inherited their dwellings from their parents. "Our forefathers were here before partition" [of India and Pakistan in 1947], noted Javed John, the local pastor. Yet the government refuses to provide public services: we "need a sewer line, we need a natural gas line," complained one. Islamabad also will not release the land and destroyed a small church which they had built. "We want a church, but the government won't allow it," says John. So now people meet in the courtyard: "there are many people, but a small place," he explains.

Why not? "This is the army's place, not your place," one of them says they were told. "The government wants us to go somewhere else," says John. The military said it wanted to build a plaza on the land. Yet the Muslim neighborhood next door is also on army property and its members have been allowed to lease their land and build a mosque. "Here is a very dangerous situation," said John. "By the grace of God we are still here, as they want to remove us." If the government would offer them some other land, they would go. "But the government doesn't offer," he noted.

Even those whose land ownership is not in doubt cannot get services for their land. Nearby in Lahore is a group of 70 families who have purchased their property on installments starting in 1993. They have built not only homes, but a church, on their land. Indeed, the latter was the first building that they constructed, even as they lived in tents. But the roads are dirt and animals, including a cow in a makeshift pen, wander the property and share courtyards with the people.

Inside their homes residents have created a clean and warm atmosphere, highlighted by pictures of Jesus and other religious images. But there is no electricity. Even though they sit astride an electrical transmission line. Nearby lie well-served Muslim neighborhoods. A Muslim mausoleum lights up at night. The poultry farm next door has power. "We have applied for electricity many times," one resident told me. But the government told the 70 families that the cost to connect would be $7000, an impossible sum. "We just can't afford it," said one frustrated man. "The government will give electricity to chickens, but not to Christians," said another resident. "It is a terrible situation."

Yet, observed Khokha as we left, "they have a strong faith in Jesus Christ. They have many problems, but retain a strong faith in him."

Worse for the future generation is the lack of education. Only about five of the residents can read. And there is "no school in the area," one resident complained. A few children go into the city for school, but others "cannot afford it."

This is a constant problem. Christian children often find themselves barred from school by local officials. "We can't get in," one of the squatters on government land told me, even though "they provide for the Muslims."

When formally free to attend, cost acts as another barrier for Christian families, which so often subsist at the bottom of the economic ladder. "Some children want to study, their parents want them to, but they can't afford the fees," said Khokha. He was late to meet us one morning because a family was threatened with having its two children tossed out of school. The husband, a painter, had been injured in a work accident, so the family could not pay the $40 annual tuition each for their two children. Many families always seem to be on the brink.

Once in school, Christian children must learn and pass the subject "Islamia," which teaches the tenets of Islam. "You can't graduate without it," explains TSA's Samuel. "And if you don't take it, the tester knows you are a Christian and you will never get through." In short, submerge your faith or suffer.

Moreover, access to government employment is also limited. In a market economy, where entrepreneurship, diligence, and investment is duly rewarded, this would represent obnoxious discrimination but not a serious financial roadblock. But sadly, in Pakistan, the state is the best option in a grossly over-politicized economy. "Government is the best job in the world," says Khokha. And it is an avenue often closed to Christians. "We apply for the jobs," even menial ones, and "we can't get them," one poor resident told me. Or big bribes must be paid—10,000 or 20,000 rupees, a year or more salary, to become a street sweeper, for instance.

The natural result of such restrictions on education and employment, with few countervailing private opportunities in a state-dominated economy, is to lock the mass of Christians into poverty. Rare must fewer than a half dozen people rely on one worker for support. Once working, they can ill afford to stop. I met an 80-year-old woman who was cleaning houses. And a 78-year-old watchman who was still working. "These are the small things that we go through every day, which most people don't hear about it," says Shagufta Samuel.

It isn't just lost opportunities, however. On top of this comes official harassment and even persecution. Although Christians are largely left alone in their own areas, not so where the faiths mix. "I can preach in our area, within that boundary. But not outside. We can make a new church in a Christian area. But not in a Muslim one." Indeed, complains Khokha, whose congregation includes about 300 families, "Muslims call if we have a meeting, and we get persecuted."

Nor can Christians count on legal protection. Samuel's TSA provides not only work opportunities for Christians, but also shelter for women. "A lot of women are molested by elite people," she explains, often the families for whom they are working. "They have no place to go and the human rights commission sends them here." Rarely is the law of much help: "they go to court over physical abuse, but no one listens to them." Muslim women are also abused, she notes, but the system is least responsive to Christians. Christians "are treated very badly by Muslims," she says.

Even worse is criminal prosecution. "It's terrible, explained Khokha. "Ten years ago you could pass out Christian literature, but now there's the anti-blasphemy law." Christians handed out Operation Mobilization materials, and the government "put people in jail."

For instance, Pervez Masih, a Christian teacher, was imprisoned last year after answering a student's questions about Mohammed's life (his marriage to a young girl, for instance); Masih was denounced by the administrator of a rival school. "A lot of blasphemy cases are brought against Christians," complains Samuel. But such trials are rarely reported in the media and are often conducted in secret.

Sometimes there is unofficial violence. Converts in Islamic Pakistan face death; for this reason Masih Yousaf, a member of Khokha's congregation, has received political asylum in America. "He can't come back," says Khokha. After significant delay, asylum has been granted and the visas finally issued to Masih's wife, Elvina, and their three children. Before that the family remained in Lahore, fearful for its safety. "I'm afraid here," she explained: "It's not safe." And for good reason. Living with her 25-year-old nephew Jabeen, whose father, a Christian convert, was murdered by a mob that pushed him off a cliff. "Everyone has a gun, everyone is angry," worries Khokha.

In March two men killed five Christians, including two Americans, in a grenade attack on a church in Islamabad. Last October gunmen stormed a church in Bahawalpur and slaughtered 15 Christians, including the minister. They screamed "blood for blood," apparently suggesting that the killings were retaliation for America's war in Afghanistan.

The St. Anthony's Church in Lahore has been vandalized and subject to bomb threats; the authorities have exhibited little interest in intervening. A small Assemblies of God church in Islamabad was destroyed after Christmas; the government proclaimed it to be a gas explosion, but did little to investigate. Just two days before we arrived in mid-January, said Khokha, Muslims beat a pastor and his family in a village near Lahore. Since September 11 it's been "very tense," observed Khokha. Though "these days it is a little better."

For instance, of their general treatment of Christians, he complains, all governments seem to follow much the same policy. For instance, under intense Islamic criticism, the Musharraf regime backed away from reforming the blasphemy law and has allowed provincial application of Sharia, or Islamic law.

But Musharraf deserves some credit even before September 11. For instance, he dropped the separate electoral lists for Muslims and religious minorities: "He said that we are all Pakistanis now," explained Khokha. Since then the Musharraf government has begun moving against the Madrassahs, the fundamentalist Islamic schools which have spawned so many jihad warriors. And he seems committed to breaking the security service's ties to militants. Observes Khokha: "We praise the Lord for Musharraf. Musharaff is from God. Sharif and Bhutto couldn't do it. But Musharraf took brave steps. He banned the fundamentalists."

American Christians can help too. One step is to reach out to Christian communities in need. Pastor Javed John said: "Please convey the message to the American people that there are so many problems with Christians" in Pakistan. Christian people are very poor. We need your help. Please pray for us. Support us." For instance, Christian Freedom International is attempting to help brickmaking families escape their servitude, provide an education for poor children, and aid families in need. What is needed is not a massive government-to-government aid program, but small-scale initiatives to make positive improvements in people's lives.

Another tactic is to embarrass the Pakistani government for its discrimination. The Musharaff regime is walking a political tightrope, but still could improve Christians' lives at the margin.

American Christians can also push their own government to stop discriminating against Pakistani Christians. Odd as it may seem, Pakistani Muslims are much more likely than Christians to receive a visa to visit the U.S. That might not be the intent of U.S. officials, but it is the inevitable result of their policies. Washington does not want anyone to come who might stay in America, and demands evidence of extensive ties to Pakistan. Since Christians tend to be at the economic bottom of Pakistani society, they have a harder time meeting U.S. requirements to show a bank account, for instance. Observes Khokha: "A Muslim has property. We don't. They say you'll stay in the U.S. In contrast, Muslims show property, business, land." And they get a visa. One of the deacons in Khokha's church has been turned down three times for a visa to visit America, despite the invitation from Christian churches.

Whether or not Islam is a religion of peace, it has clearly proved, throughout most of the world, to be a religion of discrimination. The lot of Christians in Pakistan is extraordinarily difficult. They need support and prayers from Christians in America and around the world. "Remember us in your prayers. Don't forget us," implores Rev. John.

March 2002

CHAPTER ELEVEN

Who Serves?

Serving Uncle Sam

My brother-in-law, Birkley Wical, just celebrated his 39th birthday. What makes it significant is not that he is rapidly approaching the big 4-0, though that certainly gives those of us in the family who've already hit that milestone some satisfaction. More significant is the fact that it coincides with 20 years in the Air Force.

He's now eligible to retire with a pension, though not a generous one—NCOs don't get rich in the service. It hasn't been an easy life, and I applaud him, as well as my sister, nephew, and niece, for enduring it.

Americans have grown used to nearly costless wars. The New York Times headlined one story during the war in Iraq: "Invading Forces Capture Key Bridge—More American Deaths." It left readers to ponder which was the more interesting nugget of news—that a bridge was taken, or that U.S. soldiers died doing so.

That Americans had died in battle was not considered to be news in the Korean or Vietnam Wars, World Wars I and II, and certainly not in the Civil War, America's costliest conflict. In all of those wars the casualty lists were long, hideously long. The price of serving was inevitable and evident to all.

Despite complaints about the American public's low tolerance for casualties, it obviously has accepted huge losses when it believed the goal to be worthwhile. And it almost certainly would accept even more if perceived America's survival to be at stake. In contrast, tracking down one of many warlords didn't seem worth the 19 dead Rangers in Mogadishu.

The Clinton administration thought Americans would react the same way in Kosovo when it decided to impose an outside settlement in one of the smaller of a score of civil wars around the world. Thus the bombing from 15,000 feet and refusal to mount a ground invasion.

We were lucky and the American public's willingness to accept losses wasn't seriously tested in the current war. Even some unexpected Iraqi resistance was not enough to generate the kind of carnage seen in past wars, when Uncle Sam's qualitative and technological dominance was not so great.

Yet while the casualties were mercifully low, every one left a family in anguish. And other families breathing a sad sigh of temporary relief.

Moreover, every potential casualty—that is, every serviceman or woman in harm's way—left a family worried, nervous, and on edge. With units on the move, people, including some friends of mine, could only catch TV and scan the newspapers for an indication as to the whereabouts of their son or daughter. And for evidence that their loved one was not likely the one killed, wounded, or captured.

It's an experience that I've largely avoided. I grew up a military brat, with great respect for the profession of arms but not desiring to enter it myself. It takes special commitment to be willing to turn over control of one's life to a boss as fickle as Uncle Sam.

My father was career Air Force, but he forecast weather for combat pilots rather than flew combat sorties. We were stationed stateside during the Vietnam War, so my classmates' parents also were at little risk.

Two decades ago Birkley, my brother-in-law, enlisted in the Air Force. However, he has been tasked to keep supplies moving, not drop bombs. In practice, he's been at greater risk from our erstwhile allies—he spent time in Saudi Arabia—than our adversaries. Thus, I and my family have been spared having to worry about his safety during the half dozen small-scale invasions and wars since his enlistment.

Yet the risks of military service have never seemed too far away. I'm glad my friend of more than a quarter century is now in the Air Force reserves rather than on active duty, since he would have been in the thick of any action.

My racquetball player and Navy reservist friend has been called up, but to do intelligence work for the Defense Intelligence Agency. My across-the-street neighbor and Navy commander was nearly hit by the 9/11 attack while working at the Pentagon, but at least he's far from Iraqi bullets.

Not so lucky, though, is my assistant pastor, an active duty turned reserve Marine Corps infantry officer, called up for occupation duty in Afghanistan. At least he wasn't racing into Baghdad, though several more months in Afghanistan might not be much better.

Three other members of my church, another Marine Corps reservist, also currently on active duty, a sailor off-shore, and an Army infantryman, are in the Gulf. I don't know them too well, but I thought of them when I saw casualty reports. And their families' anxiety has been evident.

The sacrifices that servicemen and women and their families make during war is obvious. "Only" 147 Americans died in Gulf War I, but I met the mother-in-law of one, still grieving a year after his death. The casualty count is about the same in Gulf War II, and the effects of death will similarly linger long after the occupation of Baghdad has ended.

Less dramatic, but more persistent, are sacrifices made in peacetime. In my family we counted ourselves lucky for lasting seven years at one posting while I was in elementary and middle school. My sister's family has not been as fortunate.

The service offers enormous responsibility: men and women not yet able to drink, legally, at least, prepare weapons for battle, guide airplanes onto carriers, maneuver in combat, and share responsibility for countless lives around them. Such duty brings satisfaction, to be sure, but little money and little more public recognition.

Life is often boring, filled with lines, meaningless rules, and long hours. Families no less than soldiers must adapt to the vagaries of service life. Especially in the post-Cold War era, with frequent deployments, occupations, and wars, spouses and children must endure long absences and suffer through sometimes difficult reunions.

Most incredible, perhaps, is the fact that so many men and women choose to join and remain. Like my brother-in-law, they love their country, long to serve, yearn for responsibility, enjoy the comradeship, and want to be soldiers. Those of us who have chosen other career paths owe them an enormous debt of gratitude. They deserve our thanks, support, and prayers—especially now, during wartime.

April 2003

Fighting Future Wars: Conscripts, Not Now, Not Ever

Until September 11, it had been sixty years since the U.S. homeland came under attack. As after Pearl Harbor, Americans turned to the military for their defense. But now, in contrast to the past, they are finding security in a volunteer military.

When the terrorists struck on September 11, they attacked the nation with the most powerful and effective military on earth. Its weapons are the most advanced; its troops are the brightest and best trained. The result is catastrophe for any opposing force, as the Taliban and al-Qaeda quickly learned.

Yet even as the military was gearing up to fight with such good effect, some analysts called for conscription. For instance, the day after the World Trade Center attack, Stanley Kurtz of the Hudson Institute wrote: "Maybe now, in the wake of this terrible act of war, we can break our great taboo and at least consider a revival of the draft." He complained that "military recruitment is in a state of crisis for some time now." Without reliance on women in the service, he argued, a draft would certainly be necessary, "And that's without taking into account the increased demands on our armed forces that the war on terrorism will surely impose."

This is an extraordinary argument: to fight terrorism America needs a mass conscript army. Ironically, foreign nations are now following the U.S. in abandoning the draft. France has dropped conscription; Russia is professionalizing its military. Other states, such as Germany, are debating the same step. Even China's strategy for strengthening its armed forces is to cut numbers and increase quality, as did the U.S. after the advent of the All-Volunteer Force. No major power is moving in the other direction. The countries most dependent on conscription tend not to be ones whose example we should wish to follow—the Taliban in Afghanistan, for instance, and Hutu rebels in Burundi.

Today, the U.S. military possesses an extraordinary ability to use advanced information and weapons technology to maximize destruction of opposing forces and minimize American casualties. Observes William Owens, former chairman of the Joint Chiefs of Staff: "What sets the United States apart from its adversaries is that we use information much better than they do. Properly used, that can be an unbridgeable gap."

Although high-tech weapons—evidenced most dramatically through aerial attack—alone are unlikely to subdue an adversary and obviously cannot occupy a vanquished foe, they can ensure the defeat of opposing military forces. And they preclude the need for large U.S. ground forces. In Afghanistan, for instance, sustained air attack was supplemented by the extensive use of special operations forces—of whom, all told, the U.S. today fields some 29,000. Also active on the ground were Marines, the smallest service branch, but the one with the toughest reputation which has nevertheless consistently had the best recruiting success.

Moreover, America fields a professional force of extraordinary quality. Soldiers today are far brighter and better educated than the draft-era force. They are therefore much more capable of handling high-tech weapons. This will become even more so in the future.

Even the army sees a need for quicker, lighter, and more lethal forces in the future. That means an elite, not mass army. And a volunteer, not draft force. Observes Philip Gold of the Discovery Institute: "the present military is an Industrial Age, labor-intensive structure ill-suited to 21st-century technologies and threats. Properly organized, equipped and with more superfluous bases closed and many support functions privatized, it could easily drop to 1.2 million or less."

The military opposes conscription, not just because it tends to resist change, as some charge, but because today's force is the best ever. Observes Gordon Sullivan, former Army Chief of Staff and current president of the Association of the United States Army: "Military commanders prefer high-quality volunteers to mixed-quality draftees."

All of the services made their recruiting goals in FY2001. More than 90 percent of Army and Navy accessions had high school degrees; 96 percent of Marine and 99 percent of Air Force recruits had diplomas. Roughly two-thirds of those joining the first three services scored in mental categories I-IIIA (out of five); three-fourths of Air Force recruits fell into that category.

Recruiting was tougher in 1998 and 1999, though there was never a crisis: DOD fell short by 6000 and 8000 recruits in those years, respectively. Even then, the military's problem was inadequate quality recruits, not inadequate recruits. The All Volunteer Force (AVF) is choosier than a draft military, rejecting many bodies; the percentage of "high quality" enlistees, that is, those with high school degrees and scoring above average on the AFQT test, has jumped 50 percent since the advent of a volunteer military in 1973. With few exceptions, the armed services today do not accept those scoring in categories IV and V on the military aptitude test, or who lack a high school degree. The military could solve any recruiting problems by simply lower its standards to that of a conscript military.

The volunteer force is superior in another way: the armed services are filled with people who desire to serve. Even Kurtz acknowledged that discipline problems would inevitably increase with conscription. And this phenomenon would permeate the force: draftees have little incentive to train, accept greater responsibility, or reenlist; yet the military must retain them, almost no matter how ill-suited they are to military service.

This explains the fact that the volunteer military has higher attrition rates. Attrition is significant in the volunteer military—it peaked at about 20 percent for the Army in 1998. But that's because it is a *voluntary* military. The services get to choose who remains; with conscription, they can ill afford to kick out even the worst malcontent since doing so would be seen as a reward for anyone seeking an out. One must ask: is a military healthier if it relies on those who desire to serve and succeed, or is forced to include those who desire to escape at any price?

Kurtz also contends that only the presence of women—33,621 out of 182,845 recruits in 2001—allows the AVF to survive. The role of women in the armed services remains a controversial issue, of course, though so far the military has performed superbly even as women have filled more roles.

Moreover, changes in the military culture to accommodate women may have suppressed male enlistment. For instance, while the propensity of women between 16 and 21 to enlist remained unchanged between 1991 and 1994, that of young men dropped by a third. Observed Elaine Donnelly, president of the Center for Military Readiness, "There is something wrong with the changes in the culture of the military that is turning off young men, and young men are the primary market."

How much the military has lost what was once part of its fundamental appeal is a matter of serious debate.

But these issues do not justify conscription. The proper question is how best to build a volunteer military, given whatever constraints are imposed by the civilian leadership, ranging from foreign commitments to military culture. Reducing the role of women, if desired, would not necessitate conscription. Rather, it would require a different approach to recruiting, including perhaps a different set of quality standards.

Since a draft would lower the quality of enlisted manpower while diverting attention from creating the specialized, professional forces needed in the future, what other reason is there to conscript? Commentator John Derbyshire suggests a draft to meet specific needs, such as Pashto or Chinese speakers. This proposal builds on more traditional plans for a medical draft, to ensure the availability of doctors and other health care personnel in a crisis.

The latter has long been justified because it would occur only in the midst of a serious war. The former, in contrast, could be implemented at any time; in theory, there might be a draft of just a few hundred people, if they were unlucky enough to possess a particular skill demanded by the military. Yet to do so, to only conscript Afghan immigrants, for instance, would correctly be seen as grossly unfair. It would also create perverse incentives—encouraging anyone with unique abilities which might suddenly come into demand to hide those skills (deny that one speaks Pashto, make a hash of interpretation duties, or refuse to speak it at all) or undertake an extended sabbatical abroad or even emigrate (Pakistan might begin to look good to someone who otherwise faced induction into a Ranger unit to be dropped behind Taliban lines).

Conscription also offers an unnecessarily complex solution to a relatively simple problem. A draft is unable to provide a long-term supply of any skill: absent life-time conscription, most draftees will leave when their tour ends. Nor can a draft quickly fill an unexpected need; even if the Pentagon had decided on September 12 that it wanted Pashto speakers, they would not have been inducted and trained in time to serve during the heaviest fighting in Afghanistan. Better to either rely on civilian contractors or military reservists to find people with skills that will only unexpectedly and temporarily be in demand.

Northwestern University's Charles Moskos and Paul Glastris, editor-in-chief of the *Washington Monthly* recognize that a high-tech military requires professionals. But they suggest a draft to acquire raw numbers for other purposes—peacekeeping duty, for instance. "This would free up professional soldiers to do the fighting without sacrificing other U.S. commitments."

Fear of maintaining expansive commitments also motivates Kurtz. Imagine, he writes, a U.S. busy garrisoning Afghanistan and preparing to invade Iraq, then having to deal with the collapse of Pakistan's government, followed by a North Korean invasion of South Korea. This "would stretch our forces past the breaking point, and almost surely force the president to ask the Democrats to join him in imposing a draft."

More sensible, however, would be to ask: which commitments are worthy of U.S. attention? More particularly, which commitments are worth meeting through conscription?

For instance, no vital national interest is at stake in policing the Balkans. The area is important to Europe, which has more than one million men under arms, not America. The artificial settlements imposed in Bosnia, Kosovo, and Macedonia reflect the opinions of international elites rather than local residents, and thus warrant no exposure of American blood. There is certainly no reason to conscript young Americans to force three hostile communities to live together in Bosnia, or ensure that Kosovo remains an autonomous part of Serbia, a position that satisfies none of the combatants. Americans' freedom should not be sacrificed so frivolously through conscription for such purposes.

As for Kurtz's slightly lurid scenario of the U.S. choosing to war with most of the known Muslim world, Washington maintains a substantial reserve force precisely to handle such unexpected contingencies. No one suggested maintaining, day-in and day-out, a sufficient active force to manage the unlikely contingency of a full-scale NATO-Warsaw Pact conflagration. Instead, in the event of war Washington would have called up the reserves while expanding its active forces.

Anyway, the U.S. could easily increase its available military resources by no longer defending its prosperous and populous industrialized allies. The U.S. presently maintains 100,000 troops in each of Europe and East Asia. The Western Europeans face no serious security threat and are able to deal with disruptive civil wars in the Balkans. Japan is capable of doing much more to enhance regional stability while South Korea can counter the sole serious regional military threat, posed by North Korea. At a time when Seoul possesses upwards of 40 times the GDP, twice the population, and a vast technological edge over its northern antagonist, Americans should stop talking about what they would do in the unlikely event of an invasion and let South Koreans talk about what they would do. Unnecessarily subsidizing wealthy client states is ridiculous enough; drafting young Americans so allies don't have to burden their own citizens is senseless.

Moreover, dubious commitments unrelated to American security have exacerbated the military's recruitment and retention problems. Focus group interviews have found young men to be reluctant to support America's increasing role as international policeman. Reported two researchers at the Defense Manpower Data Center: "youth today generally view the military as less attractive than before the end of the Cold War. A considerable number of young men indicated they did not wish to serve as peacekeepers in foreign countries. ... Some suggested that recent military ventures were motivated by the interests of national leaders—Congress or the President—but were not in the national interest. They objected to being put in jeopardy to fight someone else's battles. Parents share this concern.

Promiscuous and frivolous deployments have also harmed service retention. This may be the most important reason for the loss of Air Force pilots. A similar effect is being felt by the Navy. One servicemen complained that "We're not really fighting the country's wars; we're just acting like the world's policeman." An Army officer explained in his resignation letter: "I didn't join the Army to be a peacekeeper." The *New York Times* has reported that "the combat readiness, morale and effectiveness of the troops appears to plummet after six months of duty" in such operations. This problem is beyond the reach of conscription, unless Uncle Sam's lottery ticket means lifetime service.

Military columnist David Hackworth take a different approach, suggesting that conscription would prevent the wasteful use of U.S. lives. Regarding the fight in Afghanistan, he writes, "The draft would bring this war home to every family in America." This, in turn, would cause Americans to "better watch the threat conditions and how and where the war was being fought."

Yet the fact that the U.S. military is broadly representative of the American population means that the war is already being brought into the homes of many people. That is especially the case when reservists—often well-established members of the community ranging from cops to lawyers—are called up to serve. And volunteers have the power to hinder if not stop a foolish war by simply refusing to join; a draft allows the government to pursue an increasingly unpopular conflict, like Vietnam, through compulsory service.

Another proposal is to use conscription for defense at home. Writes political columnist David Broder: "The reality is that homeland defense in the war on terrorism is bound to be labor-intensive, as demanding of manpower as the big wars of the past. But we do not have the vital tool we used in those wars: the draft." University of North Carolina journalism professor Philip Meyer argues that "A system of universal training—military, civil-defense or related skills that could be called into use on short notice to combat terrorism—would reduce [the gap between military and civilian society] and make the USA more democratic and, at the same time, a safer place to live."

Moskos and Glastris propose a three-part draft: choose among the military, homeland security, and civilian work. This system, they write, "would focus less on preparing men for conventional combat—which hasn't been very extensive in this war so far—than on training young men and even young women for the arguably more daunting task of guarding against and responding to terrorism at home." Why pay a salary when people can be forced into uniform? They write:

> we are clearly going to need more armed federal personnel to guard dams, nuclear power plants, sports complexes and U.S. embassies; more border patrol and customs agents to keep terrorists and their weapons from entering the country; more INS agents to track down immigrants who have overstayed their visas; more Coast Guard personnel to inspect ships; more air marshals to ride on passenger jets; and more FBI

> agents to uncover terrorist cells still operating inside and outside our borders.

Others use anti-terrorism as a hook for creating a mandatory program intended to meet other goals, such as establishing a huge new federal social program. "Our schools are as important to our future as are border patrols," argues David Gergen of *U.S. News & World Report*. Cynthia Tucker, editor of the *Atlanta Constitution*, makes a similar argument. "A draft for national service," she writes, would not only allow staffing of the military and existing social programs, such as VISTA, but also new programs "to aid the elderly, the handicapped and the impoverished."

Senators John McCain (R-Ariz.) and Evan Bayh (D-Ind.) have proposed legislation for a large expansion of the (currently voluntary) service program AmeriCorps. But it appears to be a stalking horse for conscript service. McCain adviser Marshall Wittman of the Hudson Institute explains: a move to coercion "may be sooner than we think, depending on what the needs are in this war."

A civilian draft is unprecedented, however. The idea goes back more than a century, to the famous William James "The Moral Equivalent of War" essay and the even earlier Edward Bellamy novel, *Looking Backward.*

A draft is not an intelligent means to fill such a diverse set of needs. Ignoring costs means that "needs" will be infinite. After all, before the concern for homeland defense, one study estimated 5.3 million "unmet social needs." Another report figured that libraries needed 200,000 people; education needed six times as many. But such numbers were, and remain, meaningless, since the proper number of librarians, or airport screeners, or INS agents can be decided only by balancing the benefits of their work with the costs of paying for it.

Calling something homeland defense does not change the analysis. For instance, stationing national guardsmen—more than 9000 were called up after September 11—at airports across America was a complete waste. No one expected al-Qaeda terrorists to storm airport security checkpoints, the defense of which the guardsmen could conceivably contribute. The guardsmen do nothing to screen passengers, the real issue of airline security. Indeed, this diversion proved particularly costly since guardsmen play other important roles; in private life many are cops, for instance. The National League of Cities reported "a temporary loss of public safety personnel to National Guard and military reserve call-ups." Conscripting people wouldn't make the guardsmen's task any more valuable.

There are a half million bridges across America. To protect every bridge would entail at least a two-man detail at all times, with three shifts a day, plus weekend duty. That's at least eight people per bridge, or four million people—the entire number of men and women turning 18 a year. There are also 91,062 schools, 4000 water treatment plants, 3329 major malls, 493 skyscrapers, 322 commercial sports stadiums, 103 nuclear reactors, and 190,000 miles of natural gas pipeline. Nine million shipping contains enter the U.S. every day. Add in all of the other potential tasks, and, if we value people's labor at zero, no one will be doing anything else.

Nor will conscription draw people into useful tasks at acceptable cost. Not everyone is fit to be an FBI agent; some people have talents suited to work other than manning an airport security checkpoint.

In fact, a labor draft involving the four million Americans who turn 18 every year would inevitably result in poor use of manpower. Inefficient central government control mixed with the usual political porkbarrelling would ensure a failure to make serious trade-offs among competing tasks. This is the experience of AmeriCorps, which has funded "volunteers" to engage in all manner of low-value activities, including political activism. Consider the debate over federalizing airport screening. Although many people apparently felt they would be more secure with the job turned over to a government bureaucracy, most foreign countries rely on a competitive mix of airport authorities, local governments, and private companies.

Anyway, if conscription is a good idea, then don't draft the young; instead, follow Derbyshire's idea and grab cops, security personnel, private investigators, and others out of their present jobs. Not that doing so would save money. Conscription only shifts the burden of paying onto those drafted. There ain't no free lunch when it comes to recruiting soldiers, training firemen, or hiring airport screeners. A national service draft would simply foist the cost off on the young, in the name of patriotism.

Of course, patriotism and civic commitment are good things. Write Moskos and Glastris, "It's a shame that it's taken terrorist attacks to reawaken us to the reality of our shared national fate." But nothing in that shared fate suggests that we should abandon the shared principles upon which the American nation is based, most notably a commitment to individual liberty.

Especially because it is freedom that has kept America free. Columnist Hackworth advocates renewed national service because it has "kept our country free since we booted out the Brits." But it is not the national but the service that has kept America free. And it is service—voluntarily offered by brave young men and women—that will keep us free in the future.

Well, asks Mark Shields, "Should only American volunteers be asked to die in the defense of the United States?" Should only American volunteers be asked to die in arresting criminals? In fighting fires? In devoting their lives to the poor? A free society doesn't mean there are no shirkers, content to benefit from the sacrifices of others. But that is the inevitable price of freedom. Allowing the pampered elite that populates Washington to decide how everyone else should spend his or her life is far too high a price to pay for such a dubious form of "fairness."

In America, homeland defense does more than secure a plot of land. It protects an ideal, a free society built on respect for and protection of individual liberty. Renewing conscription would destroy the very thing we are supposed to be protecting.

August 2002

Strengthening the All-Volunteer Military

Three decades ago the U.S. inaugurated the All-Volunteer Force. The AVF produced the world's finest military, capable of deterring superpower competitors and destroying regional powers with equal avidity.

Today, however, the U.S. military is under enormous strain. Although the finest fighting force on the planet, it lacks sufficient strength to satisfy the demands of an imperial foreign policy. The massive troop rotation in Iraq last spring was necessary, but did nothing to reduce pressure on American servicemen and women.

The U.S. has managed so far by turning the Reserves and National Guard into de facto active duty units. But the Bush administration risks driving down recruiting and retention for both active and Reserve forces. Some congressmen are promoting a return to conscription. Warns Rep. Charles Rangel (D-NY): "The experts are all saying we're going to have to beef up our presence in Iraq. We've failed to convince our allies to send troops, we've extended deployments so morale is sinking, and the president is saying we can't cut and run. So what's left?"

Unfortunately, no relief for the U.S. military is in the offing. About 10,000 U.S. troops remain in Afghanistan. Despite dramatic initial success, Washington now most cope with increasing attacks on coalition soldiers and foreign aid workers outside of the capital. Elections were postponed as the internal security situation deteriorated.

Iraq is of greater concern. Defense Secretary Donald Rumsfeld once opined that the number of U.S. troops could fall to 30,000 by fall 2003. But the garrison currently numbers roughly 160,000, about 140,000 of whom are American. (Another 34,000 perform support duties in Kuwait.) The coalition has made progress in restoring services and rebuilding infrastructure. Yet the administration's goal of creating a liberal, pro-Western democracy remains far distant.

Polls indicate that Washington had lost the war for Iraqi hearts and minds even before the lengthy and bloody battles in Fallujah and Najaf in April and August 2004. In November 2003 the CIA warned, in a report endorsed by occupation head Paul Bremer, that Iraqis were losing faith in U.S. efforts and policies, creating a fertile environment for the insurgents. Even then one unnamed official told the *New York Times*: "The trend lines are in the wrong direction."

The Iraqi conflict is taking a heavy toll on the U.S. military. Not only the thousands of dead and wounded, but the unexpected and unexpectedly lengthy deployments to Iraq. Although administration supporters routinely complained that the media was focusing on bad news, the troops lived the bad news. A poll of 2000 soldiers in 2003, before the worst of the violence, by *Stars and Stripes*, a DOD-funded newspaper for members of the armed forces, found that 40 percent believed the Iraq mission was unrelated to their training, one-third believed their mission was not clearly defined, and one-third believed the Iraqi war was of limited value.

The administration had hoped to bring down the U.S. garrison to about 110,000 in spring 2004. But that proved to be another example of hysterically high hopes ruined by reality as the insurgency intensified. Even now, many analysts believe that more troops are necessary.

But the Pentagon has had trouble finding sufficient soldiers to man its existing commitments. In order to maintain training standards and troop morale, the Congressional Budget Office suggests "rotation ratios" of 3.2:1 to 4:1 for active forces and 7.5:1 to 9:1 for Reserve/Guard. Yet of roughly 480,000 Army active duty and 560,000 Army Reserve and Army National Guard forces, 370,000 are deployed overseas. Even this understates the problem. Only about 300,000 active Army personnel and 470,000 Army Reserve/Guard members are in deployable units.

The burden falls heaviest on reservists. Nearly 40 percent of the Iraq garrison is made up of members of the Reserve and National Guard. The average annual call-up during the 1990s was about 10,000 annually. Lt. Gen. H. Steven Blum, chief of the National Guard Bureau, admits that the "Weekend warrior is dead."

The military can handle such burdens in a temporary emergency. But speaking only of Afghanistan in March 2002, Secretary Rumsfeld observed: "it's helpful to remember that those who developed the concept for peacekeepers in Bosnia assured everyone that those forces would complete their mission by the end of that year and be home by Christmas. We are now heading into our seventh year of U.S. and international involvement in Bosnia."

Thomas Donnelly and Vance Serchuk of the American Enterprise Institute suggest that "the protection of the embryonic Iraqi democracy is a duty that will likely extend for decades." Even President George W. Bush admitted that the U.S. faced a "massive and long-term undertaking" in Iraq. Democratic challenger John Kerry spoke of trying to reduce the size of America's garrison, but nevertheless pledged to stay as long as necessary.

Which brings back Rep. Rangel's question: "So what's left?" The administration limited coverage of the return of bodies and of funerals to cut hostile press coverage, but that provided no additional manpower. By fall 2004 allied states were leaving, not coming, in Iraq, and the only serious help came from Great Britain. As Francois Heisbourg, Director of the Paris-based Foundation for Strategic Research bluntly put it: "I don't think anybody is going to jump into an American-run quagmire."

Which means Iraq will remain largely an American show. Yet the active forces don't have much more to contribute. The Pentagon admits that many infantrymen will have to serve back-to-back foreign tours. Even though deployment in countries like Britain and Germany is more pleasant than in Afghanistan and Iraq, few people will join and remain in the Army if they rarely see home.

Adding Marine Corps actives, as DOD did last spring, will help. But the Marines are a relatively small force, 175,000, which is intended to respond to unexpected contingencies. Warns the Congressional Budget Office, "If all Marine regiments were either deployed, recovering after deployments, or preparing for deployments ..., DoD's ability to quickly deploy substantial combat power in the early phases of an operation would be degraded."

Which leaves the Reserves and National Guard. But these troops are intended to supplement the active force in an emergency. Unfortunately, write Philip Gold and Erin Solaro of the Aretea institute, Washington is using reservists "not just as reinforcements for the regulars but as substitutes." The Army Reserve has been mobilized more in the last 12 years, ten times, than the previous 75 years, nine times. Today Guard/Reserve units handle everything from civil affairs to personnel services.

Extended deployments place a greater burden on reservists than on active duty forces because the former, who consciously chose not to join the active force, must leave not only family, friends, and community, but jobs. The burden has been compounded by discrimination against reservists, who often serve longer deployments than active duty soldiers but are last on the list to receive the best equipment, such as Kevlar vests. Nevertheless, the military has been pressuring reservists to waive the statutory requirement of 12 months home between overseas deployments.

Where else can bodies be found? When Gen. Eric Shinseki retired as Army Chief of Staff in June, he warned "Beware the 12-division strategy for a 10-division Army." Support for adding at least two divisions has been building in Congress.

So far the Defense Department has rebuffed such proposals. Adding forces takes money and time. Concludes CBO: "Recruiting, training, and equipping two additional divisions would entail up-front costs of as much as $18 billion to $19 billion and would take about five years to accomplish, CBO estimates. In the long run, the cost to operate and sustain these new divisions as a permanent part of the Army's force structure would be about $6 billion annually (plus between $3 billion and $4 billion per year to employ them in Iraq)."

Moreover, the armed services are having trouble because excessive and unpleasant commitments make it harder for them to attract and keep enough people. Increasing recruiting and retention requirements won't address the underlying problems.

Publicly many officials and analysts argue that there is no morale problem. Yet the *Stars and Stripes* interview found that one-third of soldiers said their own morale was low and half said their units' morale was low. Half said they would not reup once their tours end and the DOD's "stop-loss" order, which bars retirements, is lifted. Moreover, the *Stars and Stripes* reported that it was hearing "edgier complaints about inequality among the forces and lack of confidence in their leaders" than the sort of griping common among enlisted personnel.

Also critical is the attitude of service families. Worried Fox News Channel commentator Robert Maginnis, "Either we find a fix to rotate those troops out and to keep the families content ... or we're going to suffer what I anticipate is a downturn in retention." Army recruiters are finding increasing resistance from parents, especially when they seek to recruit 17-year-olds, who need parental approval to join.

So far, DOD has been making most of its manpower targets. However, in FY 2003 the Army National Guard and Navy Reserve fell behind their goals; the former ran 87.4 percent and the latter a less worrisome 98.9 percent. Although attrition rates remained low, Defense Under Secretary David Chu admitted that "Certain high-demand (high-use) units and specialties have experienced higher than normal attrition."

But the situation could easily worsen. Secretary Rumsfeld acknowledges that "the effects of a stress on the force are unlikely to be felt immediately; they're much more likely to be felt down the road." Similarly, Les Brownlee, acting Secretary of the Army, worried that DOD might have to wait "some three to six months after these units return" to judge the impact. The effect might take even longer for retentions, since "stop-loss" remains in effect for some Army active duty soldiers and many Army Reserve soldiers.

A growing economy, by providing more employment alternatives, could discourage new enlistments. And the longer the Afghanistan and Iraq occupations, the more likely problems are to arise. Beth Asch of the Rand Corporation explains: "Short deployments actually boost enlistments and reenlistments." But "Studies show longer deployments can definitely have a negative impact." Lt. Gen. Blum says that a fall in recruits and reenlistees is "the No. 1 thing in my worry book."

So all that's left, in Rep. Rangel's view, is renewing the draft. Every recent war has sparked proposals for restarting conscription. Rep. Rangel and retiring Sen. Fritz Hollings (D-S.C.) introduced legislation to establish a system of conscription-based national service. Indeed, when the Selective Service System, apparently innocently, placed a notice on its website recruiting for local and appeal boards, sparking a flurry of media stories and administration denials.

From a security standpoint, conscription would be foolish. The U.S. military is the finest on the earth largely because voluntarism allows the Pentagon to be selective, choosing recruits who are smarter and better educated than their civilian counterparts. Enlistees also are selective; they work to succeed in their chosen career rather than to escape forced service. They serve longer terms and reenlist in higher numbers, increasing the experience and skills of the force.

Since conscription would lower the quality of the U.S. military, draft advocates make other arguments. Rangel argues that lower socio-economic groups "make up the overwhelming majority of our nation's armed forces, and that, by and large, those of wealth and position are absent from the ranks of ground troops." Actually, Rangel is wrong. There are fewer children of elites, but the underclass is entirely absent, barred from volunteering.

Virtually no one who lacks a high school diploma or who doesn't score in the top three of five categories of the Armed Forces Quality Test can join. The U.S. military is overwhelmingly middle class; in fact, the test scores and educational achievements of recruits exceed those of young people generally. African-Americans are somewhat over-represented, but they disproportionately serve in support, not combat arms. Hispanics are underrepresented.

Broader national service makes even less sense. It would divert people from military service to civilian tasks, jail young men and women who prefer not to put their lives at the discretion of political officials, and waste people's lives in frivolous, pork barrel pursuits. How can one compare picking up cigarette butts in a park with patrolling the streets of Baghdad?

Although a volunteer military beats a draft force, Washington risks driving down recruiting and retention, which, over the long-term, could wreck the AVF. If forced to choose between a policy of promiscuous military intervention and freedom, an activist administration, whether Republican or Democratic, might turn to a draft. Argues *Washington Times* editorial page editor Tony Blankley, it is critical to increase the size of the military, "whether by draft or by voluntary means."

Ironically, Blankley recognizes the fact that voluntarism impedes an interventionist foreign policy. Which disproves Rep. Rangel's final contention, that "there would be more caution" in going to war if policymakers' children were at risk. The surest barrier to war is not a draft, which allowed the Vietnam War to proceed for years, but the AVF, which empowers average people to say no.

A related argument by *Washington Post* columnist David Broder is that a draft would ensure that more leaders served in the military. But conscription would not increase the incidence of military service, which was low throughout American history until World War II and the Cold War. With new accessions running only about 185,000 a year, the armed services require fewer than 10 percent of male 18-year-olds, and 5 percent of all 18-year-olds, irrespective of how the military is manned.

Ironically, while some legislators advocate renewing conscription, other nations—France, Germany, and Russia, for instance—have moved or are moving to professionalize their forces. In a world where terrorism is a greater threat than a mass attack by the Red Army through Germany's Fulda Gap, the U.S. has no choice but to build the sort of quality force possible only through voluntarism. Indeed, Congress should eliminate draft registration—the list ages rapidly and a post-mobilization sign-up would be available in an emergency—and close down the Selective Service System, an expensive and unnecessary anachronism.

What to do to strengthen the armed services? The obvious place to start is improved pay and benefits, especially for Guard and Reserve members, who are increasingly being treated like active duty soldiers. For instance, Democratic legislators have proposed extending health insurance for National Guard and Reserve members even when they are not deployed.

Improved treatment for those deployed in overseas, and particularly in battle zones, also matters. In September 2003 the Pentagon began the first rest and recuperation leave program since Vietnam, allowing soldiers 15 days at home. Congress also approved legislation to pay for the flights from Baltimore (where military flights land) to servicemen's home towns.

Resources also need to be put into recruiting. In fact, so far the Pentagon has helped staunch potential personnel losses by increasing signing bonuses, doubling the advertising budget, and developing cyber-recruiting.

The Armed Services could use uniformed personnel more efficiently. Explained Secretary Rumsfeld, "we can get some possibly 300,000 people, military people, who are doing non-military jobs out of those non-military jobs and into military positions." The strategy is sound, though civilian functions in war zones cannot always be easily categorized and civilians do not come cheap.

DOD needs to rethink the mix of duties within services as well as shift some billets between active and reserve forces. As Acting Army Chief of Staff Gen. John Keane has observed, "We need more infantry. We need more military police. We need more civil affairs."

Another creative approach, which runs against military tradition, is to bring in trained personnel laterally. The demand for civil affairs personnel, technology experts, and translators, for instance, vary by conflict.

DOD also should consider establishing a multi-tiered reserve force, with some units available for longer-term deployments, others for temporary emergencies, and a number for homeland duties. CBO suggests creating temporary "constabulary" units made up of members of the Individual Ready Reserve and people who recently left active or Reserve/Guard service, which could train for six months, deploy for one year, and then disband. Moreover, the military could offer higher compensation for reservists willing to accept more frequent deployment. In fact, the Navy uses assignment and sea pay, and the Army offers stationing pay, to encourage personnel to accept undesirable jobs and locations. Larger reenlistment bonuses also are employed for some hard-to-fill specialties.

Most important, the U.S. should drop unnecessary commitments. As part of the Pentagon's review America's strategic posture, President George W. Bush proposed redeploying 60,000 to 70,000 soldiers from Asia and Europe. Far more could be done.

But the first priority should be to expeditiously exit Iraq. Lawrence Korb of the Center for American Progress points to Gen. Maxwell Taylor, who observed that we went to Vietnam to save the country but had to withdraw from Vietnam to save the Army. Plans to turn authority over to Iraqis are welcome and reflect administration realization that, as one unnamed official put it, "The Iraqis won't tolerate us staying in power for that long." However, the administration plans an indefinite military occupation.

The administration must recognize—even if it doesn't publicly acknowledge—its mistake in invading and occupying Iraq. This is not the first time that administrations intervened militarily in potentially disastrous civil wars and irregular conflicts. But, as Korb points out, in the cases of Lebanon and Somalia "the Presidents admitted their mistakes and withdrew the military before more problems were created for the military and the country." Better to accept the prospect of Iraqi instability with equanimity and focus on preventing accumulation of weapons of mass destruction and cooperation with terrorists.

The U.S. military won the Cold War, defeated a host of small states with minimal casualties, and could overwhelm any nation. But it cannot do everything. Worries Michael O'Hanlon of the Brookings Institution, "It would be the supreme irony, and a national tragedy, if after winning two wars in two years, the U.S. Army were broken and defeated while trying to keep the peace." Conscription is no answer; fiddling with military compensation and force structure would help, but would not address the basic problem. Only abandoning a foreign policy of empire will eliminate pressure to create an imperial military.

August 2004

CHAPTER TWELVE

Who Declares War?

Declare War Before Going to War

As in most crises, the shocking attack on the World Trade Center last fall caused most people to support the government. Few people seemed willing to criticize the President should he decide to expand the war to Indonesia, Iraq, Philippines, Somalia, or Syria in the name of forestalling new terrorist attacks.

To its credit, Congress did formally authorize the President to retaliate against any "nations, organization, or persons" he determined to be involved in the September 11 atrocity. But what about a nation, organization, or person who wasn't?

This is an obvious problem for hawks who want to wage war widely: there apparently is no evidence linking even the ugliest of regimes, such as Iraq, to the September attacks. If there were, the President would probably already have struck. And he would have had legal authority to do so.

Now the administration seems to be developing a new justification for attacking Iraq: its refusal to accept United Nations inspections to ensure that it does not develop weapons of mass destruction. Nonproliferation is a worthy concern, though not necessarily one warranting war. After all, Baghdad has been out of compliance with the UN's inspection regime since 1998.

Moreover, the President has no authority to act for this reason. Congress authorized him to retaliate against terrorism, not to commence war to enforce UN inspections, or even to get rid of a nasty dictator. For that he must go to Congress.

The U.S. Constitution is clear. Article 1, Sec. 8(11) states that "Congress shall have the power ... to declare war." The president is commander-in-chief, but he must fulfill his responsibilities within the framework established by the Constitution and subject to the control of Congress.

Today, of course, presidents prefer to make the decision for war themselves. President Bill Clinton took or considered military action in Bosnia, Haiti, Korea, Kosovo, and Somalia with nary a nod to Congress. This former state attorney general and constitutional law professor announced in 1993: "I would strenuously oppose attempts to encroach on the President's foreign policy powers." Apparently according to his reading, "the Constitution leaves the President, for good and sufficient reasons, the ultimate decision-making authority."

No different was the first President George Bush. He was happy to have Congress vote on war with Iraq, but only to support his decision to go in. Lawyers had advised him that he had the authority to act alone, he explained.

President Ronald Reagan invaded Grenada on his own authority. President Richard Nixon prosecuted and expanded the Vietnam War with the thinnest of legal justifications, the fraudulently obtained Tonkin Gulf Resolution. One has to go back to President Dwight Eisenhower, a former general, to find a chief executive who granted Congress' decisive role in deciding on war.

And he was right. Today the American President claims possession of power comparable to, if not greater than that, of the head of the Soviet communist party. As then-Defense Secretary Caspar Weinberger so rightly criticized the Evil Empire:

> Now who among the Soviets voted that they should invade Afghanistan? Maybe one, maybe five men in the Kremlin. Who has the ability to change that and bring them home? Maybe one, maybe five men in the

> Kremlin. Nobody else. And that is, I think, the height of immorality.

Now who among Americans has voted to attack, say, Iraq? Should one man in the White House make that decision, it would also be the height of immorality.

The founders certainly would have thought so. One of their criticisms of the British King was that he could unilaterally drag his nation into war. President Abraham Lincoln, a "strong" president apt to act on his own authority, nevertheless reflected: "Kings had always been involving and impoverishing their people in wars, pretending generally, if not always, that the good of the people was the object."

The Americans wanted no such system for their new nation. The Constitution's framers, observed Lincoln, understood this promiscuous warmaking "to be the most oppressive of all Kingly oppressions; and they naturally resolved to so frame the Constitution that *no one man* should hold the power of bringing this oppression upon us."

Still, some Americans opposed the proposed Constitution because they feared that it gave to the chief executive authority similar to those possessed by the British monarch. Don't worry, explained that great friend of executive power Alexander Hamilton. The president's authority was "in substance much inferior to it. It would amount to nothing more than the supreme command and direction of the land and naval forces ... while that of the British King extends to the declaring of war and to the raising and regulating of fleets and armies; all of which by the Constitution would appertain of the legislature."

Particularly curious is willingness of modern presidents to work harder to get approval from the UN Security Council than the Congress. Recognizing that he faced a Chinese and Russian veto, Bill Clinton did refuse to take Kosovo before the UN—no president seems to appreciate a negative vote in any legislative forum—but he successfully sought the blessing of the U.N. for the invasion of Haiti.

The founders wrote the Constitution as they did because they feared that presidents would otherwise act as they do now. Explained James Madison in 1793, it is necessary to adhere to the "fundamental doctrine of the Constitution that the power to declare war is fully and exclusively vested in the legislature." Constitutional convention delegates did change Congress' power from "make" to "declare" war, but the intent was to give the president authority to respond to a sudden attack, not initiate a conflict. When Pierce Butler of South Carolina suggested authorizing the chief executive to start wars, Elbridge Gerry of Massachusetts said that he "never expected to hear in a republic a motion to empower the executive to declare war." The delegates rejected Butler's move.

They did so to make war less likely. The president "is not safely to be entrusted with" the power to decide on war, said George Mason of Virginia. He was in favor of "clogging rather than facilitating war." James Wilson advocated a strong presidency, but was pleased that the proposed constitution "will not hurry us into war." Instead, "It is calculated to guard against it. It will not be in the power of a single man, or a single body of men, to involve us in such distress." Similarly, observed Jefferson, "We have already given ... one effectual check to the dog of war by transferring the power of letting him loose."

One need only look at succeeding American history to understand why delegate Wilson did not trust "a single man ... to involve us in such distress." Presidents have routinely deceived the public, lied to Congress, and manipulated the political system to take America into war. Obviously, Congress can be a weak reed upon which to rely—witness legislative passivity in the face of one illegal war after another. But a congressional vote, as before the Gulf War, at least ensures some debate and accountability. Especially if the conflict went bad, voters would know whom to blame.

What argument can be made by those who would have today's presidents possess monarchical powers? Harry Truman treated the Korean War as a "police action," a three-year non-war in which the U.S. military was apparently attempting to arrest common Chinese and North Korean criminals. Lyndon Johnson and Richard Nixon pointed to the Tonkin Gulf resolution, to the extent that they bothered to defend their warmaking.

Ronald Reagan pled exigent circumstances in Grenada and his authority as commander-in-chief elsewhere. In advance of the Gulf War George Bush stated that "I don't think I need it" when asked about obtaining congressional approval. When criticized for committing to war in both Bosnia and Haiti, Bill Clinton denounced "any attempts to encroach on" his prerogatives. He would welcome a vote only if it was yes.

These are all willful misreadings of the Constitution. There always be potential gray areas; a world in which nuclear missiles can deliver destruction almost instantaneously, and in which hijacked airliners can be turned into cruise missiles for transnational organizations, is not a simple one. But most cases are easy and unambiguous.

Spend three years fighting China and North Korea? Go to Congress. Devote a decade to combating South Vietnamese guerrillas and North Vietnamese regular forces? Go to Congress. Intervene in Lebanon on behalf of the minority Christian government? Go to Congress. Invade Grenada, Panama, and Haiti? Go to Congress. Attack Iraq to free Kuwait? Go to Congress. Initiate military strikes against Bosnian Serb forces in the Balkans civil war? Go to Congress. Bomb Serbia to impose an artificial political settlement on Kosovo? Go to Congress. Hit Afghanistan to depose the Taliban? Go to Congress. Take on any number of other targets—Iraq, Somalia, et al.—in the name of fighting terrorism? Go to Congress.

Naturally, presidents and their aides have been creative in coming up with reasons to short-circuit the Constitution's clear requirement. Those who thus torture the Constitution include many conservatives who normally proclaim the importance of "original intent."

One favorite claim is that the President has some unspecified, ill-defined "foreign affairs power" that reduces the explicit warpowers clause to a nullity. That might be a good argument if the Constitution didn't speak to the issue, but the founders explicitly circumscribed the President's foreign policy authority by vesting countervailing power in Congress. Legislators are to declare war; they also raise the military, organize the militia, and implement the rules of war (such as authorizing letters of marque and reprisal and defining and punishing piracy). Congress is also to regulate foreign commerce, while the Senate must consent to treaties and approve ambassadors.

Despite one truly silly Supreme Court decision suggesting that the executive is the "sole organ" for conducting international affairs, *United States v. Curtiss-Wright Exporting Corp.*, any honest reading of these provisions suggests that whatever foreign policy powers are possessed by the President, they are not superior to those of Congress. Explains

Jack Rakove, a Stanford University historian, the constitutional provisions "that laid the strongest foundation for a major executive role in foreign policy are more safely explained as a cautious reaction against the defects of exclusive senatorial control of foreign relations than as a bold attempt to convert the noble office of a republican presidency into a vigorous national leader in world affairs."

Since there is no constitutional warrant for the pretensions of those who would supercede Congress' power to declare war, are there any legitimate exceptions to congressional the warpower? Some analysts would have Americans believe that in the modern world it is simply impractical to involve legislators in foreign policy-making. Yet experience proves otherwise: Congress has often voted on the use of force and U.S. security did not suffer as a result. The point is not that 535 legislators should be expected to manage the ensuing war—that's why the Constitution names the president commander-in-chief. But Congress must decide whether or not the president will have a war to run.

Legislators can even use a conditional declaration of war to grant the president some discretion and avoid alerting opponents to the beginning of hostilities. In fact, Congress has four times passed conditional declarations, empowering the president to use force if certain goals were not met. Three times the disputes were peacefully resolved; in the fourth, the president took America into war after Spain refused Congress' demand for a military withdrawal from Cuba. Thus, Congress could have approved a conditional declaration of war demanding an Iraqi withdrawal from Kuwait, Serbian compliance in Kosovo, or Afghan turnover of Osama bin Laden. It could now pass one against Iraq demanding, say, the resignation of Saddam Hussein and introduction of UN inspectors.

Almost everyone agrees that Presidents may unilaterally use the military for "defensive" purposes. Defensive means *defensive*, however. Constitutional convention delegate Roger Sherman of Connecticut explained that "the executive should be able to repel and not to commence war."

"Repel" does not mean, for instance, overthrowing Saddam Hussein. Not that presidential imperialists worry about the meaning of words. In 1990 Robert Tucker of the Center for National Security Law argued in favor of President Bush's authority to join the Iraq-Kuwait war: "When the president seeks to respond defensively against Saddam Hussein's aggressive war (a crime against all nations under international law), he no more becomes the aggressor than did Franklin D. Roosevelt through the Normandy landing." Apparently Tucker forgot that President Roosevelt secured a declaration of war against Germany; only then did he organize an American expeditionary force.

In an uncertain world, presidents also like to argue that they must be able to respond instantaneously to unpredictable events. Fair enough, but there is almost always time to go to Congress before going to war. The regimes ousted in Grenada, Haiti, and Panama had been in power for years; President took months to build up U.S. forces before attacking Iraq; the Balkans civil war raged for years before America intervened. Even in the case of the September 11 attack, Congress had ample time to act.

The founders understood that only rarely would the nation's security preclude involving the legislature in the decision to go to war. They refused even to give the president authority to unilaterally retaliate against other nations for committing an act of war (in contrast to undertaking war) against the U.S. "The making of a reprisal on a nation is a very serious thing, explained Secretary of State Thomas Jefferson: "Congress must be called upon to take it; the right of reprisal being expressly lodged with them by the Constitution, and not with the executive."

This narrow view of presidential authority was also held by Alexander Hamilton. In 1798 he advised John Adams' Secretary of War, James McHenry, that the president can at most "repel *force* by *force*. ... Any thing beyond this must fall under the idea of *reprisals* and requires the sanction of that Department which is to declare or make war," namely Congress.

But presidents' favorite excuse for claiming the right to wander around the world unilaterally bombing other nations is simple: everyone else does it. Those lawyers favored by Bush senior point to 200-plus military deployments without congressional approval.

The precedent is thin. Legal scholar Edward Corwin notes that these examples are largely "fights with pirates, landings of small naval contingents on barbarous or semi-barbarous coasts, the dispatch of small bodies of troops to chase bandits or cattle rustlers across the

Mexican border, and the like." Whatever their relevance, they are inadequate precedent for launching a real war against a real country halfway around the globe. In any case, the Constitution does not disappear because past presidents have ignored it and past Congresses have let them get away with doing so. Prior executive lawlessness actually increases the case for strictly enforcing the warpowers provision today.

Since presidential misbehavior seems to be a constant, the Constitution requires congressional enforcement. Yet Republicans and Democrats routinely support the right of their own partisans to engage in war at will. Then, when a member of the opposing party is elected president, they instantly and shamelessly switch sides. Members of both parties adopt the position of Senate Republican Leader Robert Dole (R-KS), who in 1993 proposed legislation requiring congressional approval for military deployments in Bosnia and Haiti. He explained that Congress should be heard "before the body bags are counted, before the caskets come home." They aren't likely to do so, unfortunately, because they are political cowards. Noted Rep. Lee Hamilton (D-Ind.), then-Chairman of the House Foreign Affairs Committee, "Congress basically wants to let the president make the decision." Then members can applaud if the war turns out well, but complain if it goes badly.

If nothing else, legislators should protect their own institutional authority from constant presidential abuse. James Madison warned that "war is, in fact, the true source of executive aggrandizement."

Still, the most important reason to respect the Constitution is to better protect the liberties of the American people. The nation's founders correctly feared that presidents would do precisely what they now do regularly, intervene in overseas conflicts often with only tangential relevance to American security. At the same time, hundreds of thousands of U.S. soldiers have died, hundreds of billions of dollars have been wasted, fundamental civil liberties have been violated, and endless government powers have been expanded. This is why the Constitution requires a vote by Congress before America goes to war. "International support is fine," explained Sen. Dole, "but it is no substitute for the support of Congress and the American people."

Lots of presidents have claimed the right to unilaterally take America into war. Ironically, one of the most qualified to do so, Dwight Eisenhower, respected the Constitution too much to do so. In January

1956 he explained that "When it comes to the matter of war, there is only one place that I would go, and that is to the Congress of the United States." He later observed: "I am not going to order any troops into anything that can be interpreted as war, until Congress directs it."

His successors should demonstrate similar fidelity to the Constitution. Whatever the target and whatever the reason, American presidents should not risk the lives of young Americans in foreign adventures without gaining congressional consent. The decision of war and peace is far too important to leave to one man, however honest, bright, or popular.

January 2002

Warpowers Hypocrisy: Democrats on Parade

In response to growing demands for a congressional vote on President Clinton's planned invasion of Haiti, William Gray, the President's special adviser on Haiti, complains that "it appears many people want to apply a different standard of constitutional law for this president," which he finds "kind of confusing and perplexing." Instead, he argues, "we can only have one standard, and so I think the president of the United States will make the decision as to what he feels is appropriate."

While it is true that many Republicans seem to be reading the Constitution in a different light with Bill Clinton as president, Mr. Gray is in no position to complain about hypocrisy. On January 12, 1991 the then-congressman voted against granting President George Bush authority to go to war with Iraq. He also backed a second resolution asserting Congress' right to decide on war: "The Congress finds that the Constitution of the United States vests all power to declare war in the Congress of the United States. Any offensive action taken against Iraq must be explicitly approved by the Congress of the United States before such action may be initiated." What a difference three years—and a job in the executive branch—make.

But Gray is not the only former Democratic dove turned hawk. White House Chief of Staff Leon Panetta recently stated on NBC's Meet the Press, "if we have to exercise the military option, the authority is there." He added: "I don't think we can sit back and allow that kind of turmoil to continue. We've got to act." However, in 1991 *Rep.* Panetta joined Bill Gray in opposing the Gulf War resolution and reaffirming Congress warpower. Indeed, Rep. Panetta went so far as to join a lawsuit with 53 other legislators seeking to forestall unilateral presidential initiation of force against Iraq.

Others allied with Rep. Panetta in that court case included Rep. James Oberstar (D-MN) and Rep. Major Owens (D-NY). But today? Both want "quick military intervention," in Rep. Oberstar's words. Indeed, Rep. Owens has long been a vocal critic of unilateral presidential intervention. Four years ago he told his House colleagues that "The invasion of Panama was illegal, brutal, and unnecessary." In 1983, after President Ronald Reagan ordered the invasion of Grenada, the congressman complained: "the invasion of the tiny island of Grenada is illegal, immoral, and a wasteful expenditure of resources and human lives. It is imperative that the Congress exercise its constitutional powers to restore sanity to our foreign policy. We must reject this new policy which implies that the United States is responsible for maintaining democratic institutions in all of the countries of the Western Hemisphere. I sincerely hope that this administration is not planning to invade Haiti where dictators have murdered, tortured, and denied basic human rights to its citizens for decades." That was then, apparently, and this is now.

Georgia's Rep. John Lewis is another fervent opponent of Republican intervention. During Congress' debate on the Gulf War resolution he declared that "I happen to believe that war is obsolete as a tool and a means to conduct foreign policy." He added, "We should give peace a chance in the Middle East, not the instruments of destruction and death." But today he thinks these same "instruments of destruction and death" should be used in Haiti.

Other 1991 advocates of congressional responsibility who are now enthusiastically promoting a presidential war when the target is Haiti include Representatives Joseph Kennedy, Nita Lowey, James Moran, James Oberstar, David Obey, and Maxine Waters. For instance, Rep. Obey has demanded the dispatch of troops to get rid of "that useless, sick, poor excuse for a government." Yet in January 1991 he advocated continuing to rely on sanctions: "How long are you willing to wait it out to save lives? My answer is, a fair amount of time." Further, Obey suggested the possibility of impeachment if President Bush did not seek Congress's warrant for war.

In contrast to the others, Rep. John Murtha (D-PA) backed President Bush's request for warmaking authority—but still voted for the resolution affirming Congress' sole responsibility of deciding when to go to war. He is currently advocating an invasion Haiti. "It would be a fairly routine military operation," he explains.

So far there have been fewer arm-chair warriors in the Senate. Sen. Clairborne Pell (D-RI), chairman of the Foreign Relations Committee, opposed military action in the Gulf and defended Congress' warpowers prerogatives. He contended that "shared responsbility for war is what the founding fathers intended." In early August, however, he strongly opposed an attempt by Sen. Arlen Specter (R-PA) to bar an invasion of Haiti; to do so, Pell warned, would prohibit "our President from taking the kinds of actions that Presidents have taken in the past." Another Gulf War dove, Sen. Christopher Dodd (D-CT), stated that "I do not want to tie the hands of a President when he feels as though he should take some action." Two months before Sen. Judd Gregg (R-NH) proposed limiting the use of federal funds for an invasion of Haiti but was rebuffed by the Democratic majority: "This is not what the Senate does in its relationship with the president, unless it is being asked to play politics," retorted Sen. John Kerry (D-MA). Kerry, too, voted against authorizing George Bush to use force in the Gulf.

Even more significant is the position of the Democratic leadership in both houses of Congress. Senate Majority Leader George Mitchell (D-ME), along with House Speaker Tom Foley (D-WA), forced a congressional vote on President Bush. Stated Sen. Mitchell at the time: "Our firm view is that the president has no legal authority, none whatsoever, to commit American troops to war in the Persian Gulf or anywhere else" without congressional authorization. "The Constitution clearly invests that great responsibility in the Congress and the Congress alone," he added. He concluded that "there must be a debate and votes on this subject." About Haiti, however, he says that congressional approval is "not legal or necessary," though he would advise it in order "to build support in the country."

Similarly, in 1991 Speaker Foley joined Sen. Mitchell in telling President Bush that congressional assent was necessary and promised liberal legislators that a vote would be held before any military action against Iraq. Rep. Gephardt went so far as to threaten that Congress might cut off funding for a presidentially-initiated war. But today? A spokesman for Speaker Foley says that "he has not addressed the question of whether the President needs authorization." As for Rep. Gephardt, he explains: "I think if there are lives being lost or there is danger as we did in Panama and Grenada you go in without the Congress." The Constitution doesn't make such fine distinctions, of course, but apparently no matter.

After spending three decades piously acting as defenders of the Constitution, many congressional Democrats are now genuflecting before the altar of presidential prerogatives.

Admittedly, Republicans seem to be having much the same sort of conversion experience, only in reverse. As Sen. Joseph Biden (D-DE) has snidely cracked, "the Republicans have found God." True, but what does that mean the Democrats have found? As Bill Gray observed, it is all "kind of confusing and perplexing."

September 1994

A version of this article was originally published in the Wall Street Journal, *September 14, 1994.*

An Acceptable Constitution?

War with Iraq likely approaches, and it may be only the first of many if the Bush administration follows seriously its new doctrine of preemption. At least Congress voted on the record. Alas, if Iraq is any guide, Congress will only wave on this president or his successors in a future case, leaving them with plenary authority to go to war. And conservatives who now speak of remaking the judiciary to respect the Constitution will be leading the parade to abdicate Congress' responsibility.

Indeed, the president never even acknowledged that he was constitutionally bound if the vote had been no. If he was not, his request for a resolution was meaningless.

White House lawyers reportedly told President Bush that he doesn't need congressional authority to go to war. Still, he sought legislative approval, or at least some form of "support," for political reasons.

But the Constitution explicitly requires the Congress to "declare war." And the Founders' undoubted intention, even while recognizing the President's need to be able to respond defensively in an emergency, to limit his warmaking authority.

Virginia's George Mason, for instance, spoke of "clogging rather than facilitating war." Thomas Jefferson wrote of creating an "effectual check to the dog of war by transferring the power of letting him loose."

Even Alexander Hamilton agreed. He reassured his countrymen in the 69th Federalist: the president's authority was "in substance much inferior to [monarchical power]. It would amount to nothing more than the supreme command and direction of the land and naval forces ... while that of the British King extends to the declaring of war and to the raising and regulating of fleets and armies; all of which by the Constitution would appertain of the legislature."

Alas, Bush 43 seems to be following in the footsteps of Bush 41. The latter stated that "I don't think I need it" when asked if congressional approval was necessary before attacking Iraq more than a decade ago. Why? "Many attorneys," he said, had "so advised me." Too bad neither Bush apparently reads the Constitution themselves.

The president is the commander-in-chief, but only within the legal framework established by the Constitution and Congress. He cannot just create a military—Congress must authorize the forces and approve the funds. Congress is also tasked with setting rules of war and organizing the militia. The president can negotiate a treaty ending a conflict, but the Senate must ratify it.

If the President can unilaterally order an attack on a nation halfway around the globe which has not attacked the U.S., posed an imminent threat, or provided a traditional casus belli, the Constitution is dead. And if conservatives treat the Constitution as dead when it suits them, they should stop complaining when federal judges, liberal activists, and Democratic politicians do the same.

Why, for instance, require congressional approval to impose taxes and borrow money? To be sure, the Constitution lists this as one of the legislature's enumerated powers, but that outmoded provision need not dictate present policy. Especially since Congress itself long ago dropped any pretense that the lack of explicit constitutional authority limited its power.

If the president sees a critical need, he shouldn't have to wait for Congress to act. Certainly not if selfish, petty, and political minded legislators say no.

Nor should the nation's fiscal health be impaired by pork-minded congressmen who lard essential bills with special interest subsidies. Whatever the merits of the Founders' scheme two centuries ago, the president should be able to unilaterally cut wasteful spending, without having to veto entire bills or fear being overridden.

Article 1, Section 8 also empowers Congress to "establish an uniform Rule of Naturalization" as well as bankruptcy and patent laws. But look at what a mess legislators have made of the first, with foreigners coming to America to kill.

Populists are doing their best to block bankruptcy reform, despite manifold abuses by debtors who want to take the money and run. Patents involving pharmaceuticals are currently subject to a bitter congressional fight. Forget the Constitution: Let the President decide.

Congress is allowed to establish Post Offices. It did so, and now Americans are suffering the ill-effects of an inefficient monopoly. Yet change is impossible, blocked by the postal unions. The President should act unilaterally.

The problem of judicial activism would have disappeared had President Franklin Delano Roosevelt been able to pursue his "court-packing" plan.

Why should some abstract constitutional provisions and congressional intransigence have prevented him from doing what had to be done?

Indeed, we could dispense with congressional approval of presidential nominations. The Senate's "advise and consent" function is outmoded; the president should simply declare his nominees to be in office.

Moreover, consider the potential of executive predominance during the ill-fated health care debate of 1993-1994. The crisis should have been obvious to all but the most reactionary partisan.

Tens of millions of people without health insurance, sharply rising medical and insurance costs, growing popular dissatisfaction with the system. Yet rather than working with the president, Congress thwarted Bill Clinton's efforts. The GOP was especially shameless, using the issue for its own electoral gain.

Now, almost a decade later, the same problems remain with us. If only the president had had the courage to act unilaterally. Consider the speech that he could have given explaining why he was putting the Health Security Act into effect on his own authority:

> "I realize that some people of good will believe that the Constitution gives this power to Congress. But there are few issues more important than Americans' health. Many lawyers have told me that the Constitution established an energetic chief executive, vesting him with final authority for protecting the public. Other presidents have shared this view, using their power to issue executive orders and regulations to solve problems when Congress failed to fulfill its responsibilities. In my view, that requires acting to assure secure health care for all Americans."

But why stop there? The Constitution's electoral scheme is notably defective. The mere fact that more than two centuries ago some dead white males concocted a system as cumbersome as the electoral college doesn't mean that we should follow it today. And if Congress won't approve a constitutional amendment to fix it, why shouldn't the President, say, unilaterally recognize the candidate who has greater popular legitimacy by winning the most votes?

What is most surprising is not that presidents routinely attempt to expand their warpower authority, but that Congress is so ready to surrender its power. Of course, the partisan pirouettes are staggering.

Democrats outraged at what they saw as persistent abuses by Presidents Richard Nixon, Ronald Reagan, and George Bush suddenly gained a strange new respect for executive power when President Bill Clinton was preparing to invade Haiti and attack Serbia. Republicans routinely defended executive privilege by "their" presidents and criticized Bill Clinton's propensity to unilaterally bomb other countries.

Still, why surrender the most important power, whether or not to go to war, to a competing branch? The U.S. Constitution says that the Congress decides what needs to be done. Today, anyway, many Republicans might prefer that the Constitution read differently. It doesn't.

The last President who understood this was Dwight Eisenhower, one of the few chief executives with command experience in the military. He respected the Constitution enough to announce: "When it comes to the matter of war, there is only one place that I would go, and that is to the Congress of the United States."

For all of the bizarre constitutional interpretations emanating from law schools, courts, and op-ed pages, most people recognize that the President's domestic powers are circumscribed by the law of the land. So too are his warpowers.

November 2002

Printed in the United States
86007LV00003B/80/A